Jaundiced

Preston Jericho

PublishAmerica
Baltimore

First printing

ISBN: 1-4241-6237-8
PUBLISHED BY PUBLISHAMERICA, LLLP
www.publishamerica.com
Baltimore

Printed in the United States of America

For Carol-Aynn

Acknowledgments

To Bob Cummins, who stuck by me through thick and thin for forty years. To Dad, may your soul rest in peace. To Mary Susan, my dear sister. Thank you for your patience. To a mom that everyone should know, and Sam for being there for her and me. To all the people throughout my life that were instruments in the hand of God to bring out the best and worst in me that I might live. And lastly—to you the reader, that you might be helped in some small way to be encouraged, have a new hope and learn the finer points of life through my joys and sorrows penned here in sweat.

Table of Contents

Introduction

Mom taught me to remember things "by association." Since she seemed to always focus on things that were good, maybe she didn't realize that a five-year-old boy would someday be a teenager and then a man. One who would fall into the clutches of temptation and self.

While having a good memory of things past that deify goodness, the compilation and the reason for this work was birthed out of the trials in my life. There are two kinds of trouble on this earth. The trouble I cause myself, and the trouble that is allowed to come into my life even while I am doing the right things. The trick is to narrow down the one side so that the other may be bearable. Who really wants to be the cause of their own problems?

The memories that I possessed, and still do, are nothing less than the greatest highs and the greatest lows one could possess. The difference now, though, is having been broken like a wild horse, I feel qualified to share the booty of my life with folks that may need a touch on the inside. After all, that is where the real work is done.

I have been embarrassed often throughout the last three and a half decades to look at other people and see that I lacked even the simplest of principles in life. Trying to stuff my ignorance and reluctance to learn something new like really caring how someone else feels or sharing my food or my time. Playing it safe by keeping my "acquaintances" to a minimum made sure that the lessons I should learn I didn't. They would have to wait until I had my fun. Then the pain starts and I feel the twist of an arm. After much prodding by people and circumstances, I finally decided to bend and be a little pliable. The potential, though, still resides in me to come kicking and screaming to the altar of change.

Jaundiced is a hybrid graft between the world of short stories and one great long exposition. There is nothing boring about it, though, my right pointing finger going numb might tell you different. *I type with two fingers.*

The book structure was designed with three stages of my life in mind. The first eighteen years as a victim of an alcoholic father, while the next "decade of decadence" following Dad's death saw myself tipping the bottle. And finally, the last twenty-six years of living without it launches me into expressing all that happened, both good and bad. Some I caused, some I didn't.

I had to go through the emotions of the events all over again, only now they are a just a mist and not the deluges of times past. Anger, fear, loneliness, jealousy, hope and joy to name a few. Having to stop typing to dry my eyes or just pace the floor to endure the further cleansings that I thought were finished produces a harvest of relief and liberation. Funny how that never stops. The little elderly lady in front of me at the grocery store that has thirty-seven coupons when I am in a hurry doesn't now get a sigh of disgust, but an acceptance that all is well with my soul.

Life has a price, and the best is only a decision away. In this book are constant reminders of the lessons I am approached with and their subsequent successes and failures. I do not get it right the first time very much at all, but as my life goes on, it does get better. The book shows progression from, not just the years going by, but the actual change, the metamorphosis of a Native North American male who does battle with his real enemy, "the monster in the mirror." I seem to be aware of anything on the outside that may harm me, but that one last final frontier, the "isle of self" that must be conquered somehow eludes me. Imperfection at its best for the moment.

People love a good ending. Whatever happens to get there, though, is not merely incidental. It all matters. I am graphic in the journey, but can show restraint. The points are really driven home if you, the reader, care about life. It is not so much about the descriptive ravages of my life, or even the high points. That all goes only skin deep for a moment. What really counts is what kind of soil is there to work with. I heard one preacher say recently, "Whatever you deem most important in your life, you will find time for."

I do not believe for a moment that all I suffered and learned was for naught. So come with me on this journey on a roller coaster that is coming slowly to a halt. May you have ears to hear and eyes to see all that is meant for you.

What Hath God Wrought

A dark cold day was fitting for that time of year. January 27th was a time of celebration in the Knott home in 1953. The eldest child and son had been born of Ronald W. Knott Sr. and Twila June in the wee hours of the morning. Mom and Dad did not know what they were getting themselves into. And certainly neither did I. It took over twenty five years to discover that I was the product of the forbidden fruit outside of wedlock, something that I resented, as if I would turn out to be an example of anything better.

I recall having my diapers changed at six months on the top of a dry sink. For the first year or so my place to bed down was a hammock over my parents bed. Dad had a necktie attached to it and would pull me back and forth until I went to sleep. I never had heard that I was uncooperative at that age and a good sleeper under almost any circumstances. The large antique wallpapered bedroom was really a loaner of the Bengson family. Aunts on Mom's side lived there for many years and had watched out for Mom ever since she was born, that is really after she escaped the children's home. That is how she had started her life. At age three she was abandoned by her father after an untimely death of her mother. She would run away from the police and come to 414 Congress Street to seek refuge with Aunt

Hilda and Julia. The home for children in Bradford, Pennsylvania, would always come and retrieve Mom until she was seventeen.

My eyes began to open quite early. Being able to remember Mom's smiling face as she lifted my legs to adjust the diaper can attest to that. Although I couldn't talk, I did look at her as if to say, "Okay, enough already, let's get this over with, I'm a busy baby." It was easy to recall crawling across the hard wooden floors because the height of vision is something that you cannot forget. Only several inches off of the floor for the first few months gave me just a redundant view of the legs of the furniture and molding around the big living room. Since I had the same name as Dad, it was easy for everyone to remember what it was. "Come here, Junior, don't go there, Junior, don't do that, Junior," echoed in my ears as I tested the limits of two people who had never had kids before.

Dad would carry me on his back around the house and in the yard. Maybe a trip down to the railroad tracks in the evening saw me on top of the world. Being six feet and two hundred forty pounds gave him strength to endure me on his shoulders for long distances. I was on top of the world. My view of everything changed on the back of someone else, in the house and out.

Mary came along a year and a half later. Trends continue in society today to be considerate and provide a sibling within a short time of the birth of the first child. I pretty much started to mind my own business after my sister came into the world. Mom would hold her up to me as if she was trying to sell her. "See, Junior, this is your little sister," she said at one point after she came home from the hospital. I could look into her eyes and hear them say, "I will wait you out, your time is coming." I just looked away and continued to do what I still do best, investigate. Mary did not get a lot of attention from me for a while. When I started to walk, it was another world. The ability to actually grab the corner of a tablecloth without help and pull everything onto the floor would get everyone else's attention. I liked that so much because they didn't know that I could understand that the explanations that were using for my behavior was that I was a baby, an excuse that I want to use to this day.

My potty training was rather tough and ended up planting the first seeds of resentment. After many plops down on the little wooden stool it came time for me to hit the big time. Dad set me on the high above the clouds white throne. I did not think that I was in Heaven, but couldn't go to the bathroom because I was nervous about falling off. A trusting or foolish father left me there and went back downstairs to let me do my thing. At two years old I felt worse now that he had felt something else was more important than saving me from a fall. His trip was cut short when his son let out a big scream. When Dad ran back upstairs, he came to see me stuck in the toilet. He couldn't stop laughing. I was crying and becoming angry that he wouldn't lift me out.

"Come here, hon!" he yelled downstairs. "Look at this. I wish I had a camera!"

Mom came into the bathroom and smiled, but would not laugh. "Ron, why didn't you lift him out?" she said as she helped me down.

Dad continued to laugh. I had been stuck so far in that the seat was around my shoulders and the calves of my legs. And one thing for sure, I did not think it was funny. My father had made fun of me when he should have helped. I obviously never forgot it.

Aunt Hilda would take me on her lap and sing that Swedish song that would get faster and faster until she would finish it up by being in my face and say the final loud words. I always knew when we were nearing the end and start laughing in anticipation of it. She would let us kids sleep on the floor of her bedroom when Mom and Dad would go out on Friday nights. We called it a camp out. Making a tent out of blankets and feeling like we out in the open prairie gave us something to do almost every week.

Dad was an Indian, Mom was white. It had created a little undercurrent that I really did not understand at the time. I knew there was some form of disapproval of it because it was in the air. No one really said anything out loud, but the comments of a few people gave me that indication. Even though Ron Knott Sr. was a favorite son and the center of attention, he apparently traveled outside of an unwritten law that brought him some rejection. It would take me a long time to even care about any of that.

Mary and I would have some problems of our own. The fights that we would get into very early became a problem for Mom and Dad. What parent would welcome it anyway? We generally wouldn't get into a lot of tiffs when Dad was home. His presence kept us in check, most of the time. But like most kids, so it seems, a blindness sets in as soon as the parents go out the door as if they aren't coming back. If we didn't do the right things when they were out, then the fear would set in. It was bad when Dad was gone and worse when they both were. Aunt Hilda, and sometimes her sister Julia, were built-in babysitters. It was handy to not have to pay a nickel for one, as well as no money needed for rent, although there was a little help with the food.

I graduated from the high chair into a stool at the table. Mary inherited my seat. She did her usual baby stuff, launching peas with a spoon across the room, or trying to shove a whole slice of bread dipped in milk into her face. My habits like keeping everything separate on the plate was quickly quenched by Dad. He had a heavy hand at the dinner table. Disturbances at that hour had to be limited. I would find later just how much.

One of the first Easter's we had a few colored chicks. They would make their little noises as they would walk around in the cardboard box. Mom, still today, likes to have some yellow marshmallow peeps around the house. It must remind her of fifty years ago. Coloring eggs was always a fun thing. The trademark smell of the vinegar kept my nose relating that odor only to that time of year. Not only the colored hot pungent smell in the white cups kept things moving, but the little tattoo-like images that you wrapped around the eggs certainly made it more fun. Things had to be done before the fluid would cool down or the colors couldn't stick. Early Easter's also saw the baskets hidden throughout the house. The big plastic wrapped real-woven handiwork from local crafters were nothing less than a joy to look for. Mary and I would get sick from eating too much candy. Those large crème-filled eggs made life worth living, and back then the solid chocolate rabbits didn't hurt any.

My ability to express what I was observing came quite quickly. We were taking an evening stroll along the creek, and I stopped everyone and said, "I think that there are going to be a lot of trees growing in that area over there," pointing to a clear patch in the woods.

Mom and Dad stopped and looked at me. The word "Area" is what got their attention. "My, Junior, you are starting to use some big words," Mom would say.

I felt like I had impressed them and got a little attention. Mary had just gone along for the ride. At age five it was quite a comeback after swallowing a marble at my birthday party that year. I don't think that I have passed it yet.

The beautiful summer days in the '50s seemed to be brighter and strangely more pure. It could be the pollution in the air or the increase of decadence in my life, I don't know which. My perception of that period began over the years. I loved to run through the fields near the house and just fall down in the grass that was much higher then me. I could hear the sharp voice of Aunt Hilda calling us kids for lunch. Even if Mom was not working at the factory, then she would use Hilda's ability to cover the distance with the volume of "Mary! Junior!" We almost always heard the first yell, even if we were at a neighbor's house. Sometimes my head would pop up like a woodchuck out of the grass and answer, "Over here, I'm coming!" Mary very often would be playing with her dolls in either yard or on the front porch.

My favorite picture of my sister and I is when we were together in our Easter outfits at Olin Mills studios. I had on a little black suit with a bow tie and Mary Susan wore a frilly pink dress. We sat together on a bench with her arms around my waist. It took thirty years for that picture to surface after Dad died.

Our house was an old two-story built back in the early 1900s. It had endured a fire many years before I had been born. The smoke-scarred timbers in the attic gave way to my imagination of what that event had been like when I had been rummaging around on one of my "explorations," as I called it. Aunt Hilda told me that the fire had started in the kitchen and destroyed almost all of it, but got put out before it ate up the roof. I loved looking around in that attic. We had two of them, but I wasn't able to get to the third floor one yet. I would wait patiently for that day.

I overheard Mom talking with day one day about school. I became concerned at the inevitable. Being an observer so young, I knew that I would eventually be kicked out of the nest. "Ah yes, he will get his shots, he has to start this September, he is getting started a year late because of his birthday being in January." If I had been an adult at that point, I would have started pacing the house. Shots, that was serious. And being away from all of this freedom of romping through the fields chasing butterflies? I hope this is all worth it. I know that what

I had feared most was the change, a principle that would haunt me for many decades.

I ended up getting the needles in my arms. Dad showed me his big scar from the polio shot that he had when he was a kid. That was interesting, but it was no consolation for my own pain. That needle I had endured had gone all the way through my body, I swear it. The days leading up the beginning of my school days seemed like a death sentence. Even though it was something that everyone else had been going through, I did not feel any comfort at that.

The big day had come. It was Junior's first day of school. Second Ward Elementary School was going to be the site of change for me for the next six years. The brick building had been built in 1929 and was still in good shape. Mom had gone into the school to check things out. She was quite familiar with the place. Having gone there when she was young made it easier for her to accept what I would be getting into. They had transported Mom back and forth from the other side of town from the children's home during those hard days of youth. Miss Maury was my teacher. I would be attending the afternoon session.

"Hello, Ronnie," she said. "I just know that you are going to like it here." Her smile covered her face and I knew it was a plot to patronize me. I had been through all that when Mom would let me win at a game of cards. Still, I was afraid.

"Good afternoon, Miss Maury," I answered. Looking around at some of the other kids walking around like they were tin soldiers made me think that they were not faking it. The kids were just as befuddled as me about what we had gotten ourselves into. The room was filled with toys, games, a rope ladder that went to the ceiling and a mat for me to sleep on. Mom had reassured that I would not be a problem. It was so easy to back up that claim when you were as afraid as I was. Even though I had gone through my moments at home, this event was going to make me appreciate 414 Congress Street all the more.

It came time for Mom to leave me. I knew it was coming and tried to mentally prepare for it, but just couldn't handle the moment. I followed her outside, clinging to her dress.

"Whaaaah!" I cried. "I don't want you to go! I want to go home!"

She stopped and got down on her haunches. We were at the base of the flagpole. "Now listen, you are going to be alright, Junior. You just have to be here for the afternoon and then I will pick you up. Okay? Now you go back in there and act like a young man. You can do it. Just behave yourself."

We stood up as I began to sniffle. She turned me around and pointed me toward the door. Miss Maury was waiting with the door wide open. Her smile seemed to be more sincere now.

"Thank you, Mrs. Knott. We will see you in a couple of hours."

I walked back into the room and took another look around. The kids were now climbing a jungle gym, and building a house out of giant building blocks. I all of a sudden saw this as a place that was fun. My classmates were actually not acting as if they were zombies. Within minutes I adjusted. It would keep me for those next six years.

I never recalled what it was like to have Mom come to pick me up. I think that the attention that I was now giving my new life was the great distraction. I was thrilled when I did get that "breakthrough." A taxi was our source of travel unless we chose to walk the entire mile to the Second Ward.

"Look, Mom. Look at what I made you," as I reached into a bag and pulled out a cardboard figure.

She examined it and gave me a big hug. "That is nice, honey. You made it all by yourself?"

A submissive young lad responds. "All by myself," I answered as I stood there with my hands behind my back. Of course, that was the first item of mine from school to go on the refrigerator.

From the time that Mary and I could walk, Aunt Hilda would take us in an old brown buggy up the street to the "Peach Man." There had been a gas station only a couple of hundred yards south of the house. A man who sold peaches came there with his big truck every week and set up the stand in a filling station parking lot. Those peaches were the biggest and best. Traffic on Congress Street in those days posed none of the threats that the byways have today. A quiet summer day with an occasional car actually going the speed limit was indicative of the slow pace of that small town. The buggy was made of some strange material that looked like fiberglas, but wasn't. A one piece tub with spoked-wheels made fairly easy pushing two kids on the gravel berm even for a woman in her early sixties.

The gas station was eventually torn down in favor of the company that had most of its property behind it. The large Zippo lighter manufacturing plant was right across the street from our house and extended up the street to a swamp. The powers that be felt that they would need further expansion on their grounds for more employee parking. I would miss the peach man. Every morning we could hear the traffic come up the street to the plant. Starting about 6:30, the cars would come and take their places in the parking lot until quitting time at 3:30 in the afternoon. Fridays at that time were like a drag race, as the many people would jockey for position on the two-lane street. They would be lined up for several blocks unable to move any faster than the people in front of them.

Mom had gotten a job at Zippo making lighters sometime during those early formative years. Dad worked at Case Cutlery making the world famous CaseXX knives. He would take me into the plant on Russell Boulevard to watch him grind and polish the bone and steel. Once in a while we would go along the creek-bed near our home and look for white rocks that made good parts for the handles on small pocket knives. Sometimes Dad would "go on strike" or be laid off. I never knew for years what either of those terms meant. All I knew was that it wasn't good because that meant he would be around a little more often than I wanted him to be. That constant check on my plans to be free to do what I wanted was a pain in the neck.

When things were tight with money, we would have to go to the local armory for food. Powdered eggs and milk, five pound blocks of cheese and food stamps to take care of the other things kept some of the food on the table. Of course, Dad was an avid hunter, who apparently had no respect for the assigned seasons for hunting. Day or night, summer, fall, and winter we had animals for meat. Deer, rabbit, squirrel, and much fish supplemented any lack for food. Once in a great while I would accompany him and a friend at night for a "deer run." The gun was usually a .22 caliber rifle. Spotting deer at night for checking out their habits just before deer season in the fall was legal. But the using of a spotlight to kill them wasn't. With a six pack of beer and a good aim we brought home many a "white tail" for dinner. The meat never went to waste. There were plenty of families to share, especially the hindquarters. I heard him say once that since he was an Indian there was no real barring him from his hunting habits. One late night we were out in an old car spotting deer. We came upon a skunk sitting on a stump next to someone's camp. The building had been covered with a white siding. That night dad had borrowed a 30/40 Krag, a much larger weapon than the illegal .22 rifle. Dad drew a bead on the skunk and splattered it all over the side of the cabin. I'm sure that the owners would not like that smell. When I was a little older, I was made to do something that bothered me later. We had gone onto a reserve for animals at a place called Mead Run. This government property was posted and had a few small lakes on it. We went there with a couple heads of lettuce. After climbing over a barbed wire fence, we walked near the water to feed the ducks. After spreading the lettuce all around the ground near our feet, the trusting waterfowl came to eat. They did not know that Dad and I each had a baseball bat.

"When they are all around us, just start swinging," he told me. "I'll give you the signal."

About fifty ducks were having a grand time doing what they had always done when people came around. Being almost tame, they obviously hadn't seen the likes of someone like us. The signal came and I did what I was told. That day we brought thirteen ducks home and passed them out to other families. I felt like a cold-blooded killer doing all of that to those helpless creatures. Mom was instilling in me things that were contrary to what Dad was trying to teach. The battle within was beginning to rage.

Back in school, I had made some friends. My first class picture was a photo of many kids that would follow me through my later years. Kirk Heitzinger was a neighbor who lived up the hill a block and a half. He definitely, even at the kindergarten age, was an instigator. He wanted to cause trouble wherever he went. During recess he would talk me into sneaking into the girl's bathroom and scream out loud to scare the daylights out of our female classmates. After a couple of times of doing that I bowed out. My conscience wouldn't let go on with it. He eventually got caught and had to spend some time after school.

Jan Gardner was pretty much my first official girlfriend. She always wore her hair in pigtails. She would give me a little embarrassment when she would talk to me.

"Ronnie, could you walk me home from school? I think I live on the way."

By the end of my kindergarten year I was walking the entire mile both ways. Her house was on the way. Our first walk to her home gave me the "willies." Jan looked at me with those big marbley blue eyes and made her move. She took her hand and put mine in it as we walked up Congress St. I didn't try to pull away, but thought about it. I hadn't reached that total embarrassment stage in my life yet.

"Okay, where do you live?" I asked. "I live all the way out by Zippo."

She dropped her books and answered, "That is a long way. Do you have to walk it all the time?"

Helping her pick up the books, I responded. "Yea, it's not bad. We don't have a car."

We got to Kane Street where she was living. She was right. Her home was on the way. I thought that she had been watching me to find that out. Not that it meant anything, but maybe it was because she grew up that way.

But she leaned into my face and kissed me on the cheek. "Good bye Ronnie," she said as she walked away. "See you tomorrow."

I waited for her to turn her back and then wiped my cheek off. "Bye," I said with an indistinct voice while scrunching up my face. Yuuk!

The following spring had brought May flowers. That year it was an especially long winter and the melting snow lasted into late April. There was a particular cement wall that I would always look at when the runoff was traveling along the grassy edge. I had liked to stop and observe closely the crystal clear water and any bugs swimming in it. It was a perfect opportunity to plant some seeds of creativity on the way home from school. I loved to watch nature in all of her glory any chance I could and that made it more difficult when I was made to do things that I didn't think anybody should.

Mrs. Hume was our school nurse. She would counsel us on how to brush our teeth. With the traditional large plastic set of chompers she would explain. "You take your brush and hold it like this." She would take the brush and slowly move up and down on the front teeth. "You have to sweep up, then down, turning your wrist like this, you see?"

I would go through the motions with her and not really pay a lot of attention. Learning the right way was important but I already knew it. She would give all of us kids a toothbrush and a tube of toothpaste.

Her pretty silver hair and nurses cap still reminds me of some poster painted on the front of a magazine except she did not have the red cross on it.

A fire drill here and there saw half of the school go up Tibbits Avenue all the way to South Avenue. Kids leaving on the other end of school would go onto Elm Street. It ran to South Avenue too, but its steep road surface made it treacherous especially in the winter. Waiting to come back in from the drill could make you tired just standing on that incline for a few minutes. The sound of the school bell when it was time to come in or leave whether it was a drill or going home had a special sound that you don't hear anymore. The nuclear fallout drills just took up time that I thought was of no use if the real thing happened. I had wondered a lot about what we had created.

Miss Maury was also going to be my first grade teacher. I came to like her. That was something that I was actually looking forward to in the fall.

Summer time had come and Mom was laid off for a while. About forty feet away from the house was an "Iron Horse." That was a name for the pumps attached to a rodline that would pump out the crude oil from the ground. Bradford was an oil town. The hills were dotted with iron horses all moving up and down. Every once in a while you could hear a loud backfire from a pumphouse piston that had built up too much pressure. I was not allowed to ride the horses when they were on. Pennzoil, Quaker State, and Kendall owned most of the big properties with oil in the ground and hadn't really adopted the legal protections that we have today. Back then if you rode a horse and fell off, you were responsible. I have a scar or two from falling off of those things over the years.

One thing that I always disliked when I was young was cigarette smoking. Dad used to buy the cans of "Bugler" tobacco and roll his own on that little mechanical device to save a few bucks. Everywhere he went he had to have a "fang" in his mouth. Camel, Lucky Strike, or Marlboro was the top shelf brands when he could afford it. By seven or eight years old I was making runs for dad to have his cancer sticks.

"Junior come here," he would say. "I want you to go to the gas station and get me some cigarettes. Don't take all day, I'm going to time you." Dad always tried to put some novelty into something that may be a burden. He would take off his watch and stare at it a moment. "Ready, set, go!"

Off I went up the hill to the City Line Filling Station. It was called that because the Bradford City line ended on that property. It was a steep hill all the way but the trip down after I got the cigarettes was easy and fun. John Stromberg owned the station and knew Dad. Once in a blue moon I would get them on credit until payday. Running back into the yard Dad would let me know how I did. I do know that at least once he really kept track because he was looking at the watch all the way up to the end of my trip and said, "come quick like a bunny, your going to beat the last time." I would drive through the finish line helping my dad kill himself.

One of my first acts of tomfoolery was to sneak into the staircase that led to the basement. On a shelf that set over the stairs was a can of bug spray. It was silver can with a label that read, "Atomic Bomb." The reason that I went for it was that I had discovered a bumblebee's nest under the edge of the house near the back porch. Aunt Hilda was sitting on a swinging bench on the front porch. Mom was doing laundry in the kitchen and I had to sneak past her with spray. I got to the nest and emptied the can all over the side of the house. The bees came out and were very angry. I did not get stung, but even if I had I probably wouldn't have felt it. I was overcome from the fumes of a spray that had been manufactured without much restriction. I fell to the ground dazed and ready to pass out. Mom came running out when she noticed me on the edge of the porch trying to climb back into the house.

"For God's sake Junior, what did you do now?" She picked me up and brought me inside. Sitting upright in a kitchen chair she started to wash my face with a damp cloth. Scrubbing a little hard from her fear, she continued her scolding. "Don't you know that you're not supposed to be around that stuff! I told you not to go near the bug spray in the first place! What is the matter with you?" Without having to go to the hospital I seemed to recover and got told about it again when Dad got home. He hadn't really started the heavy hand thing yet.

The fall of the year came and my first grade class would be welcomed by a smiling Miss Maury. Craft projects using pressed leaves and dried flowers was something that we were into when

October came around. Autumn time is my favorite time out of any of the seasons and it is clear that my love of fall started way back then. The sun hitting the gold, the reds, and burnt orange on the trees could not be matched by any artist. There has always been something about the intensity of those colors that only come that in that way.

Many of the same kids that I had in kindergarten were with me now. A couple of them had moved away but it was good to be around familiar faces. Jan of course would follow me through the next couple of years. She kept up her little puppy love for me.

Christmas was coming up and the holiday program was going to be a hit. I was just going to sing in the choir-like ensemble. "Silent Night, Deck the Halls, Jingle Bells" and all of the other favorites was something that I was already singing at home so it was going to be easy. Mom came to the program and watched me sing my little lungs out. I tried to pretend that I didn't see her, but her presence gave me the biggest boost. When we were done with our number, I watched all of the parents clapping. I loved that part. Now I could look at Mom and soak up the glory. Dad had to work.

The local radio station, WESB, had a special program on every year at Christmas time. Santa would read the lists that kids in the area would send in. Mary and I heard our lists and it was fun to be on the radio. Our tree was always a big natural one. The scent of pine throughout the house never let you forget what time of year it was. Mom and Hilda did most of the baking. Julia stayed in her room a lot of the time. Thanksgiving had come and gone. I liked that time of year because it signaled the official start of the holiday season. In Pennsylvania, the first day of buck season always comes the Monday after "Turkey Thursday." Hunters come from all over Ohio, Pennsylvania, and New Jersey. I didn't really believe that any of those guys would use the occasion just to get away from their families until there was a report of a man getting stopped on the New York thruway with a small horse in his trunk. He swore he thought it was a deer.

For the first eight years of my life I stayed with Mom and Dad. I slept with them after the deal with the hammock had gotten too old. Going to the bathroom in a five-gallon bucket started to age a little too. Moving to another part of the house was a definite problem. Both of the spare rooms upstairs were filled with things that belonged to our aunts. The trip over from Sweden in 1898 on a boat had given them a new life in the land of opportunity. Trunks filled with clothes, dolls, antiques, and newspapers written in Swedish were not to be moved.

After several months of debate and some resistance from Hilda., I ended up living in the pantry. This room was shaped like an ice cube tray, five and one half feet wide and sixteen feet long. The jars of canned goods lined the shelf near the doorway into the kitchen. With no door on the hinges, I never put two and two together that the missing door was why the jars and cans did not freeze in the winter. The heat, of course, would not go beyond the foods. Moving into that room in the summer was exciting. It stayed a little cooler than the rest of the house and no one ever had really known what it would be like there. My first winter was bad. There was frost on most of the three walls. The blankets had to be piled on very high and it became a big pain to have to go to the bathroom. I couldn't sneak into Mom and Dad's room to use the bucket. It was a long way up the stairs and back down. One night I made the big mistake of going in the kitchen sink. Dad asked me the next day if I had done it.

"Nope," I said.

"Don't you lie to me," he retorted.

Whenever I did anything wrong, if it was Dad questioning me I tried to lie my way out of it. I feared the consequences of what I did more than lying about it too. I never got in trouble for that, but maybe I would have been better off if I had told the truth. God seemed to find a way to make up for all the things that I thought I was getting away with.

The Stewardship

The school Patrols looked like they had something good working. Whenever I had to cross the street near the school, they made it clear that no one was to step out of bounds or they would be "reported." I started to like that power and authority. I wanted some of it, but would have to wait awhile. The plain white belts across the chest indicated the trainees and the bright orange ones the kids that were in to stay. Holding my classmates back to the sidewalk with a flag didn't look at the time as a great responsibility, but a little control over other people. Maybe it was a leadership quality and not being lord over someone, I'm not sure. I did know that as a little kid I wanted what somebody else had.

On our way home from school there were two candy stores. The "Sunshine Market" only a block away from the school and "Simond's Market" on Jefferson Street three blocks from school on the way home. Both stores were operated by couples who were getting up in their years. The differences between the folks were extreme. The Smiths were always kind and gentle. Being the closest to the school made the potential for more business likely. The Simonds, however, were much sterner. They wouldn't take garbage from anybody, especially Mrs. Simonds. She would sit behind the counter and watch every move that each kid made. One moment too long in the store without buying something gave her the notion that you had other things in mind. And she was right. Helen Simonds backed up her assertions with a good bite.

"If you kids aren't buying anything hit the road," she would bark.

I really didn't like that, but there were some of us who would try and steal small things. The main reason that we would go there anyway was because they had items that the Sunshine Market didn't, mainly little fireworks like the little burning black snakes, pinwheels, and sparklers. The grab bag of candy and plastic toys for a nickel made for an attraction away from Congress Street.

By the end of first grade Jan seemed to consider that I was not going to bend in her direction. Other girls on the way home from school would become interested in me. Sally Kellogg lived on the bottom of Kane Street. Jefferson Street ended at Kane and made it convenient to stop at her house and meet her parents. Their house was much nicer than ours, and as I began to get older that started to bother me. Dad had gotten away with drinking all of the time as far as I was concerned because I thought it was what everybody was doing. But it wasn't. There was actually other people out there who came home at a decent hour after an evening out or maybe did not even drink at all. The furniture, a nice car or just the way that some others were living made me see that something was wrong. One thing for sure though, not one of my girlfriends ever came near my house. I quickly became ashamed when I began to learn these things.

Sally had a big black Lab. Princess would always be at the stop sign waiting for us at the intersection of Congress and Kane Streets. That dog was proud to be an escort the rest of the way. Sally's Mom would make me a peanut butter and jelly sandwich. "Here you go Ronald," she would say. Mom knew that I stopped there once in a while for lunch and then head back to school. By that time I had been walking the mile home for lunch and then back and then home again for the four-mile total daily. A reprieve from that distance once in a while or if Mom made me a lunch to take was a relief. Winters having to do that was treacherous when you had to turn around and head back after eating a fast lunch. "Where do you live?" Mrs. Kellogg would ask. My answer was always the same. "Out by Zippo." I knew that everybody else knew where that was, only I would never give an address or describe my house.

Second grade had come and gone. A bout with measles, and having to begun to develop a little allergy to goldenrod saw me through that summer. Coming in the house sneezing a bit put Mom on watch to find out where this had started. It was believed that the bug spray had begun a compromise in my system somehow.

Mrs. McKittrick had been a good teacher that year. Her favorite holiday was St. Paddy's day. Us kids got to make just about anything in green and hang it up in the windows of the classroom. Her red wavy hair made her the vibrant woman that she was. Her job had been as an organizer of the other teachers. PTA and conference sessions to discuss the progress of the students made her a centerpiece for the school.

Third grade saw me take a turn for the worse on the inside, but I began to tolerate rather than accept Dad and his drinking. The trips to the bars became more and more frequent. Very often it was on Friday nights when Mom , if she was working, got paid and, of course, Dad with his check cashed. I understood at that age the meaning of rewarding yourself after a hard week's work. I would sit in a booth at the "Star Restaurant," a dive that continues to this day. People who had little or no money hung around there in those days. Dad's friends would be there for him when he had money. Many of them did not work and that created a lot of dissension with Mom. Our money, for many years, would literally go out the window on booze for others and not on our kitchen table. The arguments would never cease when my mother would try to stop the madness. While I lay in bed I could hear them.

"Ron, why don't you just say no? You have mouths to feed here! Why do you have to go out and spend that much money all the time! Tell them to go and get a job of their own!"

Much of the time it was the wrong thing to say because Dad was drunk when she said it. Only twice in all of those years can I remember Dad smacking Mom in the face. I heard the argument, then the slap, then silence. Mom started to cry and Dad would leave. He did apologize both times. Besides the condition of the house, the condition of my family made it very hard to consider bringing anyone around. I eventually would, but it was hard.

29

There were times when Mom would be with Mary and I in the bars on those Fridays. I would be drinking an Orange Crush and plain Wise potato chips. Maybe a pizza would do the trick. Dad's intolerance of some people earned him the reputation of the tough guy around town. I would be sitting in the booth at the "Texas Hot" bar and restaurant and have to duck while the beer bottle's flew past me. Then Dad would proceed to teach the other man a lesson. He never lost a fight that I knew of until one night he was put in the hospital by a group of men who attacked him with baseball bats. Apparently the leader of that group was black and it would plant a seed of prejudice in me. When I would get older, I would try and square up for Dad. That was the plan.

Watching how other people treated Dad in the bars made me begin to believe what Mom had been saying the whole time. "Ronnie, buy me another one. Ronnie, you got five till tomorrow." He never saw it and they knew that he would not remember because he was drunk. The smoke-filled rooms and the sound of the cue ball hitting on the pool table would pierce through the noise of many conversations going on at the same time. I would never forget the smell of booze, the cigarettes, and the waste of money in that kind of life. Beginning to develop a hatred for it started to cause some resentment. What could I do about it? The answer to that question was, "nothing."

The effect that my father's drinking problem was having on me was mounting. I didn't like to do things with him when he was drunk. A couple of beers and feeling good really wasn't much of deal. The walks along the tracks with no booze around, was the best. We sat on the rails in the fall and threw stones at the caterpillars on the second set of tracks. The evenings when the sun was going down still had a lot of meaning to me despite any other beefs that I had

After he would toss a rock he would tell me, "Junior, the only thing that I care about for you is that you would graduate from high school. That's all. Can you promise me that?"

I really didn't have to think a lot about my answer. "Yes, Dad," I responded. "I will."

Short and sweet were my answers in those days. I knew that anything else would give someone fodder to work against me somehow.

"I didn't graduate and I don't want you to end up like me. I'm not going anywhere."

I stopped throwing for a moment and thought about how it appeared how right he was.

Aware of Dad's concern about his life didn't really cushion the fall when I had to face friends and him at the same time. The Heitzinger family became a saving grace for me. Sleep-outs with Kirk on a weekend often in the summer gave me an "out." I didn't have to be around Dad. In order to accomplish something like that though, it would be necessary to have my friends accompany me often when I asked. I didn't like to get permission from a Dad who just might not be "in the mood." Dad hit it off quickly with Kirk and I was glad. Being around Mom with him during the day was safe while Dad was at work. It was the other relationship that I had the problem with. In order to get what I wanted I would have to ante up a little pain.

The trend of manipulating my Dad by offering up the presence of a buddy became my own way of life. Mark Rothwell was another neighbor a couple of doors toward the city. He had no problem coming around and thought Dad was cool in some ways. In my mind, my father began to represent everything that I did not want and to some of my friends he was an example of some of the wildness that was being suppressed by parents who knew the right way to live. I never thought of it that way at the time, I was just glad that their relationship was developing, "Now let's get out of here before he changes his mind."

The seeds of doubt I now would sow,
that Pop would ever change.
What I feared the most not that he say no,
but that my mind was drawing from below.
The descent was quick so it seemed,
when I finally realized that trip,
had been bought and paid for by my wit.

My grades in school were average except for math. I hated math. Dad would sit with me and try to explain some of my homework. I watched him in his own frustration, as he couldn't get some of what

I was being taught. His desire for me to graduate was so serious that he would get angry with the system as well as with me.

"Why do they have to teach you that crap? What on earth are they thinking? I never saw this when I was in school!"

He clearly missed out on some of the basics and now was being pummeled with some of the new ways of teaching on top of it. I felt like I was sliding out from under some of my responsibilities in learning it myself. Any opening that would make my life easier I would take. That kind of thinking was creating a monster and I didn't know it.

The winters in northwestern Pennsylvania had the reputation of being the worst in the nation at times. It seemed as though we were in competition at times to have the lowest temperatures as well. Bismarck, North Dakota and someplace else in Minnesota very often had the prestigious honor of being the coldest on any given day. I never was really bothered by that season of the year. Being a kid and being able to play in it took any edge off anyway.

The best place to sled ride was in that "Gully" next to the Heitzinger's. It was a straight stretch of a hill that ran about one hundred twenty yards, had a turn off about a two thirds of the way down, and then leveled off sharply before going over a steep sharp bank. We all prided ourselves in being able to go very fast and make that first turn before going over another steep dip into the lower end of the ravine. On occasion, Kirk and I would ride together and try some of the more daring things like to try to make the turn at the last second without going into harm's way. The wear on the right runner of all of our sleds was treacherous. The constant left turns made sure that we would either have to bend back the runner, or get a new sled. Mary had the shortest sled. It had been a gift from Aunt Hilda. She had gotten it from a friend. Me being much taller than my sister made it necessary to keep me in the longer ones. There were about thirty kids or so that would sled steadily at the gully.

Mark spent some of his time with us in the winter. His family was really a bunch of skiers though so he wasn't around us a lot in the winter. His brother Reggie, sister Deb, and his Dad had memberships to "Grosstal Ski Slopes" about forty minutes away. His mother Jean was not much of a fan of that sport.

32

One Christmas I had asked for a toboggan. It was beautiful. The other things that I lacked in my life had been compensated for by having something that many other kids did not have. I looked at this long sleek tool for the snow and went and got Mark. It was a very snowy Saturday and many of the other kids had gone home. We had a lot of fun learning to go down the hill on my new "wooden runner." There was one run, though, that brought all of my fun with this generous toy to an end. Once in a while Mark and I would have to plan where we would be going before we traveled down that hill. The toboggan had to be steered differently than a sled and there had to be a mutual understanding where you were going to go so all the kids riding it could lean in the same direction at the same time. Mark wanted to take a new path, but the only thing was that he didn't let me know until we were speeding down an ice-covered hill.

"Let's go to the right, through Freeman's yard," he yelled to me.

I was in front as the cold white spray made me gasp for breath. My face was covered with snow as I tried to steer to the right, across the lower part of Kirk's lawn, through Mr. Freeman's yard and onto the Howe family property. By that time we were traveling faster that any of us had ever gone before. It felt pretty neat flying across those yards without any real obstructions. Clear sailing and no trees gave us the feeling of being free. It was all new to us. No one had attempted to take this route before.

As we approached the property line on the East side of Davey Howe's yard I yelled back to Mark, "Don't you think we should stop?"

Mark retorted, "No, keep going into the bushes. I want to see where we end up."

The bushes that we were heading into were so thick you couldn't see through them. And you didn't know what was on the other side, although we both should have. Mark and I plowed in the bush at full speed laughing all the way. The toboggan cut through the fine brittle brush like a knife going into a cardboard box. The twigs stripped off any loose clothing that we had on. Mark's hat had been blown off, my hat was lost and the hood of my parka had been pulled back. All of a sudden we broke through the other side of that bush and there was total silence. The crackling of frozen branches being broken ceased as we were now in the air, touching nothing. We had become airborne over a steep bank that we both recognized. The back of Mark Rothwell's garage was coming up fast. After sailing many feet, we came down on the top of a pine stump that had been cut off like a quill pen. The toboggan hit with such a force that the sharp deadly object came through like a shark's tooth into an egg carton. My new toboggan split from the front to the rear. The only thing now holding it together was the rope that was meant to hold on to. The sharp stump came through my coat, two sweatshirts, and a t-shirt and just scratched my skin. My clothes saved my life. Mark continued on through the air and hit the garage. He was knocked unconscious as I tried to look around at the carnage. He laid on the hill not moving.

"Mark!" I called. He didn't move. I tried to crawl to him, but was stopped by my ripped clothes that were stuck onto the stump. I looked down at my side and jerked my bloody t-shirt away so I could crawl over to my friend. "Mark, Mark!" There was no answer. I got scared and began to shake him. "Wake up!" After squeezing his chin and shaking his face I said, "Snap out of it. Are you okay?"

Mark shook his head and looked at me and started to look around. Then he started his patented uncontrollable laughter. He realized what had happened and that made it all the more funny I guess. I started to laugh with him for a minute, but that didn't last long. After I was convinced that he was okay my concern immediately went toward my new toboggan. I knew that I would never see another one, not in this lifetime.

Mark looked at my clothes and started laughing again. "Let's go back up and look at the path that we took" he said in between his bouts of the funnies.

We would pick ourselves up and drag the remnants of my pride and joy up the hill. Dad's choice to put the shattered and splintered Christmas gift under the front porch forever was an easy one.

"That's it," he said with finality. "You had one shot and that was it. Say goodbye to that."

I was right. I never saw another one. Mark and I both recovered from our bumps and scrapes.

Summertime by age nine or ten also saw new and creative ways of having fun. Playing with matches seemed like a fun thing to do. Especially since there was this novelty that you weren't supposed to do it. And who else but my friend Mark would be fitting to get into trouble over something like that.

I don't really know whose fault it was. All I remember is that we had gotten a few of those Ohio Blue Tip matches and went up to the new log cabin owned by the Westerlund family three doors away from us. It was a nice Lincoln log structure meant for the triplets. Billy, Bob, and Steve had the best place to hang out and nobody was home at the time. Mark and I snuck into the cabin and sat down on the floor. Striking the matches against a small stone was easy to make a little fire with a few twigs. The one thing that we did not count on though was the dry hay under the floorboards. We wanted to keep our little fun a secret, but when the fire that we started had dropped through the spaces between the boards in the floor, the secret was out. The hay quickly caught fire and we could not reach it. The smoke started to fill the room and I ran back home to Mom. I was now crying, partly due to fear and some because of guilt.

"Mom, Mom," I screamed. "There's a fire in Westerlund's cabin!"

Mom looked over at the smoke pouring out of the doorway. "What did you do now? Were you playing with matches?" She answered angrily.

Her next move was to grab the wash pan and fill it with water. With her apron on she ran over to the cabin and dumped it through the floor and saved the day...but not my skin. When she came back, she threw down the pan and grabbed me by arm an made me turn around. Smack, smack, smack went her hand across my behind. She didn't stop until I started crying louder than I was already was.

"I told you never to play with matches, didn't I? Now go to your room!"

I went into my bedroom with a red behind. She didn't have to remove any of my britches to get the job done. Her hand relentlessly coming against me time and time again was sufficient. But I must confess that I remember clearly that I made her spankings a little more dramatic that they really were. I would discover, though, that I would never get away with anything. Round two when Dad got home would make up for all of my "faking it." Mark had taken off like a scared rabbit and didn't get punished. I could hear Mom over at the Westerlund's later, talking and reassuring them that this episode would not be repeated. She was right. It never was.

Summertime also meant some chores for Mary and I. We both were approaching the age that if we wanted any spending money we had to earn it. Aunt Hilda would help out Mom and Dad in the responsibility to teach us those lessons. Dad was always the iron hand in enforcing any ideas that anyone came up with, especially his. Our yard on Congress was about a half-acre or so. The back section was always deep with weeds among the fourteen to eighteen inch high grass. After years of letting it go wild, little junior became the convenient one to change all of that. Throughout the time of my early elementary years I got away from having to do anything with cutting grass. Once or twice a year Dad would take an old scythe and wack down that yard and let it lay there. The time came for me to be initiated into lawn care, as it was called. The problem with me was that I couldn't get a handle on that old scythe. I was too short. Dad felt sorry for me so he went and got a hand sickle. Now I had to do the whole thing by hand. He showed me how to cut down the grass and let me go.

"Do it right, and I do not want just a cow path," he would say.

I heard that statement for the next few years. He had to repeat that over and over until I got it right. My hands blistered time after time, sometimes until the blood would be mixed with the water. Getting older and taller year after year did help some, but that never changed my view of Dad.

My family social life was not without some of the visits of relatives from Canada. Earl Simmons was the husband of Sharon, the daughter of Aunt Evelyn who was living in Bradford at the time. "Sharon and Earl," as they were always referred to, made a trip from Toronto to the Bradford area and would stay either with Uncle Don or with us on our couch. Don had originally lived with us for a short time when he first moved to the states from the Indian Reserve where all of the siblings were from. The bombastic attitude of Earl always started in the morning. He was an early riser, we were not.

"Okay, it's time for everybody to get up!" he would shout. "Rise and shine, rise and shine!"

Dad didn't like that, but to this day I don't know why he never said anything to him about it. I know that he wasn't afraid of him. Even when Earl would stay at someone else's house, he would just walk into ours and start his yelling on a Saturday or Sunday morning. Once in a while he would come into my room and shake me even while I was awake just to be funny. I wasn't laughing though. The whole family would then reluctantly get out of bed and someone would start a big breakfast. When everybody got going the irritation would finally wear off. Earl did not really have a bad bone in his body. Maybe that was his saving grace. Hilda and Julia were almost always up early, but they were respectfully quiet about it.

On occasion it would be our turn, so to speak, to travel to Canada. It was always a good time to go to Grandma's house at the Curve Lake Indian Reservation where Dad grew up. In my life the anticipation of some things were more real than the event itself. That was true for things that I liked as well as things that I did not. We had a car off and on when we could afford it. Of course, when the booze took over we sold it and have to wait a while before we could own another one. Our first trips to Canada were in an old Packard. A yucky green of a hulk it was. That car was the closest thing to an Army tank that you could get. Solid inside and out, it had a push button transmission. Those cars never had any power steering in those days, so you had to watch out for a spinning steering wheel that could break your wrist if things got out of control.

At Grandma's house there was always this distinct odor of old wood. Her two-room dwelling was indicative of many of the homes on that reserve. Grandma's name was Margaret, though no one ever called her that. It was always "Mum" just like the unofficial title of the queen mother of Britain. She was the only one in the family who had the wrinkly bronze skin that earmarked an Indian culture. She was always unusually quiet until spoken to. She loved to laugh when everyone started telling stories from the past. Conversations were called, "chinwags." She did not like the way alcohol was taking over people's lives and would eventually learn just how bad it would get in her own family.

A ride out on the lake in a motor boat became a regular thing there. The bass fishing was good about a quarter mile out near one of the islands. The reserve was located about and hour and a half northeast of Toronto. It was the beginning of many of the little lakes scattered across the Canadian Province of Ontario. Curve Lake and Buckhorn

Lake were near each other and made for a good place to fish, hunt, or trap. My fear of deep water hadn't fully developed yet, but Dad would make sure that it did.

"Junior, would you like to go over to Merlin's and then go to the store?" Grandma would say.

Her love for the son of her favorite son was obvious, but she played it cool most of the time. She would give us a little money for penny candy and we would be off for the trading post. My uncle Merl lived only a half mile from Grandma and was easy to get to. In the early '50s you didn't have the same concerns about being abducted as you do now. Us kids traveled in packs anyway, so there was power in the numbers. That trading post would be the envy of literally any store in the country today. Everything in it was handmade and sold for a song. The commercial spirit hadn't been near Curve Lake and would not come for some time. Times would change eventually and the prices would go through the roof.

Mom was always welcomed at the reserve, but I never suspected what was really going through the minds of some people with respect to the "white woman."

One of our trips to Canada took us straight to Sharon and Earl's home in Toronto. It was Canadian Thanksgiving time and the drive on the Queen Elizabeth Highway from the border at Niagara Falls was always exciting. That straight stretch saw many speeders fly by us as Mom tried to keep a check on Dad's driving.

"Slow down Ronnie, the kids are in the car," she would say as he would try to push it.

There weren't many pieces of road like that around home and Dad certainly knew the Queen E like the back of his hand. It took a long time for me to understand that Mom's wording in situations like that was literally giving Dad a license to speed when she wasn't around. I would experience that later myself when Mom stayed home.

We got to Toronto a day before thanksgiving. I was used to seeing a turkey on the table on that big day. This one would be different and Dad would be extremely disappointed. In the small apartment there were four adults and four of us kids. Sharon and Earl had two girls to watch over. Dierdre known as "DD," and Betsy were about our age and they were a handful. I never knew what real relationship they were to us because I think there was some marriages and hanky panky involved there somewhere. I was supposed to just refer to them as "my cousins." DD was the troublemaker and she proved it over and over again. The sniveling attitude of a ten-year-old redhead disrupted the day more than once. The company in their space took the edge off a bit, but it was still a trial for the parents.

The dinner was to be a surprise, and what a surprise. Earl brought out two duck on platters. Dad could have eaten both of them himself. Mom watched him as he tried to keep it together. "We had traveled all the way here for this?" was my interpretation of the look on his face. There was a grace said at the table and the duck were cut for eight people. It was not impressive at all. We knew Earl just wanted to show off his hunting skills because a long story came with each of the duck.

"You don't know how long I waited for these two guys to show up," he bragged. "It was rainy and cold, but I got them."

The story dragged on and did not in the least bit change the fact there was not enough meat on the table for all of us. Earl meant well, but he was the only one mesmerized by his great white hunter story. That and the fact that he was the one cutting up the duck so everyone could have some. The grease on those two birds could have lubricated an Army tank, but we ate them. The only saving grace was the potatoes, stuffing, and dessert. I can still hear Dad to this day when they retired for the evening.

"Those little teeny duck, I can't believe it, I just can't believe it."

We had our holiday in Canada and came back home a little disgruntled. Dad made sure for the rest of his days that we had a turkey on the Thanksgiving table.

Back to Reality

Life on Congress Street in the summertime was special in some ways. When Mom and Dad would go out on a Friday night and us kids stayed home, Hilda again was the one who had the prestigious job of babysitting. We knew it was game time. The anticipation of being without some of those parental restrictions became almost too good to be true. Hilda, this time, would be tested farther than she had ever been tested before. Mom and Dad went out to the Star restaurant about five o'clock that Friday. Mom always gave Hilda instructions about us while Dad gave us instructions concerning Hilda.

"You kids behave yourselves," was the blunt point made on the way out the door. "I don't want to hear anything bad about you when I get home," he echoed while the door closed.

The message from Mom was usually along the line of provisions such as snacks and what time for bed etc, etc.

It was a particularly warm summer evening and we had our usual fun in the yard for a while. Hilda let me go the Second Ward Park just down the street two blocks. I was supposed to be home by dark and we would have some popcorn and watch a movie. Well, there was also the Caterpillar company depot next to the park. As a young boy I was infatuated with the tractors and everything else in that big stockyard. We were forbidden to climb on the heavy equipment, but it just seemed like so much fun. After about an hour of sitting on a few different tractors it was getting dark. One of the things that this dealership also had in stock were those big three feet wide corrugated steel pipes. Some of the pieces were twenty or thirty feet long. I climbed inside of one right at the time when I should have been coming home. Inside of those pipes were little round rivet heads that looked like metal pills the size of aspirin. I had always known they were there because I used to throw them down the pipe just to hear the sound of the echoing chink of metal against metal as each piece ricocheted off of the inside edges of the corrugated steel. Tonight I would like it so much I just sat inside the pipe and did it for at least forty-five minutes. I could now hear sirens in the distance. They got closer and closer. I thought, *Maybe there was a house fire or an accident. Nahh, I could tell if there was one. It was probably a false alarm or something.* Chink, chink, clang, clang, went the pieces of metal down the pipe. I loved to hear that sound, especially since it was dark I couldn't tell when it was going to stop. After three-quarters of an hour, I climbed out of the pipe and started home well into dark. Walking off of the lot to the street I could see police cars and fire trucks everywhere…near my house. There were people walking up and down both sides of the street, some with flashlights. It wasn't Halloween time and I just couldn't figure out what everybody was doing.

Then I heard someone yell, "I found him, he's over here." Everybody started coming in my direction.

One fireman came to me. "Are you alright son? Everybody has been worried about you."

Yelling and cheering ensued as I finally figured out what they were all doing. Aunt Hilda came to me in tears as my escort of about thirty or forty people gave me into her arms.

"Where were you Junior. Don't you know that you were supposed to be home by dark?"

I looked around at everyone as they waited for the answer. I pointed to the Caterpillar dealership and said, "I was in a pipe over there."

Without any further questions I was walked the next hundred yards without any resistance. The fire trucks left and the neighbors all took their marbles and slowly retreated into their homes. I had a short-lived moment of stardom. The well known fact that Mom and Dad would eventually come home had taken me over. When they did

I never heard a word about it. I never found out if they were told or found out some other way. The way my life was going there was no way that I shouldn't have been at least scolded or spanked, but I got nothing.

There were times when Twila and Ronnie would go out on a Friday or Saturday night and us kids got to stay up late. Our infatuation with the "Twilight Zone" or the "Outer Limits" brought us kids many a nightmare, but we always went back for more. The thrill of sitting up with Hilda as our protector and staring at monsters at midnight enraptured especially me. I had begun to develop my scientific creative mind. Mary very often would fall asleep during some of the best parts. I also think that my fondness for popcorn started way back then. Hilda always made a good batch. The intrigue of having to figure out what was going to happen next while mindlessly stuffing my face like a robot was something that I always looked forward to.

One of our favorite things to do while Mom and Dad were out was to "camp out" in Hilda's room. Mary and I would make a tent out of blankets. Draping a sheet off the end of a sewing machine and propping it on the other end with chairs made for a safe haven after seeing the uglies on the TV screen. We were "allowed" to stay there for the night. I guess that made for a little respite away from some of the residual effects from Dad's night out. I really didn't know what my little sister's position was with all of that, but she did have fun with me when I built the tents. Julia just went along with all of it. Her room was next to Hilda's and would be a place for us to visit.

Although Hilda and Julia were Swedes that had come over on the boat from Sweden in the those late 1800s, there weren't many stories about their life over there mainly because they were so young. Hilda made it clear that the main reason for their journey here was the "horn o'plenty" mentality that was sweeping the globe about America. "Our parents came here to get a good job," she said. Charles Bengson was the only brother and he had arrived a little later. August Bengson was the father that got it all started and apparently everyone had made the trip without a mother and wife who endured an early death from some disease. August had bought the house at 414 Congress Street where the sisters lived out most of their days.

The house was full of rooms that were designated by colors. The "orange room" was a forbidden place to go, so it was my favorite. A trunk that had come over on the boat was full of expensive clothing. It belonged exclusively to Julia.

"You are not to go into that room," Mom would tell me. "Those things all belong to your aunts and you are not to even touch them. The trunk is full of things that are none of your business."

That kind of talk from my mother could only come after it was discovered that I did go in to snoop around. I began to learn the craft of making everything look like it had not been disturbed. I had to get all the way into that trunk. The way Mom had worded it made it all the more a need in my life. It is one thing to just plainly tell me not to do something, but to go into detail about why not just adds a lot more novelty. The muskrat fur coat, expensive dresses, and some jewelry filled that trunk with things that Julia would never wear. On the lid was a hole that had been burned through due to the fire that had consumed the rear part of the house. That was why the charred rafters were still in the attic over the kitchen. The fire had started around a stove and spread into that attic. The house had been rescued, but had many repairs. The trunk had been originally in that attic and was obviously relocated to the Orange Room.

The "Blue Room" was now occupied by Aunt Julia herself. While each room was the color it was called, the Blue Room was eerily reminiscent of the character of Julia. Although she was mostly kind to us kids, she would have nothing to do with Dad. Julia and Hilda both were very religious, but Julia had been tempered with some resentment through a marriage that ended in divorce. Harry O'Connor used to come and visit before I was ten years old. Many a conversation would end in argument and he eventually would stay away for good. I never knew what made Julia into an angry woman, but that could have been it. She had a perpetual scowl branded into her face. I felt bad for her because divorce was almost a taboo thing back then and I knew that she had a frustrating time with it. She was "Blue" all too often. She, however, would try and keep her business to herself and inconspicuously give Mary and I some attention, explaining to us that there were important things in life that we should pursue. I felt that much of it was way out of my reach.

"The most important thing for your life is that you go to college. I went for four years and got a degree." she would explain.

The shorthand notes on pads that were scattered all over the room was indicative of one of the skills that she learned in college. She would hold one of the pages in her lap and try to help me understand what it meant.

Julia continued. "Shorthand is a complicated way to shorten the amount of writing that you have to do. Each one of these funny looking symbols means more than one thing. It can mean a letter, a word, or an entire phrase. It makes it easier to write more with less."

I looked at all of those markings and just let it all go. For a kid who hadn't even mastered sentences in plain English yet, I would just patronize my aunt for a few minutes, acting like I was really interested. She did mean well and would be responsible for planting some seeds of positive value though. Unbeknownst to us at the time, a crippling disease would set in and take over her life.

The "Pink Room" was the brightest room in the house. Not just because it was pink, but because it also faced the east. The morning sun came through the shades and lit up those walls with a natural hue that could not be duplicated anywhere else in the house. By ten in the morning, however, the big maple trees in the front yard would shade the whole house. The Pink Room was mainly used for storage until Mary was old enough to have her own room. I was now in the pantry and she needed a place of her own as well. She would occupy that room until she got older and left.

Mom and Dad's room was the bedroom on the first floor next to the living room. I have never been sure whether the first floor was ever meant to have a bedroom on it or not. None of the rooms looked like they were a place to sleep. French double doors separated the living room and my parent's bedroom. It looked like that room was supposed to be a dining or powder room of some sort, but not a place to sleep. I know the room now designated as my bedroom wasn't meant to be a place to put a bed, but there I was for the next decade and a half.

The religious life of my aunts had started to be an obvious irritant to Dad. On more than one occasion I would hear some friction between him and particularly Hilda.

"You shouldn't be talking like that Ron," she would say.

Dad's mouth was something not desired at times. He had incorporated some foul language into everyday life and certainly would emphasize those kinds of words when he was angry. The two sisters never really backed down, they would just leave him up to his own devices. They knew where he was headed and they did not want him to take us kids with him.

Very often we would have members of different faiths visit our home. Most of the time Dad wasn't home and I'm sure that was probably a planned thing. Jehovah's Witnesses, Mormons, Episcopalians, and Lutherans came knocking to spread their versions of the good word. Hilda would be waiting for them to arrive and I would get an earful of many interesting things. No one ever interfered with them trying to convince me of anything. I also had a good memory and decided to wait and watch about all those stories about Heaven, judgement, and Hell. Each denomination had its own idea of what was to come, but they all agreed on one thing. "You must believe in the Lord Jesus Christ and you will be saved." I never understood what any of the outlying differences in their belief systems were or even why they separated themselves through those differences. The similarity in their believing of a Heaven and a Hell intrigued me, though, and I would ask questions, mostly after they had left. The message of the Earth coming to an end and all of us being judged was not disputed by any of them, but rather embraced. It didn't really scare me, but was more or less fascinating. The state of the world at the time did not, in my mind, warrant what they said was going to happen, but their agreement on the message of salvation kept my attention.

One of the more unique folks to come knocking was the "Fuller Brush" man. He seemed to be always dressed in a brown suit and carried a mid-sized matching color briefcase full of combs, hairbrushes, fancy mirrors, and hosiery aids, like those long tools for slipping on your shoes when they were tight. He always called during the day. Dad would be at work and Mom would answer the door.

"Hello Mrs. Knott," tilting his hat just like in the movies. "How is your day going? I hope you are in the buying mood, I've got some great new stuff here."

He was really a fast talker, but he also had the goods to back up what he was saying. Everything made during those days had gotten more attention and held up a lot longer. Hilda and Julia usually stayed away from the man. Once in a while they would take look at what he had. Mr. Quigley always made sure that they knew he was there. "Are your aunts home too?" he would ask.

Sometimes Mom had an answer ready because she was instructed to, or maybe one of the two sisters would come and investigate for themselves. Mr. Quigley always opened that suitcase and wasted no time in informing Mom of every product that he had. The little shaving brush that Dad used with a can of "Barbasol" shaving cream lasted for many years.

There was always another group of people that would be at our door. I learned the term "Collector" at a very early age. It was one of those words that I thought everyone was using. It turns out that I was wrong. There were people out there that actually paid their bills on time. I could hear the reasons and excuses that Mom would use to ward of the representatives from the gas or electric or loan companies. "Next week, next Friday, in two weeks, the checks in the mail," to name just a few. My introduction into some truths about life would come only at the hands of me getting older and making those observations for myself. I would eventually depart from all of it for a long season. The "Collector," as he or she was called, would be shielded from my watchful eye trying to see who these people were. It was only a matter of time before the real reasons for them at my door would surface. Connecting the dots between Dad's alcoholic behavior and the unpaid bills took a while and there was nothing I could do about it when I finally did.

One of the more troublesome times was when Dad would come home from drinking. Coming home from downtown or at the factory in a taxi was almost the regular thing. Very often a deaf man, who also could not speak, would pick Dad up and bring him home. He needed access to rides whenever he drank up our cars. Once in a while when Mom got stood up on a date with Dad, or when he would come home later than her, we could hear the taxi pull up at all hours of the morning and then cough up a drunk onto the front lawn. Mom would try to drag or coax him to come the rest of the way to the house. Most of the time it was futile and we would have to endure the images of the drunken husband and father in clear view of anyone who walked or drove past the house until he got up on his own. I hated the times that Mom had to work at that situation, but stayed out of it.

My Little Space

With separation starting, frustration in my heart.
The beginning and the end were many miles apart.
Before I could escape this lonely path I trod,
the harm to come must be endured.
I knew nothing of what was to come,
but what I longed for most, was approval from just a nod.
While others fought I stood idly by, wondering who was I.
Those years laid out for me were hidden from my face.
And now I see where I was. Living, I say, living in my little space.

Beginning to drift away from all of the trouble I just would run into more of it. Refusing to mind my parents about anything would bring me much heartache, not to mention aches in other places. Dad's words did not have the sting that they once had, and even the fear of reprisal through his belt started to fade. That was dangerous, but I didn't see it that way. The episodes with drinking and all of the irresponsibility that came with it caused me to believe that "why tell me to do things that you yourself are not doing?"

The problems with Dad and the elderly sisters began to mount. The whole issue came to a head around the end of the school year in 1965.We decided...rather Dad decided, that he wouldn't take the moral heat any more, so we moved across town to High Street. It was an adjustment to a new home. It was also the first big change like that in my life. I had only known Congress Street my whole short life. I was afraid of the change. What was I going to do for fun? Who was I going to hang around with? I would have to go to another school. My friends that I grew up with were now out of my everyday reach.

Mom had recently gotten pregnant around March, and I'm sure that factored into the need to move. With the prospect of another kid in the house that had been a little too busy to begin with, probably made it all the better for Hilda and Julia when we did leave. With many things to learn and new people to meet it was finally time to go back to school. The Fifth Ward Elementary School on the opposite end of Elm Street from my old Second Ward was situated on an angle high above the city. I had been able to do something that I thought I couldn't. At Second Ward I had gotten to be a Patrol and finally had that bright orange belt with a brass buckle. Proud I was to have that responsibility and, fortunately, I did not abuse the power like I thought I would. Fifth Ward would accept me into the fold and recognize my first year as a Patrol from another school. I needed that because my goal now was to get to Washington for that annual trip, rewarding all of the Patrols in the area.

The kids at Fifth Ward were obviously new, but one thing that did make a difference was some of those kids I had met throughout the summer I made friends with. That took the edge off of my apprehensions about meeting new ones.

My sixth grade teacher was Miss Baker. A beautiful young looking blonde that anyone would have liked. She was cut out for the job as an elementary school teacher by anybody's standard. There was one question about that, though, particularly for me around Halloween time. She had decided to have a contest for the class of about thirty or so of us. She handed out brown paper lunch bags for the students to decorate. The competition was that she would judge the best creative lunch bag and that person would get a prize. We got glue, paper doilies, colored paper, scotch tape and anything else that we needed to get the job done. After each one of us finished our work we were to tape the bag onto the long run of window sills. I strained to come up with best arrangement on my bag. Back at Second Ward two years earlier I had won a citywide contest at Christmas time drawing a reindeer, so I thought I had a good chance to take home the loot here. The bags were all hanging on the sill. Everyone waited with hopeful anticipation as Miss Baker walked along the entire length of the room with her hands intently behind her back. After lifting up a bag here and there to get a closer look she walked to the front of the class and faced us. All eyes had followed her every step of the way.

"Well," she said, "I think that they are all nice. You all did a good job. But remember that I asked for the most creative one? The winner is Jack Windsor. His as the most creative."

The class was stunned. I was stunned. We all knew what Jack's bag looked like without even thinking about it. On his lunch bag was

48

nothing. He did not spend a moment decorating it at all. He just took the plain bag over to the sill and taped it up. Every person in that classroom now had a resentment. We had all worked so hard to try and win the contest and now our teacher was trying to convince us that doing nothing was creative. It was thinking that came a couple of decades too early. That newfangled abstract view of art should not have been pushed on young impressionable sixth graders. I not only felt angry, but betrayed. Jack, of course, thought it was funny. It would take at least two decades and a lot more to get over those seeds of doubt about justice.

I don't know what it was about our arts and crafts class that got me into trouble, but it followed me wherever I went. Another time of cutting out images from magazines, gluing and taping things together, the elementary class of 1965 got another round of excitement. And I almost lost my life. One of the students in my class had been transferred from Second Ward. I had known him there and also knew why he had been moved to our school. He had a few mental or emotional problems. His behavior at times made everyone at the school a little uneasy. I didn't know why anyone thought it was the right thing to do to just switch schools thinking that it would solve the problem, but forty years ago anything went. James Diblos was always laughing, sometimes about nothing. Then he would cry, often without any apparent reason.

James was sitting in his seat cutting up some paper. He saw me looking at him and he started laughing. I didn't know what was so funny, but I thought, *Hey, help yourself.* I thought like that a lot back then. I had been his friend back at the other school and there was some comfort in that for me when I had started Fifth Ward. I had been able to walk home from school with him and carry on an intelligent conversation with him when others couldn't or wouldn't. My old buddy James got up out of his seat laughing like a psychopath with scissors in hand. I wouldn't have paid much attention to those shears except that he was holding them like he was going to stab someone. He then ran in my direction.

"I'm going to get you!" he said with a grin.

I threw down my craft paper and got up out of my seat. He had waited for Miss Baker to leave the room for a few minutes before he decided to make his move. Leaving my seat like I had to rush to the bathroom, James followed close behind. I believed that he was joking and yelling with this stabbing posture he was taking. Round and round the room we went. I began to think it was sort of funny myself, dodging in and out between the desks eluding my assailant. After I determined that it was time to quit before the teacher came back, I made the mistake of stopping and was ready to resume my own project. James came from behind and stabbed me in the back with those scissors. They stuck there and just swung around as I tried to reach them. The class was disturbed to say the least. As I was now crying from the pain and looking like a dog chasing his tail, in comes Miss Baker.

"What is going on here!" she exclaimed.

Not noticing what was really happening I knew that she thought that we were taking advantage of the fact that she had been out of the room and now it was fun time. Then she saw the scissors sticking in my back. With both hands now on her face she yelled, "No, don't move, Ronald." She walked briskly over to me and looked closely at the problem. "Class, you wait here."

Miss Baker took me into the hall and yelled for help. The school nurse came and with me spreading my palms against the wall of the hallway she pulled them out. They hadn't really gone in too far. I was escorted to the nurse's office and looked at by another nurse. They decided that I did not need any further medical attention. My, how times have changed. The adjustments that had to be made with James came in the form of "Please don't do that again."

I made it through the school year alive and was rewarded for my work as a school Patrol. I was Washington bound. The anticipation of that trip was unexplainable. The prospect of that trip had been spinning around in my mind for years. I was never not allowed to think of it because every year in the month of May the meeting place for the Bluebird buses was right on Congress Street at the AAA parking lot. The patrols from all of the schools in Bradford who would be going to our nation's capital would file into the several buses that awaited them. The chaperones were always including the same two men. Mr. Arnett who was the President of the AAA in Bradford, and Mr. Dean, a car salesmen well known in the community. They were the best at their jobs with the kids. I had stood every year across the street from those buses and longed for a trip like that. And now it was my time.

Mom packed me a little lunch. The buses had their own restrooms, of course, and the trip of eight hours or so made it all the more fun. I couldn't sleep that much the night before, but that didn't make much difference. I could stay awake for anything now. We all met in that AAA parking lot and I could see the parents of the other kids and even some younger ones who maybe longed to be in my seat. This was important for me in many ways. The injustices at Sixth Ward seemed to be drowned in the sea of triumph here now. I had worked for it and I was going to get it. For a kid in the sixth grade I had the normal healthy feeling of reward for a job well done.

The journey to Washington was pure joy. The rest of the kids on my bus quickly formed their groups or clicks. We knew in advance where we would be staying for the next three days and nights, and who we would be staying with. My roommates would be Anthony Caruso and Leo Lucaster. They were part of the Italian band from the Fifth Ward area. The normal tomfoolery on the bus did not really bring much demise from our chaperone. There were four buses and each one had its own leader. The wagon train arrived near the Washington Monument in the early evening. The two motels were going to be packed full of kids for the next three days. They had been through it before, so this was not new to them.

The Harry Smith and the Ford Motels were across the street from each other and made easy access for anyone who needed to stay in contact with a friend that maybe had gotten assigned to the other motel. We unloaded our baggage and got used to the place. You wouldn't know that us kids had been in some position of authority for the last two years the way we were acting. Fortunately our times available to get in trouble were kept to a minimum. We were involved in many "get up and go sightseeing" tours that made sure we were busy. The most impressive part of the trip was having our picture taken on the steps near the Capitol Building. It was a bright sunny day for the perfect memento of a lifetime. The Smithsonian Institute, Washington Monument, Lincoln Memorial, and many other places were crammed into the tight schedule for the group from Pennsylvania.

Back at the motel at night, it was hard to get sleep with everyone sneaking around and pulling practical jokes until the wee hours. (At the moment of this writing I looked out my window and saw the President's 747 leaving Rochester Airport. It was more than ironic.) This trip had been the perfect capstone to all the standing in any weather during the school years. At the end of the trip, back in Bradford, we were exhausted. Mom met me at the AAA office and we took a taxi home.

During that school year I had a secret crush on Susan Lombardi. She had the most beautiful blue eyes and a sweet smile that melted me. If she even said one word to me, that would hold me over till the next time. Then came the big day. She asked me to walk her home from school. She lived only two blocks away down on, believe it or not, on "Rochester Street." Her cousin Mary lived only a couple of houses from Susan. I didn't care that much for Mary. She looked okay, but was a little heavy. My time to carry Susan's books was a privilege that hardly anyone got. My infatuation with Susan though would be another short-lived one. The person who really captured her eye was Leo, one of my roommates back in Washington. They were both full blooded Italians and I could not compete with the strong tradition that seemed to run through society, especially that particular community. I was aware of the marrying into your culture thing, but really didn't think that they stuck to it that much. But what little time I got to spend with Susan I made the best of. I ended up going to visit her after school, and even after dinner. There came a time when she pulled me aside and gave me the bad news. By the way she was acting I could see it coming.

"Ronnie, I have to tell you something," as she looked away toward the other end of her porch. "I know that you like coming here. But you are not my boyfriend, Leo is. We are going steady."

I looked her straight in the eye and saw deceit. They had been seeing each other the whole time and I didn't know or even suspect it. I didn't like dear John messages, but I really didn't like being led on.

"I understand, I didn't know you liked someone else," I responded. "I guess I'll go home."

Susan slid off of the railing on the porch and gave me a hug. In tears, she had been feeling the brunt of a bruised conscience. She could have done better than letting me think the things that I did and she knew it. "Good bye Ronald."

I did not weep, but I felt embarrassed to be abandoned once again. Every time someone calls me by my real name there was trouble. Off I would go into the sunset, but not feeling like a hero. This had been my introduction into the Fifth Ward. That would be short-lived too.

As fate would have it I would end up befriending Leo and hanging around him. He eventually broke up with Susan and I, of course, would have nothing to do with her. Leo lived in the opposite direction a few streets from me on East Main Street. When I went to his house for the first time, he introduced me to his mom. His parents were both full-blooded Italians, complete with the accents from the homeland. What I will never forget about his mom was her ability to twist the head off of a chicken. I had heard of that way of preparing those birds, but had never seen it. The old saying, "running around like a chicken with its head cut off," came alive for me that day. They do run around, but I had no idea that they even could. I wondered how they could keep their balance and not fall over without a head. Never found out and I didn't ask.

Leo had a thing for engines. His dad also worked at "Case" making knives, but didn't really know Dad. He had heard of him when I mentioned that I had the same name as him. By his reaction, Dad had not created a good impression. I didn't have to go far in my little mind to imagine why not. Leo's father would bring home a spare part or two for Leo to tinker with or try and build a small go-cart. Anything with a motor on it had Leo's attention. There was one interesting set of pets that the Lucaster family had. A pair of ravens stayed on the porch or in the house near the creek. Their names were Heckle and Jeckle so named after the cartoon characters. They would fly around the neighborhood and even follow Leo and I all the way to my house. I hung around Leo for a few months and then quit. He had a streak in him that produced a strange temper. As an adult he went on to spend some time in the auto dealer business.

Spotty

Pets were at times something important in our lives. There is something mysteriously soothing about an animal that doesn't have the capacity to choose like we do to things so wrong. Their unique innocence alone helps people to refrain from spending time and attention on whether you are going to get wronged. In my early years we had "Prince" the male Beagle, "Tiny" the calico cat, a few turtles and another cat gray cat.

One year, Dad brought home another Beagle puppy. We had her around for a couple of years and she got pregnant. Apparently the father was a Beagle also, for the five puppies were all that brand. I cannot remember the name of the mother, and I guess for good reason…I haven't wanted to. I had been sleeping on my bed in the pantry into the early hours of the morning. All was quiet. The mother and puppies were just on the other side of my door, quiet as a church mouse. The usual noise of Dad coming in the door at two or three in the morning made everyone in the house aware that he was home. He staggered into the kitchen where all the dogs were. His habit at that hour was to make himself something to eat or drag me out of bed by my hair and make me do it. Tonight I would get a reprieve, at least physically. The puppies awoke from the fumbling in the refrigerator. A drunken man became irritated from the whimpering of little dogs only a couple of weeks old.

Dad raised his voice. "Shut up, or I will shut you up!"

They of course didn't. I heard the water being run into the pan that he had always shaved in. Then one by one I heard the cracking of little necks and then they were held under the water to make sure death had taken over until there was silence in the kitchen. By that time I was filling my mouth with my blanket and biting a hole it. I swore that some day I would kill him. There wasn't one sound of that act that I could not hear. The mother of those pups did nothing to provoke anything further. Seeds had been planted in me that would come out slowly for decades in the form of anger, resentment, and vengeance.

The Thief and
the Penny

Probably one of the greatest examples of parallel ironies happened in 1965. There would be an attempt to get me straightened out on many fronts, compliments of the inconspicuous efforts of others. One lesson was not realized until thirty-seven years later, at the time of this writing.

"If only I knew then what I know now," is the common adage that echoes in my mind. Heard it much, said it a few times myself, but grew out of it. Being blessed with an inventor's mind probably saved me a lot of trouble and brought me some too. I couldn't stand the thought of wondering anymore if the outcome would be different had I taken another approach to life. Could have been worse. Anyway, it was taking up valuable time to wonder about it. One thing I knew for sure. Just do the right thing now and leave the past and future be where they are…but I didn't do that.

A persistent problem prevailed that year. My allergies were at their worst ever. Mom reminded me that the chronic ailment started when I got into that "bug bomb" when I was about six or seven. My prime summer months consisted of staying on the front porch or inside the house at 35 High St., which is now a vacant lot. Our landlord lived next door. A set of grandparents, a father and two children occupied 37 High St. I befriended the boy, Patrick Munday, who was one year behind me. We had many of the same interests. Science and technology were two of our most avid influences. Building model rockets, tearing apart TV's and radios became a way of life. Astronomy was also an infatuation for two early teenagers. That Christmas we both got forty power Tasco telescopes and made good use of them. This particular interest was fueled much by the creation of the television series "Lost in Space," which started its weekly debut that year. I still talk today about how funny the name "Judy" was for that monkey with the big ears.

Another interest we had in common was coin collecting. Although I had acquired quite a collection over the years, it was much more fun going over what we both had. We joined the Bradford Coin Club, which met once a month over top of the "Northwest Savings Bank" on Main Street. Always looking for that one valuable coin eventually brought trouble into my life.

Pennies were an integral part of my collection. Rolls of pennies, pennies in individual wrappers, and the traditional blue foldout coin holder, all complimented our nation's current lowest denomination in my large tin box. The box was actually an empty "Stuart Science Lab" kit. It had two fold out drawers. Perfect for what I was using it for. Although there was such a thing as a "Half Cent" at one time, I wasn't much interested in that coin, even though I had one or two. The 1909SVDB, the 1933S and the 1955S were the three pennies that were out of my reach. So, after careful consultation with Pat, we decided to try and alter a coin. Pat really wasn't too hip in the idea, especially since it would take about three months. There was only one date that would qualify. 1938. If you chip out the eight to a three, we are in the money, I thought. But wait, before you send it in it must be aged to hide the alteration. So we took the eight and made it a three, then buried it in the ground for three months. We perceived that the dirt and moisture would bring our little project back in time the five years we needed to cover. Ninety days later out came our coin and on the market it went. The anticipation of reaping what we sowed was exciting. The company sent the coin back and said it was altered. I would pay dearly for that act very soon, but never saw the connection for thirty-five years.

There was another thief on the loose in our town about that time. Although his real name was John Sikes, he had acquired the infamous title of Robin Hood. He stole from the wealthy and allegedly gave to the poor. The cops had a hard time catching him. I, along with possibly many others, were secretly admiring him for not only being a champion of the less fortunate, but for taking from the despised rich in our small town. One of the attractive qualities of his life was the intrigue of not getting caught and the fact that he stole when no one was around while using no weapons. The media had a field day with this modern day version of the "man in red." But, eventually there would come a time when he could slip up, and it did. He made the mistake of stealing a gun from the Army-Navy surplus store. As soon as the town heard that news our attraction to this man's story changed from fascination to fear. It wasn't fun anymore. I don't remember the day of the week, but it was in the summer because all the kids were out of school. The police sirens howled from all directions. The only time we ever heard that many was a major fire and that didn't seem to be the case because they were getting closer to my house. Only patrol cars, not fire trucks were quickly filling the streets nearby.

Word quickly spread that Sikes had broken out of his pattern and stole the gun to use in an armed robbery. He had taken refuge in the woods about one short block away, behind 35 High Street that had been my home for a year and a half. With all this excitement going on I had to see how it would end up. Standing in front of my house, I plotted where the authorities were concentrating their efforts. Running up the hill I heard a few shots and stopped. No more shots. I started running again and saw through the trees many spinning lights emenating from the cop cars and now an ambulance. As I climbed the last bank and approached the road there he was, on a stretcher. It had only taken a few short minutes for it all to be over. Unhindered by anyone, I walked slowly up to our Robin Hood. He had been shot in the head with a high powered police rifle. Amazingly he could hear my words and look at me.

In tears I said, "Its going to be okay."

He turned slightly to look at me with a stoic stare and then passed over to the other side. I stood to my feet and was dazed at the revelation that this was the first time I watched a person die.

Somehow in all this I should have seen that there was a penalty for being dishonest within myself, but the last person I was thinking of was me. A kid in his early teens enduring such a trauma as this had hardly the thought of learning a life's lesson.

A short time later my brother Samuel was born. The last day of the year 1965. Mom couldn't hold out a little longer to compete for the rewards that came for giving birth to the first baby of the year. It was strange having a brother, and a baby at that. His crying and keeping us up at night made me believe that this was the last of the "family increase," and so it was.

Dad was proud of Sam. As he held him he always used to laugh at the smirk that seemed to cover his face. As far as I was concerned there was never any competition for attention. My little brother would have won hands down. However, there came to be what I call a contest to see who could keep all of us awake the longest. The father of us all had this habit that only occurred at night, usually between midnight and four in the morning. He would come home and play records at any volume. The old 45s are still ringing in my ears today. "Running Bear" and "Blueberry Hill" bring me back there thirty-seven years ago every time I hear them maybe once in a while in a commercial or in a store that might be using a radio to sedate the customers. The only experience I have with those tunes is being wide awake. Over and over again those two songs were played. To the best of my recollection this went on for a few years. Not every night, but too often for someone who was told to get good grades in school. The alcohol in my father had the biggest influence on his decisions to do most of what he did, even when he wasn't drinking.

That fact came to bear some time later when my suspicions were so strong about the theft of my entire coin collection. Mom confronted him in front of me and, of course, he denied it. I didn't know for sure then because my dad stressed honesty his whole life. As far as I knew he never lied. This would have been a first. There was some compelling evidence, though, that I couldn't shake. Ronald Sr. had a drinking problem his whole adult life and he never ceased to spend money that was intended for the family to survive. He could have broken out of his "comfort zone" and broke the big rule he wanted us kids to live up to. Don't lie, cheat, or steal. To make matters worse his pride wouldn't let him admit it if he did do it. By the responses he gave and the circumstances at the time of the crime I still believe he took it. The most remarkable aspect was his reaction to the question. Very defensive for days afterward. Anyway, this message that I did not learn till decades later was that "what goes around comes around." That old cliché was driven into me any time I did something wrong.

The "penny." That "old penny." Couldn't put the two together. It was another great opportunity to learn something about life's lessons and I missed it. For the love of that altered copper I traded something that if I had that collection today I could pay off the house. My problem was that my heart wasn't changed about all that. Even when I knew I was guilty of fraud, they never accused me it. I felt safe not getting caught and didn't change my thinking. Too bad. Too sad.

The Paradigms of 12 Cedar Street

One of the two times our family left Congress Street for another address was the barn-shaped house at 12 Cedar Street. This was the next to the last move in which we ultimately returned to the house that has gripped my mother for the rest of her life, 414 Congress Street. The reasons for the move in the first place were the same as before. Dad couldn't get along living in the same home with two convicting aunts. They never said anything about being pure and holy, they just lived it, and the stark contrast between their lives and Dad's was the same as a black spot on a white wall. He didn't want to be around anything that constantly reminded him of his errors. So we moved, less than a mile from Aunts Hilda and Julia. Although Bradford was not a big town, that was still close.

The new home wasn't anything to look forward to as far as I was concerned. Although the neighborhood wasn't totally strange to me, it meant that I would have to really adjust to it, not just visit it as I had done in the past. Johnny Burton was our landlord and an interesting one at that. He was a Pennsylvania State Health Inspector and he had one of the messiest apartments I had ever seen up to that time. Living right below us on the first floor had to be a trial for him. He never really complained about any noise in our apartment or when Dad would come home singing in the early hours of the morning. On the other hand, we didn't have much to say about his little escapades with friends or women when he got too noisy. I know it wasn't even Steven, because we were much louder than most of what noise he had ever produced.

The house was a dark barn red, which accented its shape. One of the early days there I almost fell through a railing on a small four foot by four foot porch. Johnny did fix it, because he felt he was supposed to, not because of any fear of a lawsuit. Quite a difference from much of today's world.

Like many other family moves around the country, ours was planned with school scheduling in mind. We moved in the summer of 1968. I had turned fifteen that past January and the coming school year would be seeing another new high school freshman. Even back then it was a little trepidus in lieu of the fact of getting destroyed by the traditional dictatorship of upperclassmen. It went quite okay for me. I think the anticipation was worse that the actual initiation.

The house was only a hundred yards from the bus stop, which was ironically across the street from one of Dad's favorite bars. It was called Ben's. Named after the owner, Ben Idorosa. I was never really sure if that prime location had anything to do with the move since all Dad had to do was roll down the bank a few feet and he would end up near our front door. And that he did…literally, more than once. On one hand it spared me some of the shame rather than when he would sleep on the park bench in the public square, but at the same it didn't really help him with his problem It just got worse.

Dad's sense of responsibility to provide for his family took many very interesting twists during his tenure as breadwinner. I don't know if it was the Indian in him, the booze, or both, but I knew we were living in the 1960s not the 1860s. I had wished he would have remembered that at times. Like the episode when I was made to completely dress out two deer. Both were dragged up the long steep stairway to our hot summer apartment and laid to rest in the bathroom. Not only was it not deer season, but the limit was two at the time only when fall would arrive. The fact that the one deer lying in the bathtub was a bloated road kill may have given my father a note of perverted confidence that since only one deer was shot, he may have found a loophole.

The process of a full dressing of both of these animals was long and tedious. I spare myself the details, but cannot forget the hopscotch I had to play to keep from damaging the tub with the knife and hatchet. Anyway, I got the job done and nobody got sick over the "questionable meat."

Being disciplined was never fun, especially when I was wrong. I had gotten caught stealing a stick of pepperoni from the South Bradford Fruit Market, which was just around the corner a couple hundred yards. A few of us were camping out up on the hill and I took the prestigious assignment on a dare. I needed attention and this was a perfect opportunity to acquire it. Walking to the back of the store to the meat and produce cooler had drawn the attention of one of the owners. He went into a walk-in cooler and peered through a hole in the door just in time to observe me sliding the pepperoni down my pants. Ronnie Boser came running out of the cooler and yelling "Where's Bill Neatour?" Bill was the well known Bradford Township cop that we all knew. Well, as the story goes, Bill was called and drove me in the squad car around the corner to my house and escorted me up the stairs just in time to see my dad. He didn't want to do that. They never did. Everybody who had ever caught me doing anything, dreaded presenting me to my father. They knew that my punishment was going to be more than what the crime called for. Bill left, and naturally, I went sailing across the room with a backhand. Twice. My neck would hurt for a couple of days when that happened as it did happen too often. He had said, "What ever possessed you to steal?" and then the beating commenced. I was never hit, as far as I can remember, with a closed fist. The fact that I was still alive testified to that. The outright punch was reserved for the man to man fights he got into.

There once was a man named Bill Stanley, who thought it was no big thing when he made the mistake of kindly suggesting to Dad to "go easy on the kid." I was at the time just receiving strong words prior to what I perceived to be my usual physical retribution. (Never did understand why I didn't wise up). What nobody knew was that my father had never expressed to anyone that I knew that his role as the disciplinarian was something he wanted to share with anyone. After Bill made his suggestion, Dad punched him in the face.

Bill yelled out, "you broke my nose Ronnie!"

With Dad still angry, Bill was taken and thrown down that long flight of stairs. Fortunately, there were no broken bones from that fall. I believed that later on they patched things up and there was no attempt to interfere with my punishment again by anybody.

Mom was in the kitchen and heard the commotion, but never did anything. With the exception of a few times of horseplay, while I was being twisted into a pretzel, she never really did come to my rescue. Sometimes it was definitely a need when I would look up at Mom from the floor during my "predicament" and get no response that should have favored ending my pain.

Charley Shemeda became a good friend of mine. Charley lived a couple of houses away around the corner. This family of ten boasted the art of never being inconvenienced for anything. There was always someone around to pick up the slack. My new friend had a love for electronics and would show me up at times his ability to explain in detail the finer points of televisions and radios. My initiation into his world came when I discovered that it was possible to get shocked from a TV while it was still unplugged. I was so impressed that when I crossed a couple of wires our local radio station would come over the speaker. The attempt to get more stations was, I believe my first mistake.

There was something unique about the Shembeda family. Everybody was short. It was obvious that all the kids never made it to six feet because Mom and Dad were both about five foot six. There are exceptions in some families, but not this one. Charley's first cousins, the Pettinato family, lived just up the street. Yup, they were short too. I would get to know them better later on because their dad, Joe, was a carpenter and I would tend to him in the construction industry. His nickname was "Spud" so named after a little potato.

The Boser family was living in the neighborhood. Gerry, Brian, and Ronnie all resided within a couple of hundred yards of each other. Gerry and his family lived next door to us, Brian lived on the other side of Gerry and Ronnie, (the one who caught me with the pepperoni) lived up the street around the corner near the fruit market. They all had a wife and kids and shared duties at the market that their Dad had started years ago. He still lived in Allegheny, New York, just over the state line about fifteen miles from Bradford. To this day, some thirty five years later, the Boser family is still ranked as the hardest working bunch I have ever seen.

Making it through the summer in my new home obviously had its trials, but autumn was still my favorite season. The colorful foliage, pumpkin pie and football games all highlight the ringing in of harvest time. Riding the new bus to school was interesting when I entered tenth grade. New kids in the new grade and the new kids because I was in a different neighborhood. Being somewhat timid and certainly self conscious because of my social status always gave me grief inside because I felt I didn't have much and Dad's lifestyle kept a hard thumb on my ability to get close to anyone. Bringing new friends home was still almost nonexistent. It was fair to conclude that they were glorified aquaintances rather than true blue friends, but some of us still hung out a safe distance from where I lived.

Christmas that year became a haunt for me to this day and for the rest of my life. It was the eve before the big day when the world would open its gifts. I remember it so vividly as I sat in front of the television watching "Andy of Mayberry." A white striped announcement started to move its way across the screen. It read: *Another Allegheny Airlines plane has just crashed three miles west of Bradford..* Mom and I were the only ones home and I told her what had just happened. I could hear Gerry Boser next door firing up his snowmobile to be put on his truck. Dad had called home to say he was downtown giving blood. I pleaded with my mother to let me go with Gerry to the crash and she gave in. Two weeks earlier the other plane went down in a swamp a few miles away and I wasn't going to let another chance like this slip by. Getting dressed for the ride was no problem. I yelled down to Gerry asking if I could go. He agreed and off we went. I have wished at times that Mom would have said no. The snow was coming down rather heavy, which was the primary reason for the crash in the first place. We got to the crash site before most of the emergency personnel did. There were many light plants set up which lit up the whole area. The scene of this disaster was the Pine Acres Golf Course, set on top of a hill outside of Bradford.

When we arrived at the scene of horror I saw a long dark oil slick streaking across the course and ending with what was left of the plane. We got out and rode the snowmobile to the plane. There were Christmas gifts scattered everywhere. The smell of jet fuel imprinted my mind forever. Body parts became a vision which would keep me up for the next three days. When I got to the main part of the fuselage in which there were some survivors, I climbed inside and tried to pry a pair of upside down seats apart to free a man that I didn't discover that he had died until I bumped him and it became obvious that I had to move on. I couldn't get to the pilots because they had been crushed in the nose of the plane when it hit a tree.

It was a lot to ask of a person in his mid teens who didn't have a stellar social life. The mistake I made was succumbing to the hype and thrill of this anticipation in the first place. After all, this wasn't just a case of running after a fire engine. Fortunately, though, this plane was looking for the airport when it went down, so they did not have a lot of fuel. The fire was out before I got there. Every year I remember those people at Christmas time and, also, whenever I drive past the airport where I now live. If the wind is blowing in the right direction, the odor of that infamous jet fuel creeps across the highway and into my car.

Making it through the winter months brought new life with the arrival of spring. I love the sound of the birds announcing the arrival of longer days and blooming flowers. Even after having apparently survived the winter, there was still a wonderful respite from the after affects of Christmas time to be found in the springtime. Easter vacation was something all the kids looked forward to. Back in the 60's the time off from school lasted at least two weeks. Things have changed though. Solid chocolate rabbits are now hollow and the average time off is a week.

One of my buddies who lived down the street about a half mile was Duffy. We got into this habit of weight lifting. He had a basement set up with a chair, which required a spotter for bench pressing. It was one of the first days of Easter vacation and Duffy invited me over for a session. His brother Bobby was upstairs playing the stereo. It came my turn to spot Duffy. The back of the chair was curved so it held the weights well, but it had to be monitored. Standing behind the chair with my legs spread, I prepared to help "Duff" do a bench press. Putting his hands on the bar, he hesitated. Bobby had put on one of his brother's favorite songs upstairs.

Duffy said to me, "Tell him to turn it up."

I looked at the ceiling and yelled to turn up the music. None of us knew how it happened, but the weights fell off of the chair and came crashing down on both of my feet, breaking two toes on my right foot and one toe on my left. The pain was great, but not as bad as when after Duffy helped me up the stairs and immersed both of my feet in HOT WATER! I did not find out till I got to the hospital that cold water was the fluid of choice for such an occasion. He put a towel in my mouth and I bit through it with ease. Crutches were my best friend for the entire Easter vacation. Other than not wanting to be around a lot of people, I guess there was a good reason that I hesitated to go out for the track team that year. I would have been sidelined for most of the season.

It was shortly after this that my job with the pizza shop came along. Colleen, puppy love (on my part), and a new social era was ushered in.

Out a Little Too Late

The years in high school were going by too fast. I had developed an emotional security and certainly a mental dependence on just being in school. It was in so many ways a respite from the fears of the "ogre." I couldn't put my finger on the obvious contrast, there just was this continuous comfort being around people all day that to me didn't pose a threat. This environment made a lot of things possible, at least circumstantially. One of these things was a girlfriend. Up to my sophomore year I never had a girl I could call my own. I just watched everyone else and how they acted around the subject. Being sometimes envious, sometimes grateful that I didn't have a girlfriend certainly kept me at bay of ever actively seeking one. My opinion of myself was conducive only to being single. Didn't have much in the way of material things to offer and I believed that being so self conscious of my state with things at home, no girl would have me anyway. That was all about to change.

It was the summer of 1968, and I had taken a job at a pizzeria on the South Avenue in Bradford. For the next three and a half years after school and some weekends I made money for clothes and recreation slicing meats and vegetables, always followed by cleaning the floors and windows. Never got to make a pizza. The proprietors, Doug and Marlene Heitzinger had acquired the shop from her parents, Tony and Marge, who had always been in the food business in one form or another.

After work, it was customary to either walk the mile home or go to the intersection of South Ave. and West Corydon Street to hitchhike. It was only a hundred yards away from the shop, so the straight shot to my house made it very convenient. We did not own a car at the time.

The habit of sticking my thumb out on that corner made it easy for a lot of people who walked or drove that route, to watch and wonder who I was or where I was going. One of those people decided to do something about it. During my frequent visits to that street corner there was this girl who passed by after school and had lived up the street about two blocks. She was very beautiful and unknown to me had cultivated an interest in me, just saying hello a few times as she passed by. Colleen knew some of my friends because she attended their same Catholic high school. Most of my childhood cronies attended the local Parochial schools, whereas I went to the public ones.

I did not know that her smiles at me were full of more meaning than I ever could have imagined. Then it happened. One of my buddies, Bob, came to me with a message.

"Ron," he said. "I've got to tell you something. Do you know Goose?"

Goose was a new friend I had met through Bob and happened to be Colleen's older brother. How convenient.

"Yes," I said.

"Well, do you know his sister Colleen?"

"Yeah. I know who she is, but I don't know her. You know what I mean. I see her all the time when I hitchhike. That's it. Why?"

Happy to deliver the message he answered, "She likes you and wants to meet you."

I blushed. Since this was to be my first real encounter with a real girl, I didn't know how to handle it. Anyway, Bob took my "okay" back to Colleen. The stage was set and we formally met in the large foyer at Bradford Area Senior High School, the place where even the students from Central Christian High transferred buses. She had been there every day and I didn't know it. Very often I did not go there for a bus because I worked and walked directly to the A&P store or the pizza shop. I would work at both places.

Just as I thought, I was all thumbs. With books in hand she saw me and gave me her usual smile. I approached with a caution. Someone of the opposite sex was actually paying attention to me.

"Hi," I said.

We didn't shake hands or anything. I remember saying a little bit about where I lived. Something I apparently had avoided during the short hellos on the street corner. She took pride in telling me that she was an honor student and for the first time I learned what brownie points were. She said she was involved in doing extra things for the teachers. You know, more than you're asked to do? My life consisted of just trying to do what my teachers had asked so I couldn't relate to that. I wasn't impressed, which later had found out that maybe that is what she was trying to do, impress me.

Her opinion of me to my face was reflected in the things she was saying about herself. Although she was trying to meet me where she thought I was, I wasn't there. I hated studying. I hated math. Just give me a football or some sneakers and I'll be just fine.

It seemed as though she eventually did not care where I was. Junior, as she was to call me, was the object of her affection.

Don't recall too much else other than we had agreed to meet at a dance. I liked dances. I could easily get lost in all of the crowd, having been often a loner. Wearing my blue and white pin stripe bell bottoms, flamboyant orange socks, light blue short sleeve shirt with a silk tie and slip ring made me fool myself into thinking I was very special. What I really wanted was attention from other people. Maybe the fact that this was a dance and I wasn't dancing kept everybody away, I thought. The football players with their lettermen jackets were getting a lot of attention. Or maybe it was because I would sit close to the band smoking a pipe loaded with Paladin Black Cherry tobacco that made me unqualified to socialize normally. At age sixteen, that should have finished anybody off that had any reservation about being connected to me. It didn't work. It never worked and Colleen was about to sign on to a lot of things she didn't plan on.

Our first few times together were, so it seemed at the request of her father, on the back porch steps of their second floor apartment. My initial introduction to her dad was quite frightening. This whole idea of having a girlfriend was going to be work. I would actually have to meet people. These terms were not harsh, I knew inside that my inhibitions could not be locked up forever, so I tolerated new acquaintances. The desire to follow through with establishing a relationship with the opposite sex was not complicated by ulterior motives, a virtue I could not lay claim to forever.

Nearing the end of summer brought all the school "hot dogs" to try out for football. As a junior in high school, the influences of "Goose," who played quarterback for Central Christian, and my speed, played the biggest roles in giving it a shot myself. Maybe I could get a little attention. Enduring the infamous "double sessions" in the hot August sun hurt. I ran as fast and sometimes faster than the fastest and most popular kid on the team. Senior Brian Hart, one of three brothers.

One of the Friday nights behind Colleen's house, up in the woods, several of my friends had a "sleepout" complete with beer. Mark Rothwell talked me into drinking a quart of Genesee Cream Ale without stopping. I had refused this kind of "fun" for years after seeing its affect on Dad and the family. However, this time I saw something different. I was getting some attention from different people and I liked it. I had a girlfriend and was going to be a star on the team, so maybe I should go the whole way with this "popular thing."

I chugged the beer as prescribed. I paid the price. A thunderstorm had come into the area that night. My buddies dragged a limp body to an abandoned driller's shanty and lit the pot belly stove. I woke up not knowing where I was. My hand was badly burned from touching the stove. The blood in my system was so high with alcohol, what seemed like an itch was really my fingernails pulling the outer layer of skin off. It didn't hurt at all. I found my way off of the hill and went to Bob's house at seven in the morning. Sneaking into their basement, I found their big dog Tippy sleeping on a mat. Asking him to leave, the next couple of hours were uninterrupted on the concrete floor.

Eventually, that day I got my hand bandaged up and lied about the source of my ever increasing pain.Double sessions continued. Fred Melenciak stepped on my hand, but I continued.

The pampering I got from Colleen almost made it all worth it. Still seeing her every night till about 10:00 was nice. She had to study, but on occasion would sneak out to be with me.

During football season there was a curfew. Everyone was to be home at 10:30. My dad knew that. One night I being so enthralled by the relationship with Colleen I came home late.

That was my first mistake.Dad had the habit of sitting on the front porch at night, many times till I came home. His drinking pattern included "a few after work." I sometimes gave him credit for coming home, still being able to walk on his own and then go to work the next day. This night I was greeted by an irritated father who promptly told me that if I was late again I would be forced to quit football. As the story would have it, history has a way of repeating itself, the very next night. Yes, all my experiences and fears with this man would be momentarily blotted out by the need to stay one more hour with my sweetie, no matter what. It was another hot summer night, and as I left Colleen, the veil was lifted and a great horror had begun to set in. It was past 11:30 again and the walk home was a tortuous one. There was only one thing left to do. Lie. But I needed proof.

Nine houses down the street from ours was a fifty foot long concrete retaining wall about six feet high. I made a fist and pushed it against the wall. Running the entire length of this wall didn't take long to produce the desired results. My right hand was a bloody mess. I then punched myself in the face a few times and smeared the blood everywhere. Now running down the street to induce a rapid breathing and messing up my hair, I was met at the front steps by a man who was prepared to pronounce sentence.

"Dad, I got in a fight with five guys. I beat up two of them and they all left, but I got hit a few times, that's why I'm late." Dad was proud of me and proceeded to show me all kinds of Indian Judo holds he used in fighting the gorillas in the carnivals. He almost broke my back several times and I felt it was probably better to have told the truth rather than endure this. After he finished, he told me that he was a man of his word and I had to quit football anyway. So I did. In some ways it was a relief. I didn't understand at the time that I wasn't living my own life, but I was allowing the influence of others to dictate my actions and trying to cover it up. A lesson that would take decades to try and master.

My Dad had always told me, usually with a few drinks under his belt, that all he ever wanted from me is that I would graduate from high school. I never really thought that a big request, especially since

I liked school most of the time. That petition would haunt me the rest of my life.

It was a beautiful summer day in early June 1971, the year of my graduation. Colleen was gone, and my new girlfriend, Althea, had planned to go to Cleveland to visit her sister and brother-in-law. About this time Dad took sick again. His third or fourth heart attack and a couple of strokes by age thirty-seven was less than impressive since they were all tied directly to how he had chosen to live his life. My apparent devotion to Althea was greater than even visiting Dad in the hospital only once during his two week stay. I wanted to see her no matter what.

The plan was crafted. I would visit her under the guise that I was in need of searching out the possibilities of colleges in the Cleveland area. Knowing Dad did not know or recognize anyone, I felt I would not be missed. Mom let me go. I had graduated on the tenth of June and it was about eight days later that I boarded a bus for Cleveland. Althea's sister Rachael and her husband Ed welcomed me and we talked about colleges and what my goals were, or at least what we wanted them to be. A couple of days passed and I had not moved on anything. No phone calls, no attempts to visit any school of higher learning, nothing. Realizing my true intentions, Ed confronted me. I was ashamed of myself and nervous at the chiding I was about to receive.

"Ron, we don't think that you have been honest with us. You led us to believe that you were here to visit various colleges and you haven't done that. We must ask you to leave."

Ed's soft tone was something that I was not used to from my father, especially if it was under circumstances such as this. I had been deeply moved at his self control, which I guess hurt all the more. The contrast between my error and his skilled approach produced pure shame.

My last meal at this house was pork chops and mashed potatoes, then I was to be on my way. I apologetically got on the bus at about two 2 p.m. My route would take me to Erie, Pennsylvania, with a two hour wait and then directly back to Bradford.

This was my first trip away from home by myself, and so far my initiation into traveling alone wasn't making a good impression, especially because it was my own fault. The infatuation with a girl blinded me to do what I knew what was right. Wasn't the first time, wouldn't be the last.

I arrived in Erie late. My connecting bus to Bradford had just left. It was five o'clock. The dispatcher said there is only one bus per day to Bradford, and the so next one wasn't due until five p.m. the next day. So, with a quarter to my name, I put it to use by storing my suitcase in a locker. Knowing that I had to find a place to sleep that night I set out to look. Fortunately, it was summer and there was about four more hours of daylight left. Out the front door of the depot I went, like a dog searching for food and a place to lay my head. Hunger was setting in, but with no money, my lodging took priority. I could sleep with no food, but I did not want to be awake all night on an empty stomach.

Directly in front of the bus station was a park that was home to what appeared to be the annual art festival. It was bristling with people admiring the work of the artists, some local and some not. The cool shade of the trees was a respite for many, including myself. As I walked through the myriad of canvas and watercolors, the back of my mind was preoccupied with life's essentials. The sight and smell of hot dogs and hamburgers drove me away from the place. I crossed the street back to the depot and started down the sidewalk toward a main road leading to the waters of Lake Erie. About two doors away something caught me out of the corner of my eye. I found myself staring into a storefront window. Turning on a rotisserie were several chickens. The sign had a special price that I know included salt potatoes, but I don't remember how much. At the time a penny was too much.

My journey took me a couple hundred yards to the road leading to the lake. As I made the turn, the lake was in clear view a quarter mile away. I approached the well advertised public dock. A ferry service was running nonstop throughout the day taking people to Presque Isle, the main attraction in that area. Its sandy beaches on that hot day were probably a good draw for business. The waters had not yet warmed to its full potential for the summer. As I got closer to the dock, there it was. My home for the night! An old schooner in dry dock was part of a museum. Although it was surrounded by a fence, that posed no deterrent for me. When night comes I will just climb it and I'm home free. The thought that there was no real reason for this boat to be watched at night secured my decision to bunk in it. My stay there would be brief, now that I had wrapped up the "place to sleep issue" so quickly.

Back to the bus terminal I went, past those chickens in the window. Taking a seat in the travelers lobby, it was time to wait out the last couple of hours of daylight. Watching people come and go made me envious of just getting out of my seat and going somewhere, anywhere.

An old man took a seat directly across from me. He was modestly dressed and fairly clean-shaven. I was a little nervous, knowing that he chose this seat over many others that were available away from me. As he slowly sat down, he looked me over, right to left and then up and down.

"That's a nice shirt, young man, where did you get it?"

"I bought it in Bradford, my hometown, why...do you want to buy it?"

The double shaded purple and white pin stripes were attracting him like a "Renoir," but I still couldn't believe I blurted out that it was for sale. Looking straight into my eyes, he said "How much?"

I did not think very long before launching back, "Five bucks."

Without hesitation, he reached for his wallet. I stood up and said "Wait a minute and I'll go change." As he watched, I took my suitcase out of the locker, went upstairs to the restrooms and changed into another shirt similar to this one. These shirts were hard earned by sweating it out in the pizza shop, but my current circumstances made me forget about all that. Couldn't thank the man enough. Five minutes now go by and here I sit, doing some serious damage to one of those chickens in the window. Actually, it was a half of one with the salt potatoes. Best meal I had in a long time. Maybe because I thought that I wasn't going to eat for at least another day had something to do with it.

Finishing dinner brought me that much closer to darkness setting in, so back toward my seat in the lobby I went. Nearing the terminal, I noticed something different. While I was eating, a bus had arrived and had parked out front. It had a flat tire. By then it was about 8:30 and there were still people at the festival. I went in to inquire of the bus. The dispatcher was a big well dressed black man who had retained some good southern verbage.

"Could you tell me where that bus out front is going?" I asked.

"Man, that bus ain't goin nowhere for two days," he said, smiling and shuffling papers.

"Thank you, sir," I retorted as my insides were now happy that I could maybe sleep on a bus instead of a boat.

Watching the art festival close up shop, I cased the street to see what kind of environment I was forced to work around in my attempt to get on that bus. The crowds dwindled down to nothing. With suitcase in hand, just before 9:30, after looking both ways I pushed the door in. I boarded and quickly closed the door and got down low. A few feet down the aisle the clothes in my suitcase became my bed. A very quiet restful sleep kept me dead to the world until the birds started singing. I don't think anyone saw me exit the bus. They probably wouldn't have guessed what I had just done anyway.

The bathroom in the terminal was convenient for washing up. It was about 7:30 a.m. and things were still slow. A few people out for a cool morning walk dotted the streets. Looking around and knowing I had a whole day to kill, I put my luggage back in the locker. A couple of bags of junk food would be my diet for the day. Even at 1971 prices, the five dollars had been stretched pretty thin.

I walked around several blocks of the city, stopping to see it wake up and go to work. Before I knew it two o'clock in the afternoon had come. Up to this point, my guilt from why I had to come home kept me from letting anyone know I was on my way. But, since I was going to be home in about five hours anyway, I pulled out a dime and decided to call home. At this phase of my journey I was at a phone booth back down at the dock. I dialed and Aunt Hilda answered.

"This is Junior, Aunt Hilda, can I speak to Mom?"

She responded. "She is downtown taking care of business." There is a hesitation. "Did you know that your father died last night?"

To say that I was stunned was insufficient. My mouth dropped and I did not know what to say. At that moment, half of me was glad that the wicked witch was dead. I didn't have to suffer any more. The other half was very sad that my father wasn't going to be around anymore, ever. That hurt. My natural devotion clashed with the total absence of anything about him I did not like. Relief and grief kept away any manifestation of either one. I never wanted the pain to stop this way.

Of course my answer to her question was "no." I let Hilda know that I would be in Bradford at about seven o'clock that evening. I slowly hung up the phone and looked over at the waters of Lake Erie. As a youngster, just a few miles away was Sunset Bay, a place our family had visited a couple of times. We had camped out on the beach with our cousins. Dad had always loved the water.

Walking the rest of the way to the dock, I paid a dime for a ferry ticket. I now felt that these waters must be my grave. Since I never really learned how to swim, this should be quick and painless. Taking my seat on the boat, we shoved off on a five minute trip to the Isle. Fighting back the tears was interrupted by a passenger sitting directly across from me. A young man my own age had burst out into tears and was cupping his head in his hands.

"What's the matter?" I asked.

"I just found out that my mother had died," he said.

I leaned back in my seat. "My father died last night."

He looked up at me and sniffled. "Really?"

"Yeah," I said. "I just found out ten minutes ago. I had planned on jumping overboard."

Not so impressed with this irony, our thoughts became consumed with the fact that "this just doesn't happen to me." We got to the other side and walked on the beach. His name was Ed and his intention on the boat was to take his life also. We talked about our futures. That was comforting. He stayed on the Isle, and after we said our goodbyes I came back to the terminal to await the final leg of this decathlon.

Five o'clock came and so did the bus. To this day I don't remember whether it was a Greyhound or a Bluebird, but it did make a difference then. I got on the bus and handed the driver my ticket. After looking at it he said, "Sorry, son, this ticket is for Bluebird, we're Greyhound."

I couldn't believe it. I retorted. "My father died last night and I've got to get home."

But he persisted. "I've heard them all. Wrong ticket. Sorry!"

This bus was not going to leave without me, and the fact that I was now in tears and pleading with him supported that. He gave me a disgusted look as though I was lying, but he told me to get on just to get me off his back. There were about a dozen people on that bus. It was a lonely ride home. We stopped in Salamanca, New York, to drop off a couple of passengers.

Upon arriving in Bradford, we pulled up to the front of the terminal. It was located almost across the street from the funeral parlor where they had Dad laid out. The driver opened the door only to be greeted by several men in black suits. They were my uncles and some of Dad's close friends who had come to greet me at the station. The bus driver stood up. Looking at the men and then looking at me, he broke down and wept. A man about six foot four was humbled and embarrassed by a kid who was really honest. I got to front of the bus and he reached out his hand to shake.

"I'm sorry," he said. "I really didn't think you were telling me the truth."

Shaking his hand, I replied, "It's okay, sir, it's okay."

Uncle Don and Uncle Merlin helped me off the bus and we all walked over to Hollenbeck's Funeral Chapel. Gayle Hollenbeck informed us that he had never seen so many people at a visitation in all his years of business. I somehow received some encouragement from that.

Mary met me at the front of the parlor. "Junior," she said, "where were you? We looked all over for you. We drove to Erie last night. We couldn't find you."

I became puzzled. "You were in Erie? How did you know I was there?"

In tears, she continued. "We called Althea's parents and they contacted Althea. We found out you got stranded in Erie, where were you?"

It seemed as though irony was becoming my middle name. "I slept on a bus, one that was broke down," I said.

"Where was this bus," she replied.

I answered, "Oh, right out in front of the bus terminal, it had a flat tire. What time were you there?"

Mary continued, "I came up with the Swansons at midnight and we were leaning up against that bus trying figure out where you were. We couldn't find you, so we came back."

Entering the Path of Destruction

I suppose that if I were to find a segment of my life that is difficult to express it would be this one. Many of the other events in my life came from the outside, that is, to the best of my knowledge I did not cause them. They came at the hands of other people and providential circumstances. Dad had just died and I was on the spot. I didn't feel as though I was, it really became just an afterthought to help Mom get back on her feet. Even with the mail coming in from all over the country for possible track scholarships, there was no contest to whom my allegiance should belong, at least for a season.

During the visitation at the funeral home, the business agent for my father's labor union approached me and assured me that if I wanted to I could be a part of the union and he would send me right out to work. I said that I would. Don Cummins Sr. had taken care of our family by getting Dad some work when he left Case. Of course, the funds for food and bills were tapped for the alcohol scene that ravaged Dad's life. I felt a responsibility and a new importance in my life. Armed with a hatred for John Barleycorn and a zeal to play a real part in this life became a driving force to join the union and go to my first construction job. The vacuum created by Dad's passing seemed to blot out any fears of making such a drastic change. I had been sheltered from such responsibility under the mighty hand of dominance for so many years that jumping from the pizza parlor to working with all men didn't faze me. Just a month earlier it would have, and little did I know that that decision would be one that would affect so many people for the rest of my life. History would be altered for me in a span of thirty days.

My first job in the construction industry was a highway job about thirty miles away in a little town called Barnes, Pennsylvania. My ride came by way of a man named Charley Applegate. He had known Dad and I learned many new things about who my father was when he was away from the house.

Barnes was a population of less that a hundred people, but it served as a base to set up shop for the company that was going to pave the road. Sheffield was really the metropolis for the immediate area. Three or four miles down the road from Barnes, this town of two thousand inhabitants should have been considered as one town rather than two. I never understood why so many little towns so close together seek to be so separate from each other. Charley owned a Volkswagen Beetle and the gas money for my ride was cheap. He took a liking to me right away. Being a very likable guy himself I could tell that he was affected by Dad not being around anymore. He also gave me a sense of security that came with his commitment to make sure that the son of the late Ronald Knott was going to be taken care of.

The first day on the job consisted of some orientation of how the company built a concrete highway and the different crews that performed different functions. The rightaway crew, the dirt hauling and grading crew, the paving crew and many others. There was one crew that I got introduced to that turned out to be very interesting. That crew was me. Greasing steel rods by hand with a five-gallon pail of graphite grease. Before the final grading crew comes to set the grade for the big paving machine, these wire baskets are set in place on the ground every twenty five feet. There are two baskets placed end to end in one lane of highway. There was about twenty rods, one foot long that would fit just inside a toilet paper tube. My responsibility was to put on a pair of rubber gloves, gouge the grease in the pail and slide the grease onto the rod until it was completely covered, many thousands upon thousands of them. It was a two-lane highway two and a half miles long. Bent over twelve hours a day for the next ten weeks convinced me that even though I was surrounded by a bunch of good men, they made sure that the newcomer on the block got in the initiation. Nobody wanted that job, and now that I think of it, after a few days neither did I. The pay was good and I knew it would come to an end.

One thing that I had never learned how to do was drive a car. Dad let me try a couple of times, but what could a six year old kid do sitting in his Dad's lap not being able to reach the pedals? No power steering back in the late sixties didn't help any. If we would have hit a rut, my hand would have been shattered. Charley thought it would be a good time to teach me how to drive. Even though the Bug didn't have power steering either, it was finally a thrill to give it a shot. My newfound friend had other things in mind. Drinking a quart of beer on the way home was a great way to relax while letting someone drive his car who doesn't know how to drive. I managed the directions okay, but he had to grab the wheel a few of times when I would drift into oncoming traffic. Pretty soon it became a daily affair and I was hoping that someday I could get my license. Mr. Applegate was one of many people who spoke highly of Dad. He had worked with him on some other jobs and said, "He was a hard worker." Charley just confirmed what I would hear over the next decade or so. That Dad was well liked even though he had his problems. It was a testimony to people living their own lives and not meddling in other people's business. It didn't happen as often back then, but my, how times have changed.

The crew of one on my construction jobs got a lot of attention. Some days I would be out in the middle of nowhere greasing those rods. Truck drivers and heavy equipment operators watched me with interest as if they all knew Dad had just died. At least I can say that they treated me like they knew. There wasn't one man who worked for the company that I met that I could say that I disliked. Everybody was kind to me.

Denton Construction was out of Gross Point Woods, Michigan, and held more then one world record for paving highways. Once there was a kid a couple of years older than me who worked on another crew. His name was Harvey and he liked his weed. For a while he used to offer me a hit off of his marijuana cigarette and I always refused. Being out in the fresh open air made him comfortable to take in the toxic smoke and enjoy wherever the place was that it took him.

The day everybody waited for had arrived. The bulk of the greased basket rods were down and the paving crew was firing up. After testing the concrete batch plant, the grade was ready. Denton had many of these "batch trucks" that dumped their loads of concrete onto the paving machine sideways. They had also retrofitted all those trucks with used aircraft tires that they had gotten from O'Hare International Airport in Chicago. Once the trucks started running up the grade on the outside of the road, I had to get out of the way more than once rather than get run over. A couple of occasions saw a truck here and there flip onto its side either from a swaying load or a flat tire. I hadn't quite finished greasing all those rods, but they were confident that I would before they got to me.

After my stint on the rods, I got to clean some of the tools they were using on the paving crew. It kept me busy for a while because we were nearing the end of the job and I was being given duties to keep me busy. Before they finished this job, I was approached by my boss and asked if I would be interested in coming to their next job. It would be in Pittsburgh. A four-lane highway thirteen miles long between the "Steel city," and the West Virginia border. It didn't cross my mind that the job I had just finished was only a fraction of this one. Greasing that many rods never occurred to me. I must have been overwhelmed at the attention I was getting. I said to "Frank" that I would have to talk to Mr. Cummins about working in Pittsburgh because they are union down there and I know what it is like to try and go into another territory. I had been taught to respect other union halls. Don made some phone calls and I went to Pittsburgh.

Besides the bus trip to Cleveland, this trip would be the first journey anywhere by myself where I would be paying room and board. There were a few other men from my local that would be making the trip. A father and son combo ended up being my ride back and forth every weekend until the hours got extended into Saturdays too. Fourteen hours a day six days a week became the norm for the remainder of the summer and into the early fall.

Before the job started, it finally hit me. The rods! I've got to get out of the rods! I went to Frank. I was frightened to make the request. I always did what I was told and never complained to anyone, but this had to change. I felt some sense of seniority and was hoping that a kid from the Union Local in Pittsburgh would be the grease monkey. Frank told me that he would get someone else, and he did. For the next few weeks I did not grease one rod.

My new life here began with renting a room over top of "The Farm" restaurant. My room consisted of a simple setting of a lamp and a bed with a small set of drawers accompanied by a short rod to hang some clothes. What I didn't count on was a roommate. A guy named Ed Klock, who had me by about five years worked on the same job, but a different crew back in Barnes. Being from a small town not far from Bradford, he was familiar with me through my union. Being a laborer from our district meant there was not too much that people didn't know about each other, except me. I definitely knew little about the others in our Local. I think at the peak of the Union at that time there were about four hundred members.

Ed turned out to be a good egg. He also was assigned to my crew, which was a very good thing. Starting each day with a briefing kept us ahead of some of the other crews. We had to be. Our responsibilities were setting the grade for the grading machine called a CMI, as well as the big concrete paving machine. Using a transit to find the grade, driving a metal stake into the ground and attaching a line to it became a joy after my duty on the last job. Ed seemed to make it his business to watch over me. He became a good friend for a few years to come. My boss on this crew was not the same person as before, but was likable also. All I know is that his name was Jerry and he was probably one of the best foremen a person could have. He had shared some of his own life experiences with me. It gave me some comfort and a little understanding about things in my life, but even at that point no one could erase the strange feelings of not having my Dad in my life. I had discovered that no matter how a person is treated, the effect that one person has on another is not erased even through death.

For the next several weeks I worked in the hot sun for fourteen, sometimes sixteen hours a day. I hadn't gotten my driving license yet, but Ed would sometimes let me drive his car down the dirt grade for a little practice until I did. One of those days was different than all the rest. Ed had gone to lunch with some of the rest of the crew. I had packed my lunch and drove Ed's "Roadrunner" to an overpass about a half mile down the grade. It was a shady respite on a ninety degree day. Sitting down to eat my lunch I was listening to the radio station from Weirton, West Virginia, a town only a few miles away, just over the Pennsylvania state line.

What I was about to hear would put the fear of God in me. It was announced as an emergency that a hitchhiker was traveling around Weirton getting picked up by many people. The number I distinctly remember hearing was forty. At least forty drivers picked up this hitchhiker and let him get in the car. The man would use the seat belt if there was one and then driving down the road would ask each person the same question: "Do you believe that Jesus Christ is coming back again?" Regardless of what that person's response was, he would completely disappear. The seatbelts would fall limp and he would be gone. The radio on that day reported while in the very short time that all this happened it had to be that this man got around very quickly because there was no way he could get from one place to another during the time of those reports.

As I was eating my lunch, I became very afraid. It was spooky. This story has been told by me quite a few times over the years and once in a while someone will remember hearing about that incident. After telling my crew, they seemed to write it off as some kook going around pulling some kind of prank. Maybe a beer or two at lunch put them too much at ease, I don't know. I know what I heard and the testimony of so many people from different parts of the city at the same time is what seemed to make it most convincing.

One of the other days on the job saw me make a trip to the hospital. Not wearing safety glasses, I had been pounding down one of those steel stakes. A piece of steel flew off and stuck in my eye. The doctor put some of this "orange stuff" in the eye, which made it numb. There was no real damage done, but it was sore for a couple of days. On most days after I got up from sleeping upstairs at the Farm, I would come down and have breakfast at the counter. A waitress named Lisa Mikula waited on me most of the time. We became friendly with each other, but I was still a rather reserved individual, especially with the girls. That was quite a contrast from some of the men I worked around. They would try and give me pointers on how to gain access into a woman's heart for all of the wrong reasons. It really didn't matter how much the girl would take interest in me I guess. But then, how would I ever know, unless she let me know. After about three and a half months on the job it was time to go. One morning I came downstairs for my usual breakfast. Lisa waited on me what was going to be the next to the last time. I told her I was going back home for good. She turned around to pour some coffee for another customer and started crying. Then she put the coffee pot down and ran into the kitchen. I was bothered that I had said something wrong.

She came back out drying her eyes, and I asked, "What's the matter?"

Sniffling, she said, "I'm going to miss you."

I didn't know what to say. Today it seems so outlandish to think that an eighteen-year-old guy wouldn't have picked up on the fact that a girl would have had that level of interest in him. I guess it was a testimony to the fact that I was still living my own life. One that had truly still been in shock from my loss. I couldn't see anything until she let me know. Lisa had taken a secret liking to me and it was no longer possible to keep it a secret when it became time for me to be out of her life for good. I don't know what I would have done had I known anyway.

One of the rituals for the rest of the crews I worked with, especially on Fridays, was to take me to dinner. Even though we had to work on Saturday, there was this partying mood that brought the men to a long drinking stint until the bars closed. The mornings after were a sight for sore eyes from a night of bingeing. Sitting in the presence of a bunch of men who were drinking themselves silly had been a sight that I saw too often all the way back to early childhood, so there was no interest it that kind of a life. I still felt safe from all that stuff. Being able to get up, go to work and not see double helped me appreciate life all the more. The guys looked pretty rough. They would order another round, and I usually liked to order a chicken dinner and a coke. That was my night out.

We "dragged up" in late September or early October. Leaving that area gave me a peace that another job was well done. I left the Farm on a day when Lisa wasn't working, but she had left me a note. I don't remember what the note said. Maybe I should, but it's possible that it was just another event written off because I had no real feelings toward this girl. My new life was just beginning. And during my stay in this little town called "Florence," I made one interesting observation. Even though the men I worked around were spending their money foolishly, there was this sense that they were truly having fun. Laughing all night, telling dirty jokes and talking about the women presented me with some form of attractiveness. But would I have to get drunk to learn how to express myself? I would soon find out.

I really can't pinpoint the date when I decided that drinking alcohol was something that I should do. I had always known it was something I should not do. It had killed my father and countless others, the stuff tasted bad, and my own experience up on the hill in Bradford with it just once had ended with an injury. So having thought that out for a brief moment, why would I start? That answer and others would come to me many years later.

It was late 1971 and heading into the winter months. My buddies back home had been drilling on me for years to join the fun in partying with alcohol and in the not too distant future, the presentation of drugs. Fortunately for me, I never did the latter. Tried the "weed" once, and even inhaled, but it did nothing for me, so I didn't ever do drugs. It turns out that I never had to. The bubbly would do the trick.

Winter was in the air and it been my habit to think about my favorite time of year. That span between Thanksgiving and Christmas gave me the warm fuzzies my whole life. Deer hunting in Pennsylvania opened the Monday after Thanksgiving and the town of Bradford comes alive with hunters from all over the northeastern United States. Those guys from Ohio and New Jersey have been stereotyped as hunters, who were not really hunters, they just seem to come here to get a vacation from their wives. I have since discovered that it is not true, not entirely true anyway. There are some who have over the years, lived up to the billing.

The first set of holidays was tough without Dad, especially for Mom. All the cooking and preparation for that month of warmth just wasn't the same anymore. It had been said that it really didn't matter whether a person was treated good or bad by another, the cause of either will be missed. Unaware of the need to express myself in ways

I hadn't, some were dying to come out. Since I had never told anyone that I had loved them, (not even Colleen) it would mark the beginning of a new era of expression, at least for "pseudo-expression."

I had known for years that just over the state line into New York was a place called "Casey's." It was a restaurant-bar situated in the little town of Limestone, New York, less than three miles from B-town. Dad had always mentioned going to Limestone. I never understood what he saw in that place of about a thousand people. My buddies all had a head start on me in the art of drinking alcohol and Casey's was a handy place for them to get drunk. Pennsylvania had a drinking law that no one under twenty-one years of age could drink, but the New York law was eighteen. That distinction created a lot of trouble over the years and continued full force into my generation. I went to Casey's with the guys and did my usual glass of Coke. As always, it also became apparent that I was left out in the cold again when it came time for me to sincerely talk about the way I felt about anything. I wasn't aware of it, I just wrote it off as "that everybody is different." But there was always that clear sense that I was missing something. Watching people laugh and joke, hug each other and go home a happy person became an envy for me. I did not know that they all were not so happy people. I still wanted to relate along their line. It appeared to be normal, and drinking seemed to be a way to get to that place where one could relate to other people. Well, since I was already drinking Coke, why not try a "Rum and Coke." At the time I thought it could have been the best move that I had ever made. A couple years earlier I tried a double shot of bourbon, straight, and of course, the episode on the hill with a quart of beer. Both times it made me hate the taste and was convinced that I would never take up drinking that stuff again.

The rum and coke did the trick. My mind, mood, emotions and everything else were altered. Enjoying conversation, telling jokes, and relating to people had finally arrived. Giving someone a hug that you hadn't seen in a while wasn't a problem anymore either. But then something happened. When the effect of the alcohol wore off, I became my old self again. I didn't like that. It was imperative that the same scene be repeated with the people, the music, and the drinks to bring back that feeling of camaraderie with the human race. What was pent up in me, I did not understand. All I knew is that when I drank, I belonged. I was accepted. So back to Casey's I went for another round of acceptance from my fellow man. It became a regular thing.

What had started out as an attractive way to get to associate with other people, quickly became a nightmare in my life. The holidays were a perfect starting point for a drinking career. Many people were home for the Thanksgiving and Christmas break. The smiles and turtleneck sweaters made me feel like I was such a part of society, until the bar closed. In all my years of alcohol abuse, I had never wanted the night to end. That infamous "last call for alcohol" gave me an empty feeling inside. The only way out now was to continue to do what had gotten me there in the first place. Drink. If I couldn't drink I couldn't relate. No booze, no life.

Another promising set of circumstances that catapulted my ability to stay within my newfound life was that in the construction industry, at least in my Local Union, unemployment compensation was the norm for most of the members in the winter time. Jobs slowed down in bad weather and all we had to do was go and "sign up." We were making a premium wage, so the amount on our unemployment checks were near the top. None of us had to account for our time concerning looking for work because we were tied to a union hiring hall. In other words, we signed up for our checks all winter long and did not have to get up for work on any morning. The checks come in and you don't have to go to any job. An alcoholic's dream.

This new life was all new to me, but I began to like it because all the resources were there. The money, the free time, and the will to party my brains out became a perfect prescription for pure waste.

Prior to all this hoopla with drinking, I was aware that I was inhibited. Before Dad died, the years of suppression of normal human emotion and expression had a longing to come out. But I never saw it that way. I just felt "less" than other people. My home life, the constant embarrassment of having an alcoholic for a father, the condition of my house compared to my friend's homes had created in me a strong sense of unworthiness. But now my hour had come. All that was backed up, could come out, so I thought. By the middle of winter, after the holidays were over with, I was a full blown alcoholic. The last couple of months in 1971 saw me with a new addition to the family. I bought my first car. A 1965 Ford Custom. The new owner of the City Line filling station, Jim Rinehart gave me what seemed to be a deal at four hundred dollars. He didn't know that a short time later that it would be costing me a couple hundred more for an inspection, at least I never thought he did. This car now gave me a reach that I didn't have before. My rides over the state line had come from everybody else. I was learning the ropes and all the resources were there for me to surround myself with what made me now very comfortable, the affects of alcohol. I was a riot to be around. I made up all sorts of jokes, I got attention from people that had more than I did, and the overall feeling of acceptance was reaching new plateaus.

Going to other bars in New York State became a way of life. Running over the border seven days a week and it took only a few short months to get there let me know that the sky was the limit. Most of it was fun. The fact that I was single, had a car and not a care in the world opened many doors. In January I had turned nineteen and my desire for the opposite sex became increasingly apparent. I wondered, "could I get a girl now that I found myself?" At Casey's, especially on the weekend, the place was busy. The sound of music from the jukebox still rings in my years. "Knights in White Satin" by the Moody Blues, "Heart of Gold" from Neil Young, and "Thunder and Lighting" by Chi Coltrane are some of the many tunes I remember that year. Mom's teaching to recount things by association showed up very strong in the music field. I can associate many things by recalling a song.

It was a very busy weekend night at Casey's. It was Friday about ten o'clock and the waitresses were making their rounds. The owner of Casey's had hired a new girl. She drew a lot of attention from all the hotshot studs from all over. Many of them had money and expensive cars. Their attempts to get her to "go out" became very obnoxious. This well endowed eighteen-year-old wife of a marine stationed elsewhere endured too many passes by guys that didn't seem to have any concern for an answer of no. Her name was Darcy White. After a couple of weeks of heckling from all the male patrons, I became at a loss for expression. She was so beautiful and I wanted what everyone else wanted. But I knew I didn't have a chance. These guys she was rejecting had more of everything to get the job done. The clothes the looks, the cars, the whole shot, and she was saying no to them all. How could I ever even think that I would have a chance. Obviously, my morals went out the window when I started drinking. I had always believed that you "never monkey with another man's monkey." That's what Dad used to say. The rumors about my father suggested that he did not live up to that expectation. Ten years after his death I was told about one such incident by somebody who knew him well. Alcohol was pretty strange stuff. I would have never guessed that I would compromise that belief about myself.

As the evening went on, it came near the time to close. Almost everybody was gone except for a few stragglers, including our table. My sister and several of our friends were finishing up our night while Darcy was hurriedly picking up all the used glasses. When she got to our table to pick up what we weren't using, I watched her as she had worked herself into a worn down barmaid.

I said to her, "Take it easy, pace yourself, you don't have to kill yourself now, almost everybody is gone."

She stopped and looked at me with a surprising smile. Then she changed her pace of work in response to what I had suggested. That also surprised me.

I continued. "When you're done, how about sitting down for a breather?"

She replied that she would. After a few minutes of running around, Darcy took a seat next to me. I was nervous at her presence. The girl that all the hot shots had tried to get close to was actually sitting right next to me. She set down her drink and looked at me with a beautiful smile. I looked at her and she melted me. I became fidgety and she picked up on it.

"What's wrong," she asked.

"Nothing," I said.

"No really, what's wrong? What are you thinking?"

What I was thinking was not very pure and I certainly didn't want her to know that. Up to that point in my life I had never been with a girl, but I also did not want to keep it that way forever.

"I ahh, I can't say it," saying it with a nervous twitch.

"Say what?" she answered.

About ten seconds of hesitation was all I could take and then I blurted out as softly as I could, "I want to go home with you." I looked away in shame as I said it. Even though Mom and my two great aunts had taught me that you don't have sex before marriage, let alone with a married woman, there was this strong sense of following the crowd. And that night I did. Darcy looked at me with strong intent and let me know that she had been thinking the same thing.

"Okay," she replied. "All you had to do was say it."

My face dropped as she left the table to get her purse. I looked at my sister and friends, as they did not know what had just happened. My friend Bob was waiting to hear what I had to say. As I reached out to shake his hand, I expounded on the matter.

"Bob," I said. "I'm going to lose it. Finally! After all these years I'm going to lose it."

We shook hands very tightly and I went around the table to shake more hands and received some hugs. It was a celebration that the only one at the table who was a virgin finally was going to be a bigger part of that crowd. "Good luck! Wish you all the best! Go get 'em!" were some of the comments I heard as I was cheered on. Well, as the story goes, I'm not going to get into the details of the matter, but that night I was initiated into what I thought was adulthood.

There was a little problem that I was not aware of until the next day. It seems that the group of men that were sitting in the rear of Casey's before closing time had tried to get Darcy to do what I had ended up doing. These guys were the band called the "Guess Who." Every once in a while they would come down from Canada to visit the area. When Darcy and I had left Casey's that night, they had followed. Bob and my friends had watched it and followed them all the way to where I was staying. They obviously were intimidated and left. Nobody knows what would have happened, but somebody was probably jealous at my apparent luck. Maybe it would have been better for me if they would have interrupted my endeavor.

From that one encounter that night, Darcy became pregnant and I became scared. Every day I wondered how the whole thing could have turned out differently. About two or three weeks later I was introduced to her husband who came home on leave. I, to this day, do not know how she knew she was pregnant, but she definitely wanted me to know it, or believe it. I saw her again at her job and my relationship with her changed from a secret admirer to a scared young man who cringed at the thought of ever trying to support a child in a situation like this. How was I going to get out of it? I did not see her but twice after that, only to discuss the future. She would tell her husband nothing because he had come home at about the right time to make it look like the child was his. I couldn't fully accept that he wouldn't put two and two together, but what choice did I have in the matter?

A couple of months later, well after Darcy's hubby went back to the military, she was in a serious car accident. I had stayed away from her out of fear. She didn't push it, but she wanted to see me. That one time was enough trouble for me, thank you. She had moved out of town and I got a card from her. It was a sympathy card that intended to console me that she had lost our baby in the car accident. The car had struck a steel bridge girder and almost killed her, but she wasn't pregnant anymore. I felt bad. I felt good. The same feelings that I had was when Dad died, with relief and grief. She gave me her new address and wanted to see me. This time it was an Air Force base. After getting this type of communication and then her wanting to see me again I just couldn't think of a better opportunity to say no. I filed the card and quit the game I had started.

Two years later and still without a girlfriend, I found the card. I called the number she had given me and I couldn't believe that she still wanted to see me, so I drove the two hundred miles, saw her one day and left. Haven't seen or heard from her in over thirty years.

My conscience has always bothered about this whole thing. I wanted what everybody else on earth wanted and that was to be loved or love someone, but I could not see that. My warped need to be accepted or part of the crowd was so great it did not stop me from doing what I personally had believed was wrong right from the start. The drinking, the sex, the loss of dignity and respect…all of it. It was fun at the moment, but the price for me was huge. This rendezvous with the opposite sex was the start of a way of life that I secretly deplored. But for the next decade that is the way I lived. When will I wake up from my sleep and face the world with pure intention?

Shortly after Darcy had left, I went into a deeper bout with alcohol. It was still winter and I would go alone to Casey's till closing time every day of the week. Good weather, bad weather, it didn't make a difference whether I was the only person in the whole place or not. Sometimes the weather was so bad that I was the only soul out of their house. Alone by the juke box I drank myself into oblivion. Even before I went out, I would sit in the bathtub for an hour and drink a half-pint of Four Roses whiskey and chase it with coke. I was in fine shape to face life before I ever walked out the door.

For a nineteen-year-old kid I was doing all my father had done, less then a year after his death. Why? I did not know or understand why I would do the things I abhorred. Reasonably disgusted and full of disdain for how my own father died, why on earth would be off and running in his footsteps so soon after his departure from this earth? Those thoughts and more did not even occur to me, at least to the best of my recollection. A passing thought here and there, but never a serious contemplation about my nemesis. Self destruction was in the cards for me and I would do it. I know that I thought that.

The spring of that year saw a lot of rain. Hurricane Agnes brought a lot of flooding to the whole northeastern part of the country and the Limestone area was no exception. Sitting in Casey's one night with a few friends, we encountered a ghostly sight. In walked a group of men donning emergency gear carrying flashlights.

"I'm afraid you all are going to have to leave. The river is flooding."

We immediately took their advice and walked out into the parking lot. Down the road into the deep dark night we could see that the river had come all the way up to the road level and was showing its black shiny surface as it covered the bridge. I went home another way and waited to ride it out. It rained for twenty-eight days straight. Bradford itself did not experience any serious flooding, but many of the towns in the lowlands around us did. The biggest concern that got a lot of media attention was that the nearby Kinzua dam had never been tested to this extent before. With a ninety mile shoreline behind it, there was a lot of water and it was steadily rising. The rumors flew.

"The dam was cracking, the Indians that were displaced from building the dam put a curse on it," were a couple of the stories that went around the community. Some of us drove over to the dam because it was exciting to hear of the possibilities. That period of time during 1972 the dam reached its highest levels it its history, before or since. Made of part earth and part concrete, the focus was on the earthen section. It had never been tested to that level. It obviously held up.

That year I was sent on a pipeline job that passed through the area above the dam, a ten-mile stretch of woods from Warren,

Pennsylvania, to Sheffield, the town where I worked on the highway the year before. Joyce Western was the contractor. They again had a great bunch of guys to work with. The first crew to start the job went on ahead of us to clear the rightaway. Trees, brush, and large boulders had to be moved for our stringing crew. "Stringing" meant laying out the pipe end to end along the ditch.

On one occasion we caught up to the rightaway crew because they had encountered a very large group of boulders the size of houses in the middle of the line. The foreman of that crew gave me a job that I thought was the job of a lifetime. Tending the dynamite man. They called him "Charley Boom Boom." Never did find out his last name, but he was an eighty-two-year-old tobacco chewing regular with the company. He always walked with his hands behind his back unless he was handling the dynamite. It was fun at first. I core-drilled about fifteen holes deep into the rock. Then Charley and I were put up on the top together with a case of dynamite. He would drop a stick down the hole. Then another, and another. After about four or five sticks were down the hole he would take a long pole and ram the sticks down tightly to the bottom as if he were loading a cannon. I did not understand that the entire operation would not be successful without an electric detonator. I was still nervous, but the thought of watching the rock explode became my driving force to tolerate the pounding Charley was doing.

After spitting some tobacco he would look at me with a squinting eye and say, "Scared ya huh?"

"Ya, I'll be okay," I replied.

After the charges were ready to go, the hour of power had arrived. The entire crew was moved up the hill away from the rock at least a hundred yards. I laid beneath a truck and looked down the hill. Some guys just sat in their big bulldozers. They had been through this before. The charges went off and pieces of rock flew everywhere, too many of them. The blast was so great that large chunks came up the hill and hit several of the trucks. The truck I was under had minor damage, but a couple of them had significant dents in the hood and roof. After the dust settled, I looked down the hill and saw pieces that were workable with the dozers.

After the dynamite chore, I went picking blackberries. We were out in the middle of nowhere and the picking was good. I don't know if it is a cultural thing or not, but the outdoors has always been a great distraction from drinking the booze. It proved to be a bit of saving grace later on in my career with alcoholism. Deer, turkey, squirrels, and coon were plentiful almost everyday on the pipeline job. My stint on that project lasted three months to the day. I spent time with each crew. The part of the job I started began after the flooding down below. We only had a couple of rainouts that summer. Sometimes in the construction industry a day off because of the weather was welcome.

Another job I had was with a device called the "Jeep."

"Jeeping" was simply taking a hand held piece of technology the size of a shoe box and wrapping a coil wire around the pipe. It looked like a small slinky toy surrounding the entire twenty four inch pipe. You had to walk along the pipe, all the time watching and listening to see and hear a spark jump out from the pipe to the coil. There was a coating of hard tar on the surface of the pipe. If there was a crack or a small pinhole in that insulation the Jeep found it and ZAP! The sparked would jump to the coil and you would mark the hole with a yellow construction crayon. The man behind you would take a brush from a pail of hot tar and paint the hole. That tar job was mine for a while before I got to do the Jeep thing. There was a danger though. Not a great one, but the device carried one hudred forty thousand volts. You had to be careful or you could get shocked. Although the voltage was high, the amperage was low. To me it really didn't make much difference. It still hurt, as I got shocked more than once no matter how careful I was.

Cookie was the man's name that had charge of the large tar pot. His real name was George. The propane fired cooker reached a temperature of six hundred degrees and was towed behind a small tractor. For the entire summer and into the fall, Cookie's job was the one that everyone wanted. Shoving a piece of hard tar into the vat once in a while was it. The tar looked like a piece of rock candy. When autumn came, we let Cookie put a batch or two of corn in the cooker. With the husk still on, he wrapped the corn in a burlap sack. It only took about fifteen minutes and out came corn that could never taste as good any other way.

That year I began to realize that I was in serious trouble. Even though there was a lot of beautiful scenery in my life, it only made my sense of hopelessness grow deeper. The plan to help Mom for only a year was supposed to expire soon and there was no serious thought of giving up my construction jobs. Working a few months out of the year and "collecting" in the winter was too tempting a life to ever give up. I didn't really know when I would try to make a change, all I knew was that this had a great element of fun and little responsibility compared to the whines of the nine to fivers I would meet in the bars. I had it easy, but the cost was great and I blindly marched on.

Beginning to assess my opportunities to go to college, it began to look dimmer and dimmer. I had looked into the Air Force and joining the FBI during my last year of high school. Those options and higher education melted away in mind as my seemingly growing ability to want to express myself began to dominate me. People didn't hurt me, swear at me, or threaten me. I could go to bed and get up when I wanted to. I took on only enough responsibility to get by. I didn't talk as much as most people, but it did increase a bit as time went on. The late mornings at work and early afternoons were the hardest times because the alcohol effect was wearing down. The late afternoon became a time of great anticipation, thus I was showing myself as a little socialite.

"Could I help you," was a common phrase I would start to use for years. The truth was that I wasn't really as considerate as I portrayed. It was only the thoughts of heading into another time of fun hanging around the neon lights. Sometimes in life I had discovered that my preoccupation with what was going to happen made me the most agreeable person on earth. I got a lot of credit for being helpful. Dad did the same thing. After work and before going downtown, especially on Friday nights, he sometimes would even dance around the living room knowing that just a short time later he was going to be sitting on some barstool with his buddies. I have watched that same principle show up in many people that aren't even alcoholic or drug addicted. When something is going a person's way, that person can be so agreeable. Then the real person shows up sooner or later. Again, I like to call it "psuedo-peace."

My newfound sense of belonging was based on a premise that I did not even try to figure out at the time. As long as I could have my drink and my friends I was all right. But building a life around that should be obviously foolish, although it wasn't obvious to me. It is something that you have to grow into. What was really happening was that I had carried some feelings of inferiority into my adult life that had been cultivated by the life that my Dad lived. He died, left me holding the bag. I didn't know that I had this stuff in me and tried to cope with this unnamed problem. Looking around and finding other people who seemed to be having the same problem gave me some comfort. The inner turmoil always came when the people who didn't have the problem were around me. That contrast made my feelings of being less of a human being and the prospects for normality more and more out of reach. The immediate return to the fun times always rescued me from my fear of success at anything worthwhile. In the bars, people's homes, football games, or concerts, somebody would inevitably show up that convinced me that there was more to life than what I had. Back during those days it was very easy to avoid. Just get around the right people, add suds and stir. "There, it's all better now"...so I thought.

The New Era

The end of 1972 brought new hope that the pain of my personal losses were over. Aunt Hilda had passed away. She was the second person in my home to "leave me." Aunt Julia was slowly continuing her deterioration with severe arthritis. Over the next few short years I became interested in what was only convenient for me. Many nights Julia would howl for hours from the pain. I would come home in the wee hours of the morning only to yell upstairs to tell her to "shut up!" It has been one of the most cold, inconsiderate things I have done in my entire life. Mom would only make a short innocent comment to try and curb my callousness, but that would never work. I was getting restless.

A couple of years had passed since Dad had died, and I felt a new vigor to start and explore the world. My feelings of conquering came in the form of a trip with the boys around the country, followed by the introduction of what would be a serious relationship with a young woman, something that had evaded me since the Colleen thing.

January of 1973 began with Bob driving to Pittsburgh to buy a new truck. We had all gotten tired of hearing that prices were better in the big cities, so after scoping out Buffalo first, we saw the way paved for two more of us to buy vehicles from the same dealership. Don Allen Chevrolet had some great guys working for them and we never regretted getting our cars there.

A short time after Bob got his truck, he came up with this crazy idea that a bunch of us should take a trip around the country. He bought a cap for the back and that would be our motel for the trip. So sometime near the end of March five of us packed up to "see the USA in a Chevrolet."

It was a sunny, but cold day and the five of us left for our destination, California. I don't think that I could compare the exciting anticipation of going to a place that I'd only seen on the front of a "Ventures" album. The Mamas and the Papas song "California Dreamin" had come to bear. I had listened to that song over and over again for months. The trip began with the understanding that we would all share equally in the driving. It didn't end up that way, but I didn't mind. After being a late bloomer in so many things, I did not mind driving more that what was to be my share. I like to drive even today.

The recreation of choice, of course, was playing cards in the rear of the truck. That was the scene of the "traveling casino" that everybody wanted to be in. That was the reason that most of the guys didn't want to drive, especially if you fell behind in your money. You couldn't drive and gamble at the same time. I was always very frugal with my own money when I was not drinking. This trip kept me in awe so much that I only drank two beers in Rock Springs, Wyoming, and a whiskey sour in Reno the whole trip. Nature and ten days of having to pay attention to the roads kept me distracted enough to have quite the dry run. I did not miss it.

Route 80 travels across the country and we picked it up near Clarion, Pennsylvania, a couple of hours from Bradford. All the way to that route seemed only like we were taxiing up the runway before takeoff. There is something about that highway even today that brings a sense of adventure when you get on it. I think that because I know where it leads nonstop helps keep the door open for the thrill of it all.

We drove straight through to Chicago and it was pouring rain. I wanted to see O'Hare Airport because I had heard it was the busiest in the world at that time. I wouldn't have that experience though for some time to come.

The first big stop was Rock Springs, Wyoming, and even that was unplanned. Bob's truck had a defective transfer gear in the new vehicle and in the small, but growing town there was only one access to a new part. The gear could not be ordered from the factory either because it would take too long, or they hadn't any in stock, I don't remember which. Either case, what I do remember is that we had to stay there for two and a half days. The gear had to be milled down in a shop from scratch. The men did a good job because it held up for over on hundred thousand miles and with a lot of heavy work at that. During our stay there we saw a lot of construction. The town was booming everywhere and we saw an opportunity to make some money, but ultimately decided against it. We had bigger fish to fry after the truck got fixed.

Driving day and night took us straight to Reno, Nevada. That was a pleasant prelude to what we knew was going to happen later on. Gambling in the Mecca of cards and dice. Vegas would be a stop on our return trip and seeing the lights and slot machines only wet the appetite for the big kahuna to come. We stayed one night and I was particularly interested in Lake Tahoe. Its sparkling clear water looked as fresh as any mountain stream we had back east. We moved on the next day and drove through the night. Rather, I drove through the night into the Rocky Mountains. I did not really get to see the mountains as you would during the day, but somewhere up on the top about three in the morning we were almost out of gas. It was snowing heavy and we came upon a closed gas station that would not open until six a.m. It was a three hour wait. I was alone in the cab while the other four slept comfortably in the back. I would watch the deer or antelope under the parking lot lights, as well as the jackrabbits hopping along. It was a new world in the middle of nowhere. I got the gas and headed for San Francisco. Sometime during that phase of the trip one the other guys had to drive while I caught up on some sleep.

Approaching San Fran was very interesting. The Golden Gate Bridge being the main route from the east was just another example of something that I had only read or heard about. Stretching across the bay in the morning light only made it more of a wonder to behold. We got out and took some pictures while the people were on their way to work.

Chinatown was the place that we decided to rest for the night. We broke out of our mold and rented a room in a Holiday Inn. Five guys sharing the room was not really that much fun when you were as tired as I was. And my conscience was not in so great a shape either when we left that room in shambles. The boys had gone out on the town that night. I watched as a couple of women allured Bob and Rick into a bar from the outside. They had been planted there to coax men inside to buy them a drink. They fell for it. Though I did not know what was happening at the time, they certainly let me know when the night was over, which was a little early. Eighteen dollars for a draft and twenty seven for a mixed drink. They came back to the hotel with their tails between their legs. They couldn't get out of paying the money because they were being watched. When we first got into the hotel we had to park in the garage under the building. There was only one way we could park and that was by picking up a car and moving it between the pillars and the wall. The owner of that car had to either get people to do the same thing to move it back or get a tow truck. It was still there when we left, so we did not get caught.

The next morning saw us traveling to Malibu Beach where we stayed for a night, even though it wasn't the season for swimming. Traveling down the coast brought us to Los Angeles. We had lunch there near the airport. I had seen the famous control tower on many TV movies and it was interesting to see it in person. We visited my distant cousin Steve who lived in Long Beach farther down the coast. He had a nice home and my friends were welcomed in for a couple of hours. He was from Mom's side of the family, so it was a special treat to visit Steve after not seeing him for many years. We left and wanted to go to Tijuana, Mexico, but decided against it because even though we had heard of "the fun there" it made us a little uncomfortable that we could end up in a Mexican jail and never get out.

We continued across the desert of southern California toward Arizona. The sun was very hot as we pulled into an unemployment office and we all signed up for our checks, one of the luxuries that we had back in the seventies and not be accountable to anyone. Not only did we have a bye as far as looking for work because we were working out of a union hall, but there were no taxes on unemployment compensation in those days. How times have changed. I remember the temperature was 106 degrees at eleven in the morning. That was quite a contrast to the snowstorm in the mountains a couple of short days ago.

Our next night took us to the banks of a river in Arizona. It was like the old west. We started a fire and slept in the sand. Our shower in the morning was a dip in the river. Being early enough to be cool was refreshing after the heat of the previous day. We packed up and stopped intermittently on our way to Vegas. I was driving again. By the time we got about seventy-five miles away from the city, the boys were all sleeping in the back of the truck. I could see in the sky the light. It was very exciting. About an hour later I drove up over a knoll and the sight was breathtaking. The full brunt of the city lights lay before me on the floor of the desert. I stared for a couple of minutes and got out of the truck. Going back to where the guys were sleeping, I moved cautiously. I knew what was going to happen.

I tapped on the rear window of the cab, opened it up and said, "Hey, take a look up front!"

When they saw the sight through the window, I had to race back to the driver's seat. It now became a premium place to occupy. In a matter of just a couple of minutes all five of us were crammed in the front seat. We descended into the valley and found a good bright parking lot to park at a hotel/casino. Don't remember which one, but what I do remember is that it took only a few minutes after we got there for five guys to come out of the truck dressed in suits. You would have never guessed that most of us were sleeping and ragged looking within the past hour. We did what we came there for. We came, we saw, and we conquered.

Splitting up in all directions was fun. We knew where the truck was at all times so everyone went their own way 24/7 for the next two days. A couple of times I would see one of them twelve hours or so later and just wave across the street.

It was still early, but dark when we got there. About eight o'clock that night I went into a big casino. I saw three women in curlers working nine slot machines. After staying up the whole night I went back to that same casino and guess who was there? I wondered, *Why put your hair up in curlers if this is all you're going to do all night?* They were going as strong as half a day earlier. I got tired and hungry just watching them so I got steak and eggs for thirty nine cents.

After two days of running we decided to take a short hop down to the Hoover Dam. Lake Mead was bustling with travelers and the water was cool on a hot day. I just stuck my toes in the water. Those guys all swam. I still didn't know how. I constantly got ribbed about that, especially when I wanted credit for swimming in the river back in Arizona. (It was only up to my waist).

I had learned something about myself that day. About lunchtime I walked to a concession stand along the beach and ordered something to eat. Sitting in my booth alone for a couple of minutes I was interrupted by a young woman who identified herself as Bergetta. She had food in her hand and looked at me.

"May I sit with you?" she asked.

I gestured with a full mouth for her to join me. She told me she was a student from a school in San Francisco, but was in this country from Sweden studying the arts.

The first thing that she did after she peeled a hard-boiled egg was hold it up to the light and say, "This is pretty funky."

I don't know what she meant by it, but my attitude about things like that is, help yourself.

"What do you do?" she continued.

"I work construction," I said nervously. There was literally no experience in my life with sitting in the presence of a strange girl having lunch without alcohol in my system. I didn't understand that I was afraid because I had no initiative without a mood-altering crutch to give me the nerve to carry on a simple conversation with her. If I had a couple of beers in me, I would have been borderline aggressive. I wanted from her all the things that I would want in my other state.

"I never had a construction man," she blurted out.

I was mesmerized. "Oh," I said. "I build highways and pipelines," trying to change the subject.

"Do you want to go for a walk along the beach?" she said.

"Okay," I responded. Even though I knew I never would try anything unbecoming on this girl, my real comfort came from the fact a simple walk in front of a lot of people would keep me safe. Didn't turn out that way. My feeling of security was dashed to pieces when we walked down the beach to an area where no people were. I felt as helpless as a lamb being led to the slaughter. I sat on a rock and drew things in the sand with a stick while she took all of her clothes off. I was embarrassed and would not do the same. The Lord watched over me that day and rescued this helpless soul from a situation I found that I could not prevent. Bergetta immediately began to experience her flow in front of my eyes.

She said, "I'm sorry, I'm having my period, let me get dressed."

I said, "That's okay," and we left. I called it a day. I went back to the guys and finished the trip to Lake Mead to get ready for another night on the town in Vegas.

The next morning one of the guys was in pain. His fair skin had endured too much sun and it was a bright red. He was in constant agony, particularly when we over the speed bumps in the parking lots. It was that bad. We finished our stint in Nevada and headed north and stopped at Mt. Rushmore for a couple of hours and then on to Yellowstone Park. This area was the capstone to the trip. Old Faithful, the hot springs and mud pools all accented what my vision of the trip of a lifetime was for someone my age.

We got to Yellowstone in the early afternoon. Our introduction to the park was a bear in the road. We stopped the truck as he lumbered to the berm and stared at us. The signs say not to feed the animals, so I guess you know what that means. Feed the animals! Bob got a can of beans out of the truck and gave it to the bear. He sat back on his haunches and closed his mouth on the can. It exploded beans everywhere. We thought that was neat until he got done eating what he could. A frustrated angry animal got to his feet abruptly and started to chase us around the truck. I stayed on the ground on the opposite side of the bear while the four other guys jumped in to the back of the truck and closed the cap. He got up on his two hind feet and sniffed the window, dropped to all fours and slowly walked off in the woods.

Our next encounter was with the buffalo, rather, my encounter. A fairly large range fenced in by barbed wire was dotted by groups of these animals that stood almost six feet high at the shoulders. Signs everywhere made sure that the park did not want anyone going inside the fence, and the word "danger" was emphasized. Got to love it. We had the cameras, there were people all over outside the fence and I needed some attention. Over the fence I went, even at the chiding of my friends this time. Steve was the most fun this time. I loved to make him laugh. He thought I was stupid for doing it, but he liked the show nevertheless. I took a camera with me and approached a bison who was separated from the rest. The closer I got the more nervous I became. I was still that fast runner from Bradford, but the sign on the fence said that these guys could top forty miles per hour. I insanely believed I had an edge anyway. Taking a couple of shots gave me a little courage to walk right up to this guy and start talking to him. Chewing his cud and not moving at all kept me wondering what he was thinking. I decided the ultimate challenge. While everybody was watching I got in his face and tweaked his ear. I took off running and jumped back over the fence. I turned to look back and old hunchback still chewing his cud. Never moved an inch. An addendum to that story is that ten years later in the Rochester, New York *Democrat* and *Chronicle* dated March 1983 was a ten-year anniversary clip remembering a woman who was killed in Yellowstone Park back in 1973. Her cause of death? She was gored by a buffalo. I had never heard of that during the whole decade. We were there that exact month in 1973.

Our trip home was easy and slow. Tired and ready for the next adventure, we would have to wait a while. It is strange to think that I was returning to a life that I had left only ten days ago. It is as if I had a responsibility to pick up the bottle after setting it down. No one really prompted me to drink during the trip and I didn't want to, but as soon as I got back to Bradford there it was, the liquid nerve was calling and I soon beckoned.

The old Ford was worn out from a year or so of being owned by a negligent owner. I did not take care of the maintenance very well. Even though that car probably would not have lasted much longer anyway, it was no excuse to not take care of it like I should have. I still see people today that may not have much, but they are still responsible to what they do own.

Driving around Warren, Pennsylvania, off and on in my running around I noticed a car on a small lot a couple of months after I got back from the California trip. It was red and black, the colors of my alma mater at Bradford High. She was a beautiful two-door 1967 Chrysler Newport. I had passed it several times and definitely thought the price would be way out of my reach. I finally stopped and asked how much it was. The miles were okay with not a scratch on her and for eight hundred dollars it was a steal. Only one problem. Mom had to help me with part of the money. She initially said no, but came around and we went over to pick up this new gem of mine. I brought it home and had to let it sit until I paid off Mom and could afford the insurance and registration. I couldn't wait to get this thing on the road.

This was a car I was going to take care of. The sheer beauty of it all was inspiring a new sense of responsibility in me. I guess I had a little more respect for something that seemed so delicate and shiny. It was worth it. Back in those days the engines were not burdened with all the pollution control technology and the horsepower ratings did not affect the insurance rates like they began to do later on. Even in luxury cars like mine you could go over one hundred twenty miles per hour very easily and it was not a real gas hog. And I did that quite often. My six cylinder Ford could not come close to the ummf the Newport had.

I ended up getting mag wheels and air shocks when summer came. A trip to the car wash was always in order. It was an irritating thing to have it start raining after the car got clean. That was sure evidence that I wanted to take real care of it.

Throughout the rest of the year and into the winter saw many trips with my friends traveling up and down Main Street in Bradford. We called it "flaming the main." Many people did it, especially the guys with the hot cars. Main Street is three quarters of a mile long with a public square on one end and a big parking lot on the other. This made for a perpetual route that never had an end. Up and down, up and down we would go seeing the same people and the same scenery for sometimes two hours with an occasional stop to visit somebody on one end or the other.

I was invited to a party in at Edinboro College near Erie Pennsylvania, one weekend. The town itself is actually named Edinboro. I was going to meet a lot of people from Bradford in a house where my friend Paula Mclaughlin lived. She was a real hippie who had made a career out of going to school. We all thought that a dozen or so years of school was more than sufficient. She should've had five PhDs in the arts, but ended up owning a bar in Ohio.

I got up early in the morning to get a good start on the hour long trip to Edinboro. I got in my car, turned the ignition and poof! The car is now filled with smoke. Every wire inside my dashboard had burned to a crisp. All the color coding was ruined. Mom let me go in her car to the auto parts store and buy some wire. It took the next full eight hours to rewire the car's dashboard. One wire at a time had to be traced from one end to the other. It is funny that to this day I never found out what had caused that problem. During the 70s many Chrysler built vehicles had the reputation of electrical malfunctions. I got the wiring back together and to the best of my knowledge all the new wires were the same color. Why not? I knew it so well now! I also put the dash back together with just enough screws to keep it from falling outward and off I went.

Arriving at Paula's house in the early evening it was still a little light. I told my story and had a hankering to make up for lost time. In a college town like that, sub shops are the main staple of every kids diet. Today was no exception. I sat among ten people, most of whom I had never met before and ate my dinner, jealous that most everyone got a head start on me in the drinking department. One thing I had always noticed about people who did drugs at that time. They slowly milked their booze as if they were in complete control of everything, that is until the drugs came out. There was a general consensus among everyone but me that now darkness had fallen that it was time to do just that. Hashpipes and marijuana cigarettes now brought a group of people to a more subdued state. Someone put on a Chicago album and turned out the lights. The room is now filling up with smoke from all of the mood and mind altering lights flickering in the dark room

Not being a drug doer, I certainly felt out of place. What was I to do among a group of people who were doing something I could never agree to. After all, I had my booze. Why wasn't that good enough? I got up out of my chair and walked into the kitchen and sat at the table with a can of Pabst Blue Ribbon. Looking at the clock, I began to wonder. Is it really true that if you drink a shot of beer a minute that you will be in bad shape? That only adds up to five cans of beer and I could easily do that three times over in the course of a night, this shouldn't be any problem. So, for the next sixty minutes I did a shot a minute. I do not remember finishing the night. I had to rely on the tales of others to let me know what actually occurred. Everyone had to step over me to get to the bathroom. As usual, all the stories about how funny I was only fueled reasons to keep doing things that got me the attention in the first place. It was true that most of the people who were doing drugs in my life were able to maintain a little more order than myself. They got high, but could still get up, talk and function in ways I couldn't. I secretly envied them, but at the same time felt a little self righteous that I "only drank." That thinking continues even today with many. There would be many opportunities to come that would let me know that I wasn't missing anything.

Helping Mom Helping Me

There came a point a year after Dad died that I felt Mom needed a change of scenery in the house. Back then she was still very pliable and I had suggested that she let me make some arrangements with my friends and we would put new paneling and ceilings in the kitchen and living room. Though they ended up being very inexpensive and not so great a quality, it could made a huge difference in the appearance of those rooms. I still had the bug that enabled me to offer her the chance because I had some experience redoing my "bedroom slash pantry" a few years earlier.

We got to completely alter a look that bugged me for so long. With the other decision makers out of the way, Mom and I could invite at least some semblance of psychological change through the cosmetics of getting rid of those ugly early 1900s wallpapers that had seen its day, as well as the water-stained ceiling. We cut around every obstacle such as chimneys, doorways and windows. The suspended ceiling was fun, especially when you start to drop in the panels and watch all the bad stuff disappear. Personally I felt a new sense of direction for Mom just with a simple change such as this. She was appreciative of it.

The job took a couple of weeks and, of course, there is the celebration of a job well done. A quarter keg, cases of Pabst Blue Ribbon and a big card game seemed like a fitting way to reward ones self. I guess it would have been nice of me to let Mom know just how big of deal it was going to be. She knew that I was to have a few friends over for a limited time. She even disappeared for a while shopping. She came home to a big mess. One of the problems with gambling is that those who lose want to stay to get back the losses and those who win want more so nobody leaves. In the door comes Mom.

"Hi, Mrs. Knott," everyone would say.

She would set down her bags and look around. "Hello, anybody winning?"

Mom never really had to say anything to us guys. Her presence, though not dominating was convincing. She was such an innocent person that being in the same room with her under those circumstance let us all know it was time to wrap things up.

"Were going to be leaving shortly, Mom," I would say.

The boys sort of made me feel protected while I was feeling like I was doing something wrong. I still felt a need to keep playing, and asked her, "Mom, can we play just a little longer? I'll tell you what. If you take a lap downtown and come back we will be gone, okay?"

Now looking a little perturbed, she responded, "I'll be back in about half an hour."

She then leaves and now it is desperation time. The cards could not be dealt fast enough. I started picking up the garbage and playing my hands at the same time. In the end, though, those guys always respected my mother. When she came home, all was back in order.

The Newport would become my first actual victim in a long line of cars that would not make it through my life. I do not know whether it was the end of '72 or the beginning of '73 when I decided to travel in excess of one hundred twenty miles per hour downhill in a slick highway during a Pennsylvania winter. It had the potential to kill many over times over and what I ended up with was a bruised thumb hanging onto the steering wheel. That was it.

Bob had gone to Altoona, Pennsylvania, to see a girlfriend who was going to school there. I wanted to go see them at about 2:30 in the morning. Driving under the influence, I lifted myself up off the seat to put my whole body weight onto the gas pedal. The speedometer bounced off one hundred twenty and I entered a turn at the bottom of a long hill. Didn't make it. I slid through the turn and spun around and around hitting several small trees and a concrete drain abutment while climbing a high bank turn that was actually a landscaped hill fashioned by bulldozers. Though I did not flip, the car was destroyed. I closed my eyes and held on for the ride. What happened next I had only heard of and not experienced, not before nor since. A flash went off in front of my eyes. My eyes were closed and I was in an area where there were no lights at all. I saw before me my whole life in a high-speed film in less than a second. I conceived and understood everything that had happened throughout my entire existence. I still can understand that moment even today. It never left.

When all had settled down, I came to a rest in a ditch about a quarter of a mile from where I started my spin. All was quiet. I shoved opened my door and looked around. A minute later a trucker coming down the hill from the opposite direction saw me and stopped.

"You all right," he asked, looking at the mess.

"Yea, I guess so," looking back at what now is revealed in his headlights as a totaled vehicle.

"I'll radio for a wrecker. You're not going to just need a tow on this one."

I was spared the presence of a police officer and his questioning, and my pal to be Clayt Troutman showed up about an hour later to pick up the pieces and put them on the flatbed.

Clayt was well known in our community as the only one to call when you got into trouble with your car, especially the wrecks. Over the years he had the worst of them for the whole town to see on his lot. News of any violent accident traveled fast, and mine was no exception. I hated to go there the next day and see what I had done. Even though I was a star for a moment, that was no consolation. I felt guilt and remorse. But even though some folks told me to start going to church, the shock of this loss would soon wear off and I was destined to tempt fate once again.

Move Over Lady

After the incident with the Chrysler, I had to find something else to drive. I usually took my time to find the right car, but I hated it when other people made me wait. Hearing that this fast car was for sale made me wonder if that was really something I needed to get into. I had seen the car around town, but never really knew it well. Hearing the history of it made me give it an early approval. I called the current owner, a curly haired Irish kid that I had graduated with. Patrick Flanagan was always a good egg with honesty being a very strong point.

I bought the car from him and started my terror of racing other kids around the county. The wheels that came on it were authentic magnesium, but because of the way they were made they had the reputation of breaking off the studs on the wheel housings and then ultimately the whole rim and tire would come off of the car. If that happened while you driving it posed a serious threat to, not only the people in the car, but anyone else nearby when it happened. And happen it did. Coming down Minard Run Road about fifty miles per hour in the middle of a summer day the right front wheel came off. It left the road and traveled into the front yard occupied by several small children. The tire spun out of control and raced across the yard missing everyone in its path and came to rest against a tree. Keeping my eyes on the road with a wheel off and watching a threat to some children's lives was nothing less than pure fear. I never changed rims even after that experience.

Traveling over the state line to the bars took me into Olean, New York. Olean is a small town like Bradford with a similar population give or take a couple of thousand. Alleghany was a smaller town which connected Limestone and Olean that houses St. Bonaventure University. Both towns became second nature to me in my carousing. St. Bona had its underground Rathskeller, while up the road a mile was the Der Hut and Paul's Steak House. Many people that I knew died on the route to these places. All of them left this earth due to drugs or alcohol.

One evening in the Der Hut I met this girl that I became attracted to. Martha Cline had this sparkle in her eyes that again would mesmerize me. She was on a college break from Alfred Tech and had lived in Bradford her whole life. She gave me her phone number and we sometimes would talk for hours. Her parents liked me, but later we would see how much. Alfred Technical College was located in Alfred, New York, about an hour and a half from Bradford. Martha invited me to visit her there. It was against school policy to have a boy in the girls' dorms, but when the room check came Martha's way I would be hiding under the bed sipping a beer while she had a conversation with the Dean of Housing. Never got caught in several attempts on that offense.

As time went on, Martha and I would fall in love and never wanted to be apart. This eventually had something to do with her quitting school and coming back to Bradford to live with her parents. I was overjoyed to have her do that. I had no concern for her commitment to school, but was looking out again for old number one. There were several contributing factors in her decision to quit, one of which was I almost lost my life more than once. I believe that she felt if I was near her all the time I could live a little longer. One evening before she quit school we were on the phone. I was intoxicated and passed out while talking to her. I woke up the next morning with the phone cord wrapped around my neck at least twice. I called her and she was furious, partly out of her inability to reach me with the phone off the hook and the fact that she was scared that something had happened to me.

During that time of being away from each other, I had to travel back and forth to Alfred. I eventually ran into a girl on the road who was driving a black Plymouth GTX. I knew those cars were fast and I had to find out how fast. We raced down a long straight stretch of highway near Wellsville, New York, on my way home and I blew my engine. I never did replace it, but gave a friend some parts off it. I didn't need to own speed anymore.

As time went on, my late nights at Martha's became more frequent. I needed a new ride and bought a brand-new Monte Carlo. It was about February 1974 and my traveling buddy Steve Pettinato bought a new Monte Carlo the same day that I did. That dealer in Pittsburgh was quite happy that Bob had made that trip the first time. Word of mouth does sell. It was my first new car and I was happy. So happy that on Easter morning that year I passed out at the wheel, hit a telephone pole so hard that the bumper stopped only a few inches from the windshield. I got a few small cuts on my forehead from breaking the windshield glass. It happened after I had left a card game at seven in the morning. Since I hit the pole only a block from the police station, they didn't have to travel very far to investigate. I told them and the doctor at the hospital that a deer had jumped out in front of me. They had a hard time believing that, but couldn't prove otherwise.

I had my own difficulty believing the insurance company telling me that they would not total the car. The frame was bent and I had to wait sixteen weeks for Detroit to deliver a new one. Writing them letters did no good. Martha would let me use her car when she could and my friends would cart me around during the four month wait.

I finally got my brown car with the spoked wheels back from the garage. Martha slowly succumbed to my way of life. I thought I could have her and my drink, and over time that was the way it worked. You don't plan it out, you have to incorporate a girl into your drinking life. Even though I loved her, she was coming in from the outside. There wasn't really anything to dislike about me as a person. Nothing anyway that would make some girl not want to be around me. No woman should put up with what she was about to. There had been enough evidence already that I should have been dumped like a hot rock just with the lifestyle issue. She had tried many times to keep up with me in the party mode and many times got pretty tipsy herself.

Things seemed to be going better. I got my car back and off and running I went. In today's language, the car had now again become a three thousand pound weapon in the hands of a person who indiscriminately wielded it like a blindfolded man with a sword. The paint was not even dry on the hood of this car that had only twelve hundred miles on it when I did it again. Driving back to Bradford on a Friday night from Warren, Pennsylvania, I passed out on a steelgate bridge. This time I hit a family of six head on. Drunk and asleep one second, very much alert and awake the next, I ran off the bridge having no thought about what I had just done. I asked the people in the other car if they were okay. They were. I ran to a nearby Tasty Freeze and stuffed my mouth full of onions and ran back to the scene. By that time the State Police had arrived and questioned me.

"You been drinking?" the trooper asked.

"No sir," I quickly responded. I got out of what would have been much serious trouble for me. I needed a consequence, but did anything that I could to avoid it, include convince the troopers that it was the other guy's fault. That poor man pleaded his case, but it became what I knew it would, a stalemate. Our own insurance companies paid for our cars. That was better than them finding out the truth. I believe I have contributed in making some of the laws that exist today.

It is strange how some news travels. Mom had been listening to the news on Bradford's local radio station. (There is a story behind the call letters WESB). My accident was broadcast almost immediately. Mom had called Martha and they came together to pick me up. My friend Rick was with me the whole time and he could never swear to anything because he was passed out before me. Mom arrived with Martha and they were both in tears. By the description of the accident on the radio they were convinced I was at least seriously injured or maybe worse. We hugged and I took the ride home.

The next day Martha came and got me. I needed to be away from people. The guilt and remorse of it all became great. We went into the woods and I slept in the leaves, Martha holding me tight while tears ran out of my eyes. When would it end? How could I stop? I wasn't to find out right away. I have learned that emotions are just that. They may be a pathway to a lesson learned, but they do not go to the innermost part of a man. It just feels like it does. There must be a change of heart, but it would be some time before I would cross that bridge.

I eventually got rid of the Monte Carlo that year (on the premise that it was bad luck). I traded backward a year to a 1973 Dodge Monaco. Martha was getting more restless about my safety. She worked at a local bank as a teller near her home. It was very convenient for both of us since I ended up living at the same address as her. One day I decided that I had gotten tired of traveling the length of the town all the time to visit her and her parents. Since there was no animosity toward me, that seemed to be a clear indication that maybe it was time for the change. One day while Martha was at work, and Jim (her dad) was out on the road driving an oil tanker truck, I showed up at the house with all my worldly possessions. A short time earlier at Mom's house I simply loaded the car with my clothes and the double mattress off my bed and headed for Martha's.

Arriving at my new home with the mattress hanging out of the trunk was no problem. I rang the doorbell, Martha's mom answered.

"Hi, I said. Could you hold the door for me?" I proceeded to bring a few boxes of things and finally that mattress. She was polite about the whole thing. It was very surprising because I don't remember anyone but me knowing that I was going to do this.

When Martha came home from work she was flabbergasted. Not angry, just surprised that I was able to pull it off. Of course, the real test was yet to come when Jim came home and that went well too. She was glad that I would not be away from her. I had taken her bed apart, laid the mattress and box spring side by side and then put my mattress over the two. I stayed there for the better part of two years. Her Mom would just come and knock on the door when it was dinnertime.

Life among the leeches was not always easy, at least not this one. Although it was quite a bold move in anybody's book, what made it even more interesting was that they never asked me for money for food or rent…and I didn't offer. We would travel to Grandma's house up at Hornell, New York, about an hour and a half from Bradford. Sunday dinners were quite relaxing as we came to be quite a family.

I worked several construction jobs during my tenure at 1156 East Main Street. One of the things that Martha and I did the most was go to the stock car races. I had gone a few times as a kid, but really got into it during the seventies. We would drive to Drum Raceway an hour away on Saturday night and then Bradford Speedway on Sundays. Beer in the cooler was always the main attraction. I almost always drove home no matter what shape I was in. I knew Martha let out a lot of line because I was near her. I did a lot of the same things that got me into trouble it is just that she felt she could monitor me. I believe enabling is the correct term. We hardly ever had a disagreement. Over those two years her mom and dad had concerns that I knew about only twice. Once, when I was outside in the snow waiting for Martha to come home. She had gone out with the girls and at two in the morning I decided to make angels in the snow. Under the spotlight with cars driving by created somewhat of a spectacle and Jim didn't like it. The other time was when I vomited on the antique sofa. They never told me directly, it was always through Martha, and I made my apologies known through her.

One night I was awakened to some very bad news. At three in the morning there was loud pounding on the back door. I got up and opened the door. Rick was standing there in tears.

"Ron, Kirk is dead!" he said.

"What!" I replied, wiping my eyes. "What are you talking about?" I asked.

"He got hit by a car. He laid down in the road. He got into a fight with Melanie and just laid down in the road. They took him to the hospital to give him his last rights."

"Rick, Rick! Slow down. Let me get dressed," I said. "Let's go to the hospital."

"They won't let you in, I'm telling you they won't let you in. Nobody can see him."

"Okay, settle down! Just settle down!" I was nervous and scared, but I had to go and try to see him. Martha and I drove to the hospital on the other side of town. Rick was right. Nobody could see him. We had to stay in the parking lot and get any reports that would come our way. I could hear his sister Chrissy yelling at a priest who couldn't save him. Then the news came. Kirk had indeed gotten into a fight with his girlfriend and went out into the highway near the bar that

117

they were at. He laid down in the road and was hit by two different cars, breaking every bone in his body. The first car that hit him was not found for two days. The driver lived in Kane, Pennsylvania, about thirty minutes from Bradford. He had thought he had hit a deer and did not stop. The news of Kirk inspired him to call the police. The second car dragged my friend about a quarter of a mile and finally pulled over. He did not have a chance. Although he lived for about an hour or so after all of this damage, he finally succumbed at about four a.m. I was now devastated. Kirk had flirted with death for years, but now reality had set in. Martha held me as I wept. The fun kid I had grown up with was now gone. All of the memories of my childhood with Kirk and his family came rushing in. I never really gave it a lot of thought. Death has the unique quality of forcing upon you to reflect on the past when maybe you otherwise wouldn't. This was tough. I had laid beside him on my mat in kindergarten. The hunting, trapping, sleepovers, all of it came at once as a bright star and then went out, only to be kept on the shelf for reference in its new state.

The funeral was a big one. The Heitzinger family with its six kids were well known in the town. The attention for this event was overwhelming. For me, I had to attend to another loss of someone I had cared for, for so long. Every year I try to call or stop by their home on June ninth. That was the day he was born. His gravestone has on it the image of a hunter's paradise. Even that life was taken away by drugs, the very thing that he liked to do the most. I have often looked at my own life and sighed, wondering why I had seemed to escape such a fate. Later I would find out.

Mom and Sam have now had the house to themselves for a couple of years or so. They seemed to enjoy a little piece and quiet now that the wayward little Indian had moved in with his squaw. Sam was about ten years old when all of this happened and Mom kept him quite protected from all of the hoopla. Since she had started driving, the world for her and my brother was wide open. They went to the store for groceries, the mall, sometimes the laundromat, or maybe for a drive in the country. It has always been entertaining to watch her be so independent, especially behind the wheel. Sam had always had a pet Guinea pig and he named them all "Squeaks." He got that name from the noise that they made when they were happy. No matter what condition or frame of mind I was in, I also had this protective instinct that Sam should never follow in my footsteps. In my life was developing a resignation to the fact that not only was I wrong in my ways, but that I saw no evidence that it was ever going to change.

Marriage for me was a secret longing, and while never thinking that I was capable, I made it point to avoid. It was safe to only talk about, not really do. I had quite a low opinion of myself. I didn't ever admit that either, but it was important to keep up the facade. Working around the other guys in which some drank to excess, some didn't, I got to pick which role model I would use. That depended on which day it was, and if I would really benefit from it. My life was becoming one big loss. Taking and not giving, starting to live the lie in new ways had started to poke at the perceptions of other people. It was fun to refer to me as an alcoholic. Sometimes I liked it. After all, I was getting attention and accepted.

Martha and I started to have a disagreement here and there. It seemed like it was nothing big at the time, but I did the ultimate one day. I had gone to my mother's to cool off after a spat. Martha came to the door and stood there arguing and wouldn't stop. I physically pushed her away from the door so I could close it. That ended her and me. I had heard my mother get pushed or slapped by Dad and swore I would never be like that. My program of restraint got impaired by a life of alcohol addiction, and no matter what, I had just broken the rule and lost a beautiful woman who put up with more garbage than most would and the hen came home to roost. I cried for two weeks. All the pleading, promises, any tricks that I had left in the bag and it just didn't do it. I could in no way console myself. For many months later I visited bars where she was at and watched her be content in the arms of someone that had real restraint. A man from her class who led the life that all woman want. That made it worse because it only highlighted my own inadequacies. She stayed with him until they got married and lived happily ever after.

Sink or Swim

The boys and I had gotten the itch for another trip. Last year's venture to California and all of the sights sort of planted a seed that when the humdrum of the middle of winter started to settle in, we needed a break. Sunburned Mike had gotten married and wanted to keep it that way. Everyone who went on the first trip would go except him, and we would ask Bob's brother Donnie to come along. He had started to get into all the same routines as the "rest of us grownups." Being the youngest of the crew, he still had gone a few places that many people his age had not gone. The plan was to drive to Florida and maybe fly over to the Bahamas for a day or two. The trip down, of course, would be much as the same as before. "The Indian drives" while everybody else gambles. That is pretty much the way it went. About the end of March we packed up and headed south. On the way down we would stop in Atlanta and see Steve's brother Mike. He was a schoolteacher and the oldest in his family. We stayed a night and continued on to Daytona where we would stay in the parking lot of a big nightclub near the ocean. Steve had gotten angry over the loss of almost all of his money and left us for a while. Bob's taunting didn't help matters any. Anytime he saw anyone acting like a two-year-old, he would let you know about it. Either you got straightened out or you would lash out, take your pick. Steve eventually came back and Bob kept quiet about it.

Our next stop would be Fort Lauderdale. We got to the water and looked for a place to stay. A hotel called the Captain's Table was a good choice. Right on the ocean and on the strip made everything accessible. We happened to be there at the same time that they were having the kissing contest for the world's record. The people for the "Guinness Book" were there keeping score. I was not interested in making a sport out of such a thing. You would never know it, though, by the way I was acting everywhere else.

Nightfall came and the lights came on. I wanted to sleep on the beach, but there were ordinances against that. Our hotel room was a tight fit again for five guys trying to save a buck. I had gotten cleaned up and headed out for dinner. After eating a hamburger, I came back to the room and wanted to go out on the town. Everybody seemed to be tired and really didn't want to go out, but were still acting kind of punchy. A couple of them had just gotten cleaned up, but were not totally dressed yet. Bob came out of the shower and Rick thought it would be a nice gesture and snap him on the arm with a towel. That was a big mistake. Bob always had this payback mentality, even though he wasn't mad. The fight was on. Rolling up their towels into the nasty "rat tail," dipping the ends in water and making snaps so loud that it could hurt your ears. I was glad not to be a part of this as the guys kept snapping each other until there was blood everywhere. Red marks, bruises, and cuts were no reason to stop the paybacks. Finally Rick had had enough and initiated quitting all of the pain. I left and went downstairs to the disco. After getting a drink and walking around for a few minutes looking for girls, I noticed that there weren't any. I was in a gay bar and didn't know it. There were some glances my way from some of the fellas, but I never put two and two together until I noticed the common dress and body movements. My own friends had known, but didn't say anything. I finished my drink and went back upstairs to call it a night.

The morning of the next day had come and, as usual, it was going to be a scorcher. We would all hit the beach for a dip or a tan. The late afternoon seemed to be a good time to plan for a party at our place. We thought we could invite some girls and make our last day there a memorable one. The first thing that we had to do was to get the beer and the ice. The ice machines at our hotel were not working. Never really found out why. My creativeness had to kick in soon and it did.

I asked Rick to come with me to another larger hotel down the street. I was in my swim shorts and sneakers as we went up to the second floor to check out the ice machines. We found a nice big one outside a large meeting room for executives. Since we did not have a cooler or anything else to put the ice in I would have to improvise. I went into the executive room and overturned the freestanding cigarette canister. It was filled with sand and the carpet looked like a good place to dump it. I now had a perfect container for our ice. Rick was on the lookout while I loaded the ice. Someone who worked on that floor, could've been a cleaning lady, must have seen and alerted the management. Up the hall they came.

Rick spotted them and said, "Somebody's coming, quick let's get out of here!"

He expected me to drop everything and run. He did, but I didn't. With the hotel staff at my heels I ran out on a balcony overlooking an outdoor café on the first floor. With the canister of ice under one arm, I jumped out onto a decorative wrought iron post that traveled to the ground. Climbing down that post with one hand and a load in the other was very hard. I would have to let go for a second, then drop a few feet and catch myself all the way down. Every time that I did that, a lot of ice was shaken out and onto the dining customers at their tables. They were so caught up in the fact of what I was doing that it seemed to distract them for any inconvenience. Anyway, by the time I got to the patio almost all of the ice was gone, so I set the canister down and ran top speed through the crowded patrons, jumped a small wall and then down the street to our hotel. The only thing that I got out of that little project was a lot of scrapes and brush burns from sliding down the iron post. No one caught me. We just canceled the party and fudged it until we had to leave.

The following day we would pack up and go to the airport to fly over to Nassau in the Bahamas. I had a lot of concern about flying, but this trip would be especially nerve racking. Although the hop from Fort Lauderdale to the islands would only last twenty minutes, it would be over water. I had never flown over water. But this was not just any water. It was going to be a flight through the Bermuda triangle. All of my fun studying UFO's and the mysteries of the devil's triangle were coming back to haunt me. We got on the plane. I strapped myself in and looked out the window. The guys knew that

I was afraid of flying and they surely knew that I couldn't swim. We took off and they would have their fun. The view across the Atlantic was certainly breathtaking. However, it was no consolation to my fears and my friends just loved it. Every time that we would hit a little turbulence I would jump in my seat thinking that we were going down. Funny how you can so selective about where you take your risks and at the same time retain your fears about other things. My buddies looked at me and laughed.

Steve made the comment, "Look at his hands, they're shaking."

What he saw were my hands clutching the armrests as if I was being shocked to death. I started sweating profusely and looked like a panicking passenger in a plane that was really going down.

We finally landed, and because of the time zone difference, we got there ten minutes before we actually left. It took me a while to settle down and a cab would take us to the Holiday Inn on a beach. We would stay there for two nights.

The scenery in that area was everything people had told us and then some. Seeing in real life what had been up to that point only images on television or maybe pictures on a calendar was very impressive. The blue water and white sand was something that I would never tire to be around. We would not be so crude during our stay at this luxurious hotel.

Looking around at all the people in the pool, as well the swimmers in the ocean, made me a little jealous. I couldn't swim like I wanted to and faking it unfortunately was not in my book. I could die trying to pull a stunt like that off.

The guys did their usual thing of taking advantage of the facilities. I decide that it time was time to sink or swim. Avoiding the fun and all the benefits of social acceptance in my life had to come to an end. I would walk away from everyone and learn how to swim. The first thing that had to be done was get to a comfortable spot where no one was watching. There was a patch of trees separating the end of the hotel property and the spacious empty beach that seemed to go on for miles. It was a perfect spot to teach ones self how to swim in just a few minutes. About a quarter mile down the beach I acquired "no fear of anything." Behind me was another strange looking hotel. It was white and I couldn't see the parking lot or any of the people. I had wondered why no one was down here swimming like the others were at the Holiday Inn. I turned around and looked at the water. The small beautiful waves rolled in and dissipated at my feet. The sound of the ocean drew me to it. I walked out as far as I could. Just before my head went under I caught a glimpse of an unusually large wave coming. I held my breath and tried to keep my eyes open. It didn't work. The wave picked me up and spearheaded me into the beach headfirst. There was sand in my eyes. I got down on my knees in the water to wash them out, but they still hurt. What was really difficult was the salt particles that had been driven into the depths of my hair. I couldn't wash them out. Not even in the shower. It would take a couple of days before I would be free of them. My vain attempt to teach myself something was another example of the; "I can do it myself" syndrome. I learned nothing except that a person maybe should reach out for a little help once in a while. Since I would not be around water that much, it would be safe to put up with this rare moment of looking foolish that I had not yet learned how to swim.

It was dinnertime and no one of wanted to spend the big bucks on the meals around there, especially at the hotel. The ten member Jamaican band would walk through the dining area playing their native music with the steel drums and flutes. If we could have afforded it we would have eaten there. The guys would split up and go look for something cheaper. I went my own way again. It was about 5:00 and I was famished. Taking a stroll around the island I ended up in an area where there were fishing boats selling fresh fish and clams right off of the boat. It was rather interesting to watch, but the chasm between a fresh fish and the cooking pot was very wide in my mind. As I was walking along a pier trying to think about how I could turn the scene into something edible I looked up and there appeared out of nowhere a Kentucky Fried chicken in the middle of the Atlantic Ocean! I couldn't believe my eyes. Needless to say a five-piece meal went south almost immediately. I went back to the hotel and met the guys who had their own stories about what they had eaten. Settling for much less than what I had gotten did cause a little irritation. They had to spend more to get less.

Our trip had come to an end. The flight back to the mainland went a little better for me. I didn't learn how to swim, but at least I didn't disappear in the Bermuda Triangle. My friends had owed each other their money several times over during the gambling junket in the truck. In the Bahamas you had to be twenty-one years of age to gamble on Paradise Island and we couldn't con our way into that world. Fortunately we all came home in one piece with no significant financial losses.

The year1975 was a year of transition. I had gotten over Martha, I was working a big job and had taken up flag football in the fall. I played for two years and on my jersey was the number eleven and the letters AA underneath. The eleven meant that I had always wanted to be number one and I emphasized it twice while the AA stood for Alcoholics Anonymous. I had never attended a meeting. I thought it was a funny name for someone that was being touted as an alcoholic. My only intention was to patronize, but not openly admit my problem. We played around a circuit consisting of several small towns who had joined the league. I was a wide receiver and still held some speed from earlier days. In 1976, a year later, we had beaten a team by a score of 19 to 76. Hardly anyone could have matched that lopsided victory.

I started a job working at the Quaker State oil refinery building pollution control tanks. That job went from the fall into the winter. The cold days especially after winter got down to thirteen below zero with the wind chill factor being much worse. They didn't keep track of that data as much as they do now, but it really wouldn't make much difference anyway. The winds howling across the flats at Farmer's Valley were unforgiving no matter which era you lived in. My job was to arrange and tie the reinforcement steel for the concrete base and walls. The concrete had to specially treated with a calcium mixture to help it set quicker. That process was assisted by heat blowers, hay and tarps to hold in the heat while everything hardened. We never did have a problem with it. About that time I had run into a woman who worked at a local greasy spoon in Bradford. Her name was Ladonna and we grew fond of each other after a few talks on her job. She lived in an apartment near her work so it was handy to visit after she was done. She had a son, David Victor. I never knew his last name. My welcome eventually wore out with Ladonna. I guess I had discouraged the relationship when I saw that there was not real future with me in their family. There are ways of ducking out without saying the truth. She is still a friend to me though I haven't seen her in quite a while.

The year 1975 had come and gone. The New Year had begun and the spring of 1976 had brought again a sense of new life. The big problem that I had was that my perception of new life was corralled into a limited space called self. Everything had to fit into convenience for me. Part of it was pure selfishness and part of it was being trapped in a confining area that I could not do anything, but arrange things so that it wasn't out of my short reach. This was a recipe for failure in every area of my life and I hadn't experienced the full measure of that yet.

Bemus Point

The whole country had started preparing for the two hundred year anniversary of our Declaration of Independence. This year would prove to be one of the most dangerous years of my life. (As if I couldn't have said that a few times before!) The year started out great. There was talk of a good job coming up in the spring. It was a job everyone wanted. A new high school was being built in a little town forty five minutes from Bradford. Shinglehouse, Pennsylvania, lay among the rolling hills and boasted one of the best hunting areas in this part of the country. It is best known by its location in "God's Country, Potter County." A bustling community with a couple thousand folks did not make a recipe for the robust excitement of larger towns, but actually created a respite for many people who came near that area for a rest. Fishing was good as well as camping for those who wanted to escape the throngs of places like Cleveland or Pittsburgh.

The high school was obviously a long time need and construction of a building paid better that the heavy construction jobs like highways or pipelines. The laborers in our local all wanted any job that was rated "building" and especially one that would last a while. The goal on everyone's mind was always that you wanted to get a job that would last at least from spring through the fall or longer if possible so you could collect the top rate of unemployment benefits.

You not only make top dollar on the job, you would also get paid the most when it came time to snooze for the winter. No wonder there was a buzz when someone was picked to be a labor steward for that job. The steward stayed on for almost the whole duration and I got it.

The other guys picked for the job came in very handy for me. Rick Slocum had already been my running mate for bum of the year and now we had hit the jackpot. We could make good money working for quite a while and travel around the circuit getting into trouble when we weren't. The previous couple of years saw us going to Rick's cottage in Bemus Point, New York, but this year was going to be banner one for wine, women, and song at that lakeshore community, all financed by building a high school.

We began the job in Shinglehouse in late spring. I showed up a couple of weeks before Rick to help set up the foundations for the bricklayers. On the flats nestled between the hills lay an open space for the new school which brought to the community some good business for a better part of the year. Some of the workers had come from out of town and needed a place to stay. Not everyone would or could pack a lunch so we had to eat. A small diner on Main Street or Carlo's tavern about a mile out of town were the mainstay for the best subs at lunch and great dinners for all the men on the crew.

My boss was a great guy who was living in Binghamton, New York. The contractor "Strope Newton" has won the bid on the job and certainly had a good man in George to watch over things. I do not remember his last name. Every Thursday George would buy a half keg of beer about 2:30 in the afternoon for the crew. I thought I was in Heaven. And on Fridays we always knew that old George would be leaving early to make the two hundred mile journey back home. To help expedite that process we always used to ask him questions about his family in the late morning. He would show us pictures as well.

As the job started to get into full swing the crew increased in size. All of the trades started to show up after the foundation was laid. The bricklayers, tin knockers, pipefitters, carpenters, steelworkers, and electricians became part of the job landscape for the next few months. You always met some guys that you had worked with from other jobs so it was always good to see a familiar face or two.

Rick and I would share the driving responsibilities. I would drive one week and he the next. The conversations in the car usually consisted of the events from the night before or the anticipation of the weekend to come. George had to pull me aside one day and tell me something that I as a labor steward did not like to hear, but still had to act.

"Ron, could you come here for a minute, I want to show you something." We took a walk over to the inside of the building and he pointed up to the top of the scaffolding where Rick was working. He said, "See that? We can't have that around here. Take a look at the speed he is moving."

I looked at Rick, who was making the tortoise look like the hare, and said to George "I'll take care of it." I was stuck. One thing that Don Cummins had always told me. "Never give contractor a reason to fire you. Always do your best." I asked Rick to come down and we straightened out the problem.

As a steward I had the job of mixing the mortar for the bricklayers. It got a little hectic when you had to clean out the tub to change colors at a minute's notice. They all were usually kept happy. After a while I ended up giving the job to Rick while I did the odds and ends around the job. He did very well in that position, but there even came a time when both of us had to be spoken to about our garments on the jobs. Rick had on only a short pair of summer shorts and even had them pulled up and tied on the side. It looked like a thong accompanied only with clogs. I was told about my bootwear. They were in such bad shape that I had wired the soles to the uppers because they had separated all the way to the front. It was like taking a string and tying it around your arch just to hold the whole shoe together.

George said, "Come on, Ron, that's unsafe. If you get caught on something you could get hurt."

I reluctantly bought new boots. Rick took off the string and had to wear a shirt.

I got to tend the bricklayers when the walls got up so far. One of those bricklayers had a strange way about him. We were on a wall facing part of the community, and on the front lawn of one the homes was this woman who used to come out and sunbathe. I don't know whether she had had intentions to tempt the crew or not, but Bill Kristov made a comment to me that I will never forget. He was a good "brickie" who had been watching that beautiful scenery while building the wall.

With his trowel pointing at the woman, he looked at me and said, "I'm going to marry that!"

That is all that he said. Over the course of the job he met her and got married. I had heard that they lasted a few years and divorced. Bill was not really a partying person. He took a drink, but usually had things in control. I on the other hand got a lot of men in trouble with their wives. Between the drinking, gambling, and late nights, there were a few women that never wanted to meet the man who had that type of influence.

At Carlo's tavern was a very nice elderly couple who were the proprietors. Howard and Ruth Carlo always had a smile on their face and made sure that every customer got what they asked for. Rick and I went there for lunch almost every day and once in a while came back there on a Saturday night for a dinner and maybe a game of pool. Our last time there was not very profitable for Rick. What started out as a friendly game of pool ended up with me being a big winner. The first game was for five dollars. We were drinking, of course. I ended up being ahead about fifty dollars. Rick didn't like me winning as much as I was, so he thought he would say to me "double or nothing" just to get out of the debt. I said, "Okay, let's do it." I won all the way up four hundred dollars patronizing his call to get out of owing the money. He had taken me farther than I wanted to go. I needed to end up with some money. I backed off a little on the booze and finally agreed for the last time to double up. I won the eight hundred dollars from him that night. He paid me when we got home and I wasn't feeling the least bit guilty because I knew he had won more than that the night before in a card game. The only problem was that he had to break the news to his live-in girlfriend that the money was now gone. She had felt like a queen for only a day.

The time had come for me to reach that higher place,
but what awaited me was only open space.
Never had I cried so loud, and no one heard me.
My sounds had all gone south, like birds you see.
If only I had opened my mouth.

My zeal to be wayward had now increased tenfold. Means, motive, and opportunity all came together for the crime of my life. I had little respect for any principle of rightness. The money was there. I had no responsibilities of a wife or children, and the banner year was now in full swing.

Rick and I had gotten set in our routines at work and started to make the weekend trips to Bemus Point. Very often we would go there to meet some other friends from Bradford or take a few with us. The ride home on Friday nights to get cleaned up and scoot an hour or so north to happyland brought as much fun just with the anticipation of it.

The cottage was off the main street about fifty yards. The community definitely was an attraction to the folks who wanted a laid back, slow moving pace away from their labors. The Surf Club was the main venue for people my age. It boasted a good band that played '50s music, as well as many top bands that had a hit or two. The food was good, especially late at night. Across the street was the Seisure House, an old hotel with the hallmark creaking wooden floors. Behind the Surf Club was the Hotel Lenhart. This building was created into a landmark and attracted the older set. It faced Chautauqua Lake which brought it all together.

Up the lake a few miles was Goose Creek. The fish fries at the firehall there on Friday nights were some of the best around. Then there was Midway Park, a short distance farther up the road. It had one of the oldest operational wooden roller skating rinks in the world. A putt-putt golf range and go-cart track made this place a good choice for any of the Saturday afternoons. The last two favorite places to go were almost side by side only a short drive from all the other stops were the Viking Club and the Moose Club. They were both on the lake and made for easy access for boaters.

Alcohol was served everywhere, even near the roller rink. All the clubs, hotels, and anything associated with the lake made for a lot of fun. We would arrive at the cottage and immediately go to dinner. Very often we would get a sub to eat along the way so we could start drinking before we got there. Had to be in the mood to start socializing. Like our conversations back and forth to work, we talked mostly about the night life. The old story about the frog being put into a pot of cold water and how it did not know enough to get out while the water was slowly getting hot? That was me. Even though I knew right from wrong there was a long slow, subtle process to bring me down to a lower point than I had experienced before. It got worse and worse.

"What are you wearing?" Rick would ask.

"I don't know for sure, all I know is that the shirt had better have something that will light up under the black lights at the Surf Club."

Sugar sack shirts from the islands in the Caribbean were a hit at the club. They had to be the eggshell white. You got the most attention wearing those, as they lit up the night under those lights. And you have to smile, which for me was easy to do under the influence. Your teeth lit up also and you made sure that you were positioned just right for maximum affect. I had always taken care of my teeth. I learned from all my schoolmates even back in grade school to do whatever it took so that you wouldn't lose them permanently. Even during my hard days of abusing myself I spent a lot of money for fillings and crowns while taking all the dentist's advice. I did not like looking at the many mouths that had rotting teeth before we got to junior high school. It had made an impression on me that I never wanted to go anywhere looking like that.

I never met a girl from anywhere that I got to like when I went to the cottage. Nor did I ever really take one there. The last thing that you wanted to do was to take a steady to a place like that because it would interfere with getting something else.

I became increasingly tolerant of this way of life. Hangovers became few unless you drank something out of the norm like tequila or rum on an empty stomach and I rarely did that.

Most of the guys that I hung around with were Catholic, and I came to a point where I was frustrated with their hypocrisy. Not for being Catholic, but these guys would be out with me from Friday night through the wee hours on Sunday morning, crash in the bed with who knows who, and then get up to go to Mass, then come back and jump back into the party all day that Sunday. So I told them. "You guys are hypocrites! Either you stay away from the booze and get your !#%&* to church and stay there or stay away from church and get drunk, but you can't do both!" They never listened to me. Maybe I had to establish a little more integrity in my life for it to mean anything, I don't know. What I do know is that out of all of the pals I had in my life none of them drank themselves into oblivion and wasted their money as much or often as myself and I knew it. The example I had set was the last to be ever used as a positive role model. On the contrary, if you ever wanted to see everything that you should not be, I was it.

One night I had ended up alone coming out of the surf club. I reported my car stolen. There was an APB sent out for my "misplaced vehicle." I found it the next morning sitting just where I had parked it. It seemed as though every once in a while one of the guys would make a slight comment to me about just how "out of the mold" I was becoming. Everybody did their own thing when it came to drinking, but I had broken away from the rest of the pack. "You better quit your drinkin'," one would say, while another might make reference to a "problem." It never really bothered me that much and again there certainly was no evidence that I was going to quit. Actually, the more people talked, the worse it got.

One beautiful evening in the summer of that year I crossed the line...literally. I was found physically dead on the lawn of an elderly woman who had gotten up to let her cat in at three in the morning. She had called an ambulance and the paramedics had tried to revive me three times with CPR. They quit and I was gone. One of them decided to try a fourth time and I came back. Two weeks later I showed up at a stag breakfast for an acquaintance I had met at the club. As I was going to get some pancakes, I overheard a comment that was directed at me from one of the tables nearby. Although I did not recognize any of the men sitting there, they knew who I was. I stepped over to the table to see what their problem was.

"What's going on?" speaking with reserve.

One of the men spoke up. "You are crazy. Don't you know what happened to you and here you are getting ready to do it again?"

They all were the paramedics and continued to expound all the things that had happened that night. I thanked them for all that they had done and felt that this was only another tale to tell while on another barstool. The only one who would be impressed would be me. Others thought it was funny, or felt the same way some of those guys did, but no one really endorsed this story as something beneficial to anyone. I was so grateful that I continued to drink my merry way for another four years.

Traveling to other places was in order at times. Rick and I would make a trip into Canada to Cayuga, Ontario. This little town was on the way to nearby Dragway Park, a dragstrip where the best in the world would come. "Big Daddy" Don Garlits, Shirley "cha-cha" Muldowney and Don, "The Snake" Prudomme all had this stop on the circuit. We would get there and stay in the car for the night. Very often we make a run with a lot of booze on board. Although it was illegal, we would always lie about its presence. In a bold move on one of our trips we approached the border agent.

He looked in our car and asked, "Are you transporting any alcohol?"

While he was asking that question, he had to wait for me to take my mouth off of a long beanshooter that was sticking into a five gallon construction cooler. It had the lid off and was filled to the top with orange juice, ice, and vodka. I wiped my mouth and said, "No, sir." It looked like an innocent drink and certainly no one would be so bold as to try something like that!

That summer Rick decided to buy a camper to be put on the back of his new truck. It would be a pleasant addition to the already wayward life. Some people thought that it was a remarkable feat to remember that when you pushed the buttons "A1" on the jukebox back at the Seisure House you would get the song: "Carry on My Wayward Son" in 1976! How can one forget when you played it a hundred times. The only other song that I can recall the button order to from that era is "Q1"at the Westline Inn near Bradford. The song? "Fool If You Think It's Over." How fitting.

Our travels took us not really far from home, a couple hours at most. The camper slept six and saved some money if we needed to stay anywhere for the night. At the Bradford Holiday Inn, Rick started to get interested in a girl who played in an all girl band, who came to play there one summer. We all had to become groupies. Where the camper went, we went. One of those stints took us to Clarion, Pennsylvania, another town the size of Bradford that had a Holiday Inn as well. Being about an hour and a half from home it was easy to decide that the parking lot was going to be our stay for the night after a time of song and dance. We pulled up into the lot and picked our spot. When I got out of the truck, I noticed a Ramada Inn next door. That would come handy in just a short while. We went in the hotel and met the girls.

This time their parents were with them. We sat down and had a lot of talk. They all were nice people. The girls always dressed in white gowns and sang low key songs. After about an hour or so, I heard that my favorite band was playing at the Ramada next door. They were friends from Bradford. As time went on into the night I had gone back and forth between the two places. Each trip saw me shedding my sweaty shirt, shoes and socks. Finally, my pants were all that I had on. I do not know to this day why I got away with so much, but it was about to catch up with me. Both bands had quit for the night and I was very hungry. I ended up back at the Holiday Inn with the girls and their parents.

"Anyone hungry besides me?" I asked. "I'm making breakfast."

Somebody asked, "How are you going to do that?"

I took the orders and walked right into the kitchen of the nice hotel, turned the lights on and got out bacon, eggs, bread, and all the pans to cook. I stood there for about ten minutes with everything on the stove when all of a sudden I heard a stern voice.

"Just what do you think you are doing?" The manager of the hotel had caught me in the act.

"I'm making breakfast, want some?"

With his hands on his hips, he continued. "I think you had better drop everything and get out of here right now!"

Standing there in just my pants, I kept right on flipping the eggs and answered, "It's going to take a lot more than you to get me out of here."

He stared for a second and left. He came back a couple minutes later and with him were three other guys, two that were much bigger than myself. I saw them stop near the doorway and the manager looked at me squarely. I threw down the utensils and got into a karate stance. Starting to make sounds like Bruce Lee I ran at the men. Now screaming, I got to them and they parted like bystanders watching a madman. Running past them and then into the hallway, I ran all the way to the camper. As soon as I got my hand on the doorknob I heard a siren and looked over only to see a State Trooper in the air with his patrol car. He obviously had been summoned by hotel staff and I watched as he hit the pavement like it was being shot as a movie. Sparks were everywhere. Going into the camper, I locked the door. I did not know that Bob had been asleep in there. I walked over and covered his mouth and whispered for him to be quiet. "Cops!" He looked at me and smiled as the police were rocking the camper back and forth trying to get in. They eventually left. I did not hear a word from anyone with authority about the incident again. It was just a topic of discussion for years to come.

This year was going to my first class reunion and an opportunity to see how some of my former classmates had faired in the school and job market. It would also present me with another look at myself. It had been five years since I had graduated and I already knew what the circumstances were in the lives of those who stayed near Bradford after high school. At least most of them.

It was a hot July day when I got dressed up in a gray suit with a pair of silver fox slippers. The slippers I had gotten on one of my trips to grandma's house up in Canada on the reservation. There was a good turnout at the Bradford Holiday Inn. Since I was already living in Bradford, I thought it would be wise to share a room with some other guys and fill the bathtub full of beer and ice. There isn't much to say about this reunion because before nightfall I had blacked out. This was becoming a more frequent occurrence and my whole evening was spent in the dark. What did happen, though, and I have relied on the testimony from others, was that I was found in the hallway near our room without a stitch of clothing on. Some of the guys came and picked me up and put me in the ice for a minute and threw me on to the bed. When I eventually got a little sober the next day there was this sense of loss. I felt bad that I had missed potential conversation with folks I hadn't seen in a while. Although I really didn't tie it to the drinking, I believed that this was an exceptional event. It didn't happen all the time, so there is really nothing to get upset about. Denial takes a new form. Just back off a little to settle any uneasiness and things will be okay, until the next time.

The rest of that year saw concerts like Elton John, Fleetwood Mac, The Association, and the Ohio Express. The Buffalo Bills games were fun in the fall, especially when half of my buddies would get into fights with the Indians in Salamanca, New York, on the way home.

My earlier trip to Curve Lake that year to get my slippers and visit the matriarch of the band on that reservation saw me always taking it easy on the hooch around my dad's mother. Grandma Knott always smoked, but never inhaled. Her pointing finger and her thumb on her right hand were yellow from the tars in the tobacco. "Hi, Junior," she would say. She always said that in a way that was comforting. I really didn't have much conversation with her before Dad died, and it seemed as though there was hardly any contact with anyone from up there in Mom's direction. I don't know why to this day, but again I've had my suspicions. I had taken Bob with me. He had met my cousin Robert on one of his trips down to Bradford. They hit it off pretty well.

I guess the stay at Grandma's wasn't as exciting as the trip up. Curve Lake is one of many small communities scattered around that area. The lakes are as abundant as the towns in number. Bob and I loaded the car with a case of twenty-four ounce cans of Schlitz. They were twice as long as a regular can and very heavy. We got to the border, made it across the Peace Bridge and onto the Queen Elizabeth highway that runs north to Toronto. My only real memory of that highway is when Dad drove one hundred twenty miles per hour when we were taking Robert back home once when we were kids. That fear was complicated by the fact that Dad had to look around a quart bottle of beer to see where he was going. I can still see Robert and I laying down on the floor behind the seat in agony that we were going to die. Here I am twenty years later carrying on the tradition of dear old Dad.

As it got near dark, I lost my way. I stopped near an intersection and yelled over to a guy who was stopped at the light going in the opposite direction. I yelled over to him. "Hey, can you tell me how to get to the Queen E?"

He started to give me directions and the light turned green, but he stayed there until he was done, holding up the cars behind him. I thanked him, and before I started to leave I noticed a kid with his girlfriend who had been sitting behind the other guy. He didn't like what I had done holding him up and so he gave me the finger. Since I didn't like it, we chased him.

We caught up to him and his girlfriend. Running side by side at eighty miles per hour, I held onto Bob's belt as he leaned out the window and threw a can of beer into the side window of that car. It exploded inward as the driver had fear and beer all over his face. We backed off and drove north to Toronto.

It was a busy Friday night as we entered a city that I'd never driven in. I had called Robert to come and meet us so we could all drive the rest of the way. Not really knowing the town was making me nervous. Chinatown had all the makings of New York City in my mind. I now had to go to the bathroom...bad. Having been drinking all the way up and now I was driving in a strange heavy traffic all brought together that fact that now was the time. I jumped the curb and drove up on the sidewalk. I stepped inside an alley and did my thing. As I was finishing my duty, a patrol car jumped the curb and drove up behind my car. A little Chinese officer got out with his partner and walked straight over to me. I thought he had seen what I had just done.

He got in my face and with his nose almost touching mine, he asked, "What do you think you are doing?"

"I got scared, Officer. I have never been here before and the traffic scared me."

He was very angry and replied, "You people from the States think you can come here and do what ever you want! Take this car off of the sidewalk now and get out of here!"

I complied and realized that he had not seen what I had just done. By now we were all standing in it! We found Robert and left.

My Dad's side of the family really never provided much of a social outlet for me. The only connection between our family in the States was Dad. Although Uncle Don and Aunt Ev were Dad's siblings, there wasn't much attention in our direction. Either Dad initiated it or it didn't happen. This made for a stronger case that I needed attention from somewhere. And I would get it any way that I could.

One of the avenues to get attention for anyone was the Halloween contest at a bar called The Rusty Nail. That was the scene of the fight between Kirk and Melanie before he died. I had always been creative, and here was a chance to exhibit my real talents. The rules were that you had to get up on stage and show off your costume to the crowd while they played music. The loudest applause got the prize. I knew there would be many people, so I would have to make this good.

I went to the store and bought a woman's red, white, and blue one-piece swimsuit. It was very tight, as I weighed about one hundred ninety pounds at the time. I made a banner out of a sheet to make it look like one of those worn by Miss America. Franny Heitzinger did my hair up in a fall to match my own hair. I wore makeup, shaved my legs, arms, and pits. After I got all of that on, I put on a loose dress and a shawl while I carried a purse looking like a normal lady going to a store to shop. Then came game time. While they played the theme from the burlesque shows, the house went nuts. I twirled around, throwing off the garments one by one into the crowd. First the purse, then the shawl, both high heels and then slowly taking off the dress revealing the swimsuit with the banner which read: *Miss Rusty Nail*. I won a Zippo lighter and fifty screwdrivers (drinks). I was queen for a day.

Somewhere in the heart of man lies the desire to do good things despite himself. I suppose the emphasis on all of this partying and revelry can make one feel that there really was no hope. And although that would not manifest itself for some time to come, there were things that did happen that made me at least feel some kind of usefulness.

It was a warm summer night and Rick and I were riding around Bradford looking for something fun to do about two in the morning. We came upon a guy we knew from the bars. His name, Buzzy Ray, seemed like a name fitting for a famous criminal. He had been riding around in his Ford Fairlane convertible with two girls. I knew the one because I had graduated with her, but never really got to know anything about her personally.

We saw them near the Custer City intersection in a parking lot just talking with the top down on the car. This little community was so small that you would be driving along and miss it if you had read a long sentence in a magazine. A Tastee Freeze, furniture store, post office, and a gun shop are it. It is actually an extension of Bradford about two miles out. Buzzy and the girls were just sitting there in the car when we pulled in.

"What are you guys doing?" I asked.

Rick and I looked at each other and saw the perfect opportunity for one of us, but which one? The night began with me taking Rick back to his car. Buzzy, the girls and myself wanted to take a ride into the State Park. First I had to stop home and use the bathroom on the way. It was now about two thirty as we drove up to my house. I did not offer anyone the use of the bathroom because it was too late and I did not want to wake up Mom. Maybe I should have. When I came down the stairs, Mom was standing in the front doorway watching one of the girls relieving herself on our front lawn.

Embarrassed, I walked past Mom. "Excuse me, I'll be back later."

She had her hands behind her back and just looked at me, and said, "Don't you think she can pick a better place to do that?"

My answer to that was simply, "Yes, Mama." I never really talked to her like that, I was just making light of the situation.

We all left for the park. Allegany State park was a beautiful area twelve miles from Bradford. It was actually in New York, and made a convenient venue for camping, swimming and much more. It housed two small man-made lakes. Redhouse and Quaker lakes were separated by a few mountains. We went to the Redhouse side that night. But something happened along the way. Traveling to within a couple of miles of the lake I had been in the back seat with my date Nancy. As I started to kiss her, she died on me. Her heart arrested and she stopped breathing. I double and triple checked to make sure that I wasn't mistaken. Even with a good round of alcohol in me, sobriety pounced on me like a cat on a mouse.

I looked up front to her friend. "What's going on with her? She's not breathing!"

Her friend Barb looked around at me casually, and responded, "Oh, don't worry about that, that always happens to her. She's got sugar and she's not supposed to be drinking. Just slap her and wake her up, she'll come to."

I tilted my head at Barb. "Really? You think that's it?" I don't think that she ever knew just how bad this event really was. I looked at my clinically dead date, pinched her nose and put my lips to hers, took a deep breath and blew her up as hard as I could once and held it. With my free hand I gave her a hard punch in the solar plexus. That is all it took. She coughed once or twice and started crying. I hugged her and thought maybe I would get rewarded that morning, but nada. We all went to take a dip in the lake and called it a night. There are some people that called me "the kiss of death" after they had heard this story.

In a related saga, I was coming home from the Rusty Nail one night when I happened upon a severe accident. There had been a head on collision between a man from out of state and a neighbor friend of mine. Pam Sawyer lived with her mother only two doors away from me and sat unconscious against the steering wheel of her demolished vehicle. There was no one out that late night. Although the man in the other vehicle was in rough shape, he was breathing. I let him be and went to Pam's car. I leaned into the car and did to Pam what I had done to Nancy. Blew her up and punched her. She came to as I went to a neighbor's house near the wreck and pounded on the door.

"Please call an ambulance!" I begged. "They're both hurt real bad."

The lady who answered the door could see that I was not some kook. She had already called the right people and I left. I did not want anyone to see me under the influence, even in those circumstances. Both drivers made out okay. A week later I had seen Pam to tell her the whole story and she thanked me…verbally.

There were many times when I would travel around alone looking for fun, but once in a while I had somebody with me when a spontaneous opportunity would happen upon us. Our buddy Steve had bought a second car for bumming around in so he wouldn't put the miles on his better car. A bunch of us had taken a trip to Jamestown, New York, about an hour away and were on our way back when Steve made a decision. I was driving the car for him while Steve, Bob, Donnie, and Rick were playing cards.

Steve said to me with a smile, "I'm going to take the car to the junkyard."

"What do you mean?" I asked.

He continued. "I'm done using it. I want to get rid of it."

"Okay," I said. "How do you want to do it?"

Playing his next hand he responded, "When we get back to Bradford, you can do to it whatever you want and then take it to the junkyard."

My eyes lit up. I loved destroying things and he knew it. I really didn't know at the time what I would be doing, but I did know it would be fun. Upon hearing my conversation with Steve, one of the other guys pulled out a knife and started cutting up the seats and the material in the ceiling. That made Steven very angry and there was almost a fight. I couldn't understand why he got upset other than I guess he wanted do everything on his timeline. The cutting and ripping stopped and I got to do my thing when we got back.

Upon arriving in Bradford, my first goal was to take the car over to the Elm Street Bridge. The bridge went over a creek at the bottom of one end of the street. A set of railroad tracks ran across the street. That end of Elm Street was a very steep brick incline that leveled off only when you got to the tracks. My goal was to start at the top of the hill about two hundred yards from the bottom and gun it as fast as I could and hit the tracks. I wanted to tear off as much of the underside of the car as possible.

I asked, "Who wants to go with me?"

Rick got in with me while the other guys sat in Rick's car near the bridge out of the way. I gunned it down the hill and hit the tracks very hard. I couldn't see anything because of the dust in the air. That would not be hardest hit. We were in the air for quite a few feet when we landed on the bridge. Rick hit his head on the ceiling as we left many parts of the car on the tracks and road. We had a flat tire in the left rear as I started back up the hill.

The junkyard was only a few blocks away, and going back up that street was on the way. I got to the top of the hill and got to High Street. Along that street was a concrete wall about six feet high that ran for about a half mile. It was on the opposite side of the street on the way to the junkyard. The car was now very loud, as it now had no exhaust system. That was laying on the tracks and all the noise would attract a lot of attention. I drove over to the wall and slowly placed the entire length of the car on my (driver's) side against it. I turned the front of the car into it while I hit the gas. The loud exhaust accompanied by the scraping of metal against the wall had gotten noticed by a crew working on a telephone pole nearby, which, by the way, I was oblivious to. When I got to the first street I pulled away from the wall. The entire driver's side had been scraped clean of all chrome, mirror, and door handles. As I continued down the street, the rear flat tire added to the excitement because I now had the rare opportunity to drive on a flat and not worry about damaging anything. We got to the junkyard and drove up on to the scales. Walking into the office we got a big disappointment.

The junkman looked at the car and said, "You need to have all the doors off."

I looked at Rick and just sighed. "Okay, let's go and take the doors off."

The other guys followed us to another point on the property to help us with the job. We pulled the doors off one by one when all of a sudden we were surrounded by three police cars.

The officers jumped out, and one of them said, "What's going on here? Are you the guys that were just up on High Street?"

"Yes, Officer," I replied. "We were just bringing it to the junkyard."

There was no damage done to anyone else's property and the cops did not feel that they had anything on us that was worthy of arrest, so they left. I drove the car back over to the scales. After the man paid me, I held the gas and the brake down to the floor for a minute. The car was now on the bare rim and the sparks coming off the scales from steel against steel was a sight for the guys. Rick was still in the car with no doors as we went as fast as we could in to a pile of washers and dryers. My only regret at the time was that I did think to put the car to the floor in neutral and drop it into gear. I had only seen that done once and my friend had destroyed his parents' transmission.

The year 1977 had come full swing into the summer. I had parked the white Olds 442 at a new business that Bob and his Dad had bought. It was a Gulf station run by one of our other buddies that we knew primarily through gambling in the back room at the station. Ironically, John White was the guy who had had a party that one tough Easter morning back in '74 when I crashed the Monte Carlo into a pole.

The Olds had been sitting there for about two years and Bob had been very patient with me and my obvious negligence. I eventually gave the transmission to one guy and the rest of it to someone else.

For the better part of the '70s that back room at the gas station was the scene for playing the game of the decade. "Draw Burn" as it was called was a pastime that became fast and expensive. Every day at five o'clock anywhere from five to eight or nine of us got together and cramped in to that little storage room. I had ended up a winner the most during all of those years. When I quit card playing after those years I had been ahead many thousands of dollars. The reason was that I found it easy that playing with the same guys over and over gave me an edge in learning about their habits. It didn't work the other way around because not only have I always had a poker face, but my own social dysfunction made me a moving target. I never knew who I really was so neither did anyone else. Even John's mother Eileen got into the act and was a pleasant addition to our crew.

The gas customers came and went, but they got waited on. It was sort of humorous to see the guys pumping gas after they had gotten "interrupted" during a card game. I had observed and wondered what the priorities really were. The second phase of the evening was a trip to happy hour across the street at the Holiday Inn. The winter hours were always prime because the union boys were out of work, collecting unemployment, sleeping in and available for any impromptu card games. We all ran out the winters, looking for a new and prosperous year. During the first eight years of that decade there was one particular job that was recurring and everyone wanted it when it came up. The "reservoir" job. It was always "cost plus." That meant that there was never any real bidders on that project and the employer had literally an unlimited budget due to the importance of the work.

The reservoir was actually located high above the Kinzua dam on a mountain. Shaped like a deep bowl, this vessel for water had a circumference of about one and a quarter mile around. The outside perimeter consisted of a high bank of dirt. From the air it would look like a dog dish that was made to not flip over. The steep inside slopes were asphalt and it made for cautious walking if there was water below you. When this big dish was filled the water it was about two hundred and fifty feet deep. The environment to work in here was among the best. The job was only tackled in the summer months and was the most sought after job almost every year that it came up. For quite a few consecutive years during the best months you could work up to fourteen hours a day seven days a week maybe between four to six months , maybe longer if they okayed it.

In one corner at the bottom was a twenty two foot wide tunnel that shot straight down into the ground six hundred feet. It elbowed off on a slight angle and ran into the hydroelectric power station below the dam. The turbines would run in reverse during the night thus pumping water from the dam up through the three pipes that occupied that twenty-two foot space. The reservoir would fill up by about six or seven in the morning and then the great water pressure would come back down and spin the turbines during the day and generate electric power for cities that used the power. Cleveland and some other smaller localities had a large draw on the power in the summer time days because of the air conditioning units. During the seventies the utility was owned by Westinghouse.

The need for a crew on a yearly basis was unusual, but the nature of the business demanded it. The way they had built it back in the mid '60s made for a planned maintenance because at several locations around the outside near ground level were stations called "weirs." They were concrete abutments that housed three foot wide pipes which went deep into the dirt mounds that supported the outsides. Actually, being water loss monitors, these stations were used to determine the extent of leakage under the entire reservoir. The great pressure exerted by a full bowl, spread wider any cracks or fissures and made new ones that needed annual repair. The water that passed through those cracks eventually found its way to the weirs and gave the owners a measuring stick to determine the approximate need for the job. What was nice for us laborers was that the company had deep pockets and would spend anything to get the job done. There was not a great pressure to get it done at the beginning of the job, but we were let known as time went on that we could expect an end within a two or three weeks. Without getting into all of the mechanics of the job, our primary goal after the company kept the reservoir drained for the summer was to drill holes deep into the cracks on the floor and then pump grout in them until they got filled or plugged up. I had wondered how on earth a company could predict in any way when that kind of a job would end when we didn't even know where all of the fissures were. Westinghouse had to buy their power from another utility and then resell it to the customer. They were losing millions during the reservoir shutdown. When they wanted to end the job they just told our bosses to thicken the grout and leave those cracks that were left. They wanted to use their reservoir again. Even though it was no holds barred for the duration of the job we figured out that they had a ceiling in the amount of time that they would do without their moneymaker.

One of the many interesting things that we did on that job was to fish in an unconventional way. After the water was drained, the area around the tunnel had about four feet of water, (you couldn't drain the reservoir entirely because there was a five foot high wall around the mouth of the tunnel). That deep hole had been the scene of an accident about ten years earlier when a crane had fallen all the way to the bottom and killed some men. The story was that it took about four days to cut the crane apart to remove it. Dad had worked building the tunnel about that time and endured more than one cave-in. The water around that wall was occupied by all the wisest lake trout in the area. I say wisest because they were smart enough to swim against the current when the tunnel drew all the water down to the power station and became the biggest lunkers in the water. During our lunch hours we could just walk over to the water and either kick or shovel as many trout as we could onto the dry pavement.

On the other side of the bottom of the reservoir also remained a small lake that formed in a depression. In that lake was also the big fish. The biologists from the government would come out in their boats and shock the fish for "study." When the water was out of the main parts of the bottom and you stood on the top edge looking down, all of the heavy equipment looked like small toys. It was that big.

My boss, Pete Taconi, was another great man. He had been originally employed by Ashland Oil for many years. They were the first owners of the site. He always smiled and would stick out his right hand with a finger missing to shake mine. "Good morning," he would say. Needless to say that even with those kinds of hours, once in a while it was rough going because we still went out at night. Pete always knew when we did that. It was sort of hard to hide when you look like a train wreck and your boss had been around the block a few times himself.

Probably one the most attractive qualities about a job like this was the open space in the middle of the woods. Although everyone in the union was used to living in that area which was wooded there was nothing like coming to work in an environment that was not on a busy street or around a lot of the common people/city noise where building trade jobs usually were. Very often on our lunch hours we could go to the spring or see deer, turkeys, or an occasional bear. Even though most jobs required enough space that kept you away from the immediate business of other people they still were close enough to keep you in the grasp of the city "concrete and steel." You couldn't beat working in the woods.

This year would be my last for enjoying such a job. I had been there several times throughout the last few years and old Pete was the only boss that I ever had up there. I would miss him. I have learned since then people really make a job. We could have had a very undesirable person in authority and it would have ruined what was deemed as the best job around, but we had it all.

The Beginning
of the End

The spring of the following year had come and I was to be sent on a job that was eerily reminiscent of a place that Dad had worked. It was only a couple of hundred yards below the dam around the former tunnel job. A contractor needed some small projects done around their supply yard, like cleaning forms and pulling nails. Within a bowshot of the tunnel's entrance I could not, but help to look over and wonder about my father. He had come early one evening after a visit to the hospital. He had worked twelve hour shifts at night when one of the cave-ins bruised his back. I thought about all of the what-ifs. What if he had died in there? What if he was alive today? That thought of him still being here has never left me in over thirty-four years.

This little Indian wandered from place to place,
Oh if only I could see his face.
Clung to a memory from way back when,
only fueled what might have been.

The passage of time and my pondering produced no real healing in me. The ravages of alcohol still gripping my soul convinced me that I would go out like my father. While not consciously thinking about that prospect every moment, my right side had begun to hurt off and on. My skin would become "jaundiced" on occasion and I would tell no one but my friend Donnie Cummins. The son of the business agent, he eventually would begin to criticize me for my reluctance to quit drinking. My private shame was escalating, but I was crafty enough to keep the lid on it, a talent that I found out that was shared by many others.

In March of 1978 I took a bold step. One Tuesday evening a few of us were out for a trip to the Pub, a local bar that my sister Mary had been helping to run with her boyfriend and his brother. There were three of us guys as we were about to enter, I stopped the guys outside the door.

I leaned against the wall and said, "I am going in there and I will find a woman, buy her a drink, ask her for a date, and then end up moving in with her."

I was frustrated with going out all the time, having no real social life and not having anyone to care about in my life. We walked in the bar. I found a woman sitting by herself. I bought her a drink, took her on a date, and then moved in with her and her two daughters. It took a couple of months, but that is exactly the way that it happened. I did not even remember that a couple of years earlier Bill Kristov had done the same thing in Shinglehouse.

Lois Thompson had beautiful blue eyes and a sincere smile. On a dead night near the middle of the week I knew she was serious about meeting someone herself. Our first date was at a nice restaurant owned by a friend of mine. I, of course, had to show off by introducing her to Tony. That would be one of the last times that I would have to try that type of influence to win her heart. When I moved into 78 Summer Street I was still working that job below the dam. Making good money at the time, I would be asked to go to another job down in Warren, another ten miles down the river below the dam. I made even better money on that new job. The cleaning of the forms was only paying the heavy construction rate. This new project was building a new jail for Warren County.

I showed up for work and my job was working with the bricklayers. Helping unload the big trucks from Pittsburgh and delivering mortar to the brickies was the norm for about four months. I was impressed by many aspects of a job like this. The solid walls filled with mortar and reinforcement steel, bulletproof glass, and mini-blinds built inside the windows were just some of the unique features that gave this job a little novelty. One of the downsides to it all was that a pair of brothers owned the company that I was employed by. Bruce and Boyd Holcumb were like day and night. Boyd was a good-natured fellow who never gave anyone a hard time while Bruce being an angry alcoholic offset all the good characteristics of his "okay to get along with" brother. Sometimes it doesn't matter how nice a person is if someone nearby produces constant tension among people. Since I wasn't really hard to get along with, that made it easier on myself because I didn't do much to aggravate Bruce. I could still see his harshness in many other of his dealings.

The new jail was going to be attached to the Warren City Hall. It was an old pinkish brick building that is typical of small town America. One of the points humorous of my job was the introduction to the Warren County dog catcher. His office was located just inside the rear of the town hall that was to be part of the eventual connection between the two buildings. This man had been in his position for many years. Every time I tell this story people think that I am making it up, but I am not. The man had cheeks that hung down like that crime dog, McGruff. Every time he moved his face, his cheeks would swing. That in itself would be somewhat ironic, but it was his name that got me. Simon Huckabone. How much more dog related can you get. His ID tag for the county that he wore on his clean pressed white shirt spelled it out quite clearly. He seemed to enjoy it when he introduced himself. Throughout my life I still meet people that have names that are very relevant to the title of their job. A person like Cash working at bank or Drinkwater working at a filtration plant. Some folks seemed to be destined to be where they are   Back at my new address there was this optimism that Lois and I were destined to hit it off for good. One of the things that attracted her to me was that I had not seemed to pose a threat to her or the girls. And I guess I never did. However, my drinking had been curbed only a little because I was temporarily enraptured with the fulfillment of the desire of my heart. No more lonely nights. No more drinking like I was. I had finally come to that much longed for resting place.

The girls liked me, especially Kelly the youngest. She was five at the time. She used to hold her arms to me and say, "Pick me up." I loved to carry her around the house. Kim participated in all the games, but developed a distance from me. The girls had to visit their Dad on the weekends and when they came back on Sunday nights Kim was not the same. She was growing to resent me simply because I was not her father. Kelly never saw it like that. My income was a welcome sign of some commitment for Lois. She had some of the same natural longings for companionship that I had and it seemed to be a perfect fit. We were about to find out just how real it was.

I moved in around June of 1978 on a hot summer's day. It took a few months to get used to, but I liked it. Lois and I would go out to dinner. We always had a babysitter. The girls were five and seven at the time. Going to a movie, out to dinner or a bar became a regular thing, especially on the weekends. But after a few months "the honeymoon" started to wear off. I realized that I would also miss the guys and the freedom that I had when I was living with Mom. When they would see me out they would taunt me with phrases like "Ron's got a ball and chain around his ankle," or "Look who's wearing the pants in that family." I felt pressure from all fronts. I was not really capable of being my own person. I was sick and didn't recognize it as that. It was clear what I wanted, but I couldn't have both worlds. So what do you do in a case like that? Try and force it of course.

For about a year Lois had tried to see things my way. A few months of drinking heavier than she was used to woke her up. She couldn't keep up with me and yet still loved me. When stepping away from the alcohol scene did not correct my actions she had decided to seek help. But not before I had dragged her heart through the mud.

It is strange how you know beyond any doubt that you are wrong about something and even though you want it to be right, there seems to be no way out, but through the avenue of pain. I had gotten many subtle hints as well as obvious evidence that my life should not be traveling the path that it was on and I ignored them all. Now I had met my match and so did Lois. It almost cost us each our lives. Her newfound desire to keep her sanity and me was just as strong as my desire to run the two worlds together with her and my friends. I was to have one or the other, but not both.

A year into our relationship the fights started. I came home drunk, sometimes didn't come home at all or stood her up many times to go out for a simple date. I always wanted to get started early, come home and get Lois and go back out again. She would yell, "What do you think you are doing to me! I'm tired of having you treat me like dirt! When are you going to stop!" My responses were to try and get her calmed down so I could continue on my merry way. I finally got into the shouting matches with her and ultimately would use them as excuses to back out. My sister got the great opportunity to get back at Lois because she didn't like her. I got to run to Mary when I was in a fight. She would put me up for the night and get another round from me about how wrong Lois was. Building up allies against my fiancé was not a problem. What was a problem for me was that I looked like a fool going back to the one person that I was verbally blaming for all of my woes. She had her faults, but none of them were worth leaving her for. Not for a moment. Just about every one of my undesirable characteristics were directly tied to my obsession with alcohol.

One night I woke up about two in the morning , grabbing Lois by the hair and pulled her off of the bed thinking that I was saving her from aliens that I was watching fly down the street. What it really was, was that the insulators on the telephone poles were lined up just right in the street light and the fact that I was going through withdrawal. Another time I sat at the table with a knife near my hand and threatened to kill her if she moved. It was not a real threat, but intimidation. I needed to be in control and I was losing it. By this time Bob and Donnie had moved to Texas to try and start a new life. The remnant of friends kept up the pressure while I tried to figure out how to compromise, patronize, manipulate, and anything that I could come up with cut a deal with the devil. One thing for sure, I had to keep drinking, or stop. Nothing in between.

My first good intention was to stop cold turkey with no help. By this time Lois had sought professional help. Her counsel was to live her own life, take away all of the bumpers and let me feel the full brunt of my actions. Being a compassionate person and no experience with tough love made it hard going for her. I quit for one day. Drank one day. Quit for ten days. Drank for a few days then quit for a month, twenty eight to be exact. I found out that Bob was moving back and he was due on my twenty eighth day. I dropped everything and went with him as if nothing ever happened. The shock to my system was terrible. During that month that were several vain attempts to get me to go to AA or maybe a Drug and Alcohol treatment facility in Coudersport, Pennsylvania. I would say to everyone. "I can do this, I can handle it." After my binge with Bob, I woke up the next morning very sick.

Lois made a suggestion to me. "Ron, do you want me to call AA? They would send someone over to you talk right now."

I was in bad shape. Having not had anything for a whole month and then hitting it hard gave me a lot to vomit about. Cringing in pain I said "Okay. Let 'em do it."

Within an hour there was a knock at the door. My fears were just beginning to mount.

"Hello," I could here them say. "Where is he?" I was sitting at the dining room table when two men came in and sat down. "Hello, my name is Harry and this is Bob."

With my head down and my face red from a combination of getting sick, embarrassment, and fear, I slowly looked up and saw two faces that meant business. Harry began to talk to me about whether I really wanted to quit or not. He had been sober five years at the time. Bob had a year under his belt. "Yes," I answered slowly, with both hands on my stomach. I got up quickly from the table and ran into the kitchen and got sick in the sink. It hurt, and my pain was complicated by the fact that I could hear two men in my dining room laughing about my current enigma. Over my gagging I clearly heard, "I remember when," and "I'm glad that's not me." Not very encouraging for me in one sense, but there was a crack in my armor. I knew that they were right. And Harry had another weapon. He had drank with Dad and proved it by the things that he said. I was also enlightened about the things I had not known. We had a good talk and they asked me to a meeting. I said I would "check it out." After all of that hoopla I still had some reservations.

Lois had tried to hold her ground in many ways. Co-dependency or the psychological victim of another's sickness had gotten a great hold on her. I had become a great manipulator and a master at what is called in laymen's terms, head games. It was so true that the more rightness comes around, resistance from that which is wrong accelerates or sees things the right way and begins a road to change. I became like Pharoah, King of Egypt. The more he was asked to do the right thing, the more his heart hardened. It would appear at times as though there was a change of heart until the next opportunity came to manifest the real me had come. My next big attempt to do this thing myself would be my last.

Quitting drinking for five months was very strange. I had to give up going out with my buddies, mind the business of a new family arrangement, and constantly try to keep my sick head above water without help from anyone else. Getting married to Lois was something that we both believed would somehow force change on me. After all, I had a wife and kids now. While that happened earlier in the year, thinking that it was really part of genuine rehabilitation just didn't cut it.

September of 1980 had arrived. I was patting myself on the back for staying away from the rudiment elements that were destroying me. I had a small fan club that thought I was on my way to success. Then it happened. One day while mowing the lawn on a beautiful warm afternoon I stopped the mower and walked over to my wife who was digging in the flowers looked up to hear me say, "I'm going out." Although my goal was to go out and drink again, I first had to get Lois to raise her voice and get contentious. Once that happened, I was in. I would use that argument as an excuse to do what I had started to plan only moments before. If I was clean and sober with some help in my life, that drunk would have taken a longer period of time to plan. When I had no real growth and change, I was a walking time bomb all the time. She stood up and immediately challenged me. I got her to be contentious and I left while she was in tears. Even though it was mysterious then, it isn't now why that happened. Everything that I wanted in my life had come true. A wife, two beautiful little girls, nice home on a sunny day and I still was willing to throw it all away for a simple mindless drink. I had brought this innocent family to disaster.

When I came home from a couple of days away, the scene was not good. There was a sheriff sale sign on the front door of my house, Lois was sick, the bank was taking the car and the truck away, the State was now in the process of taking the girls away, and I owed many

154

dollars in gambling debts. All in one day. The girls' father had had enough of my crap and ratted to DSS. Although I had been clean awhile, I had not been as responsible as I could have. The distraction of just staying away from a drink was keeping me from normal living. With someone else's help I would have a chance, but trying to convince the world that I could go it alone just did not work. Lois had valiantly tried and failed to keep her sanity and me. No one was allowed to visit her. It was that bad. Except for death, I had reached the ultimate low a person could attain. One of the last times that I drank at a bar I had passed out on the floor in the entrance doorway. People had to step over me to get in and out. The town drunk had come to me earlier in the evening to borrow some change. Lewey Anderson had been alive at the time my father had had the dubious distinction of sharing the park benches at night with him a decade earlier in the public square.

It was that sunny day in Bradford, I collapsed on the front porch of my house in tears. While neighbors watched on, I lay on the floor and spoke. "I can't take this any more, God please help me." The emptiness was overwhelming. I had taken an ultimate risk and lost and now there was no one to rescue me from my foolishness. What I had known all along was still waiting for me. Refusing the help of other people in so many ways for so long made it almost impossible to reach out for that hand. I got up and staggered into the house a truly broken man. I went for a phone number in the house. I dialed a number that the man on the other end thought I wouldn't ever dial. His name was Ken Renshaw. Lois had been seeing him as an addictions counselor.

"Hello," he answered.

"Yes, this Ron Knott," I said. "I want to go into the rehab center."

"Is this really Ron Knott?"

Sniffling on, I made it clear the way that I had felt.

He continued. "I will make sure that you get a bed as soon as possible. This is a good thing Ron, do you understand that?"

The state of mind that I was in kept it certain that I knew that for the first time in my life I was going to win by giving up. Ken Renshaw, two psychiatrists, some AA'ers, my family and many other's were very happy that I had been finally humbled. Now I was fearless about doing whatever they would tell me.

The first thing that I did was go to work and tell my boss and then Don Cummins that I was going to give up my union card. He pulled me aside and tried to talk me out of it.

"You can stay away from it. Sure you're going to make a mistake once in awhile."

If there was a chance to rethink my position or change my mind on this whole thing this was the time. It did not even pose to me a temptation. I was going forward with the plan to change my life. I was serious from the moment of hitting my bottom. Just days prior to all of this I was asked to be the Godfather of Donnie's son Jake. I did that, but it would be a time of great trial for many people who wanted me around for a long time to come. When I decided to make this new commitment it was without reserve. I spared no one's feelings or relationship. My life was on the line.

My new start awaited me. Ken had gotten me into a place that I had only heard about as a suggestion months earlier. Maple Manor was a Rehab center that carried quite a reputation for recovery. He called me and gave me my date which was September 25, just a couple days away. Although there was trepidation in my spirit I tried to ignore it. I was now being asked to take a risk that was positive one. My track record of taking negative risks made it clear that this should be no problem if I was genuine about change.

Steve Pettinato had the privilege of driving me over to Coudersport, another small town forty five minutes from Bradford. He was about the only one at the time that could see my desperation. I never blamed anyone for not seeing things like that. I arrived at the manor with my clothes and some toiletries. The administrator, Lowell Watkins was a Baptist preacher and a good fit for the job. He was kind and very wise. Bill Weitzel came to be one of my counselors. His specialty was anger. I will never forget that he was very careful about seemingly insignificant things like caffeine and tobacco, two problems that I thought were out of my league. Bill had a problem of his own. He was addicted to saving information and putting it into a computer. He eventually told me that his family broke up because he would save boxes of articles out of the newspapers just to get the info onto the computer. His obsession cost him something as well.

The first night at my new home for the next six weeks was a comfort and relief. I looked out the window at the moon and wept on my knees saying, "I finally did it." I had a very good sleep.

I met quite a few new people who had the same problem as myself as well as those that did drugs. Some folks came and went. They couldn't or wouldn't stay. It was always a full place. One morning about three o'clock I saw flashing red lights outside and looked out the window to see a girl with her hands clinging to the wire grating on the door. The police were trying to pull her off. She wanted to get in and seemed to be under the influence of alcohol. I saw her about a week later as an inpatient.

I was in line for a whole new life. Much more than I thought. My days were marked by getting up at certain times. Meals, groups, meetings were all subject to strict time elements. I saw some people get discharged because they would not cooperate with those structures. I cannot remember if there was anything that I did not like about that place. Going to ceramics class was something that I always had looked forward to. We all went (about twenty-one of us) up to another building about a quarter of a mile away.

We started our routine by usually having to wait on a group of people that were ahead of us. They would clear up their areas, put the project on the shelf and assemble for exit. What was worth noting about these folks was that they were all mentally retarded citizens. I could watch through the door into the large room that we all have our classes in. I was observing them closely and noticed how content almost everyone was. Many were smiling and some trying to concentrate on their projects. There was always a few with the Downs Syndrome. What really touched me was the fact that they were not there for abusing any substances. They were living their life and its struggles. In some ways I was envious. I always had an unhindered capacity to make choices in life and abused that privilege. In the presence of these people I felt like I had let society down. There was a stark contrast between the circumstances in their lives and mine. For several years after, on occasion I would wish that I were retarded. I never really mentioned to anyone because I knew what I doing. I did not want to experience some of the pangs of growth.

I went to class and made the proverbial ashtrays and coffee mugs. Sitting down with all my "classmates" took a little of the edge off of the nervousness. Shaping the clay, scraping and squeezing the edges and ultimately holding up the finished work started to invoke a minor sense of accomplishment.

Mealtime back at the Manor was special, but sometimes a little embarrassing. Holding hands and saying grace for our meals was a far cry from the ungrateful waste of a life just a few days earlier. Clearing my throat and shifting around in my chair always accompanied the fear of facing my turn to give thanks for our blessings. But I did okay because I knew it was right.

I had originally been signed up to stay here for four weeks, but when it came to within a few days of leaving they had asked me to stay for another two weeks because there needed to be a focus on a young fractured marriage. Lowell came to me and made the request and watched me closely for my response.

"I told you that I would do whatever you would say," I told him. There was a little disappointment because there had been an appointed date for my discharge and I was mentally planning for that timed event. It turned out fine though. The old saying that I had heard in my youth, "God helps those who help themselves," came into play.

About three weeks into my stay Lois came to visit for the first time. I do not know what day she was allowed to leave the hospital, but it was good to see her. I was tender and very sensitive at the time. Her first announcement at the time was that she had applied for a job at J.C.Penney's as a secretary. I had a difficult time with that because it displayed evidence of a new independence.

"Ron, I have something to tell you. I got a job at Penneys."

I said "What?" I put my head down and tried to deal with it. I realized that this safe, protective covering that I had over me at this rehab center was going to be intruded upon by what appeared to be outside influences. I tried to talk her out of it, but quickly gave up. I knew that my new gatekeepers had nothing, but the best for myself and my family in mind. "Okay," I said. "I hope it works out." Trusting them implicitly from the start gave me a great edge when some unforeseen request approached me.

The standard regimen of when, why, how much, and how often became the daily thing. It was hard and humbling to finally admit in every way possible that I had a problem which I could not lick myself. Some of the sessions were brutal only because I was less than normal, not because they were wrong. There was every attempt made to test my sincerity and my commitment, both for the short and long term. While the one day at a time was emphasized, you couldn't get away from the reality of certain responsibilities. Everything had to be faced in their way and in their time.

I got to see the lives of others and some of them had very interesting situations to deal with. With people coming and going I began to wonder how my new associates would end up. Those who stayed till graduation gave me some hope. Others just scared me into a deeper commitment.

One of the items that I brought with me was a book/record packet by Hal Lindsey. I had been infatuated by the hype of current world events and how they were supposed to be related to prophecies and predictions. Orwell's *1984*, Lindsey's *The Beginning of the Battle of Armegeddon*, and other works only made my starving spiritual life even more lean. Those things were interesting, but they just did not make the grade. I had brought the material into the rehab to try and help others. I felt that they needed to be warned about some coming destruction and "Had better get right with God." That little escapade did not last long. I had met my new roommate and saw him as my first convert. To what I don't know, I just had to warn him. Jim was a few years younger than myself. A couple days into his stay I let him have it.

"You had better get right with Jesus," I would say. "There is a coming destruction and you have to be ready."

He had given me a long ear. After I had gotten done with him, he packed up and left. About an hour later Lowell came in with a team leader and took my things away. Looking at me with compassionate eyes he slowly let me know the story.

"Ron, you can't be bringing those kinds of things in here. You are here for your recovery. We have to take this away. You can have it back when you leave."

This idea had occurred to me that he was a preacher and he was doing this? How could he? I didn't ask because I knew one thing he was right about. How on earth was I ever going to be a good example of anything, given my current position in life I was that hypocrite that

I had accused my friends of being a few years earlier at Bemus Point. Those guys by the way had a grand old time while I was in there trying to save my life. I never did find out who did it, but there were many calls to Maple Manor all hours of the day and night. The callers always swore and made fun of the counselors during my six week stay. Most often my name was mentioned. Some people had to take a serious look at themselves after I had decided to step off of the freight train to Hell. It was a genuine threat to a few of them.

Eventually getting to visit Lois in the library of the Manor one on one gave me an opportunity to share some things with her that would come by that way and no other. At other times I would be prompted to make amends to my wife. That was humbling. I could have refused. Thinking about apologizing to anyone for some wrong that I had done was not really hard because of that. I almost always knew when I was wrong. What was hard was that I had to do it sober. I wasn't insulated with an altered mind, and I had to be sincere. Dad had always forced me to tell Mom I'm sorry. I had literally no experience at dealing with this with a clear head. Very often in tears I would tell my wife that I was sorry for what I have done. The wonderful people around me at that time made sure that I wouldn't overdo it and start condemning myself. I believe that I meant everything that I had said.

There was no doubt that Lois had begun to have a new outlook on our future. I had done the impossible. Surrendering to this whole thing paved a new road that she was willing to take. Many times before I had told her after a drunk that it was over. I wouldn't do it again. Especially after the time that I had broken her nose. I had been sitting on the edge of the bed moving out for the twelfth time in thirty days and she hit me in the side of the head with an open hand. The cupping of her hand covered my ear and made an air compression against my eardrum. It hurt and also scared me. Then I got angry. Standing up I explained to her that I had never wanted to hit a woman, but if I were ever attacked, that would change. The rest is history. I did something that I really never believed in. There was no excuse for it.

My wife had endured a lot. She had stuck it out and now the fruit of a lot of her hard labor was paying off. Her sacrifices gave me another chance at life. Many things would come into line. Things that we had no control over came together.

It was the fall of the year and especially in this part of the country the foliage in the autumn sun made this a more bearable experience. A couple of nights a week, once in a while during the day the whole rehab unit would take a trip to an AA meeting in some other small towns…including Bradford. My first time going to that meeting was walking on eggshells. As usual there was a greeter and a smile. We always got there early so the pain of seeing who was going to show up was prolonged. It was actually fear charged by embarrassment. Still not being totally comfortable around the potential opinion of others, my core commitment wasn't going to change.

After the ice was broken in Bradford, I discovered that there really was another world called recovery. The unseen network of groups, speakers, coffee and doughnuts was incredible. You can't see this world out in public. I had no idea that our society had created something this big and yet so obscure. Of course I was pleasantly surprised to see some people that I had known from the bars that had just dropped out of sight from that scene. That became a comfort and an encouragement to my sensitive soul.

My embarrassment was not limited to going into a meeting. There was one trip that we made during the daylight hours in which the van driver would stop at a drug store along the way. I did not really like the idea of getting off of the van with the rest of the crew to stretch my legs, but I had to. In the small towns in that area I felt that everyone knew what that van was for. So, I would step out and walk over to a storefront or street corner and stand there as if I was not associated with the "loonies" that had just arrived in Dodge. I was actually pretending to not be with them. Eventually that stigma wore off and I accepted my true position.

To start hearing the stories of others and the length of clean time that they now had was certainly inspiring. Conventions and special events were also the norm in that society. I would constantly hear, "Keep coming back, don't pick up, get a sponsor, and do service work." I took all of that literally.

We would have a meeting on Friday nights and folks from around the area would enjoy to come and to be of some help to us who were fresh into this new way of life. There was a man whom I will call John, who came faithfully to that meeting. He was a roly-poly man about five foot nine. He would come over to me with his hand out and look at me as if he was staring a hole through my head. Then he would smile. "Hi Ron, how are you doing?" Sometimes he would not let go of the handshake until he got an honest answer out of me. He knew me well in just a short time, at least about my sincerity concerning the state of mind I was in at the moment. The thing that would impress me the most about him was the peace and serenity that this man had. He was a full ten years sober and it wasn't hard to put two and two together to come up with that the path I had chosen was truly the right one. With cookie in one hand and a coffee in the other I watched him closely. I also saw others that did not have that peace which my new friend had, and even some of those men and women had some serious time under their belts. What I was being taught was coming to bear. Sobriety's principles ran on the same premise of all of society. You get out of it what you put in. What I was observing early on was that there were many different commitments, even in recovery. Some were sincere, and some not. I knew which way I wanted to go.

During the last weeks at the Manor I saw people get in fights, break down and cry about some more bad news, and also some who showed promise for a new life.

I had begun a rigorous exercise program in which I kept track of what I did everyday. Watching those who were moving on convinced me that I needed everything I could get to make it. Physical, mental, and spiritual elements were all of the things that I longed for and it had been a long time coming. Graduation day came. It was a beautiful sunny morning with all of the autumn trimmings. The birds were singing, the crisp air seemed to be alive with the announcement of my arrival. I didn't really feel so important as much as though it seemed as God had gone ahead of me to let this humiliated man know that little old me and what I was doing was important. I had heard this spoken by some people in various meetings.

What was expected of us who were going to be leaving that day was to write something down that you could read to the entire group before you left, something that you had learned during your stay. My contribution was of course unique. I had written fifty excuses that I had used to go out and drink, then read each one aloud. The most outlandish one was that I was pregnant. We celebrated by toasting my new baby in a bar. Why I chose to write something like this down was actually a tribute to my newfound sincerity. Honesty was the hallmark of recovery and I wanted to renounce anything that was associated with dishonesty.

We all assembled in the large living room. Lowell had come in to listen to what we had learned. I was certainly nervous, but excited at the anticipation of completing the program. Lois had come to pick me up and got to hear one of the first installments of my program. I read it all, Lowell led us in a prayer and then I slowly walked down to the car. I got to drive home, but before we went anywhere I had to stop crying. The safety and sanctity of such a wonderful place was now becoming only a memory. I was leaving a building that had been my home for six pleasantly grueling weeks. Two of my buddies that I had grown accustomed to sort of took the edge off of this emotional moment because they would be part of my planned fellowship out in the land of meetings. Charley and Bill the Indian hugged me as a left.

I started up the Pinto station wagon and we had quite a drive back home. Although the girls had spent a great deal of this time with different family members, they ultimately would be with us. The attempt by Denny, their Dad to take them away had failed. I had made a lasting impression on the law. In today's world the avenue that I had taken in my addiction is very much being used to just satisfy attempts by others to gain ground on an issue. Sincerity goes a long way, especially over time.

My relationship with Denny Prosser was always through other people. I made sure I hardly ever was around when he would pick up or drop off the girls. Only a year earlier I had been beaten up by his brother during one of my mouthy exchanges during a blackout. I didn't remember a thing. My future with the girls' father looked bleak. I had learned that just because you might have changed doesn't mean that the rest of the world will welcome you with open arms. The best was yet to come.

Lois and I brought my stuff into the house. I walked in and looked around. In was very strange being away for so long. One of the first things that I did was to turn the radio on. How ironic that the song in progress was "Fifty Ways to Leave Your Lover!" I looked at Lois and just shook my head. The nuts and bolts to my life were about to be tested. I would start to find out just how serious I was, what I had learned back at the Manor and what I would really do about it.

The first suggestion was for me to get a sponsor. I had shopped around during some of the meetings, but was told to take enough time to approach anyone that I felt would be assertive with me. Someone who had the nerve to tell me like it was. I had seen the results of people picking the soft soapers. Avoiding growth had been my program for so long. I did not want to go back to it. I spied a man during some the meetings who had accumulated fifteen years of sobriety. The things that he had said and the strong intent behind his words made him an attractive prospect. His name was Tom Stone. How appropriate. He was about sixty five at the time. I walked over to him after a meeting in a Catholic Rectory and asked him. Reaching out my hand to him, I made my pitch.

"Tom would you be my sponsor?"

He had known some of my history by that time. He also knew of Dad for many years. He thought for a second and accepted. From that moment on for the next couple of years he guided me through many ups and downs. We traveled to meetings together as well as the coffee shops and an occasional visit to his home. He had lived just up the street from where I had grown up. And of course, his house was made of stone, one of the only homes built like that in the area.

The second suggestion was service. I had volunteered to make coffee, set up the chairs and literature, whatever was needed. Finding a "home group" wasn't hard. Bradford's Friday night group was an easy choice. Doing the simple things in life now had meaning. And it influenced others to see the importance of doing something for someone else. It had affected me I know. Seeing the newcomers in the meetings I had attended while in the manor made me ponder doing some things that had never really been in my vocabulary. Words like help, please, and thank you come to mind.

At the time of my entrance into the world of AA it became apparent that Lois and the girls would have to make some adjustments as well. Although the idea that it was going to happen, when things go beyond just talking about them, it becomes more serious. I had run into someone that I had met about five years earlier. Jon Moore was also a newcomer in a way. He had been clean for a number of years and made some mistakes and now was starting over again. His wife Terri was an avid fan of Al-anon, the self help group for loved ones of alcoholics. I would see Jon in the meetings and after a while Lois and Terri got together and went to the other meetings for support. They even started a new meeting in Bradford in one of the churches. Kim and Kelly did not go to any meetings for help. We had felt although they had experienced my waywardness, most often they were not home and the length of their exposure to was comparably short.

I took a role in the girl's lives like no one had before. We had all put together a bulletin board for the front of the refrigerator. On the board were many squares that had a peel off piece of paper with a denomination of money written on it. On the side of the columns were chores to do around the house. After a chore was completed, each of the girls got to pull off a tab. There was always a minimum amount, but there a few one dollar tabs as well as a couple of five dollar ones. It made for a tidy house. Lois was always a good homemaker and cook. She also was a good mother. Whatever the girls did to help was certainly appreciated. I got into vacuuming and a little dusting. The yard work hardly ever was neglected except when I went into rehab.

One of the requirements for me was to commit to aftercare. I traveled with my wife back to Maple Manor, with frequent visits to offices in Bradford. Ken Renshaw and his wife had eventually even come to our home for a visit.

Of the hurdles that I had to jump after graduation, anger was at the top of the list. I had retained some issues that kept me at bay with things regarding resentments. For several months Bill Weitzel had become my confidante as I expressed myself to him. One of the most dangerous aspects of anger in my life came to a head when the right side of my body started to experience some minor paralysis. This was the result of intense hatred of the actions of another person. Psycho paralysis, as it was called, lasted about a week and was getting worse until I talked it out. Then it went away. I have not heard from it since.

When things started to get a little more settled and I seemed to carry on a little better, Lois and I thought that we would like to go into business. We knew that jumping into a big change right so soon would not be in order, so we would take some time and at least brainstorm some ideas. She had started school at the University of

Pittsburgh in Bradford for at least one semester. An administrative business degree was what she had wanted for some time. Our thoughts were leaning toward opening an eatery of some type and if we did something like that, her education would be very helpful.

I was able to collect unemployment for quite a few months. During those days there were federally funded extensions which were also tax free when your original claim of up to six months ran out. Getting a check once a week under our current conditions was quite helpful. We made it through the winter. Christmas after my rehab experience was very special. I hadn't one without having John Barleycorn around for ten years. It was enlightening.

Life had become novel. I had taken a lot of things for granted for so long, my change of thinking created one sense of gratitude after another. Seeing life through the eyes of a sober man was like waking up to a new world. They had told me the grass would be greener and the sky would be bluer. They were right and that principle has never stopped. The provisions for me to take my time especially during the initial stages of my recovery were abundant. I didn't need to work right away. There was time to spend with my family and certainly time to go to meetings and talk to Tom for some guidance.

Blue and Black

During the spring of '81, I saw something on Main Street in Bradford that made me wonder about how much responsibility I could handle. There were a couple of auxiliary police officers directing traffic. Being interested in that line of work for some time, I inquired of the men to see if they could use any more help. One of the guys was the captain. Herm Stratton was a likable guy and let me know that I would be welcome to join the force if I would qualify.

"What is your name?" he asked.

"Ronald Knott," I replied.

Herm looked around for a second. "You're Ronnie Knott's son, aren't you? Too bad about him."

"Yea," I said.

That comment by Herm was one I would hear off and on for the next two and a half decades. He invited me down to the old city hall to be interviewed. It all went well and I got to join the Special Police force. It wasn't the cloak and dagger life that I had wanted as a kid, but, hey, I could have been six feet under by now so I was grateful to get what I did.

The uniforms were a new design that year. A bright blue shirt, black pants with wide brim hats made a good run at looking like a Royal Canadian Mountie. Lois was a little uncomfortable with me when I was in full dress. She was not used to someone that had any position of authority that she cared about. Even getting to close to me was tough. It was as if I was an unknown. At least I got to strut around the house and tease the girls now that I am half a cop.

One of my first assignments was Friday night traffic duty on Main Street. I would be stationed in front of the Gleason building. Switching off every thirty minutes with my backup gave me a break. Fridays were the busy days, especially with the habitual "Flame the mainers" at night. Back and forth, up and down the street I would see the same faces over and over again. But there was one face that I hadn't seen in a awhile. Bob Cummins. Even though Bob and I went back quite a ways, he felt like he could do something that would break the law and get away with it, only because I was on duty. Here came Bob down the street in his pickup. With a can of beer in one hand and the other on the steering wheel he drives by yelling. "Hey Ronnie, look at me!" I waited for him to take another lap and then asked him to pull over. We went for a long walk and I let him know where I really stood in my new life as well as warn him about being arrested. There were a few seeds planted for later. Bob was the most receptive of the bunch.

One of my next duties was to guard the Italian Festival at night. My job was to stay awake into the morning hours. That assignment wasn't too taxing because of my previous experience of late nights.

During that first year of sobriety I had taken another interest into my life. The Bradford boxing club had been in the papers off and on and I knew a couple of guys that were in it. I decided to try and at least see what I could do. The trainer was a professor at the college in Bradford. He told me to get in shape and I could take on my first fight in a couple of months. Lois really didn't like it, but it seemed as though a lot of things were better than what we had experienced only a year earlier. I still kept track of all of my exercises. The discipline at the Manor had never ceased when it came to working up a sweat. I beat my body. Running up steep hills, pushups, sprints, situps, eat right, sleep right, you name it I did it. Watching the "Rocky" movie several times and listening to the theme song happened all the time, especially when it got closer to my first fight. I worked out hard in the gym, hitting the bag and sparring with teammates. Since I had taken Tae Kwon Do a few years earlier, it became quite an asset not just in conditioning, but in the actual fighting as well.

The first fight had been scheduled. It would be at the County Fair on a Friday night under the lights in front of the grandstand. I wanted attention, I was going to get it. For anyone's first fight this was a lot of hoopla. Camera's would roll and so would my head.

The night had come. Everyone who knew me wanted to see me try and knock someone's lights out. They thought that because I had fought a couple of Karate tournaments that I should be quite the spectacle. So did I. My fighter from Buffalo didn't show. The officials asked me if I would take a stand-in who was having his first fight. I said yes. The rest is history. I got in the ring and while the ref was giving the instructions I stared down the guy. His real name was Joel Humm. And I found out the hard way that it wasn't his first fight. The bell sounded and in ten seconds I was on my back. I got up and told the referee that I was okay. I lied. A few seconds later they carried me unconscious out of the ring on a stretcher. I woke up in a tent with Lois holding my hand. She was in tears as I came to. I looked at my wife as she was coming into focus and started crying myself.

"Honey," I said. "I can't do this to you and the girls. He could've broken my neck or something."

The thing that was remarkable about that moment was that even though I was in a stupor I knew what I was saying. Telling my wife that I wouldn't do something anymore now had (pardon the expression) "some punch" in it. I wasn't a drunk making some empty promise, I was a man that was coming away from being knocked out with a little more honesty in my life. I meant it. I quit the team and, besides, a State law forbade anyone from fighting for ninety days after a knockout. I would take on another challenge only a couple of months later with the eatery.

Pride has a way with a person. It can lie in wait and if left unchecked will spring up and try to defend itself. I would eventually be called upon again to ratchet up growth just one more notch.

That spring of '81 had seen another new hope appear on the horizon. Lois and I had finally decided to try and open that eatery in the fall. We took a better part of the year to study books, visit restaurants, and look at the possibilities of funding. When we made the decision to take on such a task there was excitement in the air for the rest of the summer into the fall. Against the advice of Tom would we go forward with our dream. One of Lois's cousins owned an

Orange Julius franchise down in Altoona, Pennsylvania. We would pay them a visit and watch how many aspects of the food service industry worked. They had been successful in restoring and selling homes for many years and continued that success in a franchise. I remember that they were very particular about every detail of that venture. They even let us look at the books. The well kept records showed just how you could really make it if you do things the right way.

Planning for such an undertaking did take most of the year especially since neither one of us had ever done anything like this before. The money part of it would be tricky. We simply didn't have any. Lois went to "Aunt." That was her official title around the house. Her real name was Florence and she could afford just about anything. Investing her money in the oil businesses in the area back during the booming days before we were all born gave her a lot of unused income and clout in the family. Lois's mother had a problem with my lack of education and if she would have had her way we probably wouldn't have gotten a red cent. Nancy Thompson was the apparent favorite niece of Florence and would have done us a favor not letting us get anything from Aunt. She had her own trials to come in which later on I would be getting a ringside seat. Aunt Florence committed to five thousand dollars. Our calculations told us we needed a total of fourteen thousand. The bank would be our next attempt.

PennBank's Carlisle Kahn was the loan officer. He was one of their younger staff, but banks seem to always make sure their folks are really ready when dealing with the dollar. He was no exception. His real position was as a liaison between the real decision makers and the customers.

We had gone to the bank armed with the committed money from Aunt and some collateral. They said no to the loan. The reason that they gave was that there was a high fatality rate of businesses in the area where we would like to go. It was true and the whole town knew it. We wanted this very much so we decided to gather more than enough collateral, literally four times the amount of the loan. We went back and got the money. It took some time to pass before we would really discover just what really had happened in the bank.

Coming out of the bank that day were two overjoyed happy campers. We had started running around like a young couple preparing for the arrival of their first baby. The place that we had picked was a little space tucked away in a run of businesses on Mechanic Street. Our number was thirteen. Bruce Hart and his partner Jim Reilly were two good landlords that saw us as a perfect fit to occupy the only space left in the building. So, with a dance studio on one side and a bar on the other, we signed the agreement to rent a space which we would eventually call "Knott's Kniche." The girls were excited. In any small town it was a big deal to get into something like that because everybody knew about it.

During the summer before the approach to Knott's Kniche, Lois and I would take a trip just over the hill into Olean to play the horses at OTB. I never cared for horses, but it was sort of fun to watch them come in. We could be seen studying the "horse sheets" to determine which pony had the best chance of bringing us home a win. Sometimes we would go to the mall next door and have lunch at the Ponderosa while we waited for the race results. It often would be a problem. We agreed that it was something that we both liked to do and doing it somehow justified the means. Not losing all of our money was sometimes nothing less than a miracle, but by the fall we had made sure that the dream was intact. By that time Lois had started to back off from the meetings. She cited a lot of reasons why and the biggest one was that I was the one with the problem. Important for both of us that I had learned to focus my own program by that time.

Mr. And Mrs. Ronald Knott were handed the keys to our business and we were off and running. The first thing to happen was to have the plumbing and electrical replaced. That is unusual because a building should have sufficient utility. However, due to the nature of our business, we needed new and heavier wiring for the appliances as well as an extra hot water tank because of the heavy usage. There had never been a business like that in the building. We ultimately decided to make the business strictly takeout and delivery of homemade foods as well as some other common items.

Anticipation during the initial work was very nice. My buddy Jim Slocum was Rick's brother. We had him build the custom benches in the front service area where customers would be waiting. He also built the counter for the television and cash register. The walls were a very expensive cherry paneling accompanied by a well lit textured white ceiling. We left those things as they were, but replaced the blue carpet with a new linoleum flooring. Installing a new oven, a hood with an extinguishing system, a custom made long stainless steel sink and a few other items brought us closer to our opening date. Looking out the front windows, I was able to see the parking spot that I had used to leave my truck for a few days during the winter a couple of years earlier. One of the parts of my earlier recovery was to get rid of that thing. It took a few months, but I finally sold it to a well pleased man for a good price.

Looking around for one last time, Lois and I had the long awaited green light to open Knott's Kniche for business. The date was October 5, 1981. A photographer from the Bradford *Era* came and took a shot of us holding a sandwich. It made the front page.

Part of our strategy was to put this business near the downtown location of Zippo. It was a good move. Not only did we get the planned business lunch crowd from the other buildings, but Zippo came through. I guess it didn't hurt that Mom and Aunt Evelyn had been working at both locations at the time. The customers stormed our business. From opening day, every business day it was almost always a packed house. There were people standing on the sidewalk waiting to get in. We had been heading into the colder season so that would become a problem.

About four weeks had passed and Halloween was here. We got to decorate our place for the first time. There also had been a rash of burglaries in the area and Lois became nervous. It really didn't affect business, but I felt we needed to take a precaution. I borrowed Bob's .357 Magnum for a few days just in case someone felt froggy enough to leap in on us. Friday night had come and the trick or treaters were out. We had an unusual number of kids for a business and especially in that location. After a couple of hours, the candy beggars were all home counting their booty. All except one. About nine o'clock one lone masked individual came in the door. It was too large too be a kid and was dressed up in an expensive Yoda outfit from the movie Star Wars. All was silent. No "trick or treat" or "hello." Not anything. I had been sitting on my stool near the cash register when silent Yoda decided not to respond to my inquisitions.

"Hello," I said. "That's a pretty good outfit you got there. Can I help you?"

One telltale sign of a real halloweener was that you always carry a bag or pillowcase for the candy. This one didn't. Continuing to stare at me and not say a word, the final approach was made to come around the end of the counter.

"Stay right there! Don't move!" I warned. By then my hand was on the revolver and I was rotating it on the shelf to follow the person's movement. Well, Yoda made the mistake of not heeding my warning and came around the end of the counter and I pulled out the 357 and pointed at the torso of this character. The person stopped inches from the gun and reached up to pull off the mask. It was Mary, my sister. (I could have killed her).

"What in God's green acres are you doing? Are you stupid or something?" I put the gun down and looked at the floor partly in disgust and partly out of fear. She laughed and didn't think it was a big deal.

November had come and the light snow had started to fly. Some of the customers were still waiting in the cold, but most of them were faithful. Others were not. Our delivery service was going full steam, but the whole business was now taxed by the fact that we were selling much of the food as fast as we could cook it. The hours had been tapered off because we had seen where the traffic would steer us. The first three weeks in business saw me putting in 108 hours a week. I was glad that was over. The girls would come in on occasion and sometimes get in the way. Kim was by now outright defiant and made me angry trying to toy with the cash register. I would have to remove her physically and plop her down on one of the benches. Kelly was still the more moderate one.

A few weeks into the opening of Knott's Kniche we were convinced that we had to have either a bigger place or buy our own building. Actually the customers decided for us. The food just wasn't being made in enough quantities and standing in the cold for a sandwich just wasn't cutting it.

Our first action was an obvious one. PennBank would be approached for money to fund the need to expand. With all of the evidence in our pocket we thought it would be a slam dunk. It took me a long time to realize that even slam dunks are missed on occasions. Sitting down with Mr. Kahn, our confidence was high. The town was abuzz with our new business, we had the receipts to back our claim and PennBank was one of our daily customers. They refused to lend us another cent. The reason? They felt that we needed more operating capital to survive the long haul. They also told us that their recovery of failed businesses was ten cents on the dollar. Of course none of it made sense to us. We were there for valid reasons in the first place and to talk about failure at that point just wasn't in our plan. We had the proof to back up those claims. Out the door we went.

The next stop would be a call to the SBA, which, by the way, was an out for the bank. They could get the loan backed by the government up to 80%. We still really did not understand why they said no, but time was important. The Small Business Administration set up appointments in Buffalo and Pittsburgh for Lois and I. The actual counseling for the business would take place in the steel city while Buffalo would be the place that we would eventually apply for the funds.

The three hour drive to Pittsburgh was distracted by the initial advice over the phone. Close our doors and hang a sign in the window stating: "Closed for Alterations." We now had started our new road to even bigger success although it was a bit scary. To go from all to nothing over a simple phone call was a shock. We walked into John Taggart's office just after the New Year. The date of our official closing was December 23, 1981, about eleven weeks into the business. Mr. Taggart was actually a counselor for S.C.O.R.E., an assistance organization for the SBA consisting of retired executives. Their goal was many fold. They would help people get back on their feet who suffered from financial distress for a variety of reasons. Taggart was a man that looked a little bit like Colonel Sanders. White hair and mustache accented a calm and gentle personality. At least that is what I branded the Colonel to be. Another smile and another handshake. It had become a big part of my life to meet such good people. "Pleased to meet you sir," I would say. Lois and I would eventually elaborate further on our plight.

The first order of business that was strongly suggested proved to be interesting. We were to do a three month long study of traffic routes and patterns in the Bradford area. Examining the business profile within a certain radius of Knott's Kniche was extensive. Every business like ours, as well as other industries and mom and pop stores all became our special diet for the next ninety days. We did everything we were asked. Some of those requests were fairly easy because they had been done to a certain extent anyway by us prior to opening our doors. However, there was one piece of information that rattled this calm and collected man. Lois and I had told John that PennBank had initially refused our loan based on the high fatality rate of business in the area of town we were interested in. What bothered him was that the bank gave us the loan when we came back with all of that collateral. Taggart's face got red with anger. It seemed to be out of character so much that I felt as if I had done something wrong.

"They did what? Why that is criminal! You two were led down the road to lose. If I were you I would sue their pants off!"

Lois and I just sat there in awe. I didn't know what to say. It was not in us to sue someone and we felt that we had come to the right place to keep our business.

Sometime near the end of our study it was recommended that we would get our money. They were pleased not just with our cooperation, but the way in which we carried out our responsibilities. I have to admit that there already had been plenty of evidence that when my wife and I agreed to put our minds to something the sky was the limit. Our goal was to be making our first million by age thirty-five.

Next stop Buffalo. Only being an hour and a half away was a little more convenient. Our meeting this time was a Jewish man who was a top man in the SBA. Mr. Edelstein was younger than Mr. Taggart by far, but had quite a reputation for investing money successfully. His track record to date at that time was impressive.

"My success rate in almost a hundred percent. I had one failed business in thirty-seven attempts and that one had some extenuating circumstances."

I thought that was a good thing for us to be in the company of such a financial general, but it also gave me a little scare. If he was having such a good success rate then that means he was also choosing very carefully who his clients would be. I figured that all those numbers couldn't be accumulated by chance. He would do just what I thought he would. He asked us questions that I could never dream up.

When the dust had cleared the hurdles in Buffalo, Mr. Edelstein gave the go ahead for the loan. Our second trip there ended with another happy return to Bradford. We had survived the studies and the scrutiny of an expert in managing money. The next step was to prepare to expand into the dance studio. The only problem was that we would have to wait some more for the lady who ran it to move out. It became a problem, but not our biggest one. Just days before we would get our long awaited SBA loan, President Reagan cut the funds off to northwestern Pennsylvania. The ride we were about to take would be rivaled only by the incident of my recovery.

The news that we couldn't get the SBA loan was beyond shock. I began to encourage Lois that we would be all right. I could not accept defeat. I had known casually a few people in town that were millionaires. My next move was to arrange meeting with some of them that I thought would be able to easily part with a fraction of their worth for a while. They had obviously all known my story. By then the whole town knew. One thing that we had going for us was that the situation that we found ourselves in did not arrive because we didn't know what we doing. The SBA did agree that we needed more operating capital, and at the same time we needed to raise our prices because of the high demand for our food. Paying our workers less was also discussed. We had decided that we were going to advocate never paying someone that we wouldn't accept ourselves, so there were numerous circumstances that were favorable to us while I exploited the need for money.

After a few meetings with some of the business people in the community and a couple conversations with the bank, we were forced to consider closing up shop for good. Now the payments for rent, outstanding loans to Aunt and the bank were in arrears. Somehow Lois and I felt that we could still make a go of it, but the money just wasn't there. There was one way of dampening the hit of course. I could try and get Mom to cosign on a loan from a loan company and pay some of the bills. But that wouldn't open the business. We couldn't jeopardize our possessions through the bank, so to Mother's house I went. That was the first mistake. I wouldn't accept no for an answer. She had watched everything unfold and certainly knew accurately what our problems were. She said no to the loan for over an hour. Finally she signed. That was her first mistake. I got the few thousand through a loan company called FBC. I had borrowed money from them before on my own and payed it back a little slow so they wanted someone else in on this application. The money would go on to keep a few people happy for a limited time only.

Spring had sprung by that time and there was no hope in our minds. We were cornered by debt. There seemed no way out. We never told the bank what ultimately happened. We really wanted to pay back everyone that we owed and if the bank was really going to get only ten percent back on the dollar like they said they do, we wouldn't let that happen. We wanted to pay back the debt in full ourselves. Selling the equipment was tough. It was a long drawn out painful process. One piece at a time, first the stove, then the fridge, on and on it went. One pitiful sale after another. Of course the money from anything we sold now had to support us personally. We would owe many places when this phase ended.

Everything was now gone. What we had studied and worked for, for so long had left us. At the time there only one option. Welfare. A dirty word in my vocabulary. Lois and I talked about it and decided that I would have to do the unthinkable. Humble myself again and reach out for help in the most unlikely place.

My next stop was actually being in the line at the welfare office. Welfare had and still does carry with it a stigma in the minds of many people. I had always felt that there were basically two groups of people who utilized what used to be called "relief." Firstly, those who had little money and looked like someone from the bowery. Secondly, people that abused the system and didn't claim what they were really making "under the table" or "on the side." Now I had to change my thinking. Although I had fallen into neither of these categories my attitude and views had to be adjusted on a few things. And it hurt. It was a good thing that I was supported by many who had experienced some circumstances that humbled them in their own lives. The most humiliating thing up to that point was that I was now standing in a welfare line with half of my customers! The only thought that came to my mind was, "I can explain!" But being just a thought, I knew I could never make anyone understand what my situation was and my feeling that I needed to explain in the first place told me that I was still stereotyping these folks. I just plain did not want to be there.

After a short wait we got some assistance and that seemed to take the edge off of the tough spot we were in. In the meantime we could never accept that this was the end of our matter. I couldn't go to work back in the union. The unemployment rate in our area at the time was the highest in the country and even this money coming in with the food stamps would not be free. Some day I would have to work it all off.

Somewhere around the end of April Lois made a suggestion. She had lived with her former husband and the girls in Rochester, New York and felt that it may a good idea to move there. I was to yet to discover another defect in my character and this was the great opportunity.

"Ron, I want to move to Rochester. We have no future here and I know that there is a lot of work up there," she said.

Rochester is one hundred fifty miles or about two and a half hours from Bradford. I wasted no time in my response. "No!" I retorted. "I'm not going anywhere!"

Lois had just hit a nerve that I did not know I had. "Why not? There's nothing here. We can't live like this forever!"

"I know we can't. Don't you think that I know that?" I became very defensive. What was happening to me had happened to so many people before. There were opportunities to move away from Bradford and they didn't take it. My home town seemed to be filled with too many folks that didn't take advantage of chances to change their lives by moving somewhere else and got stuck in a lifelong drudgery. Those who went to other parts of the country and got started with a new life had been mostly successful. It was something that I had observed for many years. Now it was my turn. "Why not?" Lois would ask. I was trapped. At the revelation that I never really wanted to leave Bradford, it very frightening. I was sober for about a year and a half and making a change like this was one big scary no-no. I knew in my heart that she was right, but I still didn't want to go anywhere. What became my plight was that I wouldn't go and I couldn't stay. "I'm not going anywhere and that's final!" That answer prompted a new call to action.

One thing that had become a great part of my life was the counsel of others. Lois would try an end-around on me and suggested we get help for our stalemate.

She calmly asked, "Would you go with me to a counselor at the family center and talk about it?"

Knowing the end result in my mind, I calmly gave her my answer. "Suit yourself." My plan was to simply agree to the counseling session and never give in to leaving. I had been set in my way and would just patronize everyone till it was over. So I thought.

Clinging to only what I knew, my mind was place to sport.
I have been humbled enough o' life I say.
Relying on my puny brain, please dispense another way!
Ah, but heart cried out to me, "The way is here to court!"

My wife and I showed up at the counselor's office only a couple blocks away. My plan was easy. Go along with all of the suggestions except one. Don't go to Rochester! Mrs. Leary was a nice woman in her mid forties that knew how to counsel. I suppose that it was important for her travel outside of her apparent professionalism when I finally got her angry during the final session. She had asked me in the beginning whether I would go away from Bradford and of course I said no. There wasn't a real attempt to find out why until a lot of things were brought up that would help what I thought was Lois's case. Somehow my desperate wife thought that this woman carried enough persuasion with her and that my potential for head games was left at Maple Manor. My stubbornness gave rise to do something that I did not want to tolerate any more of in my life. Dishonesty. I would make it look like Mrs. Leary was gaining ground for the better part of two meetings. We discussed my history, Lois's life, the kids, the union, all of it. But when it came time to submit to the last, worked so hard for question. "Will you go to Rochester?" I said "Nope!" As soon as Mrs.Leary had heard the "Nope," she lost it.

With an assertive voice she asked, "Why? Why don't you want to go?" You know it is the best thing to do."

I crossed my arms and dug my heels in. "Because I don't want to leave my family!" The counselor tries to get to my real devotions and doesn't know it.

"Who is your family?" she retorted.

I looked around the room in some kind of shame and answered her. "My mother, brother and sister."

Now furious, she leaned toward me and pointed to Lois. "This is your family! You have your own family! You don't live with your mother anymore!"

I looked at Lois in defiance and staring her down as if I had won again. "You can go to Rochester, I'm staying here, I will get a divorce over it if I have to. That's it!"

My wife now is in tears as we left the clinic. The drive is short and I know I am wrong. Not saying a word I dropped her off at the house and went for a two hour walk in the woods just beyond our yard. I felt terrible. I knew what I should do I was just too afraid to make this first time change. It was one of the early indications in my life that God somehow was doing the "accelerated plan" in my life. The walk in the woods had me in tears and talking to what I believed God to be. "I know what I should do, I know what you want me to do," I told him. "I'm afraid to move to a big city not knowing what I am going to do with a job or anything…help me." The words that I heard in my heart were, "It is right for you to go." The next thing that happened was I walked over to a place overlooking Bradford. You could see the stretches of the oil refinery down one valley and the tract of homes and businesses down the other. This view is almost the only one of its kind around there. A peace came over me like never before. It was right for me to go and now I had no fear, no reservations, nothing that would hinder me from moving away. I had undergone another change.

Taking a careful walk down the hill to my house almost made me feel like I was floating. Lois was pacing the floor as I walked in the door. Stopping to close the door I watched as a frustrated woman tried to deal with what to do.

"Lois? Can I tell you something?" She looked at me with tears swelling in those cobalt blues.

"What?"

In an unusually sedate tone I said, "I will go to Rochester. I want to go. No strings attached. I just had an experience on the walk and I am sorry. I always knew what I should do and I just didn't want to."

I took my wife and hugged her as we both wept. She was happier than I had seen her in quite a while. I seemed to grow a fraction of an inch that day. The pattern was that whatever I had acquired would be tested before I could move on, a trend that has not ceased.

Telling the girls was going to be a chore. One that Lois was better suited for than me. Of course, our concern for their father's reaction was well founded. He did not like it, but the fact that he had lived up in Rochester himself dampened the blow a bit. He still had relatives there. Kelly was the most excited, but Kim seemed to resist the notion of being away from her Dad.

Moving On

In the movie "Alice Doesn't Live here Anymore" she packs up the station wagon and heads off to start a new life. Fortunately, I did not end up like her husband. But we did have a good time breaking up some of the old furniture that we wouldn't even give away. Lois's mother held the deed to the house so that was not an issue when we left. We had been given fourteen hundred dollars to help us start over again. Nancy had tried unsuccessfully to turn her courier service business over to us in order to keep us in Bradford. She really didn't want us to go. Lois had had enough of the ties of the family influences anyway. We wanted to make it on our own.

Arriving in Rochester on the first of September we had picked a nice townhouse near the end of Long Pond Road. Long Pond Shores was a community with the property located at the water's edge of a large pond. We chose it because it was far away from all the hype of city life and driving, but still close enough to the stores and workplaces. The parkway on one side and Lake Ontario just down the road made this one of the best locations for me to get adjusted to this new way of life. It was a beautiful split level interior with new gold carpet. Furniture would not come for a while, at least that which we wanted. The girls were excited to have their own room. We had timed things for them to start school.

Getting the telephone cable hooked up produced a secret that we paid for over the next year. The outside walls were hollow. There wasn't any insulation. The story was that the plumber's union had built the place and skimmed on the materials. I never found out why no insulation was ever put even after that, but we liked the looks of the place so we stayed, high energy bills or not.

After everything was hooked up it time to look for work. I couldn't believe the number of pages in the Sunday paper that had places to apply for a job. Bradford had about one third of one page, Rochester about ten full pages. I quickly adjusted to the possibility of doing something that I had never done before. What I could do I knew for sure was building maintenance. I didn't know much about boilers, but the rest of the aspects of a job like that were familiar. Lois started looking for some secretarial work. I found my job first. It was at a place on Long Pond Road down in the heart of Greece, the actual name of the suburb where we lived. West Side Manor was an old folk's home where they had to be able to get around by themselves. Off the road about a hundred yards in a large cluster of pine trees, this property is hidden from view. The mall is just a block away and you would never know it. The landscaping, the natural surroundings, especially the trees that even helped block the sound of the traffic made this a prime location for the oldsters. Now it was time to check out the people.

My hope had taken a turn for the better. What was once a big frightening risk became a clearer understanding of some of the meaning of all this. It was important for me at times to be rescued with tangible evidence that proved I was doing the right things. Even knowing that in advance may not necessarily give me the peace I seek. But on I went.

I was hired by a family with a well known name in Rochester. The Wegmans owned a chain of grocery stores in the area at the time while the distant cousins went into the proprietary home business. My new job was taking care of the grounds as well as maintaining the interior aspects of the building such painting, carpet cleaning, some heating and air conditioning, etc. The building structure itself was shaped into the form of the letter H. The residents lived on the wings while administration, eating, and craft areas were in the center. There were two types of people at West Side, the residents and the staff. I had never experienced working around the elderly and this appeared as though it was going to be interesting.

My bosses were near the time of retirement. Damon and Onolee Wheaton had been working there since it had been built quite a few years earlier. They were very nice to me and that made it easier to adapt to the changes in my life. My co-workers in the kitchen, craft room and cleaning staff, as well as secretaries were also very kind individuals. It was rare to see such a collection of compatible people under one roof.

Jennie Fry taught crafts. Ceramics, seasonal functions, specific holiday projects and bingo on Fridays kept the people busy throughout the week. She was good at everything that she did.

The time spent on the wings where the residents were exceeded by far the time in the staff areas. My exposure to the people who had been around a lot longer than myself would prove to be invaluable. My natural quietness accompanied by just being wary of my new surroundings prompted many to test the waters to see what kind of a person I was. They had just lost their former maintenance man so I guess they were trying to make some adjustments too, after all, this was their home.

The ages of the elderly here varied from the mid-sixties to just above a hundred. I overheard a conversation between two of the women. One of them was about ninety eight years old. She said to the other, "Oh, my oldest son is seventy eight." I thought that was funny…and strange, because most of the people dying in my life did not even come close to the age of her son. The stories of many of those folks were worth the contents of a book. One woman named Edna Sears painted beautiful water color paintings. Even at age eighty four she was still holding her hand steady with the brush. The walls of her room were covered with many of the works that she had done. Another lady in her mid eighties was still a sexpot. At least she talked like it. I had to tell administration about the lewd comments she would make toward me. Between my bosses and her family they got it straightened out. Wheelchairs and walkers dotted the hallways every day. Traveling back and forth to meals and the craft room made for a time of obstacle dodging for staff several times between breakfast and dinner. There were many important and sometimes humorous events to come.

It took about a couple of months for Lois to find work. Her application at the Wegman's Corporate offices found her taking a job in which there was going to be a lot of room for moving up in the company. She would drop me off at work on her way to her job on Brook's Avenue. My first visit there impressed me. The main concourse was all glass and brass with a spiral staircase leading to the upper offices. This was something that I had only seen on TV on some drama movies.

By then it was nearing our first Christmas in Rochester. Lois had been having trouble with her heart rhythm off and on, but it had been kept in check mostly by medication. Earlier in the year we had made trips to Buffalo General Hospital to visit specialists who told us that she had a prolapsed mitral valve. Any trip to the dentist would have to be accompanied by antibiotics. On occasion Lois would have palpitations and need to sit or lay down and they would go away. Eventually she would need the valve replaced at about age fifty.

By the time the holidays came we really didn't have any money to spend on Christmas. I had applied for my retirement from the union, but had to wait two years for the money. They gave me a choice either take five thousand dollars now and pay a tax on it or wait until age sixty-two and take about one hundred and fifty dollars a month. That choice wasn't hard. I would take it now.

A few days before Christmas we were broke. We needed something, especially for the girls. I called up Bob back in Bradford and borrowed five hundred dollars. Mom and Sam would drive half way to Rochester and meet me in a little town with the money. I brought the money back home and gave it to Lois. Her and the girls were very excited to have a shopping spree especially in the eleventh hour.

One of the things that had occurred before the holidays was that my head was clearing up and a spirit of vengeance had welled up in me. I went against all I had believed in and wanted to fight again. Although I had never stopped working out, it now became apparent that I really wanted to get back at the fact that I had been beat. Even though there wasn't a realistic chance at the moment that I would box, the potential was still there. It was pure pride and nothing else. What was about to happen would clear up any misconceptions about my trek into the world of fighting again.

Lois and the girls had gone to the mall down the road about five miles. It was snowing heavy when they had left about three in the afternoon on a Saturday. I stayed home and did a few things around the townhouse. About three hours later I heard a pounding on the front door. Kim and Kelly were standing there.

Kim yelled at me. "Mom's up the road, she can't breathe! Hurry!"

I ran with the girls out of the parking lot and up the road only a hundred yards to see the pinto still running. Lois was in the back seat holding her throat.

I looked at her and said, "It'll be okay, honey, I'll get you home, just hang on."

I was afraid this time. It looked serious. We got back home and I carried her into the bathroom where she collapsed. I called an ambulance. The paramedics arrived, gave her oxygen and watched her pulse go through the ceiling. Just before she was loaded into the ambulance, I heard these words spoken by one of the medics as he radioed ahead to Park Ridge hospital. "I think we are losing her." Upon hearing that message, I believed that I was going to be without a wife before the day was over. The girls stayed home as I followed the ambulance to the hospital. Lois was taken into the emergency room as I sat in fear in the waiting room. I was the only one there and was not permitted to see her.

As I sat in my chair something strange began to happen. The room went completely dark. I could see nothing. What had happened was that the lights were still on, but a clear veil had come down from the ceiling and engulfed me. It was if as I was in a room that was all black, but there appeared this image. I was now looking out of my wife's eyes at myself lying unconscious in the boxing ring. I heard a voice say "stop." That was all I heard. I knew at that moment that my wife was at death's door. I gave a response to the voice by giving up in my heart any thought of going back to fight someone. I have played the fool by entertaining the prospect of satisfying my selfishness and pride. What I thought had ended a few months earlier had come back to haunt me in the form of getting back at someone. Now Lois was on her back and I was the one concerned and she had not gotten there by choice. About a half hour later we both walked out the front door of the emergency department. She was fine. I submitted to a better choice and my wife was healthy again. Never again would she experience things like that. I told a future spiritual mentor that story and the suggestion that God would hold my wife hostage did not shock him. There is a lot going on that no one would understand. Whatever one sees that to be, I just know that I was moved to change by a vision and Lois was alive when it appeared as if she would not be. At the time and even now that is enough for me. She would have her troubles to come, but not to that extent.

My experience in Rochester had to include my AA meetings. Support from these groups came in handy especially when things like Lois's health issues would rack my brain. I didn't walk on egg shells, but I always had a legitimate concern because the actual physical defect was here to stay. I couldn't count on a pain free life from here on in. Who could?

Back in Bradford the total number of AA groups totaled four for the whole week. Rochester had over a hundred and twenty. It was meeting mania. It readily became a big part of my life. Actually it was possible to attend a meeting almost all around the clock because Kodak and other companies had shift workers who needed something more convenient than just in the evening. It did become sort of a problem for Lois. She had backed off on the groups before we had moved and it appeared as though that wasn't going to change. Although it was understood that I had to go to them we agreed that we needed to find something that we could do together.

Before we had moved to Rochester we had come across something that we liked to do, but didn't really do it after we had come to the bigger city. It was playing bingo. Going to a couple of volunteer fire department buildings back home once or twice a week just seemed to fizzle out when we came to the big city. There was enough to keep anyone busy or distracted. We thought that we would try and revive the game and get a little enjoyment out being together. It worked very well. Too well. Within a couple of months we were going to bingo seven days a week with twice on Sunday. That was a total of eight trips to bingo halls in seven days. Week after week we went. What happened to paying the debts back from the restaurant? Ah forget it, we were having too much fun. So much fun in fact that we had a hard time paying the current bills like rent and utilities. It had become a big problem and I didn't know how much longer I would tolerate it.

Back at West Side Manor I would now be mowing the lawn on a riding mower. I would stop the tractor and look around and wonder just what I had gotten myself into this time. I was sober and around a lot of great people. To be concerned about getting out of work and getting ready to go play bingo again started to disturb me. It was time for another message from the cosmos.

One sunny Friday afternoon I was enjoying the prospect of having the weekend off. Being around the staff indoors even made it better because looking forward to the short weekly vacation wasn't limited to just me. Sometimes the anticipation of things affects us more than the actual event. That principle works for good things as well as things not so good. Friday was also the scene where the residents would make sure their medications were given on time and the thought of playing bingo during that afternoon caused them to act in funny ways.

First call for bingo happened at 1:15. What would habitually happen then was that everyone who was going would come to the lounge in the main area and wait for second or last call before going down the final stretch of hall to the craft room. What was funny about that was after last call it would be race. Everybody wanted to sit close to the caller to hear the numbers being called. It looked like a slow motion stampede. One day I happened to be working in another part of the building after the last call. I had gotten paged to do a clean up on the carpet. What had happened was that after first call to bingo, Louise VanHorn had been using the bathroom when it happened. A fully committed bingo player who had been taking a lot of iron did not want to wait to finish her duty and I had to end up shampooing a twenty-five foot long jet-black streak off of the carpet.

My testings would come in many forms. There was in each lounge on the wing extensions of the building a television for the residents. I noticed a special announcement across the screen and stopped to take a look. Flight 007 traveling across the Sea of Japan had apparently been shot down by a Russian MIG fighter. It had not been confirmed, but I went to bed that night with some deep anger that I had not experienced in a long time. I remember that I wanted to do damage to Russia. My childhood training of hiding under my desk in grade school because of nuclear weapons had taught me to believe that they and the Chinese were my enemies. It had never left me and

I didn't really know it until an incident like this almost twenty years later. My commitment to change has helped rescue me again.

On another occasion on the same television screen I was dusting in that lounge and near the noon hour was an interruption of the regular scheduled program. A live on the spot camera was recording the events at a person's home. On the front porch was a man standing with a rifle. He had been accused of shooting the lights off of the top of police cars and they did not take to liking it very well. As the camera zoomed in to see the face of the man, I recognized him. It was Rusty, a man that I knew from one of the meetings that I had been to. During the last meeting that I saw him at, about three weeks earlier, he had expressed a strong resentment about an issue and the thing that I noticed about was that he had a violent Irish temper. I got him settled down and got him to stay and listen to what was being said. He reluctantly hung around and I was convinced that he had gotten a hold on things.

Rusty was now in a bad situation. What happened next was one of the rarest events to be recorded live. The police department would be accosted for their actions. Still shooting from the porch, Rusty was being stalked by an officer who came in the back door of his house. Out the front door he came and as we all watched he shot Rusty in the head. Many people felt that though he was acting dangerously he did not deserve to die for it. Maybe if he would have tried a little harder to deal with the anger issue this would not have happened in the first place. A phrase in the groups comes to mind. "Grow or go."

Lois would have to go to Bradford on a couple of occasions to follow up for some of her problems with her heart. On one occasion she would have to stay in for eleven days while I stayed in Rochester. Adjustments had to be made with her medications.

A few months into the life of bingo we had been by now making the big mistake of leaving the girls home while we went to get another fix of entertainment. In the spring of that year they were ages nine and eleven. It was a usual Friday night and we had just come back about ten o'clock from playing a game at St. Mark's church just down the road. We had been convinced by that time that it was okay to leave Kim and Kelly by themselves because we had not only lived in a nice area, but it was only for a couple of hours. We walked in the door and said our usual "We're home!" But no answer. They were gone! A note was left by Kim on the table that said Denny's cousin had taken them and was meeting them halfway to Bradford. We had made a big mistake. Lois dropped to the floor in tears and cried aloud, saying nothing. Their father made it clear that he had a good case for doing what he did. He was right. And of course at the time I didn't agree with it.

The girls would be staying indefinitely with Denny until some new understandings about parenting would arise. It was tough on Lois, but the one consolation was that our acknowledgment of error made the blow a little more understandable. He had always disagreed with Lois on almost everything so it was especially hard to agree to something even when he was right.

We would travel to Bradford once in a while to see the girls. Meeting them in the usual demilitarized zone outside Nancy's house was again burdening. However, my wife and I would continue to go the bingo halls and now the regimen of the seven days a week thing would take over.

By the middle of the summer of '83 I began to realize just how much I had become attached to the game of bingo. Being so schooled firsthand in the subject of addiction, I felt that we should take a step back and take a look at stopping or at least tapering off. Near the end of July Lois and I would be starting to have some friction over that point. I could easily get some social life through AA, but she saw this as a viable outlet to be out around people and have a little fun at the same time. The only problem with this however was that it was ruining us. The episode with the girls and their father should have been a sufficient wakeup call, but I guess not. How far would a person have to go before they would give in to reason? We would find out.

Riding around one Sunday afternoon just killing time til the sun went down, I had had enough. We were about a block from West Side Manor when after a period of arguing about bingo, I told Lois to stop the car. I would walk the rest of the day to wherever I had to go. She eventually had gone to bingo and I walked eight miles to an AA meeting. For the next week or so, I did not go, she went alone. Walking long distances was not such a stranger to me anyway.

Only weeks earlier I had been taken to an AA meeting downtown. This turned out to be a special meeting to me because it was at midnight. It fit well into my "up late" spirit that still prevailed from the olden days. It was called "the Midnight Candlelight Meeting." I was invited by another AA acquaintance and he drove me there. We walked in the door and there were a lot of small tables around a long room with a lit candle on each table. Being the only form of light in this room, it still wasn't hard to make out that there were human bodies on the floor…and they were not moving.

I ribbed my buddy in the ribs and asked, "What's this, is this the Jonestown massacre all over again, we're just all going to drink poison Kool-Aid and call it quits?"

He looked me and filled in the blanks. "No, this is not Jonestown and we are not going to die." Pointing to the floor he continued. "You see these people on the floor? They are really alive. They are from the tunnels and under the bridges. We were there once and there were people who cared enough to be here for us so we are here for them. Even if they came for a cookie or the coffee the point is, is that they came. Do you see?" I nodded and went for a cookie.

About one thirty in the morning the meeting was ending and we all filed out the door to take our conversations in progress out to the street. Twenty-five or so AA'rs showed up that night and it had been a good meeting. People started leaving one by one until I was the only one standing there. Even my ride had left me! I didn't have any money and my car was home. No money, no phone, no car, and no ride. I looked around and said to myself, "Guess I'll have to walk." I did not know Rochester very well at all and especially being in the inner city far away from my own address in the suburbs. I started walking. Down the street was a main artery, Route 490. It went east and west. The right way for me to go was west, so of course I went east. I walked for two miles at two in the morning before I realized that I was going in the wrong direction. Back two miles I went. Now I am four miles down before I begin the right way. What made it a little more complicated was dodging beer bottles being launched out of passing cars. I eventually came upon a street name that I recognized. Mt. Read was running north and south and I would pick the right direction on this one. I walked to Ridge Road about three miles down Mt. Read. I knew I was home free now. At least I knew where I was at now. Coming to my favorite place for breakfast on the ridge was a big need at the time. I knew that I still had a long way to go, so a buffet would revive me a bit. Getting home with the sun fully up and certainly disgusted at my ride overshadowed any concerns on Lois's part. She had slept through the whole event anyway. After I got my car, I eventually got to measure the mileage that I covered. Eighteen miles was the figure that I had walked back in 1976 when Mom would not let me use her car. That time I was trying to prove a point. I could do something if I wanted to bad enough. This time, pride was not involved, I just had to do it.

I had been thinking about Lois and her plight with gambling. I wanted to spice up our marriage a little and do something nice for her that had never been done. She had told me once that she would like breakfast in bed. I never cooked at home, but I also remembered that her favorite breakfast was Perkins pancakes. The only way for me to set this all up without her knowing it was to sneak out of bed before she got up for work and drive the seven miles to Perkins and come back and set her up. The morning came and up to the ridge I went. Walking in that restaurant was pure joy knowing that my wife was going to like a surprise that I was sure she thought she would never get, at least from me.

"Can I have an order of pancakes to go," I said.

"I'm sorry sir, we don't have takeout," was the answer I got.

Getting a little upset I responded, "What do mean you don't have food to go? I've been coming here all the time."

The waitress tried to calm me down. "Sir, it is against the law for us to have food to go. We just don't do it."

I stormed out of there frustrated and angry. *Why would this happen?* I thought. I was doing a very good thing, especially when my marriage needed it.

Coming home without my gift to my wife began to eat at me. I walked in the door and went up to the bedroom. There she was, sitting up in bed with her arms crossed.

Fighting all of my emotions I looked at her and said, "Hi, honey, I'm home." I tried to imitate Jackie Gleason on the "Honeymooners." I watched him often.

Lois looked at me and said, "Where have you been all night?" My countenance had to change a million times. I went from being ticked off at an uncooperative waitress to defending myself when I felt I was innocent.

"You may not believe this, but I wanted to give you breakfast in bed," I would say.

"You're right I don't believe you!" she retorted. "Where were you?"

I sat on the edge of the bed and gathered myself together. "Listen, I know that I have never done anything like this before, you know, like even make you breakfast." It took about a half an hour of convincing my wife what the truth was. I was in tears by then. What really bothered me by that time was not that she didn't believe me or the waitress issue, but the fact that I had not done anything for so long that would have created that type of trust. I just couldn't win back something that took time to lose. It took sincere action over months and years to convince someone that had been led to think in only one way for so long. That would not be reversed with just one action. She finally agreed that I had tried to do something good for her, but I still became a little wiser that day for it.

Even though I was on the outs with the bingo issue, I would continue to go to work and Lois fortunately kept her job in all of this. We came home after a hard day and the utilities were shut off.

I got angry and told her, "If any more things are shut off, I'm history! I'll be moving out! I'm not taking this any more! Either you quit or I'm gone, that's it!"

She looked at me and said, "You have your AA buddies, I've got a place that I can go."

My response to that was, "You heard me!"

The next day I came home and the phone was shut off. I had been looking in the paper off and on for places to move to. It was a Friday night. I had called a number from a nearby convenience store. A lady answered the phone and told me that her apartment was for rent. The catch was is that I would be sharing "her" apartment with her. I drove down to check it out about five miles from where we were living. I liked the arrangement and went home. I told Lois that I was leaving. She helped me pack the Pinto. She made it clear that she did not want to know where I was living. I honored that request. Taking my things down to the apartment and then bringing the car back to her was all it took. She drove me to a place in which I would walk the rest of the way so that she wouldn't know my address.

After I had moved and had gotten settled in that night, I had plenty of time to think. In former days I would leave her many times just to go out and drink, but now I was gifted with a new confidence that this was right. I had been the master at manipulation and seemed to get away with a lot of things, but I was making sure that Lois would not do to me what I had done to her. Rationalizing, and trying to justify things just wouldn't cut it with me. I knew too much to be buffooned. I had let it come too far already.

I was able to make some calls and make it to a couple of meetings over the weekend. It was now Sunday morning and the meeting at the Mother of Sorrow's church on Mt. Read had been my Sabbath staple for quite a while. The basement was there for those of us who wanted to feel a little closer to church.

Driving into the parking lot with a friend started off a morning that had been up to that point preoccupied with thoughts of my current situation. Leaving Lois was in no way intended to be permanent. However, I left the door open to many possibilities. Sometimes in life you just plain do not know what you are going to do, but you know what you are not going to do. I guess that is the way I felt about everything.

Today would be a little different than the day before. Lois was leaning up against the Pinto with her arms crossed when we got to the church. She appeared as if she was waiting for something. I got out of the car and had noticed even from a distance that there was something different about her. She smiled as if nothing had happened.

"Good morning," she said as she reached out to hug me.

Of course I thought, *What's going on here?* Any move like that under the circumstances would normally be a patronizing one. She wanted something, what was it?

She continued. "I would like for us to get back together."

"Really?" I said. "And what is the occasion that you would ask that?" Then she told me a story.

"Last night I went to bingo. I came home feeling empty. It was bad. I needed you and I didn't know where you were. It was about three in the morning. From the convenient mart I called all the apartment complexes in Greece and nobody knew where you were. Then I decided to call your boss." My eyes opened wide, but I said nothing.

Continuing on, Lois said, "She told me that she did not know where you were living, but that she knew that you were staying with a woman. I got jealous, then angry, then depressed. The next thing I know I wanted to die. I took the car down the road and tried to hit a telephone pole. I went into the ditch and back out. I drove home and went into the bedroom. I don't know why, but I turned on the television and there was this preacher guy on. He started talking about God and I broke down and got on my knees. The man prayed a prayer and I asked Jesus to come into my heart. I can't and don't want to go to bingo anymore."

I just stood there and realized that the meeting was going to start. What I noticed about my wife was that she was not the same person that I had left two days earlier. Something had happened. But I thought to test her.

"Come with me into the meeting?" I asked.

She said, "Okay."

I was surprised and I knew that this was only the beginning of my ways to find out what was going on.

We sat in the AA meeting and I watched Lois closely to see if she was trying to manipulate me into the same old same old. She even had a few things to say when it was her turn. That surprised me because she hadn't even gone to a meeting in quite a while and now she was speaking at one. The meeting was over and I would implement test number two. Sunday night was one of my favorite meetings and there was an Al-anon meeting just down the hall in the church over on the Dewey Avenue extension.

"Will you come to the meeting tonight?" I asked. "They do both groups over there and it would be good for you." Although I was surprised that she agreed to, what interested me was how she agreed. There was something unusually and genuinely agreeable about her. And she had a glow on her face that indicated that she had some type of spiritual experience. I didn't understand it, all I knew was that Lois was not faking anything. After the evening meeting I agreed to move back home.

Around the circuit of AA meetings I had met a lot of good people of all ages, colors, sizes, and beliefs. There was this young kid about twenty-three years old named Chucky Jones. He was an addict who had seen a lot of trouble in his short life. One of the mental notes that

I had made about him was that his father was a preacher. And they lived in the same apartment complex as Lois and I. Although I never took the time to get to know any of them, Lois's experience caused me to seek out an explanation as to what may have really happened to her. She was not the same and it was a good thing. Chucky gave me his phone number and I called his Dad. His mother answered the phone and I repeated pretty much everything Lois had told me.

Her response was, "Your wife is born again."

I said, "Well, that's good, I'm happy for her."

Betty Jones was not pushy over the phone, but asked to talk to my new wife. After a short conversation we agreed to come to church. I really didn't believe in all that stuff even though I had told others to get right with God back at Maple Manor.

We ended up going to church that Sunday and, of course, the message was on the aspect of salvation. The Jones' presided over a small congregation that met weekly in an elderly living center. It was really the offices for the locations of the other facilities close by. Reverend Jones tried to hammer home the importance of coming to God through Jesus Christ.

"If you put your trust in the Lord, you'll never be the same. Everyone who doesn't will be doomed to perish. Mankind has been given two choices, Heaven or Hell." Then he read the scripture: "Whoever shall call upon the name of the Lord shall be saved."

I did not like that. By that time in my life I had not experienced any of the fire and brimstone preaching or pushiness to quote "get saved." I despised the words coming out of the man's mouth. I felt that even a girl that had been selling the flowers for the Reverend Moon had a better message than that. She was all about love and kindness. Lois seemed not to be affected at all except that it seemed to prod her into studying the Bible.

After the second week of that Heaven and Hell thrashing I had had enough. I went up to the reverend and let him have it.

"What do mean to tell me that I will be going to Hell? You don't know what I have been through! I was an alcoholic for ten years! I went to a rehab center and got cleaned up! I go to AA meetings all the time and help other people and you mean to tell me I'm doing this all for nothing? I don't think so!"

Having been a preacher for twenty-five years and once an alcoholic himself, he waited patiently for me to finish. "You don't have to take my word for it. You go home and pray to God and ask him to show what the truth is. Go ahead, look in the Bible and ask Him to reveal to you what the truth is about all of this stuff. Don't take me serious. For all you know I could be some nut just trying to get money or something. Check it out for yourself"

That was an important thing for him to say. I was still feeling the residual affect of my frustration, but there seemed to be some consolation in the man's words. He was willing to be made a fool by giving me my God given right to look into the matter further myself.

I took the reverend up on his challenge and for the next two weeks I did my best to find out what mistake I was making in my life that the Bible had claimed was all for nothing. The most important aspect that I had in me during that time was sincerity. I wasn't looking to superficially check things out and then go back and tell the preacher he was wrong. I had been given a heart that really cared about such things. Research and patience were definitely required.

It was the last weekend in August 1983. I had sought to find out just what not only this preacher meant, but many others throughout my life. That Sunday I went in tears before the congregation and spoke out loud that during my waiting on God that he had revealed to me what was the truth concerning the message of salvation. I had responded to his call to me. I cared enough to answer. Now I was born again. My eyes had been opened to a new world. How would I live it? How was I able to believe one thing so strongly one minute and not the next? Not too long before that I had been wanting to kill a man who was in the news all of the time. James Watt had been a high official in the Reagan administration and had refused to let the Beach Boys play at some function in one of the southern states. He was claiming to be a Christian. The Beach Boys were described as something that God would not want to influence our culture. The intense hatred that I had when I saw that on television was different that other anger problems that I had experienced. It was very strange. Now I was "one of them."

There would come to be a variety of observations that I would make concerning my new walk. My only experience with religion up to that point were the things that Aunts Hilda and Julia had brought

197

to me when I was younger. Mom instilled in us kids that prayer that "If I should die before I wake, I pray the Lord my soul to take." She had that picture of Jesus on the nightstand where he is piloting a ship. Many of the various belief systems that visited Julia also left me in a place that really didn't get me over the hump. As a youngster, even Bible school in the summer didn't do the trick, but I now know that some seeds were planted.

I continued to go AA meetings and the God of the recovery process just didn't seem the same anymore. While I went to church, I began to see things that caused me to do what I do best, wonder. I wondered why Chucky wasn't going to church like I was. After all, he was the son of a preacher. Lois and I would go over to the Jones' for dinner or just for a visit. We discovered that Chucky had been beating up his father and stealing things to sell for drugs. They wouldn't kick him out of the house because he was trying to change his life. He would come to church on occasion and was certainly faithful to a lot of meetings, but he was gripped by the drug scene. I knew he had been playing with fire with his apparent indecision.

My experience in recovery would play a role in the life of this preacher and his family. After the last time that Chucky assaulted his father, I had a talk with a hurting Reverend. "Frank."

I would say. "You really need to find the strength to get him out of here. You have had more mercy on him that anyone would have. He has crossed the line into new territory. He needs to be gone and you two need your lives back."

They kicked him out. He was gone for four days and they did not know where he was. This was a first. He never had been anything else other than a taker. On the evening of the fourth day I had been watching television and the news was on. Mrs. Jones had routinely called me to see if I had been around her son or maybe heard of his whereabouts through the AA grapevine. This night was different. She called during the newscast and I couldn't believe my eyes. On the television screen was a short report about the local mission house downtown. The camera was traveling around the room during the dinner hour and getting shots of those who come for a meal. There was Chucky slurping some soup. He had a smirk on his face as the closeup on him made him feel cocky. At least that is what I made it out to be.

"Have you heard anything, Ron?" She would ask.

I'm looking at her son on television and I can't say a word. Finally, "Ah yes, I did hear something. The word around the tables is that he is doing fine. I will be checking on it and I'll let you know if anything else turns up. But don't be concerned, I know for sure that he is okay." She was comforted at those words.

Over the next couple of months the Jones' would be moving into a house. I had attended some Bible studies at some of the other parishioners' homes by that time. The holidays were fast approaching and Lois and I were in a much better space. We had made a stink about the insulation because we did not want to go into another winter having to pay those outlandish heating bills. We owed some money to that cause already. Getting nowhere fast with the landlord, we decided to move ourselves. The girls had been away from us all year and we were missing them a lot. Talking on the phone had to supplement our travels to Bradford because it cost us every time we went.

Before we moved we had gotten a phone call that I had dreaded all along. Chucky was found dead along a highway. It was a very hard time in the Jones household. It wasn't really easy on me either. By that time I had taken Chucky into coffee shops more than once to try and talk some sense into him, but I didn't get through. Drugs and alcohol had chalked another one up. Lois and I had become friends with a couple in church that had owned an eatery similar to Knott's Kniche. We would go there for a sandwich once in a while. Gary and Linda Parent had their problems too. Though Gary was going to church once in a while, he became known by us rather quickly. He did cocaine frequently and struggled to keep his composure at the same time. It was clear that he really didn't want to deal with the problem as much as he should. Being addicted to drugs is hard enough, but to try in incorporate it into your family life because you gave in to it is another thing. He had called me up one time and told me that he needed to talk. I let him in the door and he sat down at the kitchen table. I went to use the bathroom and when I came back he had a line of cocaine across the glass tabletop. I got back to the room and there he was with his nose near the surface. He looked up at me and said, "I can't stop Ron." I calmly asked him to leave. Drugs would eventually take his life too.

By then we had moved into our new apartment. North Glen apartments were located far away from the comforts of Long Pond Shores. They were only off of Ridge Road about a hundred yards. The "Ridge" as I came to call it was one of the busiest highways in Monroe County. Our place was smaller, but it was neat and clean. Once in a while we would have a friend over for a visit from church or AA.

The Jones' had moved into their new place as well. It was a house that they had been looking at for awhile. Frank had been a Kodak worker at one time and had given up that job to go to school to become a preacher. They felt that after a number of years that their time had come for a house and needed to get away from the apartment scene. We would wonder shortly just what kind of new life we had stumbled onto.

Not Without Spot or Wrinkle

There had been a bone of contention that was bugging me for awhile. I had been a young Christian for a few short months and my apparent discernment had been moved up a few notches. Lois and I had been going on occasion to the Jones' for social gatherings as well as a Bible study or two. Frank and Betty were heavy smokers. I felt that they shouldn't be doing that, being in the positions that they were. It just didn't sit well with me. What especially made things worse was that one of the last times that we spent with them we were asked to watch a movie that was R-Rated. Sexual innuendo, violence, and curse words went against all that the man was preaching. We didn't say anything for awhile because we felt, like someone once said, "Be patient, God isn't finished with me yet." That obviously didn't apply here because they had been under the influence of God for a long time. What surprised me as much was that there were hardly any complaints about this issue from anyone else in the church. They kept themselves away from that stuff, at least in their own homes. We let it ride a little longer.

The girls had not been to Rochester for a better part of the year since they were taken from our place at Long Pond Shores. It was the Thanksgiving season and the time had come for a visit. Lois and I were leading an entirely different life that we had kept from the girls when we visited them in Bradford. Those times together were short and few anyway. The day had come. Kim and Kelly were knocking at the door. They had been delivered by Denny's relative. We welcomed them in as they looked around the strange place. Kim started by commenting, "It looks cool." Kelly walked into what was supposed to be their room and seemed to like it.

After the girls had gotten settled in, they were ready to hear what had happened about four months earlier. Lois took the girls into their room and closed the door. That took me by surprise. About a half an hour later they all came out.

The first thing that either of them said was, "We want to live here."

Of course that shocked me, but then it didn't. I answered, "Do you really? You know that your Dad might not like that." I was overjoyed, especially for Lois.

A couple of hours later the girls called Denny and made sure that he knew what they wanted. His response was the most surprising. The way for all of this had been paved. There was no resistance at all when the circumstances should have demanded it.

Before long our little family was back together. We went to Bradford to get the girls things and made their little abode as comfortable as possible. What Lois had told the girls was that we now were trusting God for everything. They both understand what their mother had expounded to them and had made that same commitment in that little bedroom. They wanted to go to church and meet new people...all in one day. The profound changes that they had noticed in my wife and I, were telltale signs to them that something real had occurred. We were not the same people that they had left and they wanted back in.

After a couple more trips to church I had had enough. The girls presence around the Jones' only amplified my points about the things I disagreed with. Lois and I sat down and discussed how this whole thing would be handled. We would call the reverend up and ask him to bring over with him another leader in the church. We would tell them that we were leaving the church and make clear why. I have always had the innate talent to express myself when I was pushed too far. There would be no turning back. Smoking cigarettes and compromising movies for a preacher and his wife was not acceptable by any person's standard in my book. One of the hurdles that we both had to jump was the fact they we believed that because we were new Christians, the preacher would use something like that in an argument to discredit our opinion of was of what was right and wrong. We made the decision to ignore such a contention. We were serious about our new faith and wanted to keep it as we were being taught. Many of the issues were common sense in the first place. I knew that you didn't have to be a spiritual superstar to see these things.

There was a knock at the door and I had been sweating for some time. The hallway produced two figures waiting to hear the worst.

"Come in Frank" I said politely.

Bill, an elder, accompanied the pastor with a smile.

"Bill." I nodded.

Frank refused to sit down. He had sensed that something was not right.

I started the conversation. "Listen, I know that you have been a pastor for a long time, but there is something that we feel is not right. We have been to your house and you have been a good host to us. However, we disagree with the fact that you and Betty smoke and try to show us R-rated movies. We are not going to attend church there anymore. It is not right for a man to call himself a Christian, and even being a preacher and do these things. Sorry!"

Frank was angry about the point and went for the only argument we felt he would. "What do mean by trying to judge me! Who do you think you are! You have to learn how to crawl before you can walk!"

On and on he went, but he never to my recollection ever once tried to say that what our complaint was about was unfounded. His arguments to convince us not to leave the church were vain. We were gone, and it hurt. There had been some very nice people that had tolerated all this themselves, but never would garner the nerve to do anything about it. At least that was the way I was feeling about it. Several of those fellow parishoners would follow us out of the church in search of something more agreeable.

Lois had started to become sick. Her heart was racing up and down in new ways that had not really happened before. It made her weak and feeling nauseous for quite a few days in a row. Two weeks to be exact. The toll on her future at Wegman's was starting to stir the fact that her days were limited. They understandably could not accept so many days of absence. It had happened much and too often. Finally, at the time that we needed her to work the most, they let her go, just before Christmas. My income would be the only one and we knew it wouldn't do the trick. Something had to give.

The girls were back in school in Rochester. They ended up going to NorthStar Christian Academy. Attending there was a safe haven for any student that was making a decision to abstain from the rudiment influences of the world. That school had a very good reputation and we were glad to get them in. That cost money however, a cost that would be burdening an already taxing situation. We had no idea what was supposed to happen. Our money was dwindling. We were behind a couple of months on our rent, Lois was sick and there was hardly any food in the house. We needed to find a new church and until we did, our spiritual hunger had to be satisfied. The preachers on television were interesting at the time. We had heard of the 700 Club, an organization that was run by Pat Robertson and seemed to be helping a lot of people. There was number on the screen to talk to a counselor any time of the day or night. I dialed the number one evening and asked for some prayer and any suggestion of what kind of a church we could attend. They checked their records and told us to contact the Greece Assembly of God. We "prayed about it."

Just prior to deciding to contact a new church Lois and I were feeling the pressure of losing everything again. Our thoughts of what had happened to us before were unavoidable considering the spot we found ourselves. During one of those days we had a visitor from one the other tenants at North Glen. It was a woman who been attending the same church that we had just left. We heard the knock at the door and there was this woman holding the side of her face.

In obvious pain, she said, "I have this impacted tooth that the dentist said has to come out. Can you help me? I have no money and it costs forty-five dollars."

What was interesting to us was that we had that exact amount left in the bank. That was it. We looked at each other and knew that this was something that we were supposed to do. I took the lady to the dentist and then wrote the check for the entire amount. We didn't know how things were going to change, but we were willing to go along with just about anything.

I ended up calling the Greece Assembly of God. Part of my original request from the 700 Club was expressing a need for food and maybe some help financially. Operation Blessing was the arm of the organization that helped with those things. The counselor had told me that if I would contact the church and get them to agree to help us that they would match whatever funds the church would give. I had to really think about it and bring myself to reach out in this way. Though I had been around asking for help before, my respect for the church scene was in its own way a little hard to do.

The order of things to come was nothing less in our mind than divine. Lois decided to check out the church first. I stayed home with the girls while she went to a Sunday morning service. She came home with that renewed glow on her face and made it clear that this was the place that we were supposed to be. I went to the evening service and was greeted by a man with the same countenance that my wife had. We felt good about the new place to worship.

It is difficult to start going to a new church at the same time you are going to ask for help. My first approach was to tell the whole truth. I had met a new friend and he had encouraged me to go forward with my plans. What I did not know was how fast news travels in the church arena. We never told anyone about the help that we had given the woman with the tooth, we only expressed our own needs.

A short time later, a few days perhaps, my new friend Larry was at the door. By then the only food that was in the fridge was a jar of pickles and the ice cubes. We opened the door and there was Larry with a bag of groceries.

He smiled and said, "I think you can use these. I also got a meeting set up for you with a pastor of another church. He wants to talk to you. It is a church that started up about a year ago just down the road and his office is right up behind here in the small plaza. Will you go?"

"Why, yea, sure," I replied. "I'll take whatever I can get, I guess. Thank you so much. I really appreciate it."

Larry gave us each a hug and left.

The man that I was supposed to meet had expected me around one o'clock the next day. I only had to walk about two hundred yards to get there. I walked in and there was a smiling man who I could tell loved the Lord and people. His name was Paul Colosi. In his early forties, he had obviously come far in a short time with the growth of the church. They were meeting in a fire hall on Sundays a couple of blocks away. He introduced me to Gary Smith, the youth and song minister. They seemed to be a great team.

"Have a seat," Paul said, gesturing with his hand.

Taking my chair and anticipating as to why I was there in the first place scared me a bit. I hadn't been told why I was to meet this man. And I didn't ask.

Paul continued. "I have been in prayer about something." He looked at the ceiling and thought a second. "The Lord has told me to give you a check for $450.00. I don't need to know anymore about you or your situation, that was the figure he gave me. God bless you."

I sat in shock. The first thing that came to my mind was that $450.00 was a strange figure for anyone to come up with. We had heard that God blesses in multiples, but I had no idea. Just days earlier we had spent our last $45.00 on that woman's tooth and now this! Of course, I couldn't thank him enough and I went on my way. He didn't even suggest that I needed to switch churches or anything like that. It was a pure unadulterated giving spirit that I had just witnessed. I went home on a pink cloud. Walking in that door and telling Lois what had just happened was something that was delightful. Later that day we got a phone call from Greece Assembly of God. They wanted to give us $380.00 and Operation Blessing would match it. That's $760.00 plus the $450.00 and the food we had gotten! Earlier Lois hadn't put away the groceries yet. They were on the counter and I took them out of the paper bag. In the bottom of the bag was an envelope containing a $100.00 bill! Larry hadn't told us about that one. Oh happy days! What can you say? It was like a fairytale.

We became very comfortable in our new church. In one way, with an entrance like that who wouldn't be, but we pretty much maintained our composure about all of this relating to motives and everything. I had started to read a lot of Christian books and came across one that had a peculiar teaching in it. The book was a study of the subject of faith and it covered many topics and issues for the

Christian believer. One of the topics was gambling. Now there was a subject that I was familiar with. Just don't do it. Well, the book was really saying, "not so fast." The Lotto was the new kid on the block in New York at the time. It had only been around a few years by that time and it was still reeling in new customers. The book said that you should never buy a bunch of lottery tickets, just one. Any more than one would be a demonstration of a lack of faith. Trust God for one only. Could this be a new door to catapulting us into the next level of living? It didn't take Lois and I long to decide that this disguised loophole in the commandments of God was the way to go. Up around the corner was another plaza down the street from where I just met Paul Colosi. Unknown to my wife and kids, we were about to embark on another journey that would take us to a lot of uncharted waters.

Our family agreement was to buy one lottery ticket per week. That would mean only one dollar. We would then gather around the television every Wednesday night after the news to watch the numbers being drawn. It was exciting, legal, and most importantly we thought, God approved.

Prior to all the apparent miracles with timing of events and money coming in our direction we were getting was the fact that we were wondering just how we could make it on my wages or if I would be getting canned. After Lois lost her job, the first thing that she did was travel to the Manor to tell me. I had been working in the basement and believed I had gotten a message that she was coming to tell me that she had lost her job. It would be the only time that I could claim I had an audible voice from someone that I could not see with my naked eye. And I wasn't afraid. Being so young in all of this God stuff, I wondered whether it would be easy to find out if I was only imagining this or not. I was paged by the secretary and up the stairs I went only to see a tearing wife in fear that I would be angry. Since I knew what was happening before she had told me it was easy to smile and comfort her tell her what I had heard. That is something that to the best of my knowledge has not been repeated. Some people had wanted to know why "I was so special." Maybe the fact that I told them in the first place was one of the reasons why I was shut off from that type of communication any further. On occasion, our mouths can interfere with a lot of things.

After we had gotten over that initial job issue, I was asked to participate in the Christmas play at work. I hadn't done anything like that since the "anything goes" performances in grade school twenty-five years earlier. I was not aloud to refuse. This was also the last Christmas that Damon and Onolee would spend as my bosses. They were retiring and Genny would be taking their position. *Quite a jump from the craft room to Administrator*, I thought.

My part in the play would be to be a leaping lord in the "Twelve Days of Christmas." Wearing leotards and a tight suit would certainly be up my alley. I had dressed like that at Halloween parties, but I was drunk then. Even though I had some of this experience, I was now sober. How could I do it without something to take the edge off? I knew I had to just do it. It was right.

The time for the play had come. We had rehearsed a few times in the off hours and now it was show time. I would be the grand finale. The cafeteria and kitchen were the areas where all of the residents and their families would be waiting. The main hallway to the cafeteria was the entrance for each of the actors as they came into the room. Of course there would be an applause for each one of us. I knew that my part traditionally had put upon me the most pressure purely because I was last. All of the people ahead of me made it through their parts just fine. By the time it came to me I was quite nervous. My usual sweat accompanied by cold chills when I had to reveal something about myself to others made this more difficult. Complicating matters was the fact that I felt I had to be good…very good. I couldn't let the people down. I was supposed to run down the hallway and into the cafeteria leaping like a well-stretched out ballerina. My time had come. From a distance I could see folks leaning in their seats looking for the long awaited finale with a perfectionist maintenance man in tights. I go running down the hall and leap headfirst in the door casing above the door. I hit my head, rattled all of my teeth, and pulled muscles in both legs. When I landed on my feet there were a couple of people covering their mouths in horror. I tiptoed in pain across the floor to my awaited position and received the loudest applause. The show had to go on. I couldn't let the people down. After meeting with the rest of the actors, we all took a couple of bows to the cheering crowd now standing. I felt good about that, but I hurt.

It was after that last Christmas in Rochester that our future began to be rattled. At home, a couple of months later, we were deciding to play the lottery to hit the big time, only now we foolishly thought that God himself was endorsing it. Well, what better way to be convinced that you needed the money than for you to lose your job. I had wondered about the closing of the restaurants that the Wegman family had owned. They had a maintenance man that was going to need a place to work. He had married one of the Wegman family daughters. By then Genny had been in her new position for a couple of months. I had gotten paged to come to her office. I walked in and I knew right away what was going to happen. (Not because God had told me), but because my new boss was sitting at her desk in tears.

"Ron," she said, rising out of her seat, "Phil and Ed called me and said that we have to let you go. Warren lost his position with the restaurants and he needs a place to go."

Though it wasn't a shock to me, it still hurt in a way. I had grown accustomed to these people, both staff and residents. They had been the first real tools used to help shape my new life. AA had given me some principles, church and fellow members would always be there, but this group of individuals was special. I was ushered into a new world by a nurturing bunch of real people and now I had to leave them. My words of consolation to Genny Fry seemed to dampen the blow a bit, but we still had to part in two weeks. My trip home to tell Lois was another trial in itself. She did not have the benefit of prophetic utterance. She still took it well and we would just ride it out until the Lord came through with a million or so.

Unemployment benefits was something that I had qualified for and Lois would not. The nature of the departure from her job made it impossible to collect. It seemed as though we were slowly being painted into a corner. Every once in a while there would be another slice of our pie being taken away from us.

I looked for a job and was offered a temporary position helping to build a new church. Greece Assembly had been eyeing a piece of property on Long Pond Road next to the YMCA. I was allowed to make a certain amount of money while I had applied for my unemployment benefits. The job would last for me for about two months. My chore was to help stack brick and block for the brickies, another drumbeat from the past. I had a good crew to work with. The contractor was out of New York City. He was a Christian man who came to the job once in a while to check on things. We would start work at eight o'clock in the morning and the pastor at the time was a committed man who could be found without fail in prayer walking around inside the unfinished church. The story was that he was there sometimes at six in the morning until we would start work.

Spring had sprung and with no direction as to what or where we would end up, we were sure of one thing. Whatever God wanted we wanted. The only trick to really believing that is knowing him well enough to know what that is or trusting Him when we didn't. For many reasons we had become experts at guessing and making some interesting moves when we should have stayed still.

During the next few weeks our evening ritual of watching the lottery drawing produced no real results. Always feeling like the next one was the big one is the hallmark of a person truly stuck on something. Even though it wasn't breaking the bank with a dollar a week there was more to learn about this Christian walk.

One evening Lois and I had gotten into an argument. It wasn't really a knock down and drag out confrontation. I think that I was more affected than her because I resorted to some of my old behavior. I had this streak in me that wanted to escape all I was in. Not enough money all the time had worn me down. I devised a scheme to get out of it all. I would take five dollars and go to the news stand and buy ten chances on the lottery instead of the usual dollar and, of course, I would not tell my wife. I was angry and I made a promise to myself. "Do not look at the tickets after the drawing until I was positive that I knew I had a winner." There was a way to do that.

The usual Wednesday drawing had come. I sat with my family and watched as we again did not win. By the eleven o'clock news it was announced that there were four winners. The next morning I went to work on the church, a little heavy. There seemed to be some guilt settling in with the fact that I was not being honest. The nice guys that I was working around would not ever know. Not by me, anyway. I came home and after dinner we watched the six o'clock news. They had announced that two of the four winners had come forward to claim their share of the largest pot in New York history. After being adopted as a viable form of income for the state only a few years earlier made no difference that twenty four million dollars was to be divided four ways. There were two people to go. I went to work wondering. "Could it be?" I would not look. Day three saw the third person coming forward and claiming their six million dollars. One left to go. The fourth person was a holdout. He or she would not come forward. I would not look, but what made it tough was the fact that they also had announced that the ticket was purchased in Monroe County. That was the six o'clock news! Eleven o'clock came and I was now getting very nervous about the potential that I had stashed in the closet. If I won I would leave all of this behind and take on the world. Did I need God to tell me in some audible voice that I was way off base? Never! And I knew it.

The news that I would now hear would have made anyone rush to look at their tickets. The late news that evening stated that the last winning ticket was bought at the same news stand that I bought mine! I walked out of the room and tried to calm myself. I still wouldn't check my tickets. I went to bed unable to sleep. The next morning I had to be around a lot of men who were talking about God many points throughout the day. Kicking off the workday with a prayer didn't help any. The whole day was a wreck. Even though I believed that I was a winner, there was this feeling of guilt and fear of a ruined life. If I would be a real recipient of that much money in my life at that time it would kill me. Everything that I had worked hard for, for so long would be up in smoke. Honesty, family, trust, all the things that no amount of money could buy would be gone. The day on the job was worse than any hangover. I now had a conscience that was being bombarded by bad thinking. I feared for my life now. All of a sudden the money didn't mean anything. A couple of days earlier I had quite a different view.

That evening I went home and read in the paper that the fourth man had come to claim his prize. I was elated. I felt as if I had hit the lottery! I ended up telling Lois what I had done and she didn't like it a bit. Sometimes the truth does hurt. It is like pulling teeth without any painkiller. My confession to my wife wasn't tempered by the fact that I was brave enough to tell her. We had a history and it added into her assessment of me.

Our stay in Rochester had come to an end. The landlord was trying to get money that we did not have. We ended up in court and the judge gave us a "hardship status." That status also applied to the taxes that I owed on the pension that I had received from the union. So, we packed up and reluctantly did something that Lois swore that she would never do. Move back to Bradford and in with her mother. On June 1, 1984 the little white Pinto was taking us back to the town we had left. This time we had accumulated more debt and were moving to a place that we were convinced had no real future. It was time to trust Him when we really didn't know.

We would have a ways to go before we would get cleaned up of some of the world that resided in us. We really didn't think things could get much worse, but then hey, how were we to know?

The trek back to our hometown was a solemn one. Not only were we going through the humiliation of "not making it" in Rochester, we were now going bankrupt. It was really hard to be the encouraging one this time. Moving into Nancy's house was even more humiliation for Lois. It wasn't enough that as her daughter she had failed on her own efforts, but it appeared as though she was limping back to a woman who could have easily said, "I told you so." Her mother didn't do that, but was very gracious about it all.

Our new home indefinitely became the only place left available in this three story spacious house. The third floor. It was complete with all the amenities of the first and second floors except there was a slight angle on the ceiling in the bedroom. Every one of the three full bathrooms had a unique shaped bathtub. Ours was kidney-shaped accompanied by an old high pedestal sink. Each one of the two separate antique beds we slept in were worth over ten thousand dollars each in 1984. I never had to be so careful about denting or scratching anything I had gone to sleep in before.

My father in-law Hugh was a quiet, but sociable man when he wasn't working with the family business. He, as well as Nancy, was a heavy smoker to the point that the low ceilings in the basement headquarters of the house made it impossible for a non-smoker to breathe. The only consolation to all of that was that Lois and I had much experience with that issue in all of the bingo halls, especially in the low ceiling Catholic church basements.

Phones were ringing off of the hook as couriers would call in for their next assignment or to confirm a finished one. Hugh had to fill in for some of the drivers quite often when a car would break down or someone wouldn't show up for work. One of their best workers was in an accident a couple of years earlier when we were still living on Summer Street in Bradford. It was a tough time for a lot of folks after that incident. Accidents are sometimes mislabeled. Roy Williard was a devout Christian who had made the mistake of going to a party with someone who would end up driving while drunk. Roy went from that party back into the Jeep that they were riding in to take a snooze. He didn't really want to be around the booze scene any longer. The driver came back to a sleeping passenger and drove the Jeep into a ditch, flipping it over. Without roll-bars in the vehicle, Roy broke his neck and was paralyzed from the neck down. Needless to say he was replaced at work. The Thompson family lost a great person and a good worker.

Life among the beggars had gotten off to a rather slow start. For the next fourteen weeks it would be a nip and tuck of a life. The underlying contention between mother and daughter would remarkably be kept in check. There was one time though when I thought all of hell was going to break loose when my wife referred to Nancy as "Mommy Dearest" at the dinner table. Mother in-law had the stage, but kept her cool on that one.

All of the furniture in the house was covered with a plastic sheeting, at least anything that you sat on. An antique dealer's assessment of Aunt's antiques were valued at $180,000. I know I believed that figure was accurate every night that I laid down to sleep. The four high posts on my bed were staring at me in the morning reminding me "not to touch." There was quite a contrast in my lifestyle from going bankrupt a few weeks earlier, and the environment I now found myself in.

I got the opportunity to work for Dusk to Dawn Services. Hugh and Nancy had cultivated the family business into quite a little enterprise. The two main functions being a carrier of bank data to a central location and the other being an agent for the Airborne Corporation made it quite profitable. Of course, running it right didn't hurt any.

During that summer it was an interesting job stopping at all the banks, picking up their paperwork and delivering it to a place called United Data Services located in Franklin, Pennsylvania, about an hour or so away. I would drive into the parking lot and back up to a door that was an entry into a small room. The security there rivaled only by the White House was quite impressive. As I was being watched on a monitor, a guard would come and meet me at the door and escort me in to the little room. I would have to make sure the door locked behind me before I handed my paperwork to the guard. We would sign our necessary documents and I would leave. The guard was escorted by a second guard, who would open the inner door to the building and the data would be brought in for processing. One day I made the mistake of asking if I could use the restroom. The guards looked at each other with a little frustration and let me in. I was escorted by one of them to the doorway of the men's room. I was told not to look around. Going down a hall I noticed a large room where there were many people sitting and tapping keys on computers. It turns out that they were workers hired specifically to enter all of the bank information into a main large computer that they called "mother." With all of the cameras and a helicopter pad outside in case of a breach in security this place could be very intimidating.

The other arm of the business wasn't so interesting. You had to stop at businesses and an occasional bank to pick up freight. Sometimes just an envelope or actual heavy containers of industrial products weighing several hundred pounds would at least keep in check a potential boredom. Every day was a little different.

In any job there is always exceptional circumstances along the way that made that job hard to forget. And this job would be no different. A special request was made to get a load to the airport in Pittsburgh. It was dead in the middle of the night as we pulled into the hangar at Pittsburgh International. I was tired after a four hour drive. Though this run was the only one of its kind for me, it was routinely done by other drivers. As I began to help unload the truck inside the hangar I noticed that I started to get dizzy. I stopped working for a minute and looked at the floor and everything was okay. When I would start to move the boxes again the dizziness would come back. This happened a few times and I thought that I was just overtired. Out of the corner of my eye I began to notice an entire stack of crates slowly moving. I walked a few feet to watch closely to see if I was imagining things. My helper noticed the same thing. We investigated and discovered that those crates were actually moving because they were filled with mice headed to Penn State for research. I hadn't really been dizzy, my mind was playing tricks on me because I thought things were moving even at a momentary glance towards those crates.

Things didn't always go easy for Lois's parents. Vehicle breakdowns, bad timing of meeting other drivers and slow payment from customers were some of the burdens that had to be faced all too often. But there was one event that made me quite angry. I was enjoying the fact that I was only a worker and not an owner. When Nancy and Hugh had taken over the business from her brother David he had owed a $26,000 federal tax debt. The arrangement was that Dusk to Dawn would pay a thousand dollars a week until the debt was paid off. I had moved into the house just in time to see what was going to happen next. Nancy pulled us aside one day and explained.

She said, "I've got to tell you something. When we had initially gotten an agreement with the IRS to pay back the money, it was more or less when we could afford it. After all, they wouldn't have gotten a penny if we hadn't taken over the business in the first place. We were going to sign the agreement and the agent had a heart attack. His replacement wasn't so kind, but we went along with him. We paid off one thousand dollars a week for twenty-one weeks straight, on time, every time. The agreement was that if we were going to be late on any one payment that we would call the agent's office to let him know about it. Payment number twenty two was going to be late for the first time." Nancy visibly tried to make sure that she stayed calm while she delivered the rest of the message. "I called his office and for the next two weeks he never returned the call. We found out that he had gotten the message when the bank called us this morning. He walked in the bank with Federal Marshals and took the remaining five thousand dollars out of our account. It was all that we had."

I was boiling. "You mean to tell that he never tried to contact you during this whole time?" I said…shaking. Nancy shook her head no. She was taking it better than I was and it wasn't even my business. She seemed to be glad that the tax issue was over. I went for a short walk to calm down. I had heard that there were powers that these people had, but never really had the pleasure of watching them in action. I did get things settled in my mind somewhat. I was just being moved up a notch in my growth and acceptance of things that I had no control over.

One of the intriguing aspects of living with my in-laws was the company that they had kept. Back in the '50s and '60s my own life was contrasted by the kids that I hung around with. Simply put, I had little, they had much. Nancy not only worked the business and had a full time job with the government in the forestry department, but did the books for other people. Not just any people. The history in the family included the company of millionaires. One of Nancy's clients was actually a countess. Ilka Healy was the sole heiress to Healy Petroleum, an oil business that had stretched back many decades founded by Bill Healy, her late husband. I personally saw the dividend checks come in the mail every day for thousands of dollars. For tax purposes, Ilka would have to spend thirty days per year in the United States. I would be meeting her for the first time. Her next stay would be with us. I have to admit that when we told that she was coming I was excited to actually be living with royalty for a month. I would be disappointed.

The room was readied and the countess arrived. She was an elderly lady in her early seventies that owned homes in Switzerland and England. I had a couple of meals with her during her stay, but really didn't get to know her. One morning I came down the stairs for breakfast and there was Ilka, passed out on the floor. She was a very active alcoholic and her grand entrance was a bit tainted by the manifestation of her problem. I just thought as I looked at her on the floor, "but for the grace of God there go I." Shaking my head I continued on my merry way. She never mentioned anything about having this in her life. I know Nancy didn't.

Once every two weeks there would be a delivery of special food from a truck that would deliver from Pittsburgh. Individually wrapped steaks and Black Forest Cheesecake were the two items I remember the most. It was eating high off of the hog except on Friday nights we would have pizza. I was changing my attitudes and views of some things. Lois and I would occasionally argue privately about the finances and our future. The third floor made it convenient for that forum. There was pressure mounting and we did not want to make a career out of sponging. At least it was convicting and a gnawing embarrassment living there. I could easily sympathize with my wife. She had deserved a gold medal for humbling herself to submit to that once unthinkable act of living back home with Mom.

We were nearing the end of summer and the blackberries were out. I wanted to do something that had escaped me for many years.

Picking blackberries with Mom and Dad for money was a regular thing for the Knott's. I knew where there was a good patch that had never been interfered with for all of those years. I went for a walk up on the side of the hill to that old patch. It still was producing good berries. A wonderful day in the woods picking berries and this time I was allowed to eat whatever I wanted. About an hour and a half into picking, the clouds formed and it started to rain heavily. I ran off of the hill and came in the house drenched.

I remembered after I had dried off, that on rainy days the guys around Bradford would play basketball in the Catholic auditorium. I called an old friend to see if it was on. It was and I went. It seemed as though everybody showed up. It made it difficult for me because the way it was organized was that if you lost you had to wait a long time to play again. There were just too many teams. It came time for our team to play and we were all running pretty hard. I got the ball and ran down the court full speed. When I got near the other end my legs gave out. I fell into the pipes that held the basket assembly up. My left knee hit the pipe and broke the pipe off. With my bleeding knee my friends helped me onto the stage to sit and watch some of the rest of the game. I was I pain, but I believed that I would be okay. That was not an affirmative. I jumped off of the stage and when I landed on the floor I didn't know that my leg was broken. I fell to the floor again and this time I was carried to the car. I drove myself to the hospital and sure enough, the top of my bone behind the kneecap was broken off. It was a freak break because the kneecap was not even touched. The doctor couldn't put a cast on, but gave me an immobilizer to wear for the next two and a half months. We were given an option of now living on the second floor until my leg healed. Lois didn't like the idea of living so close to where her mother was so we continued to keep our abode on the third floor. I got a good workout just going up and down the stairs for mealtimes. The most painful times were when I had to take off that support and get in the bathtub. It was excruciating when I had to lift my leg over the edge.

One of the habits that I had acquired in Rochester was making popcorn and watching television late at night, especially "The Honeymooners." Moving into Nancy's house made it a little difficult to do this all the time. We had a small television in our room, but a trip to the refrigerator was a long way down even without a broken leg.

217

Our Hamilton Beach popper was still packed, so this would require some noise. Shaking a pan on the stove at midnight in my mother in-law's house was a death defying feat, but I would try it. Even with her living on the second floor and being a light sleeper I couldn't succumb to reason. I made a lot of racket. She heard it...and I heard about it the next day. Her complaint about my inconsiderate move was the capstone to my troubles. Immediately after I had made a big batch of popcorn I looked over at the ham sandwich, glass of ice and a bottle of coke that had to go up the stairs with me. In one trip! So, with a hot pan in one hand, a ham sandwich in my mouth and the glass of ice and bottle in my other hand up the stairs I went. When I got to the first landing I had to make a sharp turn to the left. While attempting to put the crutches in a better position I started to fall backwards. The hot pan moved against the bare part of my leg showing through a space in my immobilizer. It burned very bad and I couldn't move it away as fast as I would have liked to. It was a second degree burn on my broken leg about the size of two silver dollars. I eventually made it the rest of the way without falling. When Nancy had said something about the noise, I really wanted to tell her how much I had really suffered. I wouldn't have gotten any sympathy for being so stupid in the first place. (At the time of this writing I can say with total honesty that last night, twenty-one years later I ate home made popcorn and watched TV at midnight. I have grown though. I am living on a first floor!)

Lois had put up with a lot of my idiosyncrasies. And I hers. The sum total of all of our tolerances did not add up to a very big deal at the time. I found out that I had retained a rescuer spirit when two men had broken out of prison and were terrorizing the whole northwestern corridor of Pennsylvania. They had stolen some guns and a car and were being tracked in their journey toward Bradford. The radio station was doing constant live reports as the police helicopters and law enforcement on the ground were attempting to apprehend the suspects. I wouldn't call them suspects when they had shot a few people including one of my friends while driving along the road. They had a shot another man in the chest while he was riding with his wife for a drive. Night time had come and I was pulling my hair out not being able to do anything. With my leg propped up on a chair all I could do was listen to the radio. They were closer to my mother's house and the cops had sealed off a route to try and close them in. A very concerned citizen had set a trap for the second criminal after the first one had been caught. A four-wheeler had been placed under a light in his backyard. The suspect went for it and the citizen put a gun to the back of his head.

Peg Leg Takes a Step

It was a strange time to move and my unemployment compensation was transferable, so it was now or never. The current income was not going to last forever and we needed again to get our own place. The drudgery of making it around on a broken leg to the third floor needed to end too. I was still looking for work and documenting it for New York State. I also took three civil service tests and failed them all while on crutches.

We started looking around for an apartment. Our new church was the one we knew we were supposed to be at. After looking around near the church we found a street level apartment just a few doors away from the church. I recall someone telling me that it was not a good idea, but I don't know who. I stood in the middle of the living room floor for about twenty minutes while Lois searched through the rooms and got a feel of the place. After a short sweep she agreed to get it. We put the deposit and the first months rent down and went back home to start sorting out things. We then went to buy curtains. Our second trip back into the apartment was a shock. I went into the same living room and stood there about only ten minutes this time. I became covered with fleas. My bare legs looked like someone had sprayed them with blotches of black paint. The first time we were there I hadn't seen one flea and if we had we wouldn't have taken it. I hated fleas with a passion. Brushing my legs off and returning to the car we drew the line on that place. We got our money back and started again.

Our second try would be the last. The girls had been spending a lot of time with their father when we were living at Nancy's. This new apartment was going to be a second floor deal. I didn't care about that. At least we were going to be moving away from "scrunchville" and I knew my one legged situation would be ending, so it wasn't bad. It was the around the end of September and the move would be easy, at least for me. There was enough help and I got as free ride out of it. Breaking a leg was a big price to pay to get out of moving the heavy furniture, but I enjoyed watching someone else for a change.

Twenty eight State Street, apartment number two became our new home. The landlord was a man that I had worked with off and on during my construction days. I never ran with him, but being a plumber on some of the jobs I would be a roustabout once in a while fetching tools and digging small ditches. He had known about my drinking and troubles. He also commended me for taking that giant step that no one seemed to want to. Darryl Porter became a good friend and sometimes a confidante. I was going to need one very soon.

Kim and Kelly were now established in their schools and we were nearing the holidays. The apartment was becoming lived in and my tender leg was now out of the immobilizer. It was great to walk again. The stairs would still have to be a slow piece of work as I took one step at a time. I never knew how much I would appreciate just moving around on my own two feet.

Our neighbors became friendly. I never told Lois, but the lady that was already living next door when we had moved in was that woman that had done her thing on my mother's front lawn with Mom watching back in '76. She now had eight kids and was working on her ninth. I'm glad she wasn't my date that evening. The lady living kitty corner to us was attending our church, so that was good.

We made it into the Thanksgiving season and things were looking up. Even though I hadn't found a job yet, at least I was able to get around now. One person that had become an encouragement to me was my cousin, Rose. She was living in Calgary, Alberta, for quite a few years and I hadn't seen her since she had come down with her husband Tim about five years earlier. They had visited Aunt Mary and Aunt Evelyn during one their stints on vacation. I had started calling Rose back when we were still living on Summer Street. Not really staying in touch too much while in Rochester, I thought I would reestablish some of my roots. She was my first cousin through Dad's side. She was also a Christian who would pray with me on occasion across the miles.

During my quest for a job, I filled out a questionnaire one time that consisted of 350 questions. One of the questions made you respond yes or no to the following: Did you ever think about murdering someone? Another one was: Do you ever think about homosexuality? Nobody I saw at the seminar could understand why these questions were asked. It was a very reputable insurance company looking for life insurance salesmen. I left. Another job was washing dishes. My pride would not accept the idea of doing something that menial. I had been humbled enough. After eight interviews, three of those civil service tests and 108 documented places that I had looked for work I ended up taking the dishwashing job. Every door was closed in every way. I had to do something. By now it was Christmas. I would start my new job the day after the New Year. The worst awaited me and I did not know.

> Walking now, my eyes have closed.
> I've done what I can, was there more, who knows?
> Crouching and waiting for me in the pit,
> was someone deciding to exercise wit.
> On I went like a lamb to the slaughter,
> to die to self or be sawn asunder.

Clipped Wings

It was a greeting card Christmas Eve. The snow was falling lightly, The tree was lit with all of my favorite colors. Scott Jimerson had come over for a holiday visit. Cookies and milk were served as good conversation dominated the evening. Scott was sometimes strange to me in the slant he put on certain doctrines, but that just made for new things to explore. I have made it important to hear one out no matter what they think. That night the topic of discussion seemed to be on faith. Mentioning a subject like that made me feel like I had a lot to contribute. The stories of how God spared me from a lot of calamities and provided miraculously for my family in many ways certainly came from the large storehouse that was easy to draw from in my own life. As I would learn, interesting stories are a dime a dozen, but what really matters is what those events accomplished in a life. About midnight after a lot of good dialogue between two buddies Scott made a statement.

After he had heard me tell one of my stories of faith he said, "Ron, I believe that you have a great faith."

I had never been told that before and, in fact, I still had not learned to accept a compliment. I looked around the room.

Glancing towards the bedroom where Lois was sleeping and then in the direction of the girl's room I said these words, "I believe that God could take this all away from me and I would still stay with Him."

Within the next sixty days God would call me on that bold statement. I had spoken something that was really a progress in work and I took that thing and used it to draw attention to myself. Although I was really appreciative of what the Lord had done in my life, it should not have been an occasion to make me look like a spiritual giant. Scott went home and I had a very nice Christmas.

New Year was here and I took the dishwashing job on January 2nd as planned. Lois did not like that and I did not know just how much. Maybe it was because she would have to answer questions like, "Oh, what does your husband do?" or the fact that such a job has had a perpetual stigma attached to it I'm not sure, but she began distancing herself from me. We began to argue about the money issues again. I could do nothing more to change our situation. I certainly was myself embarrassed to take a job like that in the first place, but I held out hope for change in the future. My wife would not wain from her feelings of hopelessness. My birthday was at the end of the month. I remember Lois coming home and tossing a cake on the table like a used book and grudgingly saying, "Happy birthday." By then I had grasped the finer details of doing the dishes at work and amazingly under the circumstances started to feel a sense of worth. It wasn't what I was doing that was important, but the fact that "I was doing it."

Arriving at what seemed to be an impasse, we had decided to seek out guidance from a church member that had been doing some counseling off and on. Grant Wier had the reputation from some as of being "deep" in the Lord. Lois and myself of course liked to hear that and readily submitted to hear what the man had to offer. The only problem at that time was that Lois was doing this as a last ditch effort and pretty much had the attitude of doing it just to say that she did. Grant came over a couple of times to meet with us. The appointments had to coincide with my getting home from work. Those hours fluctuated, but Grant made the effort to come when we could have him. Then he started showing up earlier. He would be there when I got home. Earlier and earlier he would be there. Well into a conversation with my wife before I even left work caused a greater dissension between this married couple. They had been talking about a lot of things that were taboo in any church. My involvement in the discussions was kept more and more superficial. After Grant would leave, Lois would start to put an accent on how much I was "not like

Grant." After a couple more sessions Grant stopped coming. He had done the damage. Lois told me that he had told her that "I would be willing to run away with you if you ever wanted to." She needed something more than what money could buy and apparently I didn't have it to give to her. A couple of short years earlier Dr. Carter had counseled Lois to "go out and have an affair with someone and that would help her marriage." She had also told me at the time that he made himself available and would meet with her if she did. He had attempted to get her to do that at least twice. We went to see a lawyer about it and could nothing because we did not have $10,000 as a retainer and Lois couldn't emotionally stand going through the courts. She would continue to see him and made sure that he would not be a recipient of his perverse counsel.

Needless to say, our marriage was rapidly deteriorating. It had come to the place where Kim and Kelly were turned against me. A few days after Grant stopped coming over I was sitting across the table from Lois eating something. The phone on the wall next to my head rang. I answered and it was Grant.

"Could I speak to Lois?" he said with his usual calm voice.

I didn't say anything. I just handed the phone to my wife. She spoke for a minute and then with a loud shriek threw the phone at me and ran into the bedroom. Not having any idea of what was going on, I walked over to look in on my emotional wife. She was sitting on the bed with her knees tight to her chest while rocking back and forth staring downward at the comforter. I asked what the matter was.

With many tears streaming down her face, she slowly looked at me. "Why is God taking away from me the only thing that really matters?"

By then I was sitting next to her and tried to give some comfort. "I'm doing the best that I can, honey" I said.

She looked back at the blanket. It wasn't what she meant. Grant had rescinded on his offer to run away with my wife and told her on the phone. When Lois told me that I was dumbfounded. She hadn't been talking about our marriage at all. I didn't know that things had progressed that far. I now had no words of comfort. In this race I didn't even show up let alone place. Back to the dining table I went, finally realizing what had just transpired.

Over the next two weeks Lois would follow Grant and try to get him to change his mind. He eventually told me that she even went to someone else's house and pounded on the door because she knew he was there with his wife for a Bible study. That tactic continued until he gave up. I came home from work one day and found a note. All it said was, *Me and the girls are gone*. No hint of where. For the next forty-eight hours I would call around, but nobody claimed to know where they were. I wasn't really worried for their safety and eventually I knew I would find out what was going on.

Going to work was a little distracting over the two days of uncertainty with Lois and the girls. There was no hint of this action. I all I knew was that we were having problems and never dreamed that she would just "up and leave."

I eventually found that the girls had been hidden from my search by Lois's sister Joan. Nobody wanted me to know where they had been staying until Lois got to where she was going. Running away with Grant Weir to North Carolina. That was the news that I was told by her sister. And she had assisted greatly in that effort. It was explained to me that Lois and Joan had gone into different versions of the Bible with the expressed purpose of finding a translation that would give Lois grounds to leave me. They both claimed to have found one and so Lois left. Abandoning her children to someone else, and leaving me was something that Lois never would have done without the help of someone else. Our problems by themselves would never warrant either one of us leaving. We argued and sometimes even yelled. I was sometimes a pain in the neck to be around. I still had an attitude at times and so did she. We had gone after what we thought was the best in life and didn't make it.

During all of this trouble there was one thing that I wasn't. Angry. I have seen all the shows on television, many friends and even relatives get into these kinds of problems and there was anger, vengeance, even murder. It was as though society had imposed upon me that I should act a certain way under the circumstance that I found myself in. I didn't have to work at it. There was a good reason why. I was happy. I was free. A secret desire fulfilled. I would have never left our situation. I had been willing to ride out all of the trouble just like I always had. Since there seemed to be reversal of the direction that this was going I became pliable and just rode it again. I didn't like the pain at the time even though it had gotten worse. I thought this was the best thing for me.

I called Rose and would talk to her for hours. She asked me to come to Calgary and I told her "No, I did not want to run away from my problems." I would stay and face what I had to and then reassess later what I should do. I traveled around with a couple of my AA friends and got more support there. Lois had rented an apartment with Grant and they both had gotten jobs. The plan was to set up shop and start a new life. That didn't happen either. Thirty days later my wife showed up at the door. She asked to come in.

"I'm not coming back, I just came for the television and stereo," she said.

By that time I had moved into the small one room apartment downstairs and had gotten rid of a lot of things.

I looked at her and replied, "You are not going to get anything."

Her response to that was, "I'm staying here until I do."

I walked over to the door and held it open. "If you don't leave now I will call the police."

She left for good.

The relationship did not last long in North Carolina. During one of the last weeks that they were there I had gotten a phone call from Grant's wife that.

"Ron, I've got Grant's gun and I'm going to kill your wife," she said.

What concerned me wasn't that she had a gun, but in telling me this she said it with a calm and collected voice. This mother of five children had every reason to be angry and her attitude to me on that phone made me really fear for Lois.

"I don't think that you should do something like that" I said with a voice of concern. "It is not worth it. It won't last. Let the Lord deal with it."

After a few minutes she would change her mind. I never told Lois about it.

The weekend that they had come back to Bradford, it was obviously a busy one for Mr. Weir He had convinced his wife to take him back and they were moving to North Carolina, all in one weekend. He had a lot of incentive to get out of Dodge. Lois had told him that I would kill him if I ever saw him and he was afraid for his life. And how would I know all of this? One of the chores that Grant had to do when he had come back to get his family was to pick up his last check at work. I just happened to be shopping in one of the aisles of Fisher Big Wheel when he did. My being there was a divine appointment. Not knowing what was going to happen I just showed up...and so did God. I was looking at some article of clothing and around the end of an aisle and here comes Grant walking right into the trap that neither one of us had set. He had a look of fear on his face while I just smiled and reached out to give him a big hug.

"How are you doing, Grant?" I asked.

Scanning the store for who knows what, a frightened man responds. "Oh , not so good. I came back to get Linda and the kids. We're moving back to North Carolina. You know something, Ron, we tried to make it down there, but the Lord was too convincing."

After explaining what had happened over the course of the last month we said our goodbyes. There was no incentive to lie about these events and many of them were corroborated later on.

It became more of a real thing that Lois wouldn't be coming home. I had no experience at divorce. I was lonely, sometimes a little depressed, and somewhat puzzled at all of these events. What could I have done differently? Why didn't Lois stick it out like we always had? We went through the rehab thing, the opening and closing of the eatery, and the loss of our jobs all had sufficient enough stress to maybe want to give up, so why now? I still had a lot of hope even under this dark cloud in my life though. At least I wasn't angry at all. The situation certainly should have called for it.

My mode of travel now had been the services of a used bicycle from a garage sale. Both cars were gone and I couldn't have afforded one anyway. Riding down the main streets in Bradford with a large bag of laundry was chalked up to just another humbling experience. By then the whole town knew what had happened, so I would just wave to people I knew and keep on going.

Friday nights at work were the worst. I had to come in for the lunch hour crowd and always prepare for the evening fish fries. One of the first Fridays after Lois was finally gone was the hardest. Washing the dishes was bad enough, but what really bothered me was when I went out among the customers to get those dirty dishes. I always thought everybody was looking at me now that this problem was in my life. Even the radio being at one of the waitress stations was playing the song: "Him" by Rupert Holmes. The words "him, him, what are you going to do about him" echoed in my mind for weeks.

Meeting new people around the town became a regular thing ever since we had moved back from Rochester. One man was Pastor Phil Palutro from church. When I had initially told him what had happened I was at work. He told me to repent of anything that I had done that contributed to the downfall of my marriage and then we prayed over the phone. He was and is still a man that was endued with some wisdom from God. Another man I had met was Frank Hill, another pastor of a church from up on one of the hills outside of the town. I had a little talk with him about my plight and he told me that "patience would be a big thing in my life." I needed to wait before making decisions, especially the big ones. He had told me how this very thing had happened to him years earlier.

My first question to him was, "How long did you have to wait before you got married again?"

Frank looked at me with those dark, black, piercing eyes and said, "Three years."

In my heart I knew what I wanted. No pain. I did not want to enter this new life without a woman. That part of my trial was very tough. I found out that even when things do not go well with your loved one, no matter what the circumstances are you will be missing something. The last time I remember experiencing that was when Dad died, relief and grief at the same time.

On occasion Frank would let me come up to the church and pray. Mom would let me drive up and I would sit in the pews alone. I had thought about working my way into becoming a preacher someday. That notion had been influenced by Jimmy Swaggart's fiery condemnation of the things going on in other people's life. Maybe my time had come. One Saturday afternoon at the church I had gotten up out of my seat and walked to the altar. I went behind the pulpit and preached a message to the pews. Finally, after forty-five minutes of "letting the world have it," I broke down for the first real time and wept. I collapsed in a heap and sobbed for a long time saying nothing. The silence of God was starting a long process of healing.

Probably one of the most encouraging things to happen was the approach of spring. With the snow gone and the birds now singing, a new hope again had arisen in my heart. Also, talking to Rose for the last few months had helped keep my sanity afloat. With no contact from my family, I knew that I had to move on, but how? What was I going to do? Where was I going to go? Rose's offer to me to come to Calgary still stood and it was looking better all the time. By then it had been four months and the hour of change had come. The middle of May had become another turning point in my tumultuous life. I was going two thousand miles away and leave my life in the hands of God. I had a hard time going two miles let alone a trip across the country.

I committed to come out to my cousin's on the first of June. I gave one glorious two week notice at work. I would be training my brother Sam to be my replacement. My boss, Connie Cavelero, liked him and hired him right away. The weather was perfect for a lawn sale. Whatever I had left would finance the trip. Two good days of that sale did the trick. I was now doing what I do best, traveling light. The next two weeks would go quickly. It was nice not to have to wash dishes during Sam's training. The Friday before my trip had come. I would be leaving Monday, June 1. That Friday would be trouble for a lot of people. The weather had become an issue for many customers. The rain and driving winds had kept a lot of folks at home. Conny would let me have whatever I wanted for dinner. I ordered pork chops. Feeling now like I was on top of the world, I went to sit in the restaurant. I was now one the customers. I sat and read the paper while the broiler was doing the chops. The winds had picked up so hard that they knocked out the power for a short while. I had to wait a little longer for dinner. That night a tornado had touched down in nearby Kane, Pennsylvania, and killed a couple of people. Tornados also destroyed many homes and killed a couple of dozen people in Barrie, Ontario, a place that I would pass through on my way to Roses.

Monday morning was here and Sam would drive me to the bus terminal in Olean. That halfhour drive was painful. I now was really doing something big. This move carried with it a feeling of "it" being over. Even though I knew things were over in my mind, this act of going away sealed the reality for me. I got on the bus for my fifty four hour trip and watched Sam as he followed me for about thirty miles.

Something in him did not want me to go, but he never said anything. This had been difficult for him.

I really did not know what was going to happen in my life now with no family, no responsibility, and no direction. That is why Rose and I agreed that I would buy a one-way ticket. My first stop was to be at the Canadian border. All forty-five of the passengers had to exit the bus and go through customs. When it came my turn to go in front of the inspectors they took one look at my ticket and drilled me. Another inspector was called over to assist in my questioning.

"How long are you staying at your cousins?" one would ask while they went through my two suitcases. One was actually a metal trunk. Then one man looked at my ticket again while he waited for my answer.

"I don't know sir, I'm just going for a visit."

They both are now staring at me like I was a leper. I never knew that it was Canadian law that you could not stay in the country for more than twenty-one days. You could leave and get a cup of coffee over the border and come back, but you had to leave. These two guys made sure that I knew that. Everyone by now was back on the bus.

"I'll tell you what," said one of them. "We are going to make sure that you are out of the country by the end of three weeks or we are going to come and get you."

I was getting nervous. My plans with Rose were definitely open-ended and I thought that maybe this would create a problem. But I submitted to their wishes. They made me sign a paper that I would have to deliver to the customs on my way back. They would enter the information into the computer and verify that I was in or out of the country.

I got back on the bus and almost four dozen frustrated people were staring me down. I took my seat and went the couple of hours to my next stop without saying a word. I had a déjà vu during that leg of the journey. I hadn't ridden a bus since Dad had died when I had got stuck that fateful night back in Erie.

Arriving in Toronto for the last and final part of my trip was like a plane taxiing up the runway before takeoff. It would be a four-hour wait and that time would go rather quickly. I got on the bus bound for the long trip across the North American continent. The anticipation of going on this trip, meeting Rose and just not knowing what was going to happen in my life now had started to crowd out some of the ill feelings that I was having about my losses. I would discover that they had only been laid aside for awhile.

The trip across the country made for a lot of beautiful country along the way. I had only seen scenery like this on calendars or in books. Along the way I would contemplate some of the people back in church at night when you couldn't see the trees and clouds. Many had encouraged me to go on with my life. Some would pray while others invited me for a meal. The sum total of it was that I was grateful to have such good people in my life. I would miss them for a while.

One of the passengers that I sat with was a beautiful woman from Australia. She was going to the west coast to take a flight back home. My conversation with her led me to believe that I was going to make it in life. She gave me her phone number and told me that when I came to Australia that she would put me up. Her job was with a travel agency. My longing for a mate made me want to try somehow and fit her into my life. As much as I wanted to I just couldn't.

One of stops along the way was at a bus depot that was outfitted with a long bar and row of beer taps from around the world. I would have never guessed for a second that out in the middle of nowhere was something like this. It was a hot day and my friend from the "land down under" and I went in to the lounge area. The setting was perfect. A beautiful day, a pretty woman, no responsibility…and lots of beer! The consequences of taking a drink appeared on the surface to be nil. But I knew better and said no to the lady who held up an ice cold foaming mug in my face. On we went.

There were an unusual number of people from other countries on my bus. The ones that stood out the most were the citizens of Pakistan. They would all carry only knapsacks and packed lunches. They hardly spent any money. Some were students while others simply were sightseers that traveled as cheaply as they could.

The bus had pulled into Calgary in the late afternoon. I could see out though the front windshield a panoramic view of the Rocky Mountains. I said to myself that I had to climb them. The only experience that I had had with those mountains was when I was with the guys on our trip in the early '70s and that was at night. This part of the Rockies looked close and I could go up them while Rose was at work. What I didn't know was that these guys were so big that although they looked close, they were actually an hour away. Rose met me at the terminal. We hugged in tears and went back to her home. Her two children Allan and Paula were there while husband Tim was back in Toronto working as an electrician.

Rose's home was a mid-size ranch on a corner of a raised lot. The furnishings were top of the line amid a compliment of white walls and curtains. It was a pleasure to be here from the start. A cocker spaniel named C2 was one of the greeters when I had arrived. Fortunately, that dog was a young one. All of my experience with that breed reassured me that they live up to their reputation as a dog with an attitude. Never knew why that was, but other people were seeing that to. Aunt Ev's dog "Coco" had bitten me when I was young. He also was a cocker the same color as C2.

The kids welcomed me as I made myself at home. They were nearing the end of their school year, and like all kids, they were excited about it. The type of upbringing that they had became evident almost immediately. I was made to feel as if I had been there all the time. Allan was eight and Paula eleven. Paula had a small streak of independence poking through in her attitude, especially with her mother. Nearing the teen years and an occasional difference in how things should be done in her life by her parents made a nearly typical childhood. The politeness and consideration for others was quite remarkable.

Rose worked as a nurse in a local nursing home. It was a job that she seemed to be well suited for. Caring for people was definitely her. The stories about how interesting and peculiar the elderly would act inspired a few tales of my own. Having worked back at West side Manor gave me a well from which to draw from. Although those folks weren't yet nursing home material, they in many ways had created a lot of things to talk about, mainly due to that fact that they were still able to get around by themselves.

My summer began with a sense of cautious optimism. Though I had no idea where my life was going I felt good about it. I didn't really pay attention so much to the demands of the border agents right away. My main job for the moment was to just simply enjoy the changes that were at my feet. I was still smarting from all of the trouble back home, while this new place that I was finding myself became clear enough evidence of an absolute "starting over." One of the best aspects of my new residence was not knowing how long I would stay. My thoughts included: *Would I live here permanently? Was I going back home? Am I really going to be a divorced man?* All these potential possibilities and many more kept me a little busy in my mind. I believe that under the circumstances I could take on a lot of thought and it would not overwhelm me. That is all I could do anyway. Had plenty of time to think.

Mealtimes were special, particularly with the kids around. Quite often Rose would have to work very hard to get them to eat their vegetables. Allan had a problem with that.

"Allan!" Rose would bark. "How many times do I have to tell you, eat it."

His reluctance sometimes got him sent to his room. Paula did not have to face that demise when it came to eating. She would have other things to deal with over time. I sat at dinner and watched the contention arise right after saying grace. The one thing about being in this new capacity that was nice was the fact that I was not their dad. I came in to the home as an observer. To hear the arguments about the food was as American as apple pie and I saw that there were no boundaries when it came to character and personality.

Rose had a lot of friends, mainly in the church. Many churches. She had visited quite few different places and it became a way of life for her. She had had a unique start in the life of a worshiper. The story was that she was on her deathbed with a terrible disease and God came to her in visions and dreams. She was miraculously healed and started to go to church. She had given her heart to the Lord and strangely did not read a Bible for two years after her conversion from nothing to Christianity. Anyone would be convinced that it was not a normal thing to come down that path and at the same time not delve into the Holy Scriptures. I, on the other hand, studied them every day. That became quite an asset for Rose. It was amazing what she really knew regardless of her lack of that type of study.

We visited many different churches, with and without the kids. She knew a lot of people everywhere we went. One lady named Josie had apparently been assigned a unique ministry. It was to go to the Catholic priests and tell them the "truth" about God. I had learned early on that the idea of being "born again" did not sit too well with some in the Catholic faith especially the leaders in that church. I was soon to be tested on that issue.

There was one group of people that Rose introduced me to that met for church in the basement of some small building. Once a week they would have a Bible study in the pastor's home. John Carlson was one of the faithfuls in that small congregation. I came to know him a little. He owned a tool and die shop and would invite Rose and I to visit him even at work. John had a very interesting gift from the Lord. I had never seen it to the degree that existed in his life, nor since. We had gone to a Full Gospel Businessmen's meeting at the Holiday Inn of Calgary. Now Rose had told me that John could peer into other people's lives and tell them something that only them and God would know. It was almost always something encouraging or uplifting and sometimes it was not. Once in a while there would be a need to chastise or chide someone and I guess it was not pretty. Dinnertime was over for the crowd of about one hundred fifty. There would be several speakers. One man came to me and told me that I wanted to be a pastor. I thought that was nice because that is what I really wanted.

Being a young Christian I was still stuck in the "show me" mode. Although I had some faith in my life, I was on occasion in need of some tangible evidence that God is really moving on something. I thought, "Maybe it should be that way all the time."

Rose pulled me aside and said: "I want you to make sure that you are near John when he goes to the door where the people will be leaving. He is going to be talking to a lot of them and tell them some things from God."

Of course I would see this as a chance to be a firsthand witness if something were really to happen. God was on the spot. Would he come through?

After the speakers were done with their sermons and testimonies Mr. Carlson went to the door as Rose had said that he would. Rose and I would follow him and stand a little out of the way. As the people started through the door John would pull then aside one by one and expound to them what "God had told him." There had to be at least twenty different people that had gone through this line. Some would break down in tears and other would walk away in plain wonder at where he got the knowledge that he had. One of the more interesting aspects of this occurrence was that some of the men and women there had known John and how he was being used. A few people had gone out of their way to approach him to get a "word from God." You had to be humble to be involved in this way and John Carlson was a great example of humility. He would himself be in tears at some of the revelations he would share. Watching closely for about a half an hour I was really convinced that this man was being used by the Lord. No one could have known what he knew, and set up the responses with people I knew he had never met.

The pattern in my own life was that I cared about people too, I just couldn't show it the way some others could. Ulterior motives can rule a man's heart and it may have been a mistake to give me a gift like that. I may have liked the attention. My track record in that area had not been the greatest, but I can recall more than once when I was given an opportunity to not "lean on my own understanding." Most often I do not know what I am really capable of. What makes it particularly hard to believe that is that which I do know.

One of our next visits would be taking us to two different places. Rose had bought a newspaper and checked out all of the church functions for the weekend.

Going down the list, she would say, "Here, this one's for you, I'll be going over here to the meeting. I will leave early and come to where you are."

This particular Friday evening while she was going down the list she stopped on this one seminar that was being held in the basement ballroom of the Ramada Inn. It would be a large gathering of Catholics complete with priests answering questions about the faith. I thought, *Here we go again.* I had had enough of trying to get anyone who didn't want to hear what I had to say about the Lord.

I told my cousin, "Why on earth do I want to go over there anyway? I'm not Catholic."

Her answer was simply, "God wants to use you there. He has something to say to the people. They are blinded."

My first reaction to that was I did not want to create contention. My second inclination was to the aforementioned problem that I thought about, even though I was a hurting individual who needed comforting myself, I just saw this as an opportunity to step out and do

236

some good. As I would discover, I didn't know myself as well as I thought I did.

Arriving at the gathering in the Ramada Inn was somewhat spellbinding. I felt a sense of worth in that maybe I could tell some people those kinds of things that John was at the dinner a week or two earlier. Walking into the large ballroom filled with people from all over I had an uneasy feeling about all of this. To ease my fears, I was met by a woman at the door who gave me a couple pieces of literature regarding the order of events for this meeting. She smiled and introduced herself as Eileen. There would be about a forty-five minute film, then a slide show and immediately following, a question and answer period from the priests.

Before the film was shown, there would be the usual custom prayer. In the front of the room was a statue of Mary. Everyone, but myself and about six others were still standing in this room of about one hundred fifty. I suspected that these other folks may have either believed as I did or had some physical limitations that prevented them from going on their knees. I started to feel a little sick. My beliefs about the accuracy of the Bible made being here very hard. I just plainly did not agree with some of the Catholic doctrine. And furthermore, I was here at the request of someone else. What had really convinced me to come in the first place was how I saw the Lord use Rose and many of her friends. I couldn't argue with almost any of it up to that point.

The rear of the room was set up to sell little images of the saints, tea leaves, rosary beads, and some books. I hated it. After everyone got up off of their knees and sat in the chairs, I made my way to the front. Sitting two rows back I wanted to make sure that if I was staying I would fully understand what was going on. The film started. It had to do a lot with the history of "The church." The different popes, church growth down through the ages, and the basic fundamental beliefs of Catholics made up a bulk of the time on the screen. Following the film was the slideshow. It featured something that I had heard about for years and especially during recent times. The manifestations of the Virgin Mary. There were many kinds of attention given to this subject at the time. Some for and some against the validity of these alleged sightings. What made this seminar a little different from the start, at least for me was the fact that now they were claiming to have caught some of these images on film. Many people throughout the years had claimed to see Mary show up in various places around the earth, but no one had photographed such a controversy. This had been a drawing point for me to come here. I liked seeing proof of things.

The slide show was impressive. I peered as close I could get to look at all of the angles and shots that people got. The primary focus was on the images presented by a person named Mary Van Louken who had reported seeing the virgin mother in Central Park quite often in New York City. That attention was not limited to the confines of the church. She also had made the news in the mainstream media. I looked closely to see if there were any fabrications or alterations of the images that I was observing. What appeared to be lightning flashes and even some profile outlines of a person did convince me that something was there. I didn't doubt that people had something to make a fuss about especially if you saw it with your naked eye. Of course by that time I had studied many of the aspects of sources of things like that, I believed beyond any doubt that the origin of these images did not come from God. In my mind they were put there by someone who wanted to distract us away from God, not get closer to Him. Even people in tears did not convince me that this was an attempt by our creator to call us to his side. I felt "compelled" to do something.

A few people asked some questions about the filmstrip and slide show. Then it happened. I stood up and walked over to the wall a few feet away. I raised my hand to ask the question of the panel of priests.

"Could I ask a question, sir? In my Bible it mentions being born again, could you please tell me what it means to be born again?"

"Why, yes," the priest answered. "Being born again means that you have been converted into the Catholic faith."

I responded by making the observation that all the people in the room had been down on their knees as a Catholic. I reaffirmed his answer to make sure that I and the rest of the people there understood the question and the answer.

"So you're telling me that once you become a Catholic that you are born again?" At that point I looked around the packed out house and with my right hand raised I asked, "Will everyone in this room who is born again please your hand?"

The six hands went up that had not bowed their knee to the statue of Mary in the front of the room. I looked at the priests and could tell by the buzzing in the room that trouble was near. It was quite a confusing scenario for the folks in the room. It appeared as though the priests were on the spot about something, at least they were starting to act like it.

In a hurried voice one of them spoke up. "There is nothing here that conflicts with Catholic doctrine!"

Looking at me, then the priests, a woman seated up in the front row defended my observation. "You know, he's got a point there."

The priest interrupted, "This has all been documented evidence."

I hadn't been referring to the film or the slides at all. I had been asking a question that required a clarification or an understanding on an unrelated subject. Another couple raised there hands to speak. The priest called on the man and what appeared to be a hope of being rescued only made matters worse.

"Yes, sir," the man said. "Born again means that your have accepted Jesus Christ as your Lord and Saviour. When you have made that commitment, he takes up residence in your heart and you are then born again."

The priests looked at each other. The second priest asked the man, "What church do you belong to, sir?"

By then the man, his wife and two children were standing up and gathering their things to leave. His family had been one of the two that did not bow to the statue. He answered the priest so that everyone could hear.

"You know, what you are teaching here is not of the Lord. You are not supposed to be worshiping anything else other than the Lord himself. We are leaving!"

As the man got out of his aisle, the room was by then bustling and could not be quieted. I started to make my way to the back of the room where the exit was.

As I got to the door, one of a pair of women approaching me asked, "Can I speak with you a second? I am a recovering alcoholic. My Bible tells me what you and the others said. I have been a Catholic my whole life and now I am questioning my own faith. Can you tell me anything that I can do to know what the truth is?"

She started to weep as I put my hand on her shoulder. "Here is what you need to do. Go home, read your Bible and ask God to reveal to you what the truth is about all of this. He will not fail you. It will be okay"

She was helped by her friend up the stairs. I never saw them again.

Rose came a little later than I had expected, but I had what I believed to be was a good report. Announcing what had just happened. "I simply asked them to explain what they believed their own commitment was. There was chaos about the exposure to the truth." Rose thought is was a good thing that I had been used of the Lord in such a way.

A few days later we went to a church that Rose had gone to before. It was a warm sunny Sunday morning. She had told me that the church had a lot of rich people there, but didn't get into any details. It was the Marlboro Pentecostal church. This was going to be right up my alley.

Many Places
Many People

Walking into the large church was pure joy, not because it was big, but because it seemed like I was now going to be around people who believed as I did. It turned out to be partly true.

My new slant on cutting across the grain of what I thought were compromised belief systems started to show a little more. I never had any inclination to confront anyone about what the accuracy of their own beliefs were, let alone a whole group of them. I wasn't embarrassed or ashamed of my last questioning and based on my own nature I should have been. I was changing.

The entrance into this building of worship took me straight to the men's room. As I was exiting into the hall a man in a dark suit approached me. Shaking my hand, he said that he was the pastor of the church.

"Hello, my name is Pastor Fenn, I am the pastor here. Where are you from?"

"I'm from back east. Originally from Pennsylvania," I responded. "My cousin lives here and I came for a visit."

I met Rose back upstairs and we walked into the sanctuary. There was a guest speaker who was a missionary to a foreign land, Africa I believe. I do not remember much about what he had said, but I cannot forget what would happen next. Pastor Fenn got up to do a short followup talk on the state of the local church, the finances, projects, etc.

As I listened, my mind seemed to wander. I thought, *This man is in trouble. He needs rescued from something. His suffering is great and does not want to be here.*

Just then there is an elbow in my ribs. Rose says, "Ron, you have a word for that man, you had better give it to him."

I looked at her like, "What are you talking about?" But I didn't say a word. I then gave her a look of disgust and tried to make light of it. "Shhh, just listen," I said.

She kept quiet for about two minutes and then again the rib thing. "Ron, he is waiting on a word from God and you have got it so to give to him!"

Ignoring her for another minute, I now began to wonder. *Is what I'm thinking actually what this man is supposed to hear? I am not qualified to be used like this anyway.* It was only my imagination, so I did not say a word all the way up to the end of the sermon.

The church started to empty out and a frustrated Rose kept me in my seat. I asked the Lord in my heart to help me. It was my turn to practice what I preached to that woman after the Catholic seminar. Ask God to show me what the truth was about all of this. If what I had been thinking was really for another person then maybe it would be a good thing for that person to come and request it from me. That would be evidence to me that I heard from the Lord. Again the Lord took me up on that challenge. Pastor Fenn was now walking toward me.

"Here he comes," said Rose. "He is going to say something to you."

I started to get a little nervous. By the time the man got to me he had tears streaming down his face. "You have a word from God for me, what is it?"

I had never seen anything like this before in my own life. I guess I was impressed that John Carlson was able to help a lot of people like that, but I was only less than two years old in all of this stuff. I shook the man's hand and said to him. "The Lord shall deliver you from all of your troubles. Do not fear anything, He will be faithful to rescue you. He has heard your cry."

Pastor Fenn gave me a big hug. "Thank you! Thank you!"

As he left I had the attitude of a child. I had just given something to someone else with no thought of it. It took me some work to get there, but it was easy in the end.

When Rose and I got into the car she explained to me, "The church being full of millionaires is a big problem. The pastor had been preaching to appease the whims of too many people who had a desire to have their ears itched. Pastor Fenn had succumbed to being swayed by the notions of man and not God. Now he had found out the truth about himself and wanted to be removed from the church."

The word that I was carrying was actually for him and I thought it was only my own imagination. The rest of that day went well.

One of our last visits to different churches was a mid-sized Mennonite worship center. This time I would be fed. The guest speaker was a beady-eyed Texan. That was how he described himself. At the end of the sermon he had an area of his ministry that was similar to what I had been experiencing. In a group of one hundred or so he would look around the room and call a particular person to come up front and lay hands on their head and give them a prophetic utterance about something only they could have known, and God, of course. I saw people laugh, and some cry at what he had expounded to them openly. After about six or eight folks had gone up, the preacher started to scan the room. I was sitting pretty far back and slid down in my seat to line myself up with the person in front of me so that he could not see me. Didn't work.

The Texan with the crooked nose leaned around and looked right at me. "You in the blue jeans who are trying to hide. Could you come up here please?"

Up to that point, I hadn't been fully convinced that this prophet thing was for real. I didn't think it was a hoax, but I believe that it was going to take something quite big to make a real believer out of me. I went up trying to look cool and collected. The man made me stand and face him.

He put both hands on the sides of my head and said these words. "You have traveled for many miles. You are in great distress.

Someone that you have loved has hurt you very much. The Lord shall be your comfort. You shall be an overcomer."

There was much more in that message. I have the tape of it twenty-five years later. He gives a copy of whatever he says to someone. Some people that I met that day had to wait for five years or more for some of what he said to come true. He hit the nail on the head. I needed something specific and persuasive for me to really believe. And I got it. Many lessons would follow that let me know that I would not always be calling the shots on what I needed. God always knows what I need, I really needed to live like I believed that. I was impressed. That man had traveled two thousand miles to Calgary. I had traveled two thousand miles to Calgary. It seemed to be another Divine appointment that I did not know I had.

During the week I had the responsibility of mowing the lawn when it needed it. Sometimes I would go for a long walk. Rose took me on a couple of commuter train rides into town. The C-train made stops all around the city and it was an interesting thing for me to do since I never rode on the inside of a train before. Jumping the train in Bradford seventeen years earlier got me almost killed and I hadn't ridden one since, so this was a real treat, and legal too! Downtown Calgary was very contemporary. Pinkish style sidewalks and wrought-iron décor accented the beautiful store fronts of an outdoor mall. Getting lunch and some ice cream was pure luxury while watching all of the uniquely dressed people doing their shopping. The fashions had always hit the big cities before they ever came to Bradford. It was something that I saw back in Rochester.

One of my favorite times was when Rose took me to the mountains. The kids had gone back east for a part of their summer so it was Rose and I taking in the sights. Banff National Park was about an hour away up in the Rocky Mountains. I had never heard of this breathtaking panorama. The town of Banff itself was nestled at the foot of a snow-capped behemoth of a rock that would not fool me again. I now knew their real size.

Our first task was to take a cable car ride up the side of a steep mountain to the top and have lunch at a restaurant. The parking lot where we loaded all of the people was very hot, about eighty-five degrees. Taking this ride was a little unnerving because like planes, my feet were not touching the ground. The tightly packed group of sightseers made for a little comfort though. Up the mountain we went, higher and higher. I did not think to try to look up to the top before I got into the cable car. Maybe it was because if I had I wouldn't have seen the top. There were clouds and snow up there. We got off of the ride onto a wooded landing. I was glad Rose had made sure that I brought a coat. It still didn't do the trick. I shook and shivered as we watched the wild rams climbing the mountainous rock The snow was flying and the wind blowing as the clouds under us hid the view of the parking lots far below. In the distance we could see a beautiful lake with a train slowly winding its way through the mountains. It is a sight that I have also seen on calendars since.

We packed in a lot of fun and much needed relaxation for me. It was getting near my time to go. I would have to leave a couple days early to make it to the border by Niagara Falls on my way back to the states. I had been appreciative of my cousin's hospitality and caring spirit.

Rose came to me and said, "I talked to the Lord and he wants you to stay longer."

"Oh really?" I said. "You know this talking to the Lord all the time is getting a little funny. So tell me, what did he tell you?"

She continued and was blunt about it. "He wants you to stay another nine weeks."

I wish I could have seen the look on my own face. "Say what? You do know that three weeks is the maximum amount of time that I can stay here, don't you? I told you that myself! They will come and get me if I don't show up at the border with the papers that I signed! Nine more weeks, that's ridiculous! How would I even begin to make request like that after what I went through?"

Rose's attempts to get me settled a bit were futile. I could not remotely imagine even bringing up such a subject not even for a one day extension. "Here's what we'll do," she added. "We will go down to the Immigration Office and tell them that you are here to help me move back to Toronto. They will ask you how much time you need and you tell them nine weeks." (Tim and Rose had finally made that decision to move, it had been up in the air for a while.)

"Rose, I don't think that there is any excuse short of death that would convince anyone to fill this ticket," I added.

She interrupted, "You will stay the whole three months, so let's do it."

Cut to the Immigration Office. Here sits one sweating nervous Indian about to meet his maker. I have never lost the respect and fear of authority, especially when they are in a position to rule my life. I looked around the large room as my cousin just set there smiling.

"What did you get me into?" I whispered. "You know this will never work."

Regardless of the situation that I was in there was still an open-ended faith that kept me wondering, otherwise I wouldn't have done it.

"I think that I will go downstairs and buy a t-shirt that says 'I Love Canada on it,'" I said.

Roses's retort was, "No! Don't even think it! Go ahead, she's calling you."

My head swung around to see a lady looking around for the next person. I had been watching people from all over the world get booted out of the country so to say that I had any real confidence at all was not very accurate. I approached her bench and she asked me how she could help me.

"Ah yes," I said, shaking, "I am here visiting my cousin and she is going to move back to Toronto. I have to leave at the end of three weeks and I need to stay longer to help her."

The nice lady said, "How much longer do you need?"

I hated that question. "Nine weeks, ma'am," I said.

With head in chin, she answered with a question. "Hmmm, nine weeks. How much money do you have?"

I thought she was asking for a bribe. "About one hundred forty dollars and some change, but I don't have it all with me."

The woman seemed to detect my fears and took a compassionate stance. "Where is your cousin, Ronald?"

I looked back at Rose, who was sitting safely at her seat. "She's over there," I said, nodding to get her to come over.

"If you get a note from her stating exactly what you are doing and come back and show me your money you will be able to stay."

I couldn't believe it! Nine more weeks and no border agents coming to throw me out! We went back to the house to get my money and showed it to the lady. Rose wrote the note and I got to stay.

My continued visit in Calgary made it necessary that I would need more than the money that I showed the immigration office. I called Sam back at Bradford and asked him for a little more. While I was on the phone with him, Mom had been coming in the door from work. She asked Sam immediately if it was me and if I wanted to borrow money. It scared him to hear from our mother something that no one had told her. He eventually sent the money and it kept me over till I would get back. My new date to be out of the country was now August 31, 1985.

The rest of the summer saw a lot of walks to the convenience store for "Slurpies," the Canadian version of the American "Slush Puppy." Coke with slushy ice became almost a daily thing during a nice hot nine-week stretch. An occasional visit to the Marlboro mall would keep our legs from getting stiff as well. That was our longest trek that year. On one occasion we ran into a little boy and girl dragging a suitcase through the crowds of shoppers on a busy day.

"Where are you going?" Rose asked.

As the six-year-old girl answered, her eight-year-old brother stopped dragging the suitcase. "We are running away," she answered.

"Really?" said Rose. "And where are you running to?"

The girl shrugged her shoulders. The boy said to his sister, "Let's go."

I jumped in the conversation. "Where are your mother and father? You know that you shouldn't be out here by yourselves, don't you?"

They were both dressed as cowboys and we thought that they had just gotten separated from their mother while shopping. That was not the case. As they were attempting to leave, I interrupted again. "Please show us where you live, will you? We will take you home."

Rose started to get a little upset. "What mother would let their kids really follow through on a the threat to leave, especially at this age! Take us to your Mommy. Let's go!"

The kids responded to gentle firm authority. When we got outside of the mall, they had a bicycle waiting in a rack. We got the bike and went to the car. The kids directed us to their home. Knocking on the door would have awakened a dead person.

Mom came and started the usual, "Where have you kids been?"

Rose let her have it. "You shouldn't let these kids go running around the countryside at their age. What in the world is the matter with you?"

The mother did not become defensive, but could have very easily. "I called the police and they are looking for you two, get in here." Looking at us in embarrassment she finally said thank you and closed the door, apparently not wanting any more of Roses's wrath.

The remainder of the warm days went pretty much as planned. Rest, healing, with a time to reflect on my life up to that point. The time had also had come to start packing for the move back east. The goal was to get to Toronto with plenty of time to unpack before I would come back to the states. It took a couple of days to load the truck. We did most of it ourselves. The heavier furniture was loaded with the help of some church friends. It became quite a sad move for Rose. She had been there for many years, and it was hard to leave everyone. She sold the car and we rode a bus back. My cousin just stared ahead in tears as we pulled out of the station. I knew it all too well.

The trip back went fine, especially with someone else driving. There is something about a bus ride. It is especially difficult to get sleep, at least for me. Of course, again, my favorite seat is the passenger side front. You can see out of the large front windshield at all of the scenery. At night it really doesn't make much difference.

We arrived in Toronto on time and went to the home that Tim had purchased. It was quite a bit suburbia within a mile of Lake Ontario. It would be a ten days stay before my departure. We went to church a couple of times and Rose started to make some new friends. One early evening I went for a long walk down to the lake. I had gotten caught in a little bit of rain. As I watched some large boats being filled with concrete powder, an eerie feeling came over me. Looking to the southeast I became emotional. I knew the other side of the lake was America, but there was something mysterious about the direction that I was looking. It wasn't straight across the lake, it was on an angle to the left. I would eventually find out what that was. Rochester.

The day came for me to leave. Rose would drive me back to Bradford. I had been told by my Aunt Mary that I could come and stay with her for a while till I got on my feet. Having always hated "airport experiences," I hugged the kids and left in my own tears.

It was a really rainy trip back home. After we had gotten across the border, Rose would make the final leg of this journey as my chauffeur while I slept during the downpour. I was awakened by Rose, who had made a wrong turn at Buffalo, and was almost all the way to Rochester instead of Bradford. After we talked about it a minute, we decided to stop and see a friend that I had met during my stay there with Lois. Es was a strange name for a woman, but that is what she is known by. I introduced her to Rose and told her all that had happened over the last few months. I met her and her family in the church that I was helping to build before we had left Rochester.

My anticipation of coming back to Bradford was not a comfortable one. Nothing had really changed between Lois and I and my thoughts of a that knock down drag out fight in court would not leave for quite a while. There wasn't any evidence that it would ever happen, I guess that I was just going by what everybody else was doing. The nice thing was that there wasn't any real property to fight over. We had decided on only one thing and that was to split the bills up the middle.

We made it back to Bradford in good time and I moved in with Aunt Mary. She had been up visiting my cousin Elly back in Rochester, so it was time to make myself at home. Rose stayed one night and left. Leaving was a hard thing to do. Rose had been so kind and caring when I really needed it and this parting would be such a sweet sorrow.

For the next few weeks Aunt Mary and I got along well. We would talk about the family of old. Dad was her brother so it wasn't hard to bring him up. She had a unique cool about her. Regardless of all of the tragedy in our family, she never really became devastated over it. Her pet bird "Reagan" was named after the President. One night she got up out of her chair and grabbed the sheet to drape over the birdcage.

She turned to look at me while straightening out the folds and said, "I've got to put the boss to bed." She laughed and put me into a little tizzy myself. The dishes that I ate off of still had the garage sale stickers on them. It was always calm and peaceful there.

I was able to acquire another bicycle and occasionally drive Aunt Mary's car. Going to the same church that I had left made the trip a little farther, but a way was always made. There was an AA meeting around the corner from my new address so it was quite convenient to walk the two blocks to be with a few folks on a Thursday evening. I met a man there that I had been a casual friend of off and on before Lois and I broke up. Jon Moore had been a staunch AA person and owned a remodeling and maintenance business. He asked me if I would be willing to move in with his family and work for him. I said yes. He lived in Olean, just a half hour away in New York. That fall I would embark on another interesting phase of life.

Up to this point there was just a moving from one place to another. Not for nothing, however, but for real reason. Everything that I did had at least a message of survival in it. Doors were opened and closed. People would come and go. All of my needs were met all of the time. Much of it I had nothing to do with. It just happened. The wind just seemed to blow me as it pleased. I was worried inside where I would ultimately end up because I hadn't been able to get a real sense of finality. Lois and I were technically married and there had been only one contact made during this time of uncertainty. The IRS had made the mistake of mailing our income tax check to her. I called her to ask for my half. She said no and that was it.

To Olean I went. The Moore home was a very large one with his entire family occupying the first floor. His wife Terri had been the woman that Lois started an Al-Anon meeting a few years earlier. There were three children. Daniel, the youngest was a year old. He was able to shove a portable dishwasher around on a shag carpet at a year and a half. His older brother DJ was about twelve with Shannon the sister being ten years old. The dog "Rags" was a nice soft light colored sheepdog.

Upstairs on the second floor was an entire living space for another family. Jon's niece Lisa Warfield had lived in a room there for a while. I eventually got the whole floor to myself. This was going to be interesting. The environment was so different than what I had been in. Mealtimes would have at least the six of us plus any relative that happened to stop in.

The arrangement for my wages were that I would make some money hourly and then pay some of the expenses for food. I was again around people that cared about me and where I was going.

It had been almost a year since Lois had left and she had been waiting to get a divorce only when she found the right man. She insinuated that in a conversation that I had when I called her to find out what she was going to do about the divorce. I finally got the papers to sign. The only catch was that I had to pay. At that point I would have robbed the Pope to get the money. I wanted this over for good. There is this final release that occurs when it is really over. I had heard of this phenomenon, but never experienced it in a relationship. You just know when it is final. It is like sitting down to rest after a long hard race.

My new job was full of things that I liked to do. Some demolition, using saws, drills, hammers, and other hand tools definitely was my cup of tea. The days were long at times. Six days a week and 14 hours a day were not unheard of.

Although the job was good and my new family nothing less than a page right out of Heaven's book, I had a new challenge. Winter was setting in and there was no heat up on the second floor of the house. That presented a problem. I had plenty of cold feet when I was a kid and now it was coming back to haunt me. My bedroom was adjoined to another large room. Actually they were originally a dining room and an adjoining living room. The bed that was in the living room was accompanied by a dresser and a few small odds n' ends. The bathroom was open with no door. I put a sheet in the doorway for any unexpected guests. As the worst part of the winter season had arrived, my room had become very cold. So cold in fact, that you could see your breath. There was no real way to get any heat up there and I was warned about that from the start. Being the inventor that I am it was time to make a way for a little warmth. The next couple of days were spent building a large bubble. With five nine by twelve sheets of window plastic I made the four sides and a ceiling out of strips of wood and the plastic. My large bed was now in the center of what looked like a makeshift clean room for asbestos removal. Aunt Mary gave me an electric heater (one of those that looked like an old fashioned radiator). There was about four feet of space on both sides of the bed. The top was tight against the wall while the bottom plastic draped close to the bed. It was all put together with tape. The seal was finished and now came the test. I brought in the heater and turned it on. I sat on the bed and watched my new home inflate to look like a Jiffy Pop. It just rocked slowly like an air balloon ready for takeoff. Eighty degrees inside and see your breath on the outside. That was my winter. That trip every night to take a bath made it especially good to get back into my bubble. I stayed that way for six months. I did run into a problem one time though. There was a Chinese restaurant across the street. It was a Friday night and I wanted to eat out. I usually didn't want to spend my money eating out if I could help and especially if you had to leave a tip. I ate General Saos chicken that night for the first time. That turned out to be a big mistake. I liked hot food, but I did not remember that I lived in the bubble. To make long story short, when I got up the next morning I had a bad headache. If someone would have lit a match inside that poor excuse for a biosphere you would have heard it in Bejing. I did not go back for that food again.

Jon had gotten a lot of small jobs to keep the workers fairly busy. He finally hit one that was going to last awhile. The family had deep pockets. That was good for us and sometimes not so good. Once in a while the money wants to call the shots just because they have the money not because it is safe or is the right thing to do.

The project was to be called "Hojo's." That was to be the name of the bike shop on the first floor of a four story building. We had gotten the whole job of remodeling every floor from scratch. It was a remodeler's dream, especially in a town the size of Olean. I was asked to go in and assess what it would take to do what the owner's wanted. The second and third floors were twenty four feet wide and ninety eight feet long and had to be made into two apartments each. There was plenty of area to do that. The original use for the building was for a newspaper called the *Olean Evening Herald*. That sign was still on the front of the building and would become the crown jewel for all of our efforts sixteen months later.

The presses had been removed and the floors were almost all original. The offices were still there as well as the rest of the partitions. One of the requests was to find the abandoned elevator shaft. It had been hidden for possibly decades by a wall built on each floor. The cost of upgrading that system obviously would have been too much in any era. Poking around through a wall suspect of hiding the door, I found it. The old scissors type gate became the subject of a lot of controversy. Being on the second floor, I broke all the way through the wall and discovered that the elevator cart itself was stuck between the second and third floor. The nice thing about the owner of the building was that any new revelations about the need for mandatory changes were met always with money and not resistance to change. Although this part of the job was not really included in the estimate it would be added in after the fact.

It was ultimately determined that the entire elevator shaft would be made into a staircase. That meant removing the whole system. We made access to the shaft on all of the floors. Cutting the cables on the fourth floor was easy and the anticipation of the cart crashing into the basement made us feel like little kids again. The cables were removed, all except one. The counterweights were taken off and stored on the fourth floor as well. The last cable was finally cut, and nothing happened. The elevator stayed where it was. It was disappointing, but we began to throw the counterweights on top of the cart. After about six or eight hundred pounds worth had landed on the top of that cart, it broke loose. The cart rambled down the shaft at full speed. The crash was so loud that the office workers in the building next door came running out into the street. This was after we had even told them that it was going to happen. After the dust settled, we looked at the destroyed cart and took three days to cut it apart. New steel stair casing would eventually occupy that space.

I was trusted to draw a rough sketch of the apartment layouts. The final drawings included much of what I had done. Ralph Housnect was the father who had backed his son Timothy in this business. Tim was going to inherit a new bike shop, four apartments and eventual ownership of the property. It was quite a graduation present for a kid that had just left college. Off and on throughout the job there were arguments about how things should be done. The Housnect family was from Batavia, New York, about an hour and a half away. More than once Ralph had to come down and settle a dispute between Jon and Tim. The most remarkable thing about any negotiation was that sometimes it would cost more to do it their way, but it was no problem for them to fork over the money. The family was the owner of a Pepsi distributorship back in Batavia.

The job went quite well considering the occasional spats that would happen. The front of the building was a real challenge. Scaffolding was erected in the winter on a main street. Putting a new face, window casings and all of the trim completely changed the look of that address. The final touch of course was that lettering for the newspaper near the top of the building.

By this time I had worked a lot for Jon. At least during the time that I was with him and his family. One Saturday morning he came upstairs on my day off and asked me if I had one thousand dollars cash. A large building was going to be razed. Louis Marra was selling the rights to his building for forty eight hours.

"We can have anything in the building and sell anything we want to the public. He is over there right now and people lining up to buy things out of the building."

I said, "Let's do it."

We went down the street to the building, which was only three blocks away and looked it over. The structure was to be demolished at about ten o'clock Monday morning. We could have or do whatever we wanted to the contents of the building.

I gave Louis the money and now it was forty six hours straight of hard labor minus the three hours that I had napped on Jon's floor. It got so bad that about three o'clock Monday morning I began to hallucinate. Seeing things that were not there was not good. I had been away from that aspect of life for a few years now, but the one consolation was that I was now sober. Jon and I felt like two kids in a candy store. We set up lighting to work through the nights. Ripping out insulation, lumber, expensive wood doors and trim, gathering some small things that were collectable made up only a portion of what we had saved.

One of my trips home to get something to eat and rest for a bit included a stop to a convenience store in the early hours. I grabbed a rotisserie chicken and ate the whole thing. I ate nothing with it and later got sick three times. We were martyring ourselves to get what we could. After all of that work we only ended up ahead only about two hundred dollars. We lost a lot because the building had to be razed.

Saturday nights in the summer I looked forward to going to the stock car races. I had gone to those events years ago, but stayed away from them after I had gotten married. It became so regular that it was a problem. Maybe it was because I could easily do it alone and I still wanted someone in my life, I'm not sure. I began to keep track of the racers and go on a Friday night if I could make it. Rainouts were tough. Becoming so dependent on this entertainment I once traveled an hour and a half to a race on a Friday night. It had been rained out and I was devastated. Having known this pastor friend for a few months in Olean, I came back to town and went to the church. In tears I had a change of heart about how I would look at going to stock car races for the rest of my life. It was an obsession, something that I could depend on for a little outlet, a little comfort. And when it didn't happen it bothered me. Thirty three years old and I still had a long way to go. At least I was open to change. I would continue to go, but with some semblance of moderation.

One evening, after work, I got cleaned up before dinner. I sat on the edge of the bed and had a difficult time with loneliness. I missed being with a spouse, but I didn't miss the trouble. I still hurt. This time was unusually bad. I dried my eyes and came downstairs for dinner.

Without telling anyone how I was feeling I said in my heart, "Lord, I need to know that you are around, give a sign. Please, I'm hurting."

I sat down to eat and said the usual blessing. As I reached for some food, Rags the sheepdog came over and lay across my feet for the first time ever. I knew I was a sheep and God had prevailed. I was comforted and went through the evening in a better space.

Thanksgiving that year saw the usual festivities in Olean. People from everywhere would come to the annual Christmas lighting that always happened the day after Thanksgiving. The Mayor gives a speech in the public square after dark and then throws a switch. The lights on all of the streets come on and then there is a parade. This was the year that we had been working on Hojo's. Since we had a key to get in the building, I thought that this was a good opportunity to get the best seat in the house for the lighting ceremony. Up on the roof of four stories gave me a bird's eye view of the throngs of people and the lights when they came on. I was leaning over the edge of the roof when people started pointing up at me. I remember someone telling me that they didn't want people on the roofs, but never heard why. I found out when the police signaled me to come down. Even though this was still only 1985 the remembrance of the sniper from thirteen years earlier made things a little different. He had killed people from the roof of a school.

Jon and I liked to eat our food. He had stopped at this place about twenty miles south of Buffalo to eat chicken wings. He came home and told me about it. A few months later I would try it. What made this place so special in Jon's eyes was that the wings were the hottest that he ever had. I liked hot food so I thought I would give it a whirl. This would be my last time.

I walked into Earl's Drive-in about one in the afternoon. I said, "I hear that you have the hottest wings around, I'd like to try them."

It was a hot Saturday and my plans were to go the races that night. I sat down to eat the first wings. After about six of them, my scalp and face were sweating, I was blowing my nose and my eyes were watering.

"Give me another dozen," I said.

After being halfway through the next twelve I saw the cooks laughing at me. It was an open kitchen and they could see the customers' reactions to anything interesting. And this was interesting. They were enjoying watching me go through my regimen of napkins, tears and discomfort. They decided to send a message to me through the waitress. If I would eat a third dozen they would pay for them.

I, of course, said, "Lets' do it."

I ate the third dozen. I did not have any real problem until I had to get up to go wash my hands. Having to hold the counter all the way to the men's room was necessary to steady myself. The hot sauce made it a little difficult to navigate. I never have had them that hot before nor since. The real trial came the next day. Did you ever see the space shuttle during liftoff? That was my incentive not to get food that hot again.

The reason that I was in the area of Earl's Drive-in was that I was in Buffalo doing a demonstration of a new invention at a large flea market on Walden Avenue. A few months earlier I came up with this idea to help kids to ride their bicycles. I watched many youngsters jump off of pieces of wood or curbs. They definitely wanted to get up in the air. After many drawings I came up with a ramp. It was only four inches high on the front, but it guaranteed not to flip. The edges were beveled to make that work. After I started saving a little money, I bought a radial arm saw. I also had to set up shop somewhere. Apparently against city code I set up my work area in the dining room next to where I was staying. That would require keeping all of the dust away from my living quarters. For about a week straight I ended up making twenty five units. All of them were sanded, finished and painted.

I had purchased a Pinto wagon to get around. It was a car that I had thoroughly trusted because Lois's had been a good car for us. I went to Buffalo with all twenty-five ramps. In one of my AA meetings I met a man who had a son that was an up and coming trick rider on BMX bicycles. He gave him permission to get into his rider's outfit and test my ramp as a promotional thing at the flea market. The fact that he was ranked number four in the world at the time didn't hurt any. His photo was in a lot of magazines.

My booth was actually in part of an extension of the rear of my car. Kids would flock to my area and watch my young buddy jump off the ramps. I was there to sell as well as advertise. Every parent that had a child there would pull them away from my booth. I did not sell one. On my way home one afternoon was when I stopped at the eatery for those hot wings.

This would not be my only attempt to market my invention. After filing a patent I would do a search for a company that might be interested in manufacturing and selling the ramp. After sending a few out around the country I discovered a company in California that was interested. They were going to take a couple of weeks or so to decide what to do. They had already had a copy of the "Ramp," so I was convinced that I should make further progress myself in the process. After consulting with an attorney I formed a corporation, hired the lawyer, an accountant, and a volunteer secretary. The accountant would do my dealing with the company. A few weeks went by and finally the company called. Their liability insurance company would not insure the ramp, therefore, they could not buy it. I thought it was strange because they had manufactured skateboards. The argument was that it "got the rider up in the air." Whatever the case was I felt a big loss. I was now convinced by that point that I should quit the ramp project. If the liability was an issue for them it would be for everybody else. I dissolved the corporation and got rid of everybody. Being the President of "Auxano Corporation" for a couple of months had become my day in the sun. That corporate name meant "increase" in the Hebrew language. The increase would have to wait.

It seemed as though I had to always have a project of some sort. During the racing season at the Mckean County fairgrounds, (the place that I had got knocked out) they were advertising a final race for that year. It was to be a two hundred lap enduro in which anyone could enter. You had to follow the guidelines and enter your car. I had always wanted to drive a racing car. Having messed up my life earlier, I felt that not all of the opportunities would be lost just because I was a late bloomer.

Finding and buying an old car was not hard. I paid two hundred fifty dollars for a 1968 Olds Cutlass. It was about the same car that I had back in the mid '70s, the Olds 442. The body style had changed a lot, but it still had a good motor. I drove the car from Bradford to where I was living in Olean. At Jon's house I removed all of the glass, lights and any metal sticking out like door handles, mirrors, etc. Gutting out the interior and removing the exhaust pretty much was all I could do. I painted the car with a brush and readied everything for the next phase. What I didn't plan on was that I now had to get the car back to Bradford. That was where my mechanic would install the roll bars and bash plates on the doors. Without telling him the problem, I did tell him that the car would be there at a certain time. Driving the car over wasn't a problem, but now all of the glass was gone and the exhaust sounded like a jet. So, I did what I do best, improvise. It was a fall evening after dark. The moon was out. That would be my guiding light. Jumping in the car, I went down a main street in Olean and took the short way up over rock city Hill to Bradford. With no lights and no windshield I weathered the cold night air blasting against my face. Oncoming traffic appeared to be startled when a dark loud figure appeared out of nowhere traveling in the opposite direction. The moon did work well because there was no other lights as I traveled through the winding mountainous roads. I got to Bradford and the pit crew got the rest of the car ready.

The race day was here and it was a glorious autumn day. I did not know or even think that I needed to learn another lesson or perhaps have another go around at an old one. I guess all of the excitement and the fact that now I was racing my own car demanded all of my attention.

Doing It Again—
An Exodus

On race day we were asked to make sure that all things were in order for the final inspection. I was nervous again at this place. Looking out through the fence at the crowd again gave me the willies. Somehow I wanted to be in the stands watching all of this rather than driving a car. That momentary thought was quickly dispelled by the announcement; "Gentlemen, start your engines." The forty plus cars sounded as loud as the other races I had attended. It was time to get excited and I was not disappointed. My blood was now rushing at hyper speed as I couldn't wait to get going. After a couple of laps to get warmed up the green flag went down. We were off! I got around the track once without being hit by anyone. Going into the second turn at the beginning of lap two, I stalled. All of this preparation and I have to now sit on the infield for seventy five frustrating laps. What made it worse was while I was watching everyone else go by, a wayward car slams into me without a warning. I have always hated the blindsided thing. I want to see it coming. The hit did not cause much damage, but it startled me mainly because of the noise it made. My mechanic came out, opened the hood up during that 75th lap racebreak and ran a screwdriver through the gas filter.

The car started and I said; "You drive this thing, I'm done!"

He gladly got into the car. He was a racer for many years who always had the "fever." The locally famous Jimmy Haag takes the wheel of car and off he went. One lap around the track and the right front wheel comes off. It was evident to me that I would not be a race driver. My place was with a hot dog and popcorn in the stands. After that race I gave the car away and was glad I did.

Sunday's in Olean after lunchtime seemed to be lonely. Going to church was all right, and certainly eating a good meal, but the quiet streets and with no one really to share my time with became the norm for too many of the days of rest after a good week of work. Taking a long walk downtown and just watching the pigeons just didn't cut it. I see that happen in movies a lot, but in real life it is different. My relationship with DJ was probably the best. He had made a commitment to God and would sometimes come to church with me. We would talk about the things that involved the unseen world. Jon had given a lot of support in many ways, but he displayed some apprehensions on some points. Playing a game or two on a rainy day would take the edge off of the loneliness once in a while. I didn't travel to Bradford as much as I could have. Being only twenty miles away made it handy, but somehow I just didn't see the town in the same light as I once did. No doubt it was because of the circumstances.

Early in 1987 I saw the jobs dwindling with Jon's company. There were not a lot of prospects for the immediate future. That fact made Jon do the thing he didn't want to. Lay me off. I did see that coming and preparations were made, at least mentally. Unemployment compensation was applied for and I was denied the claim. I made enough money to qualify, but their case was that because I was an officer in a corporation I couldn't collect. For the next thirteen weeks I pleaded my case. After two hearings, a long written presentation, and the disappearance of my savings, I finally won. The nice thing about such inconveniences is that you get it all at once. I eventually told the family that I needed to move back to Bradford and decide what I wanted to do. There was some kind of relief after I moved back in with Aunt Mary. There was this drumbeat off in the distance in my mind that Rochester was where I really wanted to be. I couldn't do anything about it at the time, but it would be a continuing thought over the next few months.

One day I had gotten a phone call while at Mary's. It was Pastor Phil.

"Ron, my mother had a stroke in Pittsburgh and I need to go down there, could you take the service tomorrow? Do you have a message on your heart?"

I think my heart stopped. "Why, yes, I always do, Phil." I said. "I will do it."

I bid him Godspeed and did what any normal first time preacher would do. At least I thought I would. This was a Saturday afternoon. It was a very nice day for the races. I immediately abandoned the idea of even going. I then got out my Bible and study materials, plopped down in the lounge chair prepared to "hear from God." Sitting for five minutes, then ten minutes, I waited. Nothing. No message, not a peep. I had just told my pastor that I had a message and I didn't. The reason that I thought I did was because I always do. I now was dumbfounded with nothing. And then the small still voice came. "Go to the races." What? How could this be? I was abstaining from anything that would be an interference of a good sermon and I hear this? *It must be from the devil,* I thought. I waited to hear it again and I did. "Go to the races." What was happening became readily obvious to me. I was calling the shots as to how things were going to be. I set the stage with good intentions and I was being shown that God wanted to be in control. Complete control. Not taking even a note, I went to my usual Saturday night entertainment. With a little notebook in my shirt pocket and my food in my hands I waited even in the stands for something that I could hang my hat on to give to the people. Even taking out that little notebook after I ate didn't cut it. I was to not work a moment on anything. I accepted that and had a good night.

The next morning I got up early and studied for the message. After about an hour and a half I was ready. The sermon was on Hebrews 12:1. It had to with setting aside the things that are causing us problems. My problem at the moment was even when something looks Godly, it may not be. I remembered the quote from Nancy. "The road to Hell is paved with good intentions." Unless there is an urgency right now, guessing instead of being still, is a big no-no. This experience was absolutely a faith builder as well. I can recall when Phil had misplaced his Bible and the sermon minutes before it was time to preach. I had the joy of watching someone else learn a little bit about this principle. The service went off as planned.

Aunt Mary needed her house painted and I needed a little break from paying the rent one of the months. So, in keeping with the tradition of unorthodox things such as price tags on the dishes, I painted the house bright blue. It was a blinding color. You could not mistake this house for any other in the neighborhood.

The itch to move on came in the form of a few tests. I began to apply for work around the Bradford area. Although the longing in my heart was steadily increasing to go back to Rochester, I did not want to make a move until I really knew it was right. I had to work and eat and did not want to over analyze something that should only be a valid common sense decision.

After a couple of applications here and there it was time. I traveled to Olean to start getting the *Democrat* and *Chronicle* from Rochester. That was as far south as that newspaper would come. It was nice to start looking at the employment pages that I was once familiar with. My last application for work around home was actually forty minutes away in Portville, New York. It was a good job as a foreman at a lumber mill. This would be the final test. I would travel to Rochester and make applications there. I ended up with two interviews. The most promising jobs that fit me were maintenance positions at apartment complexes. I ended up being interviewed first at a nice place that had some stipulations that I could not meet. I would have a three-month waiting period before I could have my own apartment which would be actually construed as a raise. It was still the end of winter and I couldn't afford to live anywhere until the probationary period was up. The cost of living was a little different up there anyway. That made my choice for a job very easy. Either I would get the place to live with the job or I couldn't do it. I knew that people did that, I just had to find the right one.

My second trip to Rochester did not happen until the end of May when I had been waiting to hear about the job in Portville. That application would the last one around Bradford. The interview in Rochester was at a large complex back in Greece, the suburb that Lois and I had lived. The apartments were called Cedar Court Village. The well-landscaped community of 360 apartments made this quite a challenge just from its sheer size alone. The manager of the property met me and gave me basically some of the same news that I had heard at the other place. There would not be an apartment coming with this job and not any probationary period either. The person who took the position would have to wait until someone else left or a position opened up. By then it was warm out and I was thinking a lot of things. The man, George Vogt had given me a high rating based on my interview and wanted to hire me. That was tough. I told him I would go back home and think about what I was going to do.

"I have this application in at a lumber mill as a foreman," I said. "I need to hear from them what their answer is. If it is a no I will call you."

I had to do something. My test would come at the hands of a silent phone over the next week. This would be my sign that it was time to move. But just how I didn't know.

I called George and he hired me over the phone The solution to the problem as to where I would live would have to be solved after I got there. In one way it didn't make any sense to move to a big city and start a job without a place to live, but then I had taken bigger risks than that in my life. And much of that was without even considering God for a moment.

Arriving in Rochester for my second tenure was one of the most wonderful experiences that I ever had. By then I knew it was right. I was introduced to the crew and took a look at what I just signed on to. My Pinto wagon had all of my worldly possessions in it. George pulled me aside and told me that if I wanted to I could stay in my car at the maintenance shop. I gladly accepted. For the next several weeks that is exactly what I would do. Every weekend I traveled back to Bradford to stay at Mom's and then go to the races on Saturday. After church and then lunch on Sunday I would make the two and a half -hour trip back in my mobile apartment. My showers after work were taken at the YMCA at two bucks a pop. Needless to say that my paycheck was just enough to keep me afloat. My meals obviously were all eaten out. Cousin Elly took me in for a week at her house to help me out, but that was only a slice out of the pie. I couldn't stay too long. Mooching with me had its ends. I never want to feel like a burden to anyone so it was my decision to go back to the shop.

My responsibilities at my new job were many. George and the crew made sure that whatever I didn't know, they would teach me. I had gotten by, fixing a washer or dryer only a couple of times, but never some of the other things that I would undertake. There were ninety buildings with four apartments in each building. That made for a large volume of appliances alone. There were 360 each of air conditioners, stoves, refrigerators, garbage disposals, and dishwashers. Then came the ninety washers and ninety dryers. That was all a part from the regular building maintenance with painting rooms, carpet cleaning, replacing screens, windows and so forth. Work would never end. The guys on the crew were stellar. Every one of them was a nice person to be around. Cliff was the oldest. He was originally from Long Island and said that back in the '60s he was a drummer from a famous band called the Blues Image. I never found his name on any of the albums yet, but I'm still looking. He was the crudest of the bunch. As soon as he found out that I was a Christian he made sure that he would comment on things in such a way that should have "gotten my goat." He and his wife Linda were already living onsite. Tom Luke was the superintendent. For a guy in his position he was a very adult twenty something. He knew the project inside and out. I liked to make him laugh because he was so loud.

My first days on the job were a little trying, at least in my mind. Pleasing those who hired me was important and the fact that these guys were special made it easier on one hand, but on the other, I felt a little pressure not to disappoint.

The arrangement was that all of the maintenance crew would be on call every third week for seven days. Of course I couldn't be simply because I lived in my car. The apartment for those who lived there came with a price.

I learned a lot of tricks as many of the calls from the tenants presented something new once in awhile. I should have kept a personal log of some of the wild requests that we responded to. Everyone was patient, both my co-workers and tenants alike. Even Donna who worked in the office had a good demeanor.

The stay in my car became a burden. Summer was at its best and so was the heat. What complicated things was the fact that the maintenance shop was near a swamp. The mosquitoes would swarm my car. I had two choices, heat stroke or hundreds of little bites. After a couple of nights like that Tom let me fabricate screens on my windows out of the stock in the shop. It gave me some relief. Even with the windows down the temperatures were unbearable and even a skinny mosquito could squeeze through the screen and nail me in the night.

I would read my Bible using the dome light in the car. To this day I have a blood spatter on one of the pages after I had tweeted a mosquito that had bitten me and landed on the good book. One of the nights would bring about another change in my circumstances. The temperature was about ninety degrees and I had tried to fall asleep. It may have been hotter in my car, but my body was starting to shut down. Before I could get out of the car, I started to get dizzy and very disoriented. The heat was catching up to me. I had to go for a walk and try to cool off. It was unbearable. Getting out of the car and using the door handle to steady myself I looked around at the quiet swamp. The only noises came from the peepers on the water and the sound of the air conditioners scattered throughout the property. That was a relief so close yet so far.

Standing outside of the car for a few minutes I gained a little sanity. Locking the doors, I went for a walk. The trip around the complex was eight tenths of a mile and that was quite accurate because many residents had been using it for their daily walk. It had been one of the hottest nights of the year and taxing a sleepless night with exercise at 3:30 in the morning would make for a more difficult day at work.

Eight o'clock came around and the usual gathering of the guys at the maintenance shop happened on time. One of the irritants that they had provided for me was the radio station that blared from the moment any of the workers opened up shop, including George. WCMF was a rock station that had a couple of disc jockeys that had unusually foul mouths as well as some of the guests that they had on the air. I never had heard some of the things that these people said on the radio. Living in such a small town my whole life kept me away from a lot of these types of things. It was a rude awakening.

George brought us donuts to jumpstart our hectic schedule. He did that very often. He also did something else that day. My boss pulled me aside and told me that I could sack out in an empty apartment until it was rented out. Then I would just move to another one. I was elated. No more sleepless nights! No more mosquitoes! Although it would be an occasional move from one place to another, so what? I was in Heaven. Not a peep came from me about how my night went. Common sense said that it would be hot, but the problems that I was really having no one knew. I had been rescued. The foam cushion in my Pinto had been my bed for many weeks and now I could move it to a place that had air conditioning.

Somewhere about that time I had invited Mom to come and see me. Never really wanting to stay anywhere overnight, her trip would be just for the day. I was excited to show her what a nice place this was. This visit would be a memorable one because it would be the only one ever. I took her on a tour of the walkways and landscaping between the buildings. She was a shopper, so I took Mom to the Marketplace Mall. She had never seen anything like it before. The perimeter of that place was well over a mile. The enormity of the property was overwhelming. So overwhelming in fact that when she got back in my car she got sick. That unfortunate accident became so complicated as it all went down the vent on the dashboard in my car. I guess that was part of the influence that she wouldn't come to Rochester again. At least that is what she says to this day.

Finding a new church wasn't hard. I had met quite a few people during my first stay in the "Lilac City," so named after the abundance of lilacs that grew each spring up around Mt. Hope in central Rochester. For the first few months I went to a church that I had heard about in Brockport, just a half an hour from Cedar Court. My visits there were mainly during the week and maybe once in a while on a Sunday night because the weekend trips to Mom's took me to my home church in Bradford on Sunday mornings. I made a few friends at Brockport and one family in particular had an unusual amount of suffering. Losses of loved ones and other personal tragedies commanded a lot of attention from the other people in the church. I took to liking that family mainly because I could relate and understand some of their plight. Having lunch or dinner at their home once in a while was interesting. The beautiful house was almost the same design that Lois and I had picked out if we would ever have hit the big time. John Zagata and his wife Sue were wonderful hosts and the lives that they led were a true example of how everyone should live. Peace and harmony within their family became a good model that I could never forget.

After several months on the job, it was heading into the fall season and I knew winter would be coming before you knew it. Surprises in my life came in all ways, both good and bad. This time would be a pleasant one. George pulled me aside once more and announced that I would be getting a promotion. My job would now be onsite, which meant that I could pick out any apartment that I wanted and it would be my free of any charges. My actual payment for such a perk would come in the form of being on call that every third week, but that certainly wouldn't faze me after what I had been through. By that time I had learned some of the ropes about the problems that tenants would have that required a response from the man on call.

I would take about two weeks to decide where I would live. It was a nice thing to be able to take my time and be so picky. Waiting for the right apartment to open up was not a long one. I wanted one that faced north and south. It had to be an upper for security reasons. It also had to be the one that was over the boiler room and near the basketball court. After fifteen days of waiting, I found 760 apartment D open. It was perfect. A new paint job, new carpeting and most importantly a new air conditioner. I installed it myself. It was going out of the season for cooling the rooms, but I would have the cat's meow for next year.

I moved all of my stuff into the apartment. The foam cushion would still be my bed for awhile. My neighbors were good ones. I would have a lot of conversations with each of them, some for hours at a time. Furniture would come easy for me. I had first shot at just about anything that was going to be for sale or thrown out. The inside scoop in the office gave me the big edge on who was going to move out and when. Having been in all of their apartments and getting to know them a little made it fertile ground for harvesting the best bed, sofa, or anything else that I needed. And that is just what I got. Some of the standards that people have still escapes me. I had heard that people threw out good things, but never really saw it for myself. It was another thing that just didn't happen in Bradford. I bought a sofa, loveseat, and bed with a matching dresser that was fit for a king. I paid twenty-five dollars for the robin egg blue living room set. After having it for two years I sold it for two hundred dollars. My own apartment started to take shape. Curtains, bathroom accessories, and kitchen utensils now occupied empty spaces. I was starting to live.

One of my new friends was the cleaning lady. Sandy Miller had her own business and making sure that each apartment was spotless after a tenant moved out was sometimes a very big job. With people moving in and out of 360 apartments, she and her sister were busy women. What made the job harder at times was that some people left their apartments in a real mess. Even if there was money coming out of the security deposit, it would be no consolation if you have to scrub your tail off around the oven or the bathtub. My job was shampooing the carpet, painting the rooms if they needed it, and replacing any incidentals such as new burner pans on the stove or fixing leaky faucets. We eventually became a team making good time on our chores not bumping into each other all of the time. I would end up going to Sandy's place for a lot of visits. Her two daughters made quite a life for this single mother. The youngest one became quite unruly both at home and with other people. The older girl was the good quiet one while her sister the flip side. The police had to play a role more than once in their young lives. The constant bickering between Sandy and her ex-husband only fueled the matters all too often. The usual manipulations and dishonesty between many divorced couples was something that I wasn't grateful about. At least it wasn't happening to me.

I began to feel a lot more at ease with my life. Meeting new people and liking my job seemed give me a fresh outlook on things. After things go a certain way for so long, when they do change it takes a while to get settled into that new environment.

Some of my service calls both on duty and on call were sometimes very interesting and sometimes dangerous. I got a call to go to an apartment to look over and secure a mess that the FBI had just made. Although this apartment complex was one of the better ones around you still had your troublemakers. And they would come in all forms. The apartment above Sandy's (she lived onsite as well)had been apparently been used by a Jamaican to house the drug dealer. No one had known that he was living this double life except the Feds, who had been watching him for a long time. The FBI agents entered through the door by using an ax. That door was splintered from top to bottom. Then they went into all of the rooms and turned over everything. The bottoms of the all of the living room furniture and the beds were cut up looking for drugs. The drawers and cupboard contents were emptied out. There had been no warning for this job and did not catch him for some time.

I had been somewhat dormant in many ways regarding any real trials that would create a problem for me. I guess that even though I believed that this job was the best ever it still would not always be a walk in the park. Winter was here and the snow would fly. The maintenance crew had the responsibility of plowing and keeping all of the sidewalks clear. We would start at four or five in the morning and have to work all day into the evening to only start it all over again. Being on call 24/7 for your appointed week on top of that made you really think that the apartment was not a freebie. Replacing broken hot water tanks and cleaning up water soaked apartments happened often enough to appreciate your two week hiatus from that pager. Just during the day at times when everyone was working made for quite a test.

Quite a while after I moved into my place I found out that a storage area came with it. I had either forgotten or was not told about it. I really wouldn't have had any use for one anyway, but my visits to other tenants to cut a lock or clean it made me think to ask if I had one. I went in my area and found a stack of magazines. There were a 128 of them from the 1930s through the 1960s. Most of them were "Look" and "The Saturday Evening Post." I had always been around antiques and wondered if there would be any real value to these. In this stack of old periodicals was one issue that had gotten my attention. Since quite a few of them had Norman Rockwell's art on the front cover, I guess that is what initially made me think "dollar signs." This one painting was that of a young serviceman who had been sleeping on a high post bed. His trousers were hanging up on one of the dowels at the bottom while his duffle bag lay on the floor next to him. He was a serviceman home on leave or whatever. The interesting aspect of this issue was that it was dated December 6, 1941, the day before Pearl Harbor. I went to Tom and asked him if those magazines were legitimately mine. He said that I could keep them. The former tenant had been long gone. I ended up selling them all to an antique dealer for one hundred fifty dollars. I had a strong inclination to hold back that one magazine, but ultimately gave him all.

One of my more dangerous calls involved responding to a request from a tenant to fix an air conditioner the following summer. I had enjoyed a good season without anyone seriously rattling my cage so apparently it was time to move on to some more changes on the inside. The outside had been taken care of in stellar fashion for a while. Going to the upper apartment with my tools I came to a man that I had had a few conversations with off and on. He was about fifty-five and held a job as an armed security guard. In all of my talks with him he had always been friendly. Today would be different.

The air conditioner in 280C was blowing lukewarm air. I could tell that the man had been drinking as I reached for my pointed thermometer and slid it into the coils of the unit.

"How ya been doin," I would ask, making light conversation.

"Pretty good. I finally got a day off and its too hot," he answered.

I personally did not like the smell of booze on his breath. I pulled the thermometer out of the coils and said, "Looks like it may need cleaned."

He would take the probe out of my hand and hold it a couple of inches away from the coils and then tell me, "This is how you hold it, you don't stick it all the way in, you have to hold it out here like this, see?"

I said "No…the fact that it is shaped like this and the fact that I was taught this way is really how you do it."

He then snapped at me. With an angry tone in his voice, alcohol on his breath and a revolver on the table, I had a flashback. The last time that I had been in a situation like this was when Dad would come home and commence the same treatment. This man was in trouble and he didn't know it. I stared at him for a moment and stopped short of picking up and throwing him out of the second story window.

I calmly said to him, "I think that I had better leave now. Someone else will be over to take care of the problem."

He did not argue or resist any of what I had said. I just left and went back to the shop and told George, "You had better take care of that man's service call. He was drunk and he almost lost his life."

My boss never really knew how mad I had gotten. I learned something about myself that day. The hurt and torment that had become part of my life many years earlier was not fully gone. The challenge to rise up and now defend myself would be accented by the fact that I knew I wasn't the sniveling little runt that could be knocked around any more. But the biggest thing that happened that day was not that I had my chain jerked, but that there was some control in my life that I had never had before. And it was time to get a little stronger in the values that I was preaching to everybody else. Things like true forgiveness. I was shaking like a leaf and in a cold sweat by the time I had told George and it would take several hours for me to really settle down. I eventually would talk to the man again only on better terms. The issue was never brought up again by either one of us, and I came away with something that no one would be able to take. When you exit away an ordeal like that it is a feeling like you had just gotten sick and now you are starting to get better.

Once in a while the trouble would not confront me directly, but may come through the trials of another person. I was more or less an observer and once in a while a little more. Sandy had called me one day after her ex-boyfriend had threatened to come over and "just wanted to talk to her." Obviously she didn't want that, so she included the police in her quest for help. He had been simply refusing to listen to her pleas to break off the relationship and did what he wanted to. Today there would be a life changing event for him. When I got to Sandy's apartment he had gone to his car to take off. She had been in tears and I didn't know what had happened. As I approached the car a cop drove up and jumped out. Steve was supposed to be arrested and getting behind the wheel complicated things. The officer ran over to the vehicle and tried to stop Steve from turning on the ignition. As the two wrestled I stood a few feet away and watched.

The officer glanced at me. "Help," he said as he was attempting to pull the man's hands from the steering wheel.

I shoved myself by the cop and grabbed the key in the steering column and broke it off. "How's that?" I answered.

I stepped back a second and then deduced that he could not get Steve away from the car. A second time I reached in and grabbed Steve and pulled with a great force and out he came. He complained of an injured wrist, but I didn't ever really found out what had happened. He never called or saw Sandy again.

My work relationships with the guys got to a fairly good place, but there was a limit too because I would not go along with some of the swearing and innuendo that made their life seem so fun. Cliff and I got into a conversation about unidentified flying objects. He asked me if I believed in them and I simply told him that UFO's are exactly that. They are objects that are flying and simply have not been identified. The problem with the whole subject is that many people fill in the blanks and try to label what that thing was and pass it off to the rest of us. We are supposed to be convinced that the object has been "Identified." But, "Yes," I told him, "I believe that many flying objects have not been assigned a reason for what they really are." I started to tell him the story that I had created one when I was a kid. In my heart I knew it was not something that I was to repeat to anyone, at least at the time, but foolishly I did.

It was very cold, I said. A below zero night back in Pennsylvania. I was about thirteen years old and by then had some knowledge of the "flying saucers." It was exciting to do what so many other folks were doing back then. Painting a picture as to what had been sighted here and there around the world, had become almost a pastime for me. Certainly an incident with by cousin and bigfoot along the creek didn't help the cause any when it came to the hype of the unknown. The wind had been stilled and I knew that once in a while hot air balloons would be the cause for an occasional concern for air traffic controllers. The height and slow speed of those kinds of objects made it quite easy to identify. But that wouldn't deter me from getting in on the action. I felt that since there wasn't any real thing like that going on around Bradford I maybe should create one. After getting my hands on two or three plastic dry cleaning bags and a crosspiece for a kite, I fashioned a hot air balloon. The light thin material meant to just keep dust and dirt off of the clothes made it a good source of material. The balsa wood from the kite did not add much weight as only a few strips of scotch tape was applied. In the center of the crosspiece I stapled a small chicken pot pie tin and put three tablespoons of "Sterno" canned heating fuel in the center. After lighting the gelled material, the balloon filled up with hot air and began to rise. It went out of sight, but I never really got a rise out of the guys at the airport twelve miles away. At the time that I was telling Cliff this story I got an ill feeling in the pit of my stomach. To many people, telling a story like that is totally harmless. I guess in my own mind I felt that way too, but in my conscience it certainly didn't feel that way.

After the tale of my UFO escapade we went home from work. It was a beautiful summer evening and all was going along pretty much as it should. I had my usual quiet time, watched a few minutes of the eleven o'clock news and went to bed. About two hours later I got up to use the bathroom and started to return and lay down. Walking past the small kitchen, I glanced out the window facing the south. What appeared to at first an aircraft coming in for a landing started to make no sense. I knew where the airport was and even though the planes routinely would swing out over the lake, they didn't move as slow as this thing and also did not ever appear as though they were burning. I wiped my eyes to watch it as it was headed my way. There was a bright yellow-orange flame burning brightly as it moved about ten or fifteen miles per hour toward the lake. I got dressed and called the police. They hadn't gotten any reports yet. The UFO center wanted the description and no one had contacted them either by this point. After the phone calls I wanted to know where this object was going to come down. Now I am wide awake and getting in my car. Its elevation seemed to be only about a couple of hundred feet and I had to follow it. Driving and keeping it in sight for about four minutes finally I lost it. It had traveled over the swamp all the way down to the lake and I never knew where it went. By that time the police had gotten a few calls, but no one could claim to know what it was. Needless to say I went back to bed with the lights on. Repeating that story the next day did not keep me from learning my lesson about certain things.

Lunchtime generally saw all of the guys go to their apartments and the shop most often had gotten locked up for about forty-five minutes. Break time at ten in the morning however brought us all together for an update on the maintenance issues or an occasional story from an experience with one of the tenants. I was walking into the shop area and I noticed a couple of the guys jumping around as if they were dodging something. The entrance was actually a three car wide drop down doorway. Cliff was sitting on the picnic table and squirting the workers with a cleaning fluid from a bottle with a hand pump similar to one that uses Windex. As I walked past Cliff, he pointed the bottle nozzle toward me.

I had believed that cleaning fluid in your eyes would not be a good thing so I looked at Cliff and said, "Don't do it."

Cliff put on a very devious grin and let it loose. It sprayed up and down the front of my uniform. I got very angry and walked over to a five-gallon pail of the stuff. Ripping off the top, I jumped up on the picnic table in front of him and gave him my response. He was soaked from head to toe. I didn't care about anything else other than getting him back. Fortunately his eyes were not affected, but as much fluid as there was there should have been. He was becoming angry, but it subsided when George came and interrupted what could have gotten worse. Cliff and I never became enemies over that, but to the contrary we became better friends.

One of the tenants called in to have a bathtub unplugged. I went over to her apartment and met a nice young woman who kept her place in pristine condition. Her boyfriend had recently lost his life driving off of the pier a few months earlier. She was still smarting and was a tender soul that wanted answers to mental and spiritual questions. While I sat on the edge of the tub turning a wrench she became very friendly in asking where I had come from and ultimately shared her feeling about certain subjects like God, relationships, etc. I listened to her and got into quite a long discussion about various possibilities for answers to her curiosities. We became friends and once in a while I would go to her place and help her with a little reassurance for her life. She had a back injury that was getting worse and the pain was on the increase. A helping hand for an hour or two was gladly welcomed as she would wince from the pain for months. She eventually would recover and move away.

My mode of transportation needed a change. I was tired of the Pinto and wanted something bigger. I sold the car to a couple who had been in the business of asbestos abatement. They were making a lot of money. During those years asbestos was the big thing. The federal and state governments were initiating many mandates to make sure that the removal of this dangerous substance was expedited everywhere. After a long talk with this couple I decided that I wanted to learn more about it. I bought a bigger car. A full sized Ford LTD station wagon. It was loaded, rode smooth and was well worth the eight hundred dollars that I paid for it. Obviously it could not compete with the Pinto in gas mileage, but the spacious ride was like a boat.

I signed up for a course to become certified as an Asbestos Abatement Worker. The new laws required extensive knowledge of the law and asbestos' physical affects on the human body. It was scarier than what I had ever thought. I had played around that stuff as a kid and like so many other people I never knew that it was harmful.

The school for my training would come at the hands of an extension of Niagara Community College in Lockport, New York about an hour away. I scheduled my vacation time in the summer so that I would not miss work. After passing the workers course I would go to the next level and get certified to become a State Inspector. An attorney from the infamous Love Canal Case, an endocrinologist, and several other professionals taught the various aspects of asbestos awareness. The demand for workers was so great that even while I was sitting in the classroom I had gotten a call from a contractor who wanted to hire me. Answering the call, I told the man that I couldn't do it. The money was nowhere near what I had heard people were getting. I would wait it out. The last and final phase of learning about this new threat would be to become an architect assistant. This would command a higher dollar and I wanted it. My vacation time was up and the schedule for me did not work. I would have to stay at the inspector level. I never did anything with any of it. Chalk it up to just gaining a little experience in another field.

That summer was going along just fine. The pool on the property was full every day and it was only walking distance from my own apartment. Getting up late Saturday morning, going to the pool and then on to the races down in Canadaigua became the regular thing that second summer. I felt like I was living like a king. The races were forty-five minutes away and these cars were faster than the one's back home so my visits back to Bradford became a little more infrequent. That was the summer of 1988.

One evening I got a call from Mom. "Junior, your grandmother died yesterday. Do you think that you can go up and sort of represent the family?"

In some degree of shock I responded with a "yes." The event caused me to reflect a lot on my childhood and once again, Dad. He had been Grandma's favorite son and it certainly bore out at his funeral when she cried out loud over his body. Now that my reprieve from all of the former deaths was over it was time to get back in the swing of things. Grandma had been two things. Firstly, she had been the matriarch of the family for all of my life and before. When she died, the glue that would keep what was left of any unity in the family would be gone. Hardly anyone called Mom after Dad's death and now this would seal that fate. Maybe there was still a secret disdain for my Mom being "white" I never knew, but I do know that unless Dad was around she would be out of the picture.

I drove up to the reservation and stayed at Grandma's house. Staying upstairs where Dad had slept as a kid was not eerie, but comforting. A walk down to the lake and looking out across the water made me feel like a real Indian. The sound of an occasional little boat going out for fish still echoes in my mind today.

Dad's side of the family had all gathered in the main room of the house into the late evening. With only the small third room added on, it didn't take much to fill up the space that was home to the family leader for a better part of her eighty-four years. The way to the second floor, which was actually more of a loft, was by a ladder that was on a very steep angle. There were steps on it instead of just rungs. I happened to be climbing up the steps when Uncle Merlin asked me a very interesting question.

With everyone in the room looking on he said, "Junior, is there anything that you know of in the Bible that you would like read at the service tomorrow?"

I stopped and thought for only a second. "Yes," I answered, "there is. Do you want me to read it to you?"

With almost one accord they all approved. When I went to my room I had wondered why I was asked. I hadn't talked with anyone at all about my beliefs. Maybe Rose had said something. Whatever the case was I now was being called to at least contribute something for Grandma. I got out my Bible and came back partway down the stairs. I sat and read to a captive audience these words:

Who can find a virtuous woman? For her price is far above rubies. The heart of her husband doth safely trust her, so that he shall have no need of spoil. She will do him good, and not evil, all the days of her life. She seeketh wool, and flax, and worketh willingly with her hands. She is like the merchants' ships; she bringeth her food from afar. She riseth while it is yet night, and giveth food to her household, and a portion to her maidens. She considereth a field, and buyeth it; with the fruit of her hands she planteth a vineyard. She girdeth her loins with strength, and strengtheneth her arms. She perceiveth that her merchandise is good; her lamp goeth not out by night. She layeth her hands to the spindle, and her hands hold the distaff. She stretcheth out her hand to the poor; yea, she reacheth forth her hands to the needy. She is not afraid of the snow for her household; for all her household are clothed with scarlet. She maketh herself coverings of tapestry; her clothing is silk and purple. Her husband is known in the gates, when he sitteth among the elders in the land. She maketh fine linen, and selleth it, and delivereth girdles unto the merchant. Strength and honor are her clothing, and she shall rejoice in time to come. She openeth her mouth with wisdom, and in her tongue is the law of kindness. She looketh well to the ways of her household, and eateth not the bread of idleness. Her children rise up and call her blessed; her husband also, and he praiseth her. Many daughters have done virtuously, but thou excellest them all. Favor is deceitful, and beauty is vain, but a woman who feareth the Lord, she shall be praised. Give her the fruit of her hands and let her own works praise her in the gates.

This scripture from Psalms 31 had been on my mind for some time and I knew immediately what I was carrying it for. Rather for whom. My uncles and aunts were now wiping tears off of their cheeks. It was an overwhelming consensus that this was the choice. I closed my Bible and turned to start back up the stairs.

"Junior?"

I heard my name, then stopped and sat. "Yes?" I said.

Merlin asked. "Will you do the service tomorrow? The Indian woman pastor will do a service in the Indian language after you do one in English. Do you think that you can do that?"

"Whatever you want," I responded. "I will do it. Thank you for asking."

That night I lay awake pondering my new role in all of this. The odor of that room from the exposed wood hadn't changed in all of my life and if there were any example of spiritual, mental, and emotional mix this was it. Another beautiful hurt. A sweet sorrow. It was worth the price to pay to be here. I could have been long gone by now and would have been only a byword, just a fading memory like so many others, but I am granted another moment of life in the sun.

She's Gone
and So Am I

The next morning was accented by cloudy skies announcing the passing of a great woman so dearly loved. In my mind was a conglomeration of many different thoughts. I usually like to pick what I think about, but today would be a blast from the past. I was hurting from my grandmother's death, afraid to preach at her funeral, and just happy to be alive. It's too bad that the uncomfortable feelings aren't smoothed out by the good ones.

The middle-sized church was packed out. There were people standing everywhere. The side yards and on the sidewalk belonged to those who could only remain still to be able to hear what was going to be said from the altar. To say that I was nervous is an understatement. At least I had the scriptures to read from and maybe jump start something more. As I got up to speak there was Grandma right in front of me. Having never been in this position before and especially being one of my own made it all the more baffling. Most if not all of the funerals up to that point of my life had been done by people other than a family member. I guess uncle Merlin was living up to his billing of being a little tough under the skin.

Looking out at the throngs of people I noticed a group of individuals that looked like they did not have much. I believed that many of them were perhaps the men that I was told about throughout the years. Grandma had kept her doors open to anyone who needed a place to stay, food, or on occasion a little money. She had been appreciated by some, used by others. It appeared as though there were folks from both groups waiting for some message of consolation to ease the pain of conscience. I began by thanking everyone for being there. I commented on my own experiences from my childhood on with grandma. Then I read Psalms 31 and made it clear that she believed that there was more than this life in store for us. It wasn't too late to get squared up with God and with each other. It was quite apparent that many who had been on the using side of Grandma felt guilty and needed to know that all was not lost just because she was no longer with us. My talk took about twenty minutes and then the Indian woman Pastor did the other service. Of course I did not understand a word she said. Dad's attempts to teach me the language were almost nil. I think that he did not want to spoil the secrecy he had within the family.

After the services concluded Merlin came to me and asked me if I would ride to the cemetery in the hearse. I obliged and took my seat in the passenger side front of course. There were a lot of firsts that day. This was another one. Never had I seen the inside of one of these vehicles before, but I was getting broke in with my own Grandmother. I suppose doing her funeral service wasn't enough.

After waiting a couple of minutes for the driver he finally came and sat beside me. "Hi, I'm Pastor Smith," he said. "I own this business. It was good to hear you. Are you a Christian?"

Reaching out to shake his hand, I said "Yes, I am a Christian. The name is Ronald Knott Jr. My father came from here."

The man started the engine and paused a moment. "I am a Baptist, what are you?"

Looking straight ahead and answering; "Pentecostal," I didn't like any conversation that accented differences in denomination.

Beginning to wonder why he asked, he began to explain, "We have been trying for years to get in here to the Indian people. You are our way in. The Jehovah's Witnesses are doing a good job of making converts here, but we haven't been able to. Do you think you can be a part of our effort?"

I was a little impressed, but I knew that there had been some pushiness going on. "I don't think so," I answered. "I have my hands full back in the states, but I appreciate the thought. Thank you anyway."

We drove to the cemetery and I had decided to leave after some of the people got there. That part of the ceremony was done in total Indian fashion and I wanted no part of it, so I hugged a few people and went home.

It was a relief to be back in the saddle again. At least I wasn't as confused about all of this like I was when Dad died. The whole event did produce some lasting affect however. It reminds me of jet lag. Your mind and spirit continue on in a busy fashion long after the trip has ended.

Back on the job, we used to watch George wash his boat all the time. He was a clean freak. Everyone, including his wife Phyllis, agreed that scrubbing that water craft was a little excessive. He gave us indications that he believed it somewhat himself. He was also a volunteer fireman. At any given moment he would just up and dart off to the firehouse down the road. Car accidents, fires, anything that required his services he was always there. This day would be different. On the other side of the swamp was Russell Station, a coal burning facility for creating electric power owned by Rochester Gas and Electric. There had been an accident there. A man had lost his legs getting run over by a train. George told us that man was totally conscious while everything was going on.

Another call came at night when we were not working. A car had slid into a large water pipe and pinned the man inside the vehicle for two hours. He lost his legs as well. A pickup truck had tried to miss him and went airborne for over a hundred feet landing on the hood of another car traveling down another road. It was almost inconceivable how it all happened. This part of George's life seemed to be exciting to him.

I wondered just how much, so I asked him. "George, what is it that you like most about being in the fire department?"

The fifty plus year old man answered, "I like going through the intersections with the red light on."

I just shook my head.

One of the tenants needed some work done in their lower apartment. David and Minnie Coy were a couple that I had not experienced before. He was white, and she was black. David eventually told me that the success rate for this combination was exactly the opposite of the husband being black and the wife being white. Almost 100% success for his type of relationship while the contrary did not fare so well. They were a nice Christian family. Dave wasn't quite there yet, but there were people praying for him. Their children were two girls with a boy on the way. Holly and Crystal were to fine examples of well-behaved children. We became friends, as they would invite me over for dinner and lunch once in awhile. It was rather convenient, having this arrangement since I just lived a few buildings over.

I had started a Bible study in my place on Monday evenings. For five months I met every week with a few people from church as well another one or two from the complex. I chose Mondays in the summer to get the most committed to come. The day right after a church day and all of the fun going on in the warmer months would sort out those who were more serious about growing, at least that was my thinking at the time. I never was without at least one person who would come over. At times, my buddy Frank from church would stop over for at least some good conversation about the principles of life itself. I would be getting to know Frank and his family better later on. I also had a news letter ministry for two years. As a message would come to me I would write it down and have it typed up by another tenant and send it out to a couple of dozen people around the world. I had gotten reports that it turned up in places that I did not send it.

One of the new friends that I met would come through an introduction by Dave and Minnie. They had been attending another church and invited a woman that they knew for a while over to dinner. They had planned out the introduction for me. I did not like meeting people that way. Minnie had never struck me as a matchmaker. The woman's name was Judy Kinz. She was a delightful person to be around, but I would not try to make anything of it right away.

Throughout the two and a half years at Cedar Court I met a lot of different people. On occasion one of those families would be members of the church that I was attending at the time. Debi Lamb was the piano player at a small congregation that I was a part of. She also had a beautiful voice to match the sounds that would come from the accompanying keyboard. She was enduring a very tough life as a single mother and dealing with an ex-husband who liked to make a lot of trouble for her. Our friendship would take me on a trip once in a while to pick up or drop off the kids at his house. She felt that she needed protection once in a while. The children were all small. The three of them ranged in ages from five to ten. Two girls and a boy made Debi a very busy Mom. I had taken her to a Christmas Eve candlelight service and it was one of the most peaceful nights that I ever had.

The pastor of the church we were going to was a woman. Cheri Brandt had started the small congregation and was meeting in the Moose Club on Sunday mornings. Once in a while the place would smell like booze and the men who cleaned it sometimes showed a little conviction when it wasn't done right. Once in a while we go to Cheri and her husband Ted's for a dinner or a Bible study.

A couple of months into this part of my life I finally met someone that I could care about. She was a Hispanic girl that had been introduced to me by a member of another church. In the church world there seemed to be a lot of moving around from one place to another so meeting new people was not a problem, even if you were the one who remained still. Zoriada Crespo had a good attitude toward life and a fine character to match. Her brothers and sisters were all Christian. Mom and Dad were some more folks who were being prayed for. She was living with her sister and brother in-law at the time I had met her. It was in a small house on the other side of the swamp near Russell Station. We fell in love and I had to be around her as much as I could. There were a couple of problems though. Not with her, but me. I did not have the type of job that would benefit her moving out of where she was at and that became a little issue with her. I never saw the real need to be a doctor or lawyer to be able to support a family. Although she accepted what I had really chosen she also felt that there should be something in my life with more stability. She was earning good money in the educational system and justifiably did not want to be the ultimate breadwinner. Sori, as she was called, became willing to accept where I was at. The second problem was my attitude. When the pressure was really on about something, I reacted with a sour taste. She did not like that and shouldn't. I was wrong. After a few months of dinners, walks, and talks, we decided that the answer to most of our frustrations was to get married. So we set a date.

For the next few months preparations were made. Announcements, who would do the wedding, even the Crescent Beach Hotel was rented for the occasion. That was the best environment on a sunny day for anyone to get married. The white wrought iron gazebo next to the high class restaurant was used by many tying the knot. The closer the wedding got the more pressure there seemed to be. What appeared to be a resolution to all of our problems actually presented an uneasiness in Sori's spirit. Finally she couldn't take it any more and called it all off. I had felt some of that pressure, but wrote it off as something that came with the territory. At the last minute of what I thought would be a new life together it was over. The deposit on the hotel was lost, all of the other work done to prepare would be written off as another chapter in this life. We broke up and stayed that way. Sometime later she went on to marry someone else.

One of things that that I always look at in my own life is the question; "What could I have done differently? What are my motives for what I do?" The real problems began right after I had met Sori. She didn't agree that a woman was supposed to be a pastor. I disagreed with her and although we would come to terms on some of these issues there would be some buried reservations. That would eventually become an issue for me as well, but not until trouble would make me think that. During the year before my engagement to Sori, I endured perhaps the most heart wrenching loss of my life, even more than Martha, Dad, or Lois. I had run into the pastor that I once met a few years earlier. Paul Colosi was the man who had given me the check for four hundred fifty dollars when Lois and I were really down.

He said to me, "Ron, I would like you to consider applying for the role of associate pastor at our church. Would you do that? Take a week or two to think about it."

Having attended his church for awhile I was elated. Preaching to five hundred strong was a dream of mine. It would have been nice having the right motives about such things.

After a week of thinking about it I said yes. I was supposed to write three papers. One each on Grace, the Holy Spirit, and Love. I did so and turned the papers in. Paul had told me that there was another candidate in the running and that his father in-law would be on the Church Board that picked the man for the position. I didn't give that much thought. God would put in who he wanted in. There would be an interview scheduled for Saturday morning in one week and another one in the afternoon on the following Saturday. Mine would be the second week. I was with a friend of mine from church at the time. He had to pick up some building materials from a lumber yard for the church. But first he had to stop at the church and get some information from the pastor. I knew that the interview for the other guy was in progress at the time and did not want to go in. My buddy, Floyd believed that the meeting was over and went in. He came back out and signaled me to come in. The meeting was over and I went in the foyer. Paul was sweeping the stairs while he was talking to Floyd. He was his usual friendly self as I said hello. Of course I wouldn't be asking any questions about how the interview went. We talked for a few minutes and we would see each other in church the next morning. Floyd and I went and took care of a few things and then I went home. The next morning I awoke to a phone call.

"Is this Ronald Knott?" the voice said.

"Yes," I answered.

"I am John Riley, one of the board members for the church. I was asked to call and inform you that we have selected the person for the role of associate pastor for the church. We did not want you to hear it for the first time when we announced it to the congregation this morning."

"Thank you for telling me," I said, slowly putting the phone down. I had to think about what I had just heard. Was it Saturday or really Sunday? Was my interview not even going to happen? After I got that straight it wasn't hard to figure out that Paul knew while I was standing there talking to him in the foyer and he said not a word. The feeling of abandonment, rejection, Paul being a traitor, Paul not having enough of something to tell me in the first place was a sample of what was going on in my mind. I got dressed for the big day.

Arriving in church on time was never a problem for me, but even going there today was a big one. I tried to make sense of it all. None of it added up to any sort of wisdom. The announcement was made and Frank Hilbert was installed to much applause as the new associate pastor. We went through the normal service routine and I went to lunch, but not alone. Having a midday meal with a woman I had talked out of suicide the night before made my landing an lot easier. But, for the next forty eight hours I experienced a pain that no one could reach. Taking a walk around the apartment complex kept me in a state of total numbness. The same questions kept going over and over in my mind. But the prevailing perception was that God knew what he was doing. I was very glad on one hand that I did not cause this trouble and very sorry that someone else had. I traveled to Bradford the following weekend and Pastor Phil said that this definitely "was from the Lord." It would take many months for me to digest this trial. And I would never question anyone about it and have believed that I wasn't supposed to.

In the spring of that year the feared sale of Cedar Court would take place. We didn't know how things were going to go with the new owners, but if George's conversations with the secretary in New York City were any indications, it would be rough sailing. I had never seen him that angry before. Milton Klein was the primary investor and the man to lead the group that would slash all of the good things that had been created over many years. Running on a skeleton crew. Doing more with less. All the while putting up a cosmetic affect to draw more people. We saw it as an effort to actually make things bad and try to make it look better. The sale occurred in March and the demands began almost immediately.

While the friction was mounting between the management and the owners, I just went about my business. The apartments were abuzz about any possible changes that would occur for them as well. My visits to tenants to take care of their needs didn't change much.

There was one thing happening though that had gotten my attention. Debi Lamb had been living across the hall from a family that I had gotten to know quite well. A father and son lived there for a few years and aspired to the drinking and gambling world. The Dad did not drink, but the son did as they both would play the ponies and have card parties. What bothered me was that Debi was letting the son Tony bring a case of beer into her apartment and gamble on her table. Not too long after I discovered that I told her about it.

"You are playing with fire, not only by sending the wrong message about what is right, but are exposing the kids to it,." I said scoldingly.

She listened, but seemed to write it off as a tool to show him that he wasn't being rejected by the love of God. As the weeks went on it got worse. She started to have a relationship with him. I had inquired what Cheri the pastor had thought about it and based on what I started to see in that situation I wasn't surprised that she not only endorsed it, but promoted it.

As weeks turned into months I endured a little pain and a little frustration with the Debi thing. Staying away from their apartments was easy because now Tony was hired to be a maintenance man. Now he could do all of their fix-its. When I heard that they had finally gotten engaged I couldn't believe it. After several warnings about marrying "outside the faith," Debi Lamb became the wife of Tony Burgess. She had claimed that he had made a commitment to the Lord and changed, but I knew better. It was a botched attempt to accomplish God knows what. My worst fears were yet to come.

We had gotten word after a quiet weekend that there was an accident. Debi, Tony, and the three kids were driving to a relative out of the state and Tony fell asleep at the wheel. The car swerved and hit an abuttment on the passenger side where Debi was sitting. By that time Tony grabbed her and pulled her to himself. The hit was so violent that his right arm was injured from the far-reaching force of the enbankment coming into the vehicle. When the car had come to a rest, the two girls in the rear suffered only minor injuries. Debi was at death's door with massive internal injuries. Her ten-year-old son, who had been lying at her feet, was killed instantly. Sometimes I hate being right, but I never tell people "I told you so." God knows how often I haven't listened to wise counsel myself and I paid for it with long-term suffering. Debi would recover after months of rehab. They would divorce and go their own ways.

By the end of the summer the investment group from New York was doing its damage to the crew. Just the attitude that Milton's assistant had made for a few people want to quit. The maintenance guys were getting fed up with the demands and started leaving. It wasn't too hard to find a job like that in the area and they knew it.

After replacing some of the crew we took another blow. Tom wouldn't take it anymore either and so he left. I got promoted to the superintendent's position. It seemed as though there was a lot more responsibility than I thought. Even the unforeseen circumstances would visit me and keep me in my place. No one had to remind me of my newfound position, life would meet me halfway…head on.

One of my first calls after I was promoted was to escort the marshal to an apartment where he and his crew would forcibly remove all of the furniture and possessions. When we got there I knocked on the door. "Hello, anybody home?" We could hear a baby crying and no one would answer the door. I had with me the bolt cutters, and after we pried open the door I cut the chain lock on the inside. It was protocol not to break the door down for fear of injuring anyone who may be near it on the inside. We walked in and there stood a young lady with a new baby in her arms. I hated that. The marshal spoke kindly to her. He had been doing this for over twenty five years.

"We know that you are not at fault here, ma'am. Where is your boyfriend?"

With a subdued face she answered. "I don't know, but he should be back this afternoon."

The marshal asked her to get her coat and go wait in her car. It was cool outside and she would only be in the way if she stayed. The crew who worked with this man were all Christians. And so was the marshal. The most intriguing thing about him was that he had two things going for him in his life that were not easy to acquire. The first one was that he would not carry a gun. In the business that he was in he should have, but trusted that all would go well with his soul. The second was his claim to not to ever of had a fight with his wife in over thirty-four years of marriage. When he told me that he knew that I would question it. They had "disagreements, but never a fight," he said.

A short time later I would be playing a game of basketball outside of my apartment on the court. The surface had just been replaced and everyone wanted to get in on a game. There were a couple of visitors there who had been guests of some tenants across the way. One of them was a girl who had obviously played the game before. About twenty-five years old and a little stocky I had learned very quickly after I had moved to Rochester not to sell any one short of anything.

Good players come in all shapes and sizes and she was no exception. After a few plays she fell down. She had gone up in the air to shoot a basket and came down wrong on her foot, twisting her ankle badly. The ambulance took her away. It would be almost three years later before I would find out that it would not be the last that we would hear from her.

My duties got more and more tough. I had helped hire a painting contractor, which basically consisted of himself, and an occasional helper for the bigger jobs. What impressed me most about him, was his calm demeanor and the fact that he said he was Christian. He would come and paint an apartment before any new occupancy, but I would inspect it first. Once in a while he would be in the rooms at the same time Sandy was cleaning the appliances. While she did her best to time things a little differently there were instances when the rush demanded a tight squeezed corporate effort. I had been told by Sandy on a couple of occasions that she was being approached by "Paul the painting man" in the form of sexual innuendo. I wanted to make sure that there was clear evidence that something was going on so I told her to "wait for one more time." That time came and it was a doozy. He had physically pushed himself against her into the bathroom sink. She came and got me immediately. I went back to the apartment where they had been working and I asked him to set down his roller. I then got in his face as angry as ever. So angry that I had scared Sandy. After making him apologize to her he pleaded with me not to tell his wife. I had no thoughts of doing anything like that, but made it clear that the thing that he had better take care of was the claim of his relationship with God as well as the other "obvious problem." After his tears had gained a little mercy, he stayed a couple weeks while longer and left the complex.

Despite all of this trouble that other people were having I felt that this was still the place to work. It wasn't what it once was, but things hadn't really discouraged me yet. Finally George could take it no longer and gave his notice. He had been contemplating going into business with an old friend and I guess with all of the pressures going on at the time he "saw an out." For the next two weeks I would now learn some of the duties of the manager. Donna, the secretary, would assist in the effort and even when I see her many years later she still refers to that position as hers. She was the last of the original crew that had been there many years. I now was carrying the helm of many positions and the new owners loved it. Taking advantage of people quitting would become a opportunity that would be seized by many companies not to replace or at least be slow about replenishing the work force.

The only time that I had ever gotten anyone mad at me was for something quite stupid. A new hire that was a treasure hunter was talking to me about some of the prime spots that he felt was holding silver or gold. Most of it was legend, but there were some places that still produce a coin or two. What got his goat was when I would not tell him the location of that rock back in Pennsylvania that I believed had millions of dollars worth of gold coins under it. Lois and walked away from that for good only after an intense search. After I told "Walt" the story he wanted to know why, "if you aren't going after it why don't you tell me?" Simply put, I wouldn't tell him and he got mad. To this day fifteen years later he still brings it up when I see him.

One of my weekly chores was to collect all of the quarters in the coin boxes on the washers and dryers. It would take the entire day. I would envy Tom when he used to do it, but I didn't know how much a small bucket of quarters weighed. They were heavy! Even in the best weather it was work. It was during one of my collection days that I was asked to lie about how much money we were paying Sandy to clean the rooms. The group in New York wanted to take the next step into what I thought was not only immoral, but illegal. When that request came in I continued to deliver the checks to Sandy and was not yet put into a position to deal with that. One of the new maintenance men that we had hired a couple of months earlier had been living in Phoenix, Arizona. He had tried to convince me that it was the place to work and live. Originally from Rochester, he had moved out there and told us many stories about the abundance of work. He was planning on going back out in the near future. He had planted some seeds in my mind earlier, but I had buried my head in Cedar Court.

Shortly after I was asked to lie, it was apparent to me that it was better to leave than to stay and be dishonest. In my mind the southwest began to take on a better look all the time. I would ask "Big John" about the prospects in Phoenix and he gave me some leads. I knew a friend that had moved out there a year or so earlier. Chuck and Theresa wanted to get away from the main stream of influence in their own families. Not that they were bad, they just needed a change. Sometimes I had wanted to know things that seemed to be obvious to others. My time was coming.

I called Chuck and arranged to stay at their place in Phoenix. After a few calls I got a couple of interviews. Even though I hated flying I went to Arizona by plane. Having not seen that part of the state before would be rather exciting. Camping out in the southwest rim with the guys sixteen years earlier didn't give me much of a real view of that area. When I arrived, they took me to dinner. Their home was a very nice apartment that was all southwest. The stucco building, the palm trees, and warm sun was quite a contrast with the early weeks of November back east.

My first interview went well and they wanted to hire me if I would come back. Some of the conditions weren't so attractive, so I just said, "I'll think about it." That job was close to a church that I wanted to attend. The second interview was the one that went the best. I would get my apartment and a salary in a company that had a good reputation in the community. The people who had interviewed me at P.B. Bell were the kind of folks that anyone would want to be around. The place where I would live and the conditions were acceptable. I said, "I'll take it." I was now off and running to open another chapter in my busy ever changing life.

On to Loneliness

The preparation for moving to Arizona was really complicated by owning or transporting a lot of things. I never really owned much and what I did have could easily be sorted out and kept, sold, or given away. My large Ford had served me well and now it was time to get something that had less mileage on it as well maybe getting more miles per gallon. That big boat did cost a little more to operate, but I never really went much farther than Mom's anyway. I put an ad in the paper and got immediate responses. One guy came and looked it over and asked a lot of questions.

He said, "I have few places to go yet and I may be back." In my mind that was a statement that everyone used, including myself. I didn't expect to see him again.

After a few hours of meeting interested parties, my man did come back. He looked at the car again and without trying to talk me down a penny he made the simple announcement, "I'll take it. I'm going to take it for one reason, because you told me everything that was wrong with it. Most people don't do that. I don't like surprises." He gave me the eight hundred dollars and left with the car. I got exactly what I had paid for it. It didn't take long for me to get another one. An elderly couple sold me a 1982 Olds Cutlass Supreme station wagon. It was in almost mint shape and had less miles on it.

The last two weeks at Cedar Court were rather uneventful. I said my goodbyes and drove to Mom's for Thanksgiving. I would stay there for the night until after the holiday meal and continue on to Phoenix. That departure was a little difficult emotionally. She had given me some extra maps and wanted me to call her from every place that I could during my travel across the country. My goal was to drive straight through, but I would have to stop and rest once for three hours. I brought a cooler with milk and cereal. Passing trucks while I was pouring milk into the bowl on my lap was not the smartest thing that I had done although maybe it was! Not stopping for any trips to the restroom and staying awake became just a mere habit. My car would get filled up with gas again every three hundred miles. I would use the bathroom only when I needed the gas. Making it to Flagstaff, Arizona, took thirty six hours, including three hours sleep for the two thousand mile stint. I averaged fifty-two and a half miles per hour non-stop. Calling Mom was no problem, as her and Sam would be watching on a map of their own where I was at when I called. All day and all night they faithfully stayed awake with me.

I pulled into Phoenix and drove straight to Orangewood Apartments on East Thomas Road in Tempe, a southern part of the city. Unloading my car was not a big job. I was grateful to have only a few things. Watching all of the tenants back at Cedar Court load and unload those big trucks full of furniture did not make me very envious.

After an hour or so of moving things into my apartment, I took a walk around the property. Stopping at the laundry facilities I went in to talk to the lady who was the attendant. It turns out that she was from a small town outside of Rochester.

"I'm from Holley, New York," she said.

"Really, I'm just moving here from Greece. Small world isn't it?" I answered.

We talked awhile about how we had come to move so far away from home. I never really got to know her although she had asked me later on to deliver a message to her family.

I checked in with my new employer and they would assign me a position down in Mesa, about thirty minutes away. My first assignment was a maintenance man groundskeeper at a beautiful apartment complex that was very different from what I had experienced. They were spotless inside and out. Stucco facing, expertly designed landscaping and two swimming pools that needed maintaining in the winter months was a real change.

If I were pressed to nail down any problems that I was having with this change it would be obvious. This would be my first Christmas away from Bradford. All of my life I had enjoyed the presence of my kin for the holiday that I aspire to the most. Next to Thanksgiving it would be hard. Harder than I thought.

The people that I would be working with were especially nice. That was a trend in my life. There would be good and kind folks wherever I went. My boss Barb at age fifty-three had been through a few trials of her own. She was married only a few years earlier after coming from a violent relationship. Enjoying the new life made her someone that anyone would like. Mike and Bill were sort of a Frick and Frack. I had walked into a quaint little clique as they seemed to be a compatible crew. One of my first jobs was to paint the inside of the office loft. It would take almost a week. Located on two floors was the main office and one of the model apartments on the second floor. The model was immaculate, something that I would have lived in, in a second.

My relationship with my new friends became a good one. We treated each other with respect and dignity. Any one of us could be sent to any chore at any time and there was not a lot of complaining about it. We were quite a team from the onset. Leniency during the lunch hours was one of my favorite perks. I would go next door in a plaza to Bacha's Grocery and eat fried chicken almost every day. Since I am a slow eater that was a good benefit. Cutting the grass and treating the pools as we neared Christmas started to wear on me more. I began to get lonelier by the day. Christmas tree lights around cactuses and no snow just didn't make the grade. To take the edge off a bit it was mandatory to come into work on one of the nights before Christmas day and go caroling around the apartment complex. I had never done anything like that before and there was something about it that I didn't want to do. Going from one dwelling to another singing at the top of our lungs we would read off of a song sheet. People would come out and watch us, then applaud. It was interesting, but not really fun. I was still carrying a shy streak and afraid to let a little line out about myself.

I had been going to that church a few miles from where I ended up living. Phoenix First Assembly was a congregation of 4,500 members and sometimes more than that would show up on Sunday morning. I had never been to a church that large before and the staff of eleven full time pastors had their work cut out for them. They boasted the largest bus ministry in the country. When I had first visited there I thought that the parking lot holding all of those buses was just occupied by visitors from elsewhere. Tommy Barnett was the senior pastor and quite a good one. I recall a message that he gave mentioning the origin of the vision that he had for the church. Starting out in a small building that attracted two hundred people almost immediately, they had to move from place to place until they ended up with the present nine million dollar building. At the time, a one and a half million dollar teen center was being built.

What made it all interesting was a comment that Tommy made in which he said, "We will never have a large bank account." The reference was to spending on the Lord's work and not hoarding.

Sunday night services were accompanied by a couple of ongoing ministries. Out the back of the building would be a long line of people coming for two things, a haircut and a meal. There would be several members of the congregation cutting hair in the hallway and many more serving the hot meals to folks who were less unfortunate. You can't forget those things.

I acquired a new friend back at the apartment. A friendly cat used to come around my place. I knew where he had lived, only a couple of doors down. I didn't have much to offer him other than a small bowl of milk, but maybe he was just acting like a dog coming back for more. I would invite him in and once in awhile he would stay for the night. Since I slept on the floor with my foam cushion it would be convenient for him to be next to me. On occasion he would sit on the vanity and patiently watch me shave.

One night I was watching the television about eight o'clock and I heard what sounded like a helicopter. During the day I knew that the military would test the new Apache choppers that were made just outside the city, but this sounded loud and sustained. I went out the door onto the sidewalk and a blinding light hit me in the face. Shielding my eyes from the helicopter's spotlight, I was able to see a police officer down on one knee with a gun. My first thought was,

Brother, what have I done now? The cop wasn't really facing me, but I went to try and see what was going on.

Before I had gotten too far, the officer yelled to me. "Go back in your home, we are trying to corner an escaped convict."

That message didn't take long to sink in. I withdrew back into my apartment and found out that the man had murdered someone and skipped out of jail. They caught him and the community was safe again.

One of my evenings out was to Sun Devil Stadium for the State High School football championship game. I hadn't been to a venue like that for many years and it was refreshing to attend a function like that without being messed up.

The businesses in my neighborhood were teeming with people from all over. "Snowbirds" was the term used to describe the people that would come to that area from up north in the winter and I would meet quite a few of them in the local mall. One small group of shops was called the "Borgata." I had heard about this place, but it was really a sight to behold. Dresses went for over ten thousand dollars. To eat lunch there I would have to be very picky. Rubbing elbows with people whose clothes on their back were worth ten times more than my car was intriguing. Watching the couples look over art, jewelry and the latest fashions made me ponder a lot of things. What am I going to end up doing? What does he do for a living? Would I want to ever live like that? I was of course content to be where I was, at least the overall acceptance that I couldn't afford some of the things that I was beholding at the moment. However, there was this growing yearning to be back home for Christmas. That seemed to be more of an attraction than a distraction.

One Sunday morning in church there would be an announcement that a box would be sitting on the altar with a bunch of names in it. Written on small slips of paper would be individuals that could be visited in nursing homes for Christmas. It was advised to bring that person a small gift. It came at a perfect time. Maybe sharing this Christmas with someone who had literally no one else in their life would help my own loneliness go away. I have been always called on the real intent of my heart and this occasion would not be exempt. I drew a man's name out of the box. It gave a couple of circumstances about his life. He was only sixty four and had no family to visit him.

Early physical problems caused this man to be confined to a nursing home and apparently he was depressed and lonely himself.

I bought a gift and paid the man a visit. He was certainly grateful that anyone cared. We had a small chat about where he and I had come from in our lives. The future wasn't discussed and I was glad. Mine seemed better than his, although I had doubts about how my life was going to go. It was being clouded at the moment by contemplating reversing my decision to make Arizona my home. I didn't tell him that, of course. I would shake his hand and leave. My attempt to feel better was vain. The man's seemingly hopeless situation could not dispel my own concern to be with family and friends again. I went home to the cat and had a talk.

It was a good thing that I was on a probationary period with my employer. After the company Christmas party I made a decision to leave. The founder of P.B. Bell and all of the other supporting cast could not be better to work for and were rivaled only by the original working crew at Cedar Court.

My boss was a little sad about it. She explained that she knew something was going on with me. I gave my notice and agreed to stay through the New Year. Packing again was not a chore. I had decided that Arizona was a nice place to visit, but not live, at least for me.

On my way to work every day I could look over across the valley and see Superstition Mountain. Until I had moved there I thought that the use of that name was fictional. I never knew that the mysterious setting in the Hardy Boys novels was a real place. This landmark would be a perpetual reminder of my short residency in the "Valley of the Sun."

One last hurrah for me would be a New Year's party at an AA convention. I hadn't really been going to any meetings since the church days started, but the people around that atmosphere was something that I needed at the time. I don't know if it was a deep calling to the times past in my life or what, all I knew was that just being among those people at that time helped me.

My last day at work was a Friday. I got my final check and went back to the apartment to pick up my things. One of the last items had been packed and obviously all of the anticipation of driving back to New York during the rush hour made me forget something. I did a final walkthrough of my place to make sure it was completely empty.

The front door had been open the whole time. I turned to head toward the front door one last time and there he sat in the middle of the living room. The cat looked around at the empty space and then stared up at me. He knew. I picked him up and explained one last time what I was doing. That was hard to do. Any prison movies where I see a man with a mouse or something else as a pet or friend reminds me of that cat. I would take him outside and say goodbye forever.

My next stop would be the bank. I would close my account and start my two thousand mile trek back home. I tore away my check from the stub. After handing the signed check to the teller she gave me the cash and as I was counting it she was cashing my stub and I didn't notice that she gave me twice the amount on the check. She really did cash the stub too! In all of the confusion I recounted the money when I got to the car. There was twice the amount that I should have and I went back to tell her. She was the happiest teller around. She apologized and said that she would have had to pay it out of her own pocket if the books didn't add up after her shift. She was well along in her pregnancy and that could have made a lot of unneeded stress. I finally got in the car and headed north.

Tail Between My Legs

Coming back to Rochester was not as a time oriented job as the trip out. I could take my time. My first stop would be an hour away at a Kentucky Fried Chicken. That initial sixty minutes was punctuated by an unforgiving mass of drivers that were anxious to get home after a week's worth of work. After dinner it was drive till I couldn't drive anymore. By then it was dark and the farther away from the city I got the more the traveling throngs would thin. Driving most of that night, I was able to grab a four hour sleep in which I would wake up to a freezing car in a rest area. There was much to think about on my way back. The usual pressure to drive with cereal on my lap wasn't there and I wasn't watching the clock every minute. I began to wonder what I was going to do. There wasn't really any trepidation about it. I again just knew what I "wasn't" going to do. Live in Arizona. My second night saw me stopping at an all night café in Powhatan, Indiana. This pint-sized town was named after the Indian who apparently was the father of Pocahontas. The people in that diner had been out on the town for a while and some of them were a little bit loud and rowdy. My order of bacon and eggs was hitting the spot, but I did keep one eye out for trouble. All went well and I continued on the final leg of the trip.

I arrived back in Rochester in one piece. Getting a hold of my friend Frank made it easier for the question of where I was going to stay. He had invited me to stay at his place with him and his wife Kay. While I would look around for a final place to land, they made sure that I was comfortable most of the time. The next two weeks at the Gaslight Square Apartments taught me a lot though. Be very selective about anyone I would get married to. Kay would turn the lights on in the middle of the night and argue with Frank relentlessly. Pointing out every little thing that she disagreed with could not wait until the morning. That happened all too often. Fortunately I been through the recent experience of getting little sleep at all so I wasn't really as inconvenienced as much as Frank thought.

I found a little boarding house in the city near an intersection that would take me in any major direction I wanted. North to the lake, west to the mall and south into the city, twenty eight Palm Street would become a launching pad for a whole new life. I moved out of Frank's and into a one-room space. There would be access to a kitchen, living room, and then the bathroom on the second floor. Five people would occupy the home. Each had his or her own room. I had never lived like that before. Cedar Court was a far cry from owning your own home, but at least you had some privacy. This was very tight.

George Holt the landlord was quite a good man. He was happy to have me as a tenant. As time went on I would find out why. The people that we both had to put up with over the next four plus years made me never want to own a place like that.

From the beginning of my arrival back in town I had began to look for work. I had enough money to hold me over for a while. The rent was forty-five dollars per week and that fit nicely into my budget.

I occupied my room in the middle of January 1990. I had searched for a job and found one at another apartment complex ten minutes away as a maintenance man again. Charwood Circle was a fairly small place to work compared to the others and gauging the people who would be my peers there were nice to work for and be around. My duties were painting, snow removal, and all the regular maintenance that the tenants needed. My immediate supervisor was also a "Ron." He had been a victim of the big layoffs at AC Delco, one of the General Motors affiliates. He was waiting for years to get back in if business picked up. Many of the people who lived there were very good to work around. The ones that were picky about things or just plain nasty I would be forewarned about. That came with the territory and I knew it. The job obviously did not come with an apartment and neither did the pager. That agreement in the beginning would eventually become a bone of contention. Meanwhile, I was glad to have a job.

A couple of days after I had moved into my room, another guy took the empty room across the hall. George had had a tough time keeping tenants and wanted some good people who stay around a while. Joe would end up being a fun tenant for me. We had some of the same interests. Basketball would become our common denominator for some time to come. He was six foot six and sometimes that became a problem for me. He would immediately be picked by everyone everywhere we went and on occasion he would make a condition that I had to be a part of the team, otherwise I would have to wait a while.

Before George would end up with a full crew of compatible tenants we would have to go through a gamut of unlikables. Drugs, prostitution, thefts, threats of violence and eventually murder would be a landlord's nightmare. I went to sleep many a night enduring the sounds of people doing things in their rooms that this unmarried man was tempted by. Covering my ears with pillows just didn't do it when you knew the whole time what was going on. Answering the front door and having a strange woman there who turned out to be an under aged prostitute didn't help my cause any. We would complain about those risky conditions, but they eventually ironed themselves out with some serious prayer.

For the next three months, Densmore Heights also called Charwood Circle became the other stellar place to work. My supervisor Linda who had her office in the center of the property was a smoke fiend. Her and Ron had that place so cloudy that you couldn't see anything. I often wondered why anyone would rent there with such an introduction like that hitting them in the face when they walked in the front door. Her demeanor must have overwhelmed them all because it was easy to get them to sign. She was a kind person.

One day I was called to the office. "Ron," she said. "The people down in New Jersey want you to go on call, but you won't be getting an apartment."

I responded, "We had an agreement from the start that an apartment comes with being on call. Why anyway would you ask me to drive here from where I live to answer every call? Isn't that the reason for a place to live on site in the first place? Ron already lives here and he has a place to live."

You could tell that she did not like doing what she was asked to. She came out and told me that she agreed with my assertion, but that is what they wanted. She would try and change their minds. The problem was that Ron was on call all of the time and he needed a break. I sympathized with his predicament, but was not willing to go that far to help him out of it.

I had been getting this feeling in my spirit that a big change for me was on the horizon. Not knowing what really sparked it off, I wanted to take care of people who were sick. I didn't tell anyone about it, I just knew that helping other people in a new capacity was something that had been coming up in my mind off and on. Could have been the guy in the nursing home back in Phoenix or a feeling of returning a debt to society, I never really found out. I had been told that my job was over and I was given two weeks notice before I would be replaced. This was another occasion that some said I could have sued because of the original understanding when I was first hired, but I wouldn't have anything to do with doing something like that. One of the last maintenance calls that I responded to was a nice woman who needed some work done on her sliding patio doors. She was a nurse for the Park Ridge Health Care System who worked as a supervisor at a nursing home. Her vocation certainly got my attention especially because I didn't know what direction I was going when I would leave my current job. I always knew that in my line of work it would always be easy to find a job, but this time that didn't seem to be an option. I wasn't tired of it, I had just acquired another direction for my life. Barb Sanor would help me understand some of the "mechanics of healthcare" in our conversation. I told her how I started to feel about the new direction for my life and ended up going to talk to her after hours as well. She said that the nursing home was always looking for good help and that I should consider making that change. I was given plenty to ponder.

It was just days before the last of my job and again a tearful supervisor who liked me was getting ready to say goodbye. It was especially hard for her because we all had started to click during that ninety-day stretch. Barb had told that she would be checking into the possibility of getting me a job as a nursing assistant.

She called me and said, "Ron I talked to my supervisors and out of the three nurses that I mentioned this to one of them said she didn't want to give you a shot at it because you have no experience at all in healthcare. But the other two were willing to interview you. But one thing, in order for you to work there you would be sent to school to get your certification. You need that by law to take care of those people."

I thought for a moment and let her know that I would do it. If it was meant to be, it would happen. The evidence in my own mind was enough, but it was still another risk that I would take not knowing where I would end up.

I left Densmore Heights and would wait a couple of weeks before the final answer would come in concerning my new adventure. I was still interviewed three times by the different nurses and it was certainly true that the one nurse Helen did not want to give me a chance.

"Don't take it personal," she said. "I just think that you are taking quite a giant leap from fixing washers and dryers to caring for a human being."

I couldn't have agreed more especially since I was the one doing it. The other two overruled Helen and I was in. I filled out my papers and my entrance in to healthcare was by a commitment to work at Park Hope Nursing Home. My education would be a month long stint at the local Monroe Community College on the other side of town. Park Ridge would pay for the schooling as well as a small wage. After I would actually start working, then over time my wage would increase.

The change of just going to college in itself was something to experience. This was the first of June in 1990, almost twenty years after I had graduated from high school. I was nervous and excited at the same time. I also knew that millions of people had gone through this in their lives so that was a comfort to me to some extent. Summer classes at that college were quite filled up so I got to get the feeling that I was back in high school. That part was "cool." I'm now forty years old and walking around the halls with kids almost half my age. There were some people my age and even older who were trying the same venture as myself.

When I got to my class it was a continuous flow of students who would graduate every Friday afternoon. New students would be put in a different area of the large rooms to learn the charting and hands on care of nursing home residents. One week I am new and the next one a "sophomore.' My two instructors were good at what they did. They both had Registered Nurse Licenses and complimented each other as they brought us students one day closer to graduation. Learning how to use a Hoyer lift, charting the input and output, recording skin integrity and many other things were taught in the classrooms. We would be moved from one place to another to learn new skills. My fellow students were also a new way for me to get know some new people.

Some of our training included three or four actual trips to the nursing home to watch how it was really done. I would see the hands on reality that many people wouldn't be cut out for. Even today I can see and understand why this field is not for everyone. The closest thing that I had gotten to just the odor in this place were the outdoor port-a-johns on the construction sites. I had been truly going through a change and I didn't know it. This environment would make a believer out of you. Either you had it or you didn't. It was not something you could fake or just pass off until something better came along.

Probably the only thing that I did not like about that college was that the county controlled the parking lot with its strict parking rules. I had seen more than one car with the "Yellow Boot" on the right front wheel. It was put there so that the owner had to pay their ticket or overdue parking fees before they got their car back. It made me angry just thinking about what I would do if one of those things was ever found on my car. Of course I had taken care of all of my responsibilities in that area.

The big day had come and graduation day was here. I dressed up in a suit and went forward to get my "little scroll." That ceremony meant more to me than taking the course itself. Just having gone to a place that I thought at one time was out of my reach forever became a wall that came down on the inside. It was quite a personal victory. Even having no one there from family didn't make a difference. It now had planted a seed that it was quite possible for me to think that college could become a part of my life if I chose it. After the course was over it was time to put all that I had learned into practical experience. Taking care of the elderly was something that I would have never dreamed of, especially after the way I had treated Aunt Julia in her nights of pain and never visiting her in the nursing home for years.

What had become an apparent career in healthcare was actually another phase of my life stealthed with lessons for stimulation to grow. I have felt that it was strange to look at life with such a limited vision, but have since discovered that it was only the tip of the iceberg. Life really is more than just thinking of how I could gain in the material sense. And one doesn't really have to reach for a lesson it has its own unique way of finding you. Just do what you believe you are supposed to and any corrections along the way may come from unexpected sources.

My initiation into taking care of other people seemed more like a hazing than a crossing over a "Welcome" doormat. At Park Hope I was a white man in a black woman's world. I never saw that coming during my visits there from school. I was called into the office one of my first days and asked to sign a paper that had a creed on it. It read: *I will maintain my integrity regardless of the limitation of the patient*. That was a good promise for me to keep, and quite easy at that. What I didn't count on was the limitation of the staff, mainly my fellow nursing assistants and the tolerance of their actions by administration.

My immediate superiors were all women. White women. The charge nurse and nurse manager did their jobs well, but like me had to put up with things like mass absenteeism. Missing work chronically by anyone should have resulted in immediate discharge. One aid missed sixty eight days in one year while another didn't come to work for thirty five. It didn't take long to find out what was going on when I had to absorb their assignments. My workload was heavy enough, but to take on another's became routine. I began to question it and always got the runaround. The day eventually came when enough was enough.

I started at seven a.m. and left at 3:30 in the afternoon. My responsibilities included everything that I was taught. I wasn't disappointed there. It was just the amount of it that blindsided me.

The residents sometimes kept me from thinking about myself and how much I was suffering. Names and faces are branded into my mind of those who maybe like the man in Phoenix that had no visitors or didn't know where they were at. Spina Bifida is a problem that kept a wheel chair bound man on my mind everyday. I had become grateful that I could walk and talk, unlike most of the folks at that address.

The day would start with a handwritten assignment. I then went and woke my people up. Toileting, washing them from head to toe, maybe a bath or two and ultimately getting them dressed for the day all had to happen before breakfast. It was a relief to have one person that required less care in some ways. Those were like gold to a nurse's aid in a place like that. Although there would be abuse of the "new kid on the block" I was rescued many times by other aids who saw what had been done to me. My worst nightmare during my tenure at Park Hope was when one day none of the other aids came to work. My normal assignment was eight residents. That day there would be twenty-four. The nurses working that day had to pitch in.

One of the ladies that I took care of on a regular basis talked incessantly about working at McCurdy's. That store, as well as Sibley's, had their heyday around Rochester in years past. Even though I wasn't around for those stores I felt as if I had been by the time I had heard of them a hundred times. One woman every morning used to stare at me when I walked in the room and yell, "Help me!" There was nothing wrong she just said it as loud as she could. Her voice had been as loud as an auctioneer's. Maybe because she had been doing it for so long, at least it kept her lungs strong.

Feeding time was sometimes humorous. A lot of people had to be fed because of dementia or maybe a medication like Haldol kept them "zoned out." One pleasant lady who was blind was also a Christian.

This African American woman had such a sweet spirit and it would appear as though she did not know what was going on. While I would feed her she would act like a lot of others. They often wanted to work their way quickly to the dessert. Like a child sometimes it was necessary to make sure that they would eat more of the nourishing items on their tray before moving onto the sweets. And most often they would let you know about it.

My experience at West Side Manor with the elderly didn't really help me when it came time to give "hands on care" to people who couldn't get around on their own. That wide space between fixing washers and dryers and doing what I was now doing made Helen's point come home to roost. I wanted to quit too many times. My goal from the beginning was to end up in the emergency room or Intensive care in the hospital setting. That part of the vision would have to wait. There were some things that I would have to learn now.

Coming home from work was like prison release. I had to go back the next day and get a dose of some strange confinement that I had signed on to. Reflecting on my job one day gave me the desire to give school another shot. I wanted to become a nurse. The only way to do that was to enroll at MCC again and start my prerequisites. I needed biology, chemistry, and the dreaded algebra in order to get into the nursing program. The college would accept my biology grade from high school, but I also needed the other two courses. I signed up to take algebra. That course was my nemesis in high school. Having failed it three times and leaving it all behind I would never dreamed that it would come back to haunt. I am a person who always wants to do the hardest thing first. At least that came into my adult life. So I took the course and got a high B. My confidence grew because now I knew how to study properly. Now, instead of being a nurse I thought about being a doctor. After the algebra course I went over to the University of Rochester and had an interview to see where I would sit with respect to becoming an MD. The counselor looked at what grades that I did have and encouraged me to take the path that I was contemplating. It would mean seven years straight with no break for the school part of it. Then there would be three years of residency and paying back about $200,000. I was flattered that I was qualifying in this man's mind, but by the time I had gotten to my car after that interview I was a mental wreck. I wouldn't start making any serious money until after age fifty and that didn't sit well with me. I thought to myself; *Who am I kidding? I want to do what I have always wanted. I want to be an inventor.* That, of course, would require a commitment that would maybe end up taking longer than going to school to become a doctor. I would find out.

Life at home started to change a bit. George found a couple of likable tenants who would hang around a while. Gary Precicci was a thirty something Italian who like to laugh and had a calm spirit. Al Mazolla was another Italiano who like Gary brought a lot to the table of humor. Gary liked to make Al laugh and that made our home a little more fun to be around. A twenty-three year-old kid named Paul who worked at the Red Lobster would occupy the fifth and final room. His sneakers would stink so bad from being around that seafood that he we made him keep them outside. Before we had gotten to the place where the house had been full and stayed that way for awhile it was touch and go with a lot of riff raff. George decided to open up the garage and rent to a man who called himself "David Love." We eventually found out that he was using that name as an alias. Authorities in the northwest had been looking for him because of some financial scheme.

At work I became friends with one of the nurse managers. She was a Christian and carried a big burden concerning what was being tolerated by the people above her. We had talked on several occasions about the risks to the patients and compromising of the attendance records of the other aids. She ended up getting fired for trying to change things. It was just a link in the long chain of nurses who had been fired for "rocking the boat." Terri Mayka was a quiet person who I felt had no place to be treated like she was and I eventually would set out to do something about it.

A couple of weeks after the firing of yet another nurse I took the responsibility of documenting four pages of problems that I had experienced or personally witnessed at Park Hope. The number one offender of course was the lack of support that the nurses and compliant nurses aids got from above. I then wrote four pages of resolutions to those problems. I hand delivered the entire document to the President of Long Term Care at his office. His secretary took the papers and I never heard a thing from him. The next day, however, was a little different. The administrator for Park Hope, Todd Spring called me into his office slamming the door behind us.

A very angry boss looks at me. "What do you mean going over my head with this stuff?" He continued to yell at the top of his lungs. "Who do you think that you are going outside this facility with it, huh?"

My response was simply; "I knew I couldn't come to you in the first place. You have been approached by others and they got nowhere. People take off work whenever they want to and the policy is clear. Three warnings and you're gone. The patients are put at risk and no one does anything. That is why I did what I did."

The man who would be king sat down in his chair and looked out his window. "Get out of here" he said. Within a few months he was gone. Nothing was done at that point. I got no satisfaction and went to my nursing aid instructors. They said to ride it out and wait to see what would happen. "Change takes time" they told me.

About five months after I had started work as a Certified Nursing Assistant my little ship of rescue came in. It came in the form of a meeting consisting of nursing professionals from Park Ridge Hospital. They had met in a conference room on a wing near mine. Although I wasn't invited, I had overheard what their agenda was. They were looking at recruiting people for the Emergency Room and the Intensive Care Unit. I got very excited. I did not know how to handle what I thought would be an intrusion into their closed door conference. I asked my immediate supervisor if I could ask them a couple of questions. After getting permission to do so I went and inquired about the possibility of transfer. Every six months in the healthcare system you can apply for a change anywhere you want if there are openings. I was delighted to hear that both places had vacancies for Technicians. The only requirements were that you had to be a nursing assistant and have some experience. I now had both and I wanted this bad...for more than one reason. It was my ultimate goal when I came there and now I also needed someone to rescue me from the clutches of incompetence. Getting away from Park Hope and working in a environment like Intensive Care would be my dream come true. I spoke with an instructional nurse that I had met in my classes at MCC and she got an ear to bend for me. She had given a good reference to them about me. It would take about a week to decide who would fill the position in the ICU.

What would be my last seven days at Park Hope was quite the airport experience. One that I would love/hate again. I definitely would miss the staff who were supportive and certainly the residents. I had no reserve for those who had caused the whole place many problems. Getting the go ahead to transfer into the hospital created a one-man exodus from the "Afflictions in Egypt." It became one of the best pieces of news that I have ever heard. To this day I can say without exception that the job I was leaving had been the hardest ever in my life. As the short seven month stretch at the nursing home became just a memory I hoped and prayed that things would turn around for those who wanted to do the right things.

My initial trip to the ICU at Park Ridge for orientation was met with a few rubber necked nurses who stared me down. I really didn't know how to take what they were doing. As I sat in this new white, clean, sterile looking environment, the prospect of taking care of people who were in a different state of health was intriguing and a little frightening.

One of the nurses who was watching me as I sat at a bank of monitors came and sat near me. "Don't be bothered about the other ones gauking at you," she said. "They are just wondering what kind of person they are going to have to work with."

I had to give her an answer just to give myself a little confidence. "Well, I hope that I don't disappoint anyone, but it seems to be quite a different place than what I'm used to."

I realized that she was doing what all the other nurses were when she was talking to me. Scoping me out. She eventually would be giving her report to them. I got the gut feeling that she was comfortable with me.

My new nurse manager came out of her office and greeted me. "Hello, my name is Karen Burnhart, you must be Ron," she said.

"Nice to meet you" I responded. Karen was a nice woman who had had her share of troubles akin to Barb in Phoenix. She had been a nurse for many years and loved the responsibilities of managing a place like this. The tour around the unit gave me an opportunity to see what really went on in that setting. There were eighteen rooms outfitted with technology that I had only heard about. The constant bells and whistles of ventilators, monitors, intravenous pumps and oxygen saturation machines could have easily overwhelmed me, but it wouldn't. I had chosen to take things one day at a time and this was a good time. I knew nothing about any of this equipment, but I was guaranteed that I would be taught. Much of what I would learn in this setting was meant to be on-the-job training. I found out that much of it wasn't even taught in the colleges at the nursing level.

New Friends

My church life would take me to a New Testament church in Greece at the building where Reverend Jim Crowley was preaching. I had heard of that church when I had first moved to Rochester and was driving to Brockport and attending Christ Community Fellowship. Many churches are connected by belief systems claiming to be non-denominational, but they are just another created denomination. The mindset of exclusiveness always creates division, something that anyone knows God would not approve of. I would spend some time in Greece meeting new people and attend functions here and there for a couple of months.

I decided to call Terri Mayka and try to discover just what happened when she was fired from Park Hope. She was surprised that anyone would care. I found that many of my hunches about what really went on there was true. She had been a victim of power and money play while attempting to support changes to how things were being handled. They simply got rid of her because she was doing the right thing. Terri had wondered if anyone besides her would ever give a hoot. We ended up talking many times and became fond of each other. I would go to her home and have dinner and eventually fell in love. During this time there had been the most terrible ice storm of the century around Rochester. I came home from Terri's the night that it started. When I drove into my driveway a very large limb had broken off from a tree and would have killed me had I been standing there any earlier. Many thousands of people would be without power. My first night was without power as well. Terri, fortunately, was not affected where she had lived and happened to be going out of town for a whole week. I could live there for a few days until things got back to normal on my block. It would take almost two weeks before that area was back in full swing again.

Operation Desert Storm had begun and I was bothered by all of that. Watching those first images of Baghdad being bombed at night scared me. I felt some patriotism on one hand and fear and hurt on the other. Never believing that war was right between people, we had become involved in something that may have serious consequences. I guess it was the live action of war on television that scared me. It was not make-believe any more.

It had become apparent that Terri and I wanted to spend the rest of our lives together. By late spring I asked her to marry me. We would drive to a small town near New York City and meet her mother. Her family was seemingly approving of me although that would eventually change with her sister. The wedding was planned for the following June, a year later. We would take walks together and discuss the possibility of me going back to school to be a nurse. Even though I had other aspirations now, I could change with the flow if I needed to.

During the last few weeks leading up to the wedding I started to get a little nervous and contentious. There was nothing really that Terri was doing that made me irritable, I was just becoming moody underneath. I would go with her to pick up her children from her ex-husband's home a few miles away. That situation had become a nightmare for her. He was a lawyer and created problems that kept her in constant wonder at what was going to happen next. I didn't like the antics that he was pulling and the manipulations had showed up in the kids. (Where have I seen that before?) Beginning to know my wife to be, I could see how she was just another soft heart that was taken advantage of by a devious ex.

I attended church with Terri at a congregation she had been used to for a while. A young pastor who started the church became well liked by the fifty or so parishioners. Jim Pannagio's father had been a famous local basketball coach from the semi-pro league called the

Rochester Royals many years earlier. Jim had gone to a Bible school and was starting the new church. I hadn't gotten rid of some of my legalistic ways of times past and I didn't know it. There was nothing going on in my life that would reveal it until I was invited to go to a Halloween party for the church. I was a staunch supporter that anything to do with dressing up in a monkey suit for this occasion was not a good thing. Jim Pannagio would be having the party at his house and when I got there I would find him dressed up as a Roman gladiator. I hated it and got into a bad mood about it. Terri and I had a tough time about the beliefs of Halloween. She was influenced because Jim was a nice guy. I understood that, but didn't think we should be acting like what we were preaching against. Although we got some of that straightened out there were seeds planted about what neither of us would give up on.

Back at work, I was getting the work over. I don't know which was the hardest mentally. The change into the nursing home from remodeling and maintenance or the switch from Park Hope to the ICU. Alan Parr was appointed to be my mentor. His job became easy because all he would do was show me something once and then go off and leave me to do it myself. He was a likable guy, but the nurses had been in a job relationship with him that seemed to overlook things that I would have fired him for in a second. Taking many cigarette breaks throughout the day and having a conspicuous liaison with a nurse did not help matters. My care for the patient was ratcheted up because now any mistake that I made may cost someone their life. I was becoming a nervous wreck. Going to the nurses for support so early was humbling. I did not learn things as well as I wanted with the training I was getting. They knew it, but didn't or couldn't do anything about it. Alan had gained their confidence in him at least up to a point. One thing that seems to happen in every work environment is that many people talk about others when there is a problem, but do not confront the issue with the person that they have the problem with. That, I would find out, was commonplace in the hospital.

One of the nurses who was prone to like to teach came up to me one day and said, "Ron you care too much."

Lori Kennedy had changed my life with that statement. She was right and I had not interpreted my concern for doing the right things in that unit as caring too much. My nerve wracking response for making a mistake was nothing more than self imposed fear that I had to walk on eggshells or somebody was going to die. She saw that I cared, she also saw a guy that did not have to beat himself up at all the prospects of making an honest mistake. From that day forth I was liberated from that. Alan became more tolerable as a mentor even with his deficiencies. Learning CPR, using an EKG machine, putting in a Foley catheter, setting up lines that go into the body under pressure became the norm. Cleaning up many messes called "brown alerts" was also part of the job. At least Park Hope taught me that.

The staff became a little more comfortable with me. I never really knew for a long time that they were really concerned about me for another big reason. They would have to trust someone new with their patient. Could I really produce confidence that could be counted on in the long run? Every nurse was responsible for my actions. It wasn't just cleaning up a patient for the day. It was making sure everything was in order. Monitoring vital signs, input, output, any remarkable changes in a patients status that could not be caught by someone else at the moment were just some of the many aspects that a person with a nursing license needed to care about. I would not disappoint, but it became a lot of hard work. One of the other techs was quite a character. Beth Nickler called herself the "Urine Fairy" after draining out so many catheters. I was given a plaque when I left the job full time with the inscription on it, "Pee King."

My relationship with the nurses, doctors, and other techs grew as time went on. We had a cramped lunchroom that made it difficult to have very many people in. Representatives from the drug companies and any meetings at all would leave a lot of folks standing. A tiny refrigerator for our lunch was insufficient. This all, of course, just made us get a little closer, at least in my mind. That little fridge had to go. I collected enough money from about thirty-five people and spent five hundred dollars on a new large one. It was a long needed item.

The ICU unit was one big room that measured about seventy feet long by thirty feet wide. Off of this large room were all of the eighteen patient rooms. It was easy access from any point. If anybody needed anything all they had to was stick their head out the door of a patient's room and ask for it. Like the lunchroom I believe to this day that the mere confinement of that environment had something to do with the

315

reason why everybody came to be as close as they did. There was always your usual serving of bickering and complaining, but the overall camaraderie among that crew was nice. Once I was accepted into the fold it became a wonderful place to work.

Gaining a little experience in the critical care setting gave Terri and I both a sense that maybe there would be a future in my own life there. We had made it through the following winter and were headed toward the altar. We had rented a facility for our wedding reception and were actually decorating it when Terri would sit me down and call it all off. Here we go again.

"Ron, I can't do it. My family and a couple of others are not comfortable with you. I can't take your negative attitude every time something happens that you don't agree with. I think that it's better this way for both of us."

I looked around at the streamers hanging from the ceiling. I took a deep breath and simply said, "Okay, I will have to get on with my life I guess, what about you? What are you going to do?"

Her response was too fast not to have been thinking about this long before we were standing there talking about it. "I want to become a missionary down south," she said.

I shrugged my shoulders and said, "Well, I guess I'll be going."

She told me that I didn't have to stay around and take the stuff down. I left and that was it. It was another example of a person unwilling to communicate how they were feeling about something until they had to absolutely. I could and would eventually learn to change and be changed about things in my life, but I had to be very careful about what and whom I would get involved with.

My tail wasn't really between my legs on this one. The pride was hurt a little. I did not want anyone to know that what had been uncorrected in my own life was a cause of my breakup with Terri. I went my own way and assessed the situation. I think that there was some relief about it all anyway. I did not give up on what I had believed and that seed had grown into something like this. It was okay.

One of the things that had been ongoing was the reality of past debt from my marriage to Lois. I was communicating with the IRS and several other people who were holding portions of what I owed and promised them all what I would do. Paying each one month after month for years, I began to see the light at the end of the tunnel. And it wasn't a freight train coming at me either. I was feeling the nearness of a debt free life headed my way.

The summer was in full swing in 1992 and basketball was almost a daily thing. Joe and I would travel up to the court on LeGrange Avenue every evening and get it on with many guys that came from all over. I had a lot of fun up there and I have to admit, sometimes you don't know how free you are until you are away from whatever may be bogging you down. I never really looked at my relationship with Terri that way. I felt some contention at times, but didn't think it was anything else than pre-marriage jitters and minor aspects in our lives that needed adjusting. I felt again like I was a monkey out of the cage.

Learning to improvise on my meals for lunch at work I first used to cook enough chicken for three days. It was cheap and it would keep in the fridge. The guys at home had become quite a good bunch to be around. George, on the other hand, would once in a while be an aggravation under the influence. He was always kind to me and the guys, but if there were even one person that was chronically late on their rent it would become a problem. He used to drink at a local bar and on occasion with one of the tenants. One evening I came home from work and found my room in a completely different arrangement than when I had left it that morning. All the furniture had been moved to different parts of the room. The bedding was rolled up and placed against the wall. The first I thought when I looked at was that I did not pay my rent. This room was the premium one that everyone wanted and I waited a long time for it. Confused, I just put down my things and went to the kitchen sink to wash my hands. I heard someone come in the front door and wheeled around to see George standing there looking at me.

I could tell he had been drinking and the first words out of his mouth were, "What are looking at? I told you I was going to do it!" His voice was loud and angry.

I had done nothing to provoke that kind of dialogue. Turning to the sink I answered, "What are you talking about, George?"

A snapping landlord retorts, "You know what I'm talking about! Your room! I moved things around to look like it was a living room."

I didn't remember him saying anything about my room, but that was okay. The inspector from the city had been scheduled to drop by and inspect the claimed status of the dwelling as well as the code compliance. George felt that he had to make one of the bedrooms look like a living area because the law stated that a living area had to be provided for a certain number of occupied rooms. He didn't have one.

I calmly stated, "That's okay, just take it easy."

He made a slight gesture that he was going to come my way for a fight. I turned around all the way to face him. He stopped, looked at me, then my open door, and walked out of the house. A couple of days later he apologized. He came back and let me know that, "I was scared that they would find something wrong and shut me down. I wanted to keep everybody that I've got." We shook hands and it was over.

There was another room that actually had been rented out before I came there. The guy in that room was really the sixth tenant. George had not wanted to alter the room and make it into a living area, but he ended up doing that. This would make my room on the first floor the only one.

One of the rooms on the second floor had become one of change. More tenants moved in and out of there than any other room in the house. One particular man had a problem with flashbacks from Vietnam. He would on occasion drink too much. That would be an impediment to many things at our home. Most of the time he was polite and courteous. I began to believe that he was suffering the very things that he claimed he was. When he was sober he would talk of being a sniper and making "intimate kills" through the scope of a rifle. It was his job and he became good at it. What he hadn't counted on was its long-term effects. His soul had become tormented by the taking another human life, and in his mind that fact was irreversible. One night he came home a little under the weather and started shooting his mouth off about how I wasn't as tough as I thought I was. I never had any negative conversation with him about anything prior to that relating to me. I did not answer him at all, but went to my room. When I got up the next morning there was a three-foot high trophy from a karate tournament on the kitchen table outside my door. I thought there was supposed to be a message in there somewhere, but I wouldn't give it too much thought.

Being back at church on Kuhn Road that year gave me the opportunity to run into Judy again, compliments of Minnie and David. I spoke to her and we ended up beginning a long-term relationship. She had been living with her Mom and two sons in Hilton, another little town outside of Rochester. The boys were about three and five years old. She had been another single mother trying to make ends meet. They had all been victims of a bad life with the boys' father. When I met them he had been pulling a lot of the same stuff that many other unscrupulous men had been doing to women I had met around the county. There definitely was a trend. Even though the divorce rate was climbing as the carnage of wrecked lives evidenced, those who had never married were experiencing breakups too. I was all too glad again that my situation from a few years earlier had not created some of the long lasting effects that many other people were going through. I naturally wanted to intervene, but didn't.

Judy's mother was a high school counselor and had her own set of rules around the house. One of the initial things that had gotten Joy Kinz and I off to the wrong start was that I had been the son of an alcoholic as well as one myself at one time. The second thing was an old haunt. My education. She did not like the fact that I had not gotten a degree of some sorts. She had gotten a master's degree and at the time was pushing her daughter to get hers. Joy was never unkind to me in any way, but wanted to make sure that Judy and I would have no thoughts about marriage. Her private talks with her daughter made that all too clear. At the same time she would not discourage what we did have. I became confused about all of that, but would come over as often as I could. Eventually, saturday night was the only time I would see her. She would come into the city and visit me and then go to a movie or out to eat. Mom would watch the kids and once in a while the boys father would take them for a weekend.

Before I had met Judy I had began to feel lonely off and on. The span of time between her and Terri was not really long, but leaving someone that you thought you loved creates a vacuum regardless of any new freedoms that you may experience. During that time I remember the song by the Beach Boys where the lyrics included "in my room." A fruit fly had been in my room and bugging me for about a week. I, for some strange reason did not attempt to kill him. They aren't as fast as a housefly and ridding myself of this aggravation wouldn't make for insurmountable odds. Apparently he came in by way of a banana and would stay on my night stand near the bed. I began to watch him closely. The condensation from any glasses of cold drink that I had sitting there would be a constant source of water for him so he never wandered too far from that surface. I eventually accepted him as my friend and he wouldn't disappoint. For the next three months he hung around and kept me company. I made sure that he plenty to eat. One good crumb would last for days, so the expense of feeding another mouth didn't break me. The most interesting aspect of this relationship with a fruit fly was when the phone would ring and he had been sitting on the receiver, he would ride it all the way to my head and would not fly off. After he had been around for the ninety days he would then go away. I never saw him again.

My new friend Judy had a talent. Her drawings were some of the best that I had seen. She showed me a collection of ants that she had drawn a year earlier. They were definitely marketable in my mind. In our early relationship she would not develop the same opinion of her work that I would. Being very critical of anything that she did may have contributed to it going nowhere at the time. The attention that the boys needed may have had something to do with that as well. She was bogged down with a lot of responsibility. Her sons, Colin and Patrick, were developing into young boys that every parent would want. After they went through the terrible twos and headed toward a double digit age group they would maintain their wonderful character and integrity. Their mother had not been working at the time, but was pursing all of the possibilities of college.

I would eventually attend some of the boys' soccer games or play with them in the driveway and maybe putting together a "Transformer" on the carpet. After a year or so I noticed that their father began to request them less and less. I could do nothing about it as they would begin to suffer greatly at the hands of someone that should have given them much and gave them little. The wall of disdain for any future with their mother by Joy continued to grow, but she wouldn't do anything about it. I knew that she felt she had a grip on her daughter.

Toward the end of 1992 I became attentive toward the thought that I wanted to start a business. Having been seeing Judy for a while and talking on the phone for long periods of time we sort of just drifted apart for the time being. The first month that we had gabbed on the phone I kept track of the time. For those first thirty days we had talked eighty hours. Her mother seemed to instill in me a longing to make more money. I had made the decision to be an inventor and certainly could not afford to support a family as planned. Even over the long haul Judy would become the first casualty of my decision not to go to school.

For the next two years off and on I would try something different. The personal section of the newspaper. And although I had hated any suggestion of what I called "synthetic" relationships I would bow to the forces that demanded some quality companionship in my life however that would happen. Just change the rules. That's how I saw it. I should have stayed with rule number one.

My first crack at media love was to answer an ad for a woman who said she was good looking and loved to cook. All the kids were gone and she needed some companionship at age fifty-three. I was forty at the time and kicking it up a notch or two didn't bother me, but she had to be exceptional if I was going to compromise on that point. I ended up getting a call and we talked for a while, discussing our interests. When we arrived at what we thought was a dinner date we made it. She invited me to her home and would prepare a meal for the two of us. I knocked on the door and was very nervous at what I would see. The door opened and there she stood. Everything that I did not want was now staring me in the face. She looked at least sixty-five and I'm being generous. She didn't tell me she was Japanese with coke bottle lenses. When she smiled she looked like a World War II pilot doing a Kamikaze run for the Emperor.

"Come in" she said.

I tried to swallow the lump in my throat. For the next hour and a half I put on the greatest show of my lifetime. I did not want to offend her. Being a polite and kind person she obviously was a good example of what I believed to the norm in eastern culture. We had a meal in a very dark room and talked about light and safe subjects like where we wanted to go in life. I guess that any subject would have been safe except the one where I would call her again because after din-din I was history. And that is exactly the way that it happened.

My next two attempts at finding a friend in the newspaper were duds as well. The fourth one became something more. I met the

321

thirty-five-year-old woman in a restaurant. Bonnie Dame was another single mother that had a son and a daughter. She was very protective of the kids and made sure that I did not know where she had lived. After we met a couple of times, she invited me to dinner, but not just any dinner. I would meet her and the kids in a parking lot of a mall and she would drive up to Mendon Ponds, a large park setting on the south side of Rochester. We did that often. It took a couple of months in the fall to convince her that I was worth letting me come to her home. I felt privileged. She was fairly nice looking woman and another female who was suffering from the abuse of an ex spouse. I don't know what it is, but everyone I was running into fell into that category that is except the "Princess from the orient."

We made it through a lot of unspoken questions and answers. Bonnie was unusually wise. The children both liked me, but had some allegiance to their father regardless of the rift between their parents. We still got along well. At the park Aaron and I would play catch with a baseball while Mom did all of the barbecuing. She would make a great meal every weekend. She had been an employee of the local telephone company and her hours gave her the time to put some special attention into packing that cooler with chicken, ribs, steak and anything else that was good. When winter did come I finally was trusted to come into her home. The holidays went well and we loved to talk about a lot of things. She had been in a relationship prior to meeting me and still had feelings for this guy, but that seemed to be tapering off. What I liked most about Bonnie was that she would never press me into a place where I had to say anything about my future or hers. To keep things at the "friend" level was a good thing for the both of us.

A while after the holidays I decided that I wanted to start a business. Making a trip to the lumber yards off and on I knew there became an opportunity to do some woodwork. In order to do that I would have to tamper with my current job and hours. I made a decision to leave the full time position at Park Ridge and go part time. The folks at work would have a going away party for myself, and another person's birthday at a friends house. I got a lot of good byes, but pretty much worked a lot of hours anyway. I gave up my benefits, but at least got to choose my hours.

I picked making shelving for my business. When spring came, Bonnie would let me use her garage to make special shelves out of wood. After designing six different kinds of shelves I made five of each. Transporting back to my room and storing them wasn't easy, but tolerable. Having gotten a need for a different car at that point I started looking. The station wagon had served me well, but it was time for another change. My business needed a more reliable transportation.

Almost everything in my life has had some drama in it. Even the most potentially bland or mundane experiences could not be complete without something interesting going on. If it was just the pen of a good writer that made a story worth reading I think that the person should find another job. There must be real creativity.

Before I could continue on with "Knott's Shelving" I had to find that other car. My search took me to a man who advertised a 1983 Mercury Grand Marquis. I thought that they were a smart looking vehicle if they were in good shape. The contours on the body and the extra chrome made them more attractive than many cars. They were also big, but that didn't stop me before. The man had stated in the newspaper ad that the car was in mint shape, had 68,000 miles and was thirteen hundred dollars. The only catch was that the engine was blown. Why would I want to monkey with a car that had an engine blown? There was something funny about the way that he worded the ad. It seemed like he may be willing to negotiate on the money. I thought if I could get it dirt cheap and the car was really mint then maybe an engine was a possibility.

I called the number in response to the Marquis ad. I asked him what made him think that the engine was blown.

He said, "I've had three mechanics look at it and they all said that the motor it shot. You can hear the rods knocking when you start up the car. Oil had not gotten to the bearings and they are gone. You can take a look at it if you want."

I asked him, "Is the car really in good shape?"

"It is in mint condition just like I said it was," he responded.

My final comment to this man on the phone before I came over was, "You know, it is possible for one person to be right and everybody else wrong don't you?"

I went to take a look. The man's home was in a very nice section of Greece. He opened the door to his garage and there it was. To me, even with no engine at all, this car was worth every penny. I hadn't been fully convinced that I would be willing to spend money on a motor even then because of time constraints.

"Can I start it up?" I asked.

"The keys are in it," he answered.

I fired the car up and waited to hear the rods knocking. All I could hear was a small pinhole in the exhaust that sounded like a little more than what it was. The car was beautiful. I couldn't hear anything like they all were saying.

"I'll tell you what, under the premise that I may have to replace the engine I will give you eight hundred dollars for it."

With his head resting in his hand, he said "Okay, under one condition, it goes "as is. I don't want to be responsible for anything."

I shook hands and went to call my mechanic. I towed the car to him and all he to do was install an oil pump for fifty-eight dollars. The car ran well after that. No damage was done to anything. What the mechanics were hearing was the pinhole in the exhaust and maybe they did hear something else after it ran a while, but not today. Not ever again.

Rescued Again
and Again

I made the shelves and now it was time to try and sell them. This work was a little more intimidating now that I had made that commitment to leave one place and start another. Selling something on an ongoing basis was different than just putting a car in the paper.

Renting a spot in a local craft gallery for six months was to be my first official showcase. "The Yellow Door," as it was called, had a high potential traffic volume mainly because it was a couple of doors down from a Wal-Mart. I have been taught since then to piggyback any business like the big boys who had done all of the research and felt it right to put a business in that locale. I got the traffic, but still lost out in the end anyway. My sales at that place did not come close to breaking even, let alone making a profit.

By July fourth of that year I had been through about half of my time at the gallery. My next venue would be the Family Fun-Fest at the Brighton High School grounds. This was literally a large festival with crafters, rides for the kids and plenty to eat. Many people came out to exhibit their wares and the projected hot day would not disappoint. It was ninety plus degrees all day long and a lot of visitors weathered the heat. From eight o'clock in the morning until six at night I sat under an umbrella watching hundreds of prospects stop, look, maybe give me a compliment and keep going. In ten hours I did not sell one shelf. My display, the number of people and the work that went into the pieces all convinced me that this would be a good day for sales. George had been kind enough to transport all of my things in his van and when he came back at night it was embarrassing to have every one of those things left.

The day was not all lost despite the bad sales. The food there was good and I like to watch people. About one in the afternoon something happened that made it all worthwhile. There was a band playing all day long accompanied by the sound of all of the carnival rides. As I was sitting and listening to the music, a group of bag-pipers came and marched around the grounds. I have always liked bagpipes and there was one song that was synonymous with that instrument as far as I was concerned. "Amazing Grace." I wanted to hear that sound. The men dressed in kilts came by my booth playing all kinds of songs, but not the one I liked. As they made a circle to the other side of the property I strained to listen hoping that they would finally play my song. The sounds of the band and the rides eventually drowned out their music. All of a sudden the men with the bagpipes stopped. The music stopped from the band on the stage. Believe it or not the rides shut down all at the same time. The only sound now was the people walking in the soft grass looking at the crafts. Then it started. The bag-pipers let loose the most beautiful rendition of Amazing Grace that I had ever heard. There was not interference from anyone. Even with the men on the direct opposite side of the field there would be nothing to drown the sound of that song. Unless there was someone else wanting to hear from God that day through that song I felt like everything was stopped just for me. With tears streaming down my face the prospect of selling anything to anybody was the farthest thing from my mind. Although I had been enjoying myself, there was still a loneliness and dejection from everyone saying nice things about my work, but not buying anything. I had now been comforted.

A woman who was working in the town government asked me if I would make her something that I did not have for sale. She showed me what she wanted and I made it for her. After bringing home all of my shelves and nursing the sunburn that had made its way through the umbrella I accepted my losses well. During the summer I had showcased my work six more times and did not sell one shelf. They eventually went into storage and, of course, Mom would help me out and bought a couple of them from me. It has been over ten years and she still hasn't put them up yet. She doesn't want me to hang them because she hadn't "decided" where to put them.

The woman who wanted me to make that custom shelf put an idea in my mind. Why not craft everything "made to order?" Since no one wanted what I did make maybe people could let me know what they did want. I would start by telling the nurses at work and a few other professionals around the hospital. That was a good move. I had all the orders I wanted. My first big project was for a nurse at work. She wanted a large shadow box for her nesting doll collection. She needed thirty individual spaces to house all of those egg-like collectibles from Russia. It had to be oak. I was excited to make that shelf. It turned out to be five feet high and four feet wide with its own stand. It took two men to lift it onto a truck. The nurse really loved it.

A couple of my projects that year did not turn out so great. Through the many orders there had to be a couple of duds that I would have to endure. The first came in the form of a very special mantle that a nurse and her husband wanted over their fireplace. They were remodeling their home and needed a custom piece of work to accent the stone and wood around the centerpiece of the large living room. I came to the house about twenty miles away and measured the space. I wrote down the length as an accurate nine feet one inch, written in pencil. They accepted my suggestion of making it out of black walnut and I would then wait for them to call me when the remodeling got to the point when I could install it. Three months later I got the call. Of course by then it was done so I wrapped it up in bubble wrap and with the end of it sticking out of my trunk, delivered it. It was a beautiful piece that had been brought to pristine shine with hand rubbed oils after it was sanded. There was no need to stain wood like that. The natural color sold itself. I got to the house and unloaded the shelf and the mounts. Walking into the house and laying the piece on the floor in front of the fireplace I got this sick feeling. Even though it had been wrapped for protection something wasn't right. It felt short. I re-measured the space and then the shelf, and sure enough it was a twelve inches short. What I had written in pencil had gotten smeared into another measurement. Instead of nine feet one inch, it read ninety-one inches, just about a foot short. I hated that. My friend felt sorry for me and understood that I would make another one. I did and took the hit. I made a second mantle and kept the first one until I sold it for a song a year later.

My second mistake that year was taking a job that I said I would never do. Refinishing something that required leaving part of the object that was not to be refinished. Matching anything to its original color was almost impossible in my mind. Even painting a whole car depending on the amount of damage and the color was necessary because to try and match a small part was not good. This little elderly gentleman asked me to refinish his tabletop of an antique table in his dining room. I reluctantly said yes and brought it home. To make sure that I would not err in the match, I would take it outside and work it in the bright sunlight. The same light at the same hour every day would produce the best possible environment to keep everything the same. So I thought. In the sun was one thing, but when I delivered it to the man the gross difference between the top of the table and the legs was offensive. The little man did not see it that way though. He liked it and accepted it as a good job. He seemed to feel that I was being hard on myself. Then I remembered what Lori Kennedy had told me when I started working in the Intensive care unit. "I cared too much."

It was tough to make the money that I wanted on a project when these things would happen, but the number of orders and satisfied customers would increase all the time. And of course I would on occasion receive money from an unexpected source. I came out of the house one day and noticed that I had some damage to my car. It had been sitting in the driveway only a short while and it was easy to recall where I had been and I knew that it had to have happened where it was parked. I looked around to check out anyone next door. One of the guys who lived there had the reputation of coming home drunk. He was loud and sometimes threatening even to his brother. I could hear them arguing quite often even to the point of fighting under the influence. I noticed something interesting though. He had parked his car across the street in a driveway of a house that was for sale. Since there was plenty of room at his mother's house where he was living I thought it was strange so I went over to take a look. Sure enough, there was some minor damage to his van. The paint chips and the ripped metal all told me that he was the man. I went next door through the fence gate and walked up to the swimming pool that he was in.

"Hi, Frank, how are you doing?"

He shook the water off of his head and without provocation became a little defensive. "What's up?" He said.

I answered with intent. "There is a little damage to my car and the damage on the van shows that they are a match. Do you know anything about that?"

"No, does it really? I don't think I did it. Let me take a look."

We went out to the vehicles and the evidence called the shot. He couldn't get out of it. After scratching his head a second he gave in. "I'll give you my insurance info. Sorry about that, I must have been drunk."

I knew that he knew all along, but the fact he was going to pay kept my mouth shut. It came to two hundred fifty dollars and I certainly could use it. Less than a year earlier I remembered that when I went to the Cornhill Festival I had only a dollar twenty-five in my pocket so this was getting better all the time.

It would seem as though my life wasn't as full of excitement as times past, but again what would be a lull would always turn into drama. It was a Friday night about eleven or so and I heard sirens, a lot of them. Sirens were frequent wherever I lived, but every time there was a lot of that familiar sound and would last a long time it would get my attention. They were coming from everywhere. I walked out of the house and looked around to see what was going on. After determining that the action could not be far away I decided to take a walk to the end of my street. Looking down Dewey Avenue I saw where the problem was. All of the flashing red lights and people gathering near an intersection told me that it was an accident rather than a house fire. I approached the scene and saw a man laying in the road with his right arm severed off. He had been driving a motorcycle and hit a car that had turned in front of him. He hit it so hard that the left quarter panel was laying further down the street next to his bike in which the front wheel has almost crushed closed. He was drunk and shooting his mouth off to the paramedics. They got him to the hospital and saved his arm. A month later I had taken care of him when he was transferred to Park Ridge for Rehabilitation. What he told me made me a little mad, but I kept it cool. He said that he was guilty of driving without a license and being drunk, but that driver of the car was negligent in pulling in front of him so he was "suing for big bucks." He said that the impact from the damage caused the odometer to stop and proved what speed he was going. I didn't tell him that it was a wrong assumption. Never found out what the outcome was. I felt he should have been grateful to just be alive.

After working in the ICU for a couple of years I started to get more into my inventive mode, not that it ever really left. Every morning after starting my shift I had to level a device on each patient that needed things lined up with technology on an IV pole. It was frustrating that I had to use a conventional level to accomplish something that should have a more state of the art way of doing things. I was enjoying the fact that all of my debts were almost all paid off and now it was time to finance an invention. I invented a leveling device to replace the archaic ruler that I was using at work and got an attorney to help me file a patent. Owing the man twenty-three hundred dollars and ultimately getting rejected by the patent office was only the beginning of a long road in the wonderful world of paying for my creativity. The only way that I could challenge the decision was to pay a lot more money to the lawyers and dispute it with no guarantee that I would win. I have always believed that I am a true inventor so instead of fighting it I would have to come up with more ideas and also find ways of cutting costs in the process.

Still working in Bonnie's garage making my shelves, she would always be an encouragement to me as well and of course making me all of those wonderful dinners. We continued to discuss on and off our future, but there seemed to be none really in sight. My lonely Sunday walks after church near my home was never really alleviated by any plutonic relationship that I had with a woman. I wanted more.

At home I could always count on a little action to take the edge off of a little boredom. We had a tenant who came to live there for a few months in that cursed vacant room. His name was Todd and with a very high IQ and he acted like it. We would sit and talk sometimes for hours about exciting topics like Area 51 or other government secrets. There was no evidence of anything wrong with this guy until I came home one day and found that he had smeared feces all over the wall in the bathroom upstairs and was running down the street naked. He had an ailment that he hadn't told me much about. What he had left out was what could happen if he didn't take his medication. The police brought him back and he took a breather in some psyche unit for a couple of weeks. That problem resurfaced a couple more times and he eventually left. The main group of us guys were still at 78 Palm Street were still intact and it was events like that that always kept us in good conversation for a few days afterward.

Back at work I began to earn a reputation for doing a good round of CPR on patients who needed it. By that time I had plenty of experience doing what I called "thumping" on somebody's chest. Using my natural intensity and the ability to focus my mind on a small area, the results that I got to help restart a heart was rather good. As I watched others do the same thing I could see a lack in even the most seasoned veterans. During the times when I would float to other places in the hospital, one of the favorite places to be was the Emergency department. That, of course had been my first choice when I was still working at Park Hope. At the time I had been working in ICU and the call came. The request for my form of CPR in the emergency department happened at about 1:30 in the afternoon. I walked briskly down the hall past the rooms that housed any psyche patients and into a trauma room. A thirty-eight year-old male had suffered a heart attack at work and was in a bad space. I put the gloves on and began to thump. The table was surrounded by many doctors and nurses all taking and giving orders to try and save this man's life. That certainly was the norm under the circumstances. What I did not expect to happen was the fact that someone had given the man's wife permission to sit beside her husband and hold his hand while I was doing CPR. In the intensive care unit that never happened. In fact, even if a relative was in the room at the time the patient "went down" they were asked or told to leave. For the first time I was witnessing a wife watch her husband leave this earth. I was soaked from head to toe with sweat throughout my scrubs. No one could tell the dripping sweat from the tears that I was shedding for this woman while I was working. The docs called the event about thirty minutes or so after we had started. I was thanked for my part in all of this and walked back to ICU. Sitting down in the lunchroom I put my head in my hands. I was alone with the door closed and the doctor for the unit slowly opens the door.

"Can I come in?" she asked.

I looked up and I knew that I probably looked like a train wreck. Joanne Hessney was a good doctor who championed the nurses if they ever needed support for anything.

"Yea," I answered.

She walked over to me and gave this hurting tech a big hug. I do not remember all of what she had said, but she knew what had happened.

"How are you doing? Can I get you something?"

I looked her straight in the eye and responded. "I'm fine. It's just that I have never seen this before. Why did they let his wife sit there? We don't do it, ever."

Rubbing my back, she agreed in principle, but said, "They can't deny her request to be there. They can try, but they have to let her do it. Most people wouldn't want to anyway. I'm sure it was tough on her. This all comes with the territory."

This had been the first and only time that I witnessed such an event. I washed my face and changed my scrubs and went back to work.

A short time later I was called to the Cath lab, the place where the doctors run a dye into the arteries and determine if any of a person's vessels are blocked. A fifty-seven-year-old woman had a heart attack on the table during the procedure. It was totally unexpected. I had to wear the heavy lead shield and do the CPR with my arms almost extended straight out under the special scope for observing the contrast in the person's body. For forty-seven minutes I worked the hardest that I ever had to save this woman. She died, but though I wasn't emotionally attached to this event, it was the hardest physically that I had encountered. Again drenched with sweat I changed my clothes and went back to work.

Very often wherever I went throughout the hospital I had become accustomed to be mistaken for a doctor. I always had a clean short cut with bright colored scrubs and wore a stethoscope. Being "only a tech" I would naturally point patient or family in the direction of a nurse or doctor to answer any questions that I was not qualified to answer. One fine day I had been floated to a wing in the hospital that everybody hated, especially the staff in the ICU. Many patients who left our unit would go to 3300 unit to continue with treatment while on a ventilator. If our unit was slow some of our staff would be sent to "Ventilator Alley" to work for the day. What made it tough was that when you got your assignment you would end up with all the patients that had "vents." That would be a very heavy workload. The staff thought that we would know those patients the best so why not give them away? I had been standing outside a room documenting some of the day's work for a particular patient. A group of three family members came up to and asked a question thinking that I was a doctor. I put my finger on my chin indicating that I was thinking about the question. Before I would point them toward a doc or a nurse I wanted to enjoy just for a second that fact that they thought I was a medical doctor.

They ended their question and before I could answer, a nurse walked up to me and in front of that family asked, "Ron, could you empty the bedpan in room four?" The family looked at me then the nurse.

I said, "She can help you," and then walked to room number four with my tail between my legs.

Holidays in the hospital were always special. In the ICU the nurses never lacked for decorations on anything that would hold them. Thanksgiving time had come and I was scheduled to work. During my entire life up to that point I had never missed that holiday with Mom back home in Pennsylvania. This would be a first and I wouldn't like it. Every year since my boyhood I got a drumstick all to myself. I began to love all of the staff that I working around, but not that much that I should miss my annual hind-quarter off of a gobbler. For a little compensation one of the nurses said that she would be bringing in a turkey for us. I felt some limited relief when I had overheard that statement. Thanksgiving Day came and I waited for the delivery. That nurse was not scheduled to work that day and I thought it was nice of her to go out of her way to do it. My scheduled time to work was from seven in the morning until 3:30 in the afternoon. Lunchtime came and no turkey. A couple of nurses brought in some pasta for lunch, but I wanted the good stuff. Quitting time came and now I was hurt. I never said anything to anyone, but even at my age I was still emotionally hurt that I would miss it all on Thanksgiving. As I left work that day I would take one last look around to see if I had made a mistake. When I got into my car I started to weep. Driving home was very lonely. Walking in the door of the house I started to smell something that was familiar. A turkey was in the oven. One of the new tenants named Louis from Puerto Rico had spiced up a bird and was now taking it out of the oven. Everyone else in the house had gone home to be with family, but Louis and I were there and he was the one with the turkey. My first thought was that God was rubbing my nose in my trial by letting me be so close and yet so far from this spectacle. My room, of course, was just off of the kitchen. I looked at Louis while I was getting the right key for my door. He had just taken it out of the oven and was cutting off a leg.

"Happy Thanksgiving," I said as I intentionally took my time opening the door.

"Happy Thanksgiving," to you too, he said while finishing the cut.

As I opened the door, I heard these golden words. "YOU CAN HAVE THE REST."

I whipped around instantly because I had my finger on the trigger just in case he would have made any suggestion or hint that I could have any of his turkey.

"What did you say, Lou?" I asked inconspicuously.

"I just want this leg and you can have the rest." I stood in awe like a kid catching Santa on Christmas morning. All he had taken was a leg and I now needed a reaffirmation that I heard him right.

"Are you sure, the rest of it?" I asked.

"Yep," he answered.

"Thank you very much!" I retorted. "Thank you! Thank you!"

Louis picked up his plate and went upstairs. I shoved my stuff in my room and came out with a big knife, and Tupperware containers to hold the meat. In no time flat I stripped that bird so that it looked like that steer head lying on the desert floor. Not enough meat left on it to choke a sparrow. I ate and ate and ate. I had been rescued from my pit of despair. Calling Mom and wishing her and the family was more of a joy now than a sorrow. I learned some things again about myself that day. I needed to grow a little more in yet another area of my life. Priorities, emotions, relationships, and much more continued to await me as long as I live.

How silly of me to think that now,
I had been abandoned.
Again and again I am tempted,
To give up when I don't see,
By Him who I've been branded.

After the winter was over the spring again was faithful to bring new hope to me. I had made it home to Mom for Christmas that year and then my birthday in January. The buds were now on the trees and the return of the geese could be heard as the daylight hours lengthened. My next door neighbor had gotten sick and was getting worse. The elderly lady on the other side of her was at one time a patient of mine at Park Ridge. She had just passed away and now "Gerri" was at death's door. She finally succumbed to years of smoking and gave up the ghost. This lady had been sort of a motherly figure to us guys living in the house when she was outside doing yard work or sitting on the front steps. We would miss her. What we wouldn't miss was the fact that everyone in the house was afraid that one of us was next. Our house was number three on the list of people that were dying. My former patient, then Gerri, then who next? I personally didn't think anything much about it, but just in case anybody had any ideas I prayed that the death angel would pass over us. I did that rather casually and didn't take it seriously. The only place that I had heard of anything like this was in the Bible in the Old Testament and I really believed that this kind of stuff was over. That is until the guy on the other side of us died two weeks later. The rest of the guys in the house now had some things to talk about.

We had a new neighbor move in across the street. That house had been sitting unoccupied for a couple of years and the family coming to our neighborhood believed that they could make something out of it. Frank and Phyllis Lauriano were a nice couple who had a son and a daughter in their mid and late teens. They quickly became our friends and I would enjoy going over to help with some advice on remodeling or maintenance. Getting dinner or lunch once in a while with this Italian family was nice too.

I was glad that Todd had moved on to another part of the city by that time. It wouldn't have been a good thing for the introduction into our neighborhood by seeing a crazy man running down the street naked. His replacement would turn out to be much worse though. He was Joe number two. He boasted about his ability to build a house from scratch and showed us his photos from projects of the past. I appreciate good work, but never took to a lot of "blowing your own horn" about it. Joe would come home drunk once in a while and when he was at his best he would help Frank across the street with a job or two. On one occasion he was accused of holding a knife to the daughter's throat and demanding her to be quiet about what he wanted to do. She escaped and told the authorities. He of course, denied everything and there just became a lot of hoopla about it. It was her word against his and most of it became unimportant...until he got arrested for murdering another woman a short time later. I had many a conversation with him about a lot of things and there was no indication that he would do either of the aforementioned deeds. I felt bad for everybody and a little betrayed. Fortunately I was not living there at the time of the murder and he had moved to another part of town as well. Frank and his family did a lot of work on that house and ended up moving a few miles down the road to an apartment. They had had up their ears with trying to maintain a house and certainly had their fill of the Tenth Ward by that time. Drugs and other problems started to come into our area in full measure and there was no let up in sight.

I was becoming more and more grateful that I made some of the choices that didn't result in what I was watching in the lives of others. At work I also would see the results of what people just chose to do. It was a well-known published fact that 80% of health care dollars are spent on choices that people make. The other problems are "appointed." One of the other Technicians in ICU had a longing to be married. She was a beautiful young woman at the age of twenty-two. She had found a nice guy that was apparently approved by all of the nurses in the unit. (If you can make through that crew and be accepted, you are in). Ann Marie got engaged and then married. We wished her well as she went into the Adirondack Mountains for her honeymoon. Her twenty-eight-year-old new husband had a heart attack and Ann Marie tried to revive him, but to no avail. I came to work one morning and heard the news. The whole unit was somber. She had kept herself from a lot of the things of the world in her wait for the right guy and now this happens. A few days later on a Friday afternoon after work I would be visiting the funeral home on my way out of town to Bradford. All of the staff from many parts of the hospital were there. I gave Ann Marie a hug on the way out and drove home to see Mom. Even though it was a fine sunny day, it was also a time for me to reflect on what I had been given. Life, friends, family and much more dominated my thoughts on the way to Bradford. I stayed at Mom's and as every Sunday afternoon I drove back about three o'clock after church and lunch. It had continued to be a cloudless warm weekend as I drove the two and a half hours back home. Traveling on Route 490 about twenty five miles outside of Rochester I came upon a car upside down in the middle of the road. There was no one else around so I obviously was the first person on the scene. A man and a woman were lying on the ground far away from the car. Both were dead with no chance of recovery. The woman had been cut in half and the man's head was shattered open. They had sheared off a metal utility pole and flipped the car. Some other people came as well as an ambulance. The paramedics rushed over in their usual quick fashion. I pointed to the victims and said, "they're gone." I left the scene and all the other people that hung around trying to figure out what had happened. It was a long straight stretch of highway on a beautiful sunny day and I knew what had happened. They had just left the road for a moment and hit the soft new berm that pulled them into the pole. Two weeks later the planned removal of all of those poles had commenced. They had missed a possible second chance at life by fourteen days. As I looked in my rearview mirror it hit me all at once. Ann Marie's husband on Friday at the funeral home and now I stumble on something like this. The tears began to well up as I hurt for all of the people and I guess for myself. It was weekends like this that can make a big difference in how you view life.

At home my basketball buddy Joe started to become a little of a problem with his girlfriend. They couldn't hide very easily in the house. Everyone had to be careful about what they had said, but most of the time that rule of thumb wasn't followed. I didn't pay attention to things like that when it wasn't my business. However, I would make a mental note of it because Julie was such a nice girl and it appeared as though Joe was going through some changes. He eventually would share some details about how she was becoming a pain in the neck with nagging about a good job or marriage. Little did I know that it was mostly rhetoric to throw me off from what was really going on. Joe had started using drugs and I did not know it. Every once in a while I would smell marijuana coming from upstairs and I had believed that it was one of the other tenants who had gotten caught patronizing the young escort when I answered the front door. I wouldn't assign any drug use to Joe. The truth was that he hadn't been using the whole time I knew him and that track record would now be tarnished. When we would go play basketball he seemed to be talking a little more about things that normally wouldn't be important. That should have been a warning sign, but wasn't. One afternoon he came to me with a football card that was encased in a plastic container held together with screws.

"Look, Ron, a Joe Namath Rookie card. I got it from an old man. I was walking down the street and I saw him taking out some garbage. It looked like he needed some help so I asked him. He said he was cleaning out his attic and asked me to help him carry some boxes to the curb. He showed me a box of sports cards, a big cardboard box that was full. He said that I could take one card, any card as payment for helping him move his stuff. I saw this one and I knew it was worth something. I'll tell you what, I owe you two hundred fifty dollars, ninety dollars for doing my taxes and one hundred sixty dollars cash. I swap you even, what do you say?"

I examined the card and it seemed to be worth something more significant in my mind. Nobody gives a card this much attention to protect it for nothing.

"Let me call around and we'll talk."

The first two places that I called told me that they would pay as much as eight hundred dollars for it. I got off the phone and thought how I couldn't do this to Joe.

Lessons and Stalked

I called Joe back downstairs and told him what the card was really worth and he said we could still call it even anyway. I offered to at least give him a hundred dollars extra for his troubles. He agreed. The card shop that I had chosen was in the Creekside Plaza. When we got into the parking lot he would not go in. He would make up some excuse so that he could stay in the car. I, of course, did not see it as an excuse, but as something innocent. He waited while I went and sold the card. I felt pretty good about the profit that I had made on the sale that day. Joe and I were square and there was some to boot.

A couple days went by and my normal routines in life carried on as usual. I was fortunate that I was not a big spender just because I had a few extra dollars. I got an interesting call two days after I sold the card. Joe's mother was on the other end.

"Ron, I have a concern about something. Joe's best friend called me today and told me that he had a football card missing out of his collection. He thinks Joe might have taken it. Have you seen or heard Joe talk about something like that?"

My mouth dropped. "What kind of a card was it?" I asked.

"It was a Joe Namath rookie card." she answered.

I looked away from the phone a second and said, "I know where it is. He obviously did take it." I told her the entire story and reassured her that the card would be recovered.

She was glad about it, but hurt and angry because, not only did he return to an old lifestyle, but did this deed to his best friend from his youth and now me. I got off of the phone and pondered about my relationship with Joe. Before I could tell him, I had to call the card shop and straighten things out. The police had already been involved and an angry card shop owner threatened to get a lawyer and sue me if I wouldn't come in and take it back. I don't remember saying anything to him that would make him take that kind of action, but I would take care of it. I called Joe downstairs and had a little talk with him. He had started doing crack cocaine in his room, an expensive habit that too much of America is familiar with. His efforts to keep the lid on this new path had been blown off in the form of doing things that he normally wouldn't do. I was caught off guard and had to pay for it. On top of all of this, Joe didn't tell me that he wouldn't be getting any money back on his tax return. He had owed money from the past and the money that I was owed for doing the taxes was supposed to come out of his return. He knew it and lied. My talk with him brought that all out. He said that he was sorry, but couldn't stop. Our friendship started to take a new path, one that I didn't like. His next feat was to get caught stealing a television from his mother and selling it for drugs. It was time for me to consider moving, but this would not be the last that I would hear from Joe. He was starting down a very dangerous road.

One of the nurses that I worked with in ICU at the time had learned that I was looking for a new place to stay. My neighborhood was beginning to slide into the clutches of the drug trade and the recent events at my current home made life a little uncomfortable to say the least. Michelle Newland was a fairly quiet nurse who had a son and a dog. When she told me what she was offering I had to snatch it up. She was living back in Greece in her own home. I paid a visit to check it out and fell in love with the setup. She had another roommate who was getting ready to move out and I would be a replacement. I would be staying for some time anyway until he left. I said yes to the proposition and told George. He tried to talk me out of it, but understood that I had to move on with my life. He also knew that things were going in a bad direction on Palm Street so for that he couldn't blame me.

I moved in with Michelle, Ryan, and the dog. They had a fence around the yard and good neighbors on both sides. It was the best location with access to direct routes into town, the malls, and the lake, all while being in the suburban life that I had longed for after I had moved back to Bradford. Michelle never had to lock the doors on the house or her car if she didn't want to. That location and its people were that nice and trusting. I wouldn't dream of doing anything remotely close to that back in the city. "Casey" was a beautiful white husky that Michelle had rescued from an animal shelter. We became friends immediately, probably because I would pander to scratching his tummy and make his left leg do the "bicycle twitch."

My room was on the second floor and I had access to the whole house, but in a better way than before. I didn't have to share the bathroom with many other people that had questionable sources of who knows what. Sharing the driveway wide enough for one car was sometimes tight, but that would never really be a problem. Being schooled in fending for myself with the food made all the easier to live what I called a dream life compared to where I had come from.

I still would work a lot of hours at the hospital. They got a lot out of me and didn't have to pay me benefits at the same time. My floating to other areas continued.

Before I came to my new home I had needed to supplement my income for a few months. The shelf sales had a lull and tech money couldn't support some of my invention projects forever. I wouldn't start anything new for awhile until I could get some extra cash. Taking a job temporarily at another nursing home would help a bit. The interview went well and my assignment would be working on the sixth floor at St. Ann's on Portland Avenue in the city. It was located right across the street from Rochester General Hospital so it made it quite convenient for a lot of emergencies.

I humored myself at the thought of ever working in a nursing home again, especially after the experiences that I had at Park Hope. But here I was again, shaving, cleaning, dressing old folks in another nursing home. There were a few things different though that made it easier. Almost everybody actually came to work. I worked every other Saturday and Sunday. It bothered me to miss church, but in the back of my mind I knew that this was not going to last forever.

The staff that I worked with was somewhat different than before. When I came to work on Sundays there were church programs on the television rather than conversations about family members being involved in crime. Almost every resident had their radio on at seven in the morning and it was turned to the African-American station DKX playing the African beats. Music on, hearing aids out and still sleeping would tell anyone who had worked the night shift. I was surrounded by black women again, but this time they were mostly church going and would actually let me do only my own assignment. It was hard enough, but at least I wouldn't have to take on another dozen people every other day.

My folks were occasionally funny the way that they acted. I had always wondered what the difference was between a Sister and a Mother in the Catholic Church. I was raised around the Catholic faith because most of my friends went to the Parochial school in Bradford, but I hadn't given it much thought about the differences between the two until I got older. In my mind it was obvious that the similarities with society and the church seemed peculiar. A mother is the older of the two...somehow. Taking care of a retired Catholic priest now gave me the opportunity to find out just what is going on with this difference pertaining to the ladies in the church. Father Smith, as he was called, had some cute quarks in his life. He always laid out certain clothes at certain times and very often made sure he could wear his black priestly garments as often as possible. He wasn't always with the program so he had to be reminded of many things. I waited for the most opportune moment right after he had gotten dressed for the day.

"Can I ask you a question please?" I asked.

He looked up at me with his head cocked to the side looking over the top of his glasses. I almost laughed at that shot. I wished that I had a camera. Glancing back at the floor he answered, "Yea, go ahead, what do you want to know."

I continued. "What is the difference between a Mother and Sister in the Catholic Church? How or when does a woman become a mother? Is it that they are elevated or something?"

The man got up off of the bed and started fumbling with some of his other clothes. I wasn't sure if I was being ignored or if he had even heard me. Maybe I had offended him. I didn't know. I waited as he walked around the room for a minute, but didn't press him for an answer.

Finally, in a fluid motion he held up a shirt to look at and said, "Those girls are always trying to break into the inner circle."

I turned around to laugh so he couldn't see me. That ended that conversation.

One of the goals in my adult life is to not miss a message that is meant for me. Whether it be bitter or sweet I need to know. Whenever an opening occurs for me to walk through I usually go for it. One of my other residents on my assignment was a ninety-two-year-old man who had been a retired painter. Old Ed had his left arm permanently crunched up to his body and was blind in one eye. His wife was ninety-one and lived next door in the Heritage Home. She was in a better space than Ed and dwelled in a place that people could get around pretty much on their own. A milestone was going to happen to this couple that year. In June they were going to be celebrating their seventieth wedding anniversary. I was impressed. That kind of longevity in relationships is a dying breed and I was happy to be taking care of someone who had been around the block a few times and was able to talk about it. Ed had all of his faculties and was able to talk freely. One morning I had gotten him all cleaned up for the day. His wife came in and stood at the bottom of the bed.

Standing alongside of him I had to ask. "Ed, I have to know something. You both are going to be celebrating your seventieth wedding anniversary this coming June. Not many people can lay a claim like that. You must have learned a lot. What kind of advice would you offer a young buck like me if I were ever to get married? What is your secret that your marriage lasted so long?"

Old Ed looked at his wife with his one good eye, then he looked back at me and said, "Keep your mouth shut."

I said, "Ohhh, okay."

At first I thought he was telling me to shut up, but then I knew what he meant. It became serious and funny at the same time. It has been many years and I still remember it, so it meant something to me.

During my short stint at St. Ann's I had also never lost a desire for a spouse. Obviously my questioning of Ed had evidenced that it was something that was on my mind. I gave in to another newspaper ad just one more time to find someone interesting that maybe I could be serious about. I found an ad which read: *Woman. broke, blind, and ugly. Willing to share my life with same.* I looked at it a second time then a third. I couldn't believe that anyone would say that about themselves, especially in a newspaper. Since I came to believe that it was a ploy and she was not really in the kind of condition that she said she was in, I would give it a shot. I eventually talked to the woman on the phone and questioned her about the validity of her claims.

"Are you really blind and broke?" I asked. I didn't ask about the ugly part. I feared that I would find out about that soon enough. We wouldn't talk about anything that could give away knowledge of where we lived or worked, but I ended up putting the whole thing on hold. What had bothered me most was not that she wasn't really blind, but that she had thick glasses. My flashback of the other woman with thick glasses made me reconsider ever calling her. So I didn't. The following weekend I went to work and discovered through an overheard conversation that the person I had talked to on the phone was actually my boss! I couldn't believe it. She had thick glasses, not much money and though she was not really ugly to me, I believe that it was just her opinion of herself. She was a nice woman who talked freely in front of me about her conversation with this nice guy, but he didn't really seem interested. I couldn't control myself any longer listening to compliments about me.

I interrupted. "That was me," I said.

She stopped talking. "What?" she questioned. "What do you mean? Are you serious?"

I enlightened her about what we had talked about and it all went well. I found it hard to believe what the chances were that it would have ended up being someone that I worked with, but we ended it all on a good note. I wished her well and I was rescued again because you can't have a relationship with a co-worker! Happy days are here again.

After moving into Michelle's I was quickly having pleasant memories of having my own family again. I sat in the back yard in the hot sun thinking about being back in 1983 with Lois and the girls and how many things had changed in my life. The circumstances at the moment could do nothing less than bring back thoughts of similar moments in time. I was very happy to be where I was and surely felt promoted having endured the problems at my former place in the city.

Ryan and I would play around the house or in the yard. I took him once in a while to the game room or to the mall. I don't think that I did as much as I could with him. Still having that streak of independence in me kept me at a distance from many people. Once in a while that aspect of me was too much. I would on occasion feel guilty about my lack of social life. I was very much aware of the candidness of other individuals to reach out and either meet new people or interact with current friends. I definitely still lacked in the social department. It would be just once every few years that anyone would comment on it.

Being sort of an observant loner at times also had its perks. I didn't get into trouble with girlfriends and arguments with anyone who had gotten too close to me. Living in my new home and working in the hospital gave me a lot of opportunities to watch others go through their troubles in life. Much of it I wouldn't want under any circumstances. At the same time I would hear that old saying come back to me that I believed would eventually apply to me someday. "It is better to love and lost rather than not to have loved at all." I knew the day would come when I would have to give up my staunch independence and take another chance at love no matter what the end of the matter would be. But, for the time being I was feeling free.

I got the now enjoyed privilege of mowing the lawn and looking like I was a completely settled man in his suburban dwelling. Casey would thump and prance around the yard while the lawnmower would run. I think he enjoyed its sound the way he would act. Once in a while we would take a walk around the neighborhood on the leash. Very often Michelle and I would be working the same shift in the ICU so it was easy to compare notes about the day. With so many patients coming and going and the lives of the other staff being so well known, we did not lack for conversational fodder.

I would have my trials with relationships though, even on a strictly professional level. Some people may not see the world the way I do and I would have to be bent a little to see that point. It wasn't always right, but I nevertheless would be thrust into situations that would grind that very point home.

There was a slow unit that day and I was sent to the ambulatory surgery area to fill in as a tech. I had been there many times before and so I was familiar with the people and routines. I was always happy to go there and work. The patients mostly had cataracts removed, shots in their spine for pain or minor surgery on a foot. Whatever the case was, they would all go home the same day. Part of my job was to help monitor them when they came out of surgery. Surgery-prep, stocking supplies, dressing and transporting patients were also included in the daily routine. This day would be different though. A nurse that I had worked with quite often had been standing nearby when a patient dropped a glass of ice chips onto the floor. I immediately got down on my haunches to clean it up. When I did that, the nurse came up behind me and reached underneath my bottom and struck my in the groin area! I couldn't believe it. The pain was pretty bad as I tried to reactively stand up. The patient saw it and I became embarrassed. I took a walk without saying a word. What I experienced the next two days convinced me that only people who had been violated in similar ways including rape could understand. Mental pain, embarrassment, fear, and a reluctance to socialize only touched on the feeling resulting from that one event. Over the years I had become an opponent of the frivolous lawsuits that seemed to be sweeping our nation. This event would not be told to anyone in authority for two weeks. I was ashamed to the point that I felt like I was guilty of something even though I wasn't.

The nurse apologized superficially believing that maybe this was a way to maybe start a relationship. I'm not sure what she thought. My explanation to three nurses in administrative positions at the same time gave me a little comfort, but didn't change the way that I felt. What frustrated me most about addressing my concern was the question, "Why didn't you come to us sooner?" No matter how much you try to drive home the points about fear and embarrassment it took a while to understand that they did not understand. Each one of them would have to go through the same thing in order to get the gist of my delay in telling them sooner. It didn't get swept under the rug, but I could have done more if I wanted to and chose not to. I never look for ways to make a fast buck even under those circumstances. I took my lumps and went on with my job. She was transferred to another area and eventually left or got fired.

My next ordeal was along a different line. I wouldn't get hurt, but I could have a lot more than the last time if I would have given in to certain demands of a stalker. I received a card in the mail. It was a card from what was signed as a secret admirer at first. The "funny" was that it came in the mail at Michelle's house. I didn't get mail there. I had used a post office box ever since I have lived in Rochester. The woman sent a couple of cards afterward and what had been a pleasant initial experience of attention quickly developed into what I felt was obsession. I couldn't answer the mail, but my "spy instincts" had been turned on. At any cost I would find out who this was. Investigating any leads or evidence that I could get she eventually called me. Even though I didn't have caller ID at the time it would not have made any difference. Her line was blocked. I answered that phone and she hesitated, just like in the movies.

"Hi, Ron," she said. "I guess you're wondering who this is, aren't you?"

My heart was pounding as I strained to play it cool. My goal now was to get her confidence that we would end up together.

"Well, yes, I believe anyone in these circumstances would wonder that is going on. So tell me, who are you?"

Hesitating again, she finally answered. "Do you think I'm going to tell you right now?"

I interrupted. "Okay then, what do you want? You must want something."

She replied calmly, "I want you. I've been watching you for weeks. You know who I am, but I can't tell you just yet."

I questioned her further to get more results. "If you are really interested in me then why didn't you just come up to me and tell me of maybe drop a hint through someone that I know so I could get to know you? Did you really have to go to all to all of this trouble to get my attention?"

That was easy for her to answer. "I had to do it this way. I'm married. My husband is a pastor and I am not seeing life the way that he does right now. I need someone else and you are it."

"Hmm," I replied. "I see your predicament. How can I help? Do you really want to meet with me or are you just infatuated? If you are it will just fade away."

She did not like the prospect of losing me to an admission that it was all wrong. "I'll tell you what. Let me think about it. I'll get back to you, okay? I'll call you later."

She hung up and I was convinced that I had planted some seeds that would produce some fruit. She had mentioned that she worked at Park Ridge, but did not work with me. That hospital was a big place, but I would try and sniff out who it was. For the next two months I heard nothing from her. During that time I had watched closely every female that I saw. I told Michelle to keep her eye out. She was the only one I told about this. I also became concerned about safety. "Play Misty for Me" was one of my favorite Clint Eastwood movies and now it was time for me consider how my own experience would play out. Clint had been stalked and there was a lot of violence. Even though I didn't think anything would happen to me, this woman's silence over the next sixty days provoked a lot of thought. She finally called.

"Hello" I answered.

"It's me, Ron," she said.

I now gave the hesitation. "Oh, hi, where have you been?"

She was a little exuberant. "I want to see you. I've been thinking about it and it's time."

I felt like she was in my sights rather than the other way around. "I will meet you anywhere, anytime. You pick where. What do you think?"

Backing off a bit, she gave me the answer that she was fighting with. She was grappling with her conscience. "We can't meet around my house. Is there anywhere near your place?"

I scanned my mind quickly to answer that question. "Yes there is. Hoover Drive School is just around the corner. We can meet at six in the parking lot. There won't be anyone there. Can you handle that?"

Her last words to me on the phone were, "I'll see you at six."

Five thirty came that day and I was sitting in the parking lot waiting to see if anyone would be scouting a little early. The coast was clear all the way up to the six o'clock hour. She had told me what car she would be driving and she kept her promise. The car was new and all of the glass was covered with the black tint so you couldn't see inside. There had to be mystery all the way up to the end. As I sat in my car she pulled up alongside of me and I watched as the power window came down revealing who this person was. I was surprised. She had delivered paperwork to the secretary in the ICU everyday and would go back to her office.

"Well, what do you think?" she said. "Did you think it would be me?"

I started to feel some sense of relief. "No, you aren't someone who I would have guessed about. Do you want to talk?" I asked.

"Yes, get in," she answered, looking around to see if anyone was watching.

I got in her car and we talked. My first intention was to make sure that she knew that she had more hope for her own situation than with me. I knew all along that I could have told her that she should just leave me alone and I could have gotten the authorities involved if she refused, but I didn't do that. Deep down inside I needed some attention, but getting it this way was not the best. Besides, I was confident that I could bring this all to a close by myself although it could've been handled better. The most dangerous thing about it all was that she was not anyone that I would have a relationship with under any circumstances. I just plainly was not attracted to her. What scared me was if she really had been.

I got in the car and told her that I was not available. I was a Christian and couldn't have a relationship with someone else's wife.

"What you need is to go back home and get close to God. Be faithful to your husband and listen to him about matters that you have refused to. He hasn't done anything wrong to you. You told me that yourself. I don't buy this mentality that you just drift away. You have to do some intentional neglecting to get to where you are today. I'll see you at work, but for now there is nothing between you and I. Are you listening to what I am saying?"

She looked away from me out the window. "You're right," she said. "I just gave up when he wasn't giving me the attention I wanted."

"Well," I said, "if he needs to pay more attention to you, isn't it okay to tell him about it? He is not the kind of guy to shun you when you need to talk. I'm sure that he has given more than one sermon on communication to the flock. He can make a mistake. He's only human. But you can't use that excuse here. Now go home."

She looked at me straight in the eye and said, "You're right. I'm sorry. I think that I can make it okay. Thank you for listening to me."

She left and that was the end of that. I see her once in a while for no more than a simple "Hello" in the hallways.

There were a lot of messages in these experiences for me. I continued to look for them and they never really stop. One of the following days in the ICU would be a deal breaker if I questioned whether there was really such a thing as an angel from Heaven. As I was making my rounds taking care of hourly documentation outside of the patient rooms I noticed out of the corner of my eye a pair of men in dark suits enter room number thirteen. At the time there was a man who was dying in that room. We most often knew approximately when that was going to happen. Sometimes the day, once in a while even the hour we could predict when a person was going to pass on. I had been in thirteen just a few moments earlier and the man had no visitors. Any family or friends who should have been there for this part of the man's life were not. I watched to see when the men would leave. What was of interest to me was that they were moving like they business to attend to. It was not a casual visit that they were presenting. They were acting like they were going to an important meeting of some sort. A couple of minutes later they came out hastily and left speaking with no one on the way in or on the way out. I went over to look in the room. The man was now dead, but the had a smile on his face. No alarms had gone off when his heart stopped. They should have because he was still hooked up to it. The secretary sitting outside the room said she did not see anyone go in. If she just slid her chair over a couple of feet she could touch the wall outside his room if she wanted to. She was that close. I never found out who those guys were, but I wonder even today where they came from.

In September of 1996 a new idea had come to mind as an invention. I have always been interested in vehicular accidents. Some of them should never have been called accidents in the first place, but the way people have been getting maimed or killed prompted me to come up with some way to prevent forces from penetrating a car in a side impact related accident. I drew up a sketch of the idea and set it down for a couple of months. Thanksgiving time came and I was traveling to Mom's for the holiday. I had bought a newspaper before I had left and when I had gotten about an hour outside of Bradford on Route 17

I got a little edgy and wanted to scan the paper. (Nice thing to do when you are in the process of inventing something to help with accidents.) I picked up the paper and on the front page was an article about an accident in a parking lot of a grocery store somewhere in the Midwest. A mother had watched her little daughter be decapitated when the front airbag went off during a slow moving collision with another vehicle. I threw the paper down and my spirit was rekindled about working on a new technology to address the problem. Although this type of accident was not the same type that I was giving attention to it certainly was the wake up call I needed to get to work on my own project. I was going to get a royal workout in the art of inventing…for the next nine and a half years just on this one project.

At the time that I would be enjoying turkey in Pennsylvania I began to take another stock of myself. How was I doing in life? Where was I in regards to the vision that I had a few years earlier? What did my future hold? Probably the most important point to make second only to my relationship with God was my relationship with people. Ever since I was in Maple Manor seventeen years earlier it was important for me to look at whether I was maturing as a person and what kind of affect I was having on others. I had been taught to monitor what I took in and what came out in my life. The real story is what comes out. That can be an indication of what I had taken in. Being a self declared expert observer it was easy to see in many ways what the norms were in society in many ways. To compare myself with those standards and discover much of where I needed work never took a stalker to reveal it.

Messenger am I in the deepest sense,
Angel I dare say.
My influence to others is good or bad, who knows?
Me! I had better, lest I sit on the fence.
May God deal with me so and knock me off,
While now all through me, my breath still blows.

After I had come up with LifWeb pronounced "LifeWeb"(the name for the side impact device) I also had something else going on in my little mind. Back in 1984 I had a fleeting thought that someday I would like to write a movie. That thought never came back to me again for over a decade. Writing had never been one of my finer points. All I ever did was sign my paycheck and wouldn't have had the patience to learn anything beyond that anyway.

In my mind was a plot for a movie. I knew enough to keep it sort of a secret, similar to an invention concept. Even though I knew nothing about writing I had this desire to have the idea crafted onto paper somehow. By 1996 there had been some semblance of order in my life and I did have more patience than fifteen years earlier. Even with some more confidence, it was a snag in my mind to commit to writing a hundred pages or so on a typewriter or computer. I could handwrite anything, but it had become easier to just pay someone else to do the typing. I "jotted down" two hundred pages on the "Sin in America" only a couple of years earlier. A mutual friend from church where Terri was going had typed it up and critiqued that work. She was brutal on every point. I did not like hearing every correction from an expert. She had gotten a degree in college for the art of writing, but I still wouldn't surrender to sound counsel at the time. Being an inventor I would have to find a new breed of typists. Knowing nothing about screenplay writing would be a snag.

I would need on occasion a letter typed up to send out to a company here and there with the invention ideas that I was working on. After finding a couple of women that had put their names on some local bulletin boards I ended up with one that I could stay with for awhile. One day when I had gone to pick up a piece that I had paid her to do I asked if she would like to try and tackle typing a screenplay.

"No, I wouldn't go near something like that. I'll just stick with the short stuff," she said. Then I saw a light go on in her head. "But, I remember someone from high school who had gotten into that area. His name was Nick Dibella. I don't know where he is at, I had just heard that he was doing that kind of thing."

To make a long story short, I tracked down Nick and had discovered that he was my man. He quickly became my mentor for a while.

Writing down my ideas was always easy, but when it came time to bring it to the standard that others accepted it would cost me dearly. Either I would have to learn to type or pay out the nose to have someone else do it. I'll take the latter please. It is amazing the lengths that some people go to, to get out of doing something that may require a little sacrifice. I guess I was no exception. By this time I had just been asked to take a look at working a job at the drug and alcohol treatment facility for Park Ridge. The job had been posted and I hadn't really been looking to switch. But I took the job and ended up going back and forth between the ICU and the drug unit every other day. Cheryl Martin was the director at the time and my interviews with her went well. She became the Mother Theresa of rehabs to me. Her willingness to welcome just about anybody through the doors had ticked off many a worker whose comfort zone had been shaken. One of the staff at rehab was a secretary who would end up typing my first screenplay for me. It took a couple of months for me to write by hand every word that I wanted. I had bought a couple of suggested books to learn the format so I could teach "Rosanna" how to organize the structure. It cost me hundreds, but she did it. I knew it was going to be expensive and before I gave the work to her I would give it one last shot to try and do it myself. I hated computers in every sense, nevertheless, I would give a word processor a whirl. I found one for sale in the newspaper and drove thirty miles in a rainstorm to pick it up. I set it up on a desk and had a new round of confident enthusiasm. I set it up, turned it on, read some of the directions and lasted about five minutes. I almost picked it up and threw it through the window. Two days later it was gone. Rosanna was going to be making some money on the side. We worked hard together for about three and a half months going back and forth to finish what I called the final draft.

Two weeks after I had celebrated writing my first screenplay, Rosanna came to me at work and said, "Ron, your movie is out in the theatres! It's in the papers!" She showed me a large article written by one of the local movie critics and sure enough there it was. My screenplay, "The Beat Goes On," was about a woman who was a nurse. Her husband had a brain hemorrhage and was on life support until the doctors declared him brain dead. She painfully donates his organs to society and faces the world a widow. The only problem is that she cannot accept his death. With the aid of a friend they try to find out where his heart went. She goes to the man who got it and he turns out to be a Saudi Prince incognito who paid a million dollars to be moved to the top of the recipient list. They eventually end up together in the end. The movie that came out on the screen was with the same premise. David Duchovny and Minnie Driver starred in "Return To Me," a movie where she as a woman who had gotten his wife's heart and ended up falling in love with him through a series of mysterious events. I was at a loss for words. This had happened too often to me in the inventing world and now I get shot down coming out of the starting gate over a simple idea that I had for a movie. "Return To Me" was a remake of an old movie, so they couldn't have known what I was working on. My experience with dealing with ideas that other people had would pay off though. It was time to think up another movie that was more difficult to copy.

My personal life was in fairly full swing with Judy at that time. I had left her company for a while and now I was back. Looking for love in a newspaper and getting stalked by married women just wasn't cutting it. We would pretty much do what we had always done. Go out to eat or take in a movie. I had a straight shot down the Parkway, which would take me to her home in Hilton. Her mother though showed no signs of relinquishing up her views about any future with me for her daughter. She was fixed in concrete about that. In some ways it was comfortable and convenient to visit those Saturday nights and not be tied down. My income still would not tolerate the entrance of a family into the picture anyway. Although it was convenient to have a setup like that, I still wanted more.

Traveling to Bradford to see my family had become again a little less frequent. Mom had almost stopped completely calling me by that time and started acting a little goofy. She would forget things and even swear up and down that something was so when it wasn't. Alzheimers had entered her life and I didn't know it. My trips to Bradford still consisted of staying overnight on the weekend, but trickled to just a few times a year. Sam would call me once in awhile, Mary not often at all. It was becoming quite apparent that if I didn't make the effort to see my family or talk to them first then it just wouldn't happen. I didn't resent it and no one showed any problem with me there just was this drifting apart. Mom hated the big cities, Sam agreed with Mom and would once in awhile drive to Buffalo just to get out of the house. Mary had a new boyfriend who either liked to fish, hunt or stay home. This would be a recipe in the making for a lot of problems in the future.

My job at the rehab center was going quite well. Cheryl had welcomed me from the start and so did the rest of the staff. Every day was different. The patient population changed all the time so it was far from boring. Drug addicts from New York City and Albany as well the local alcoholics and addicts kept us all on our toes. The story that each person had to tell is amazing. Running from people who wanted to kill them, every crime known to man as well as the usual broken families, finances and health issues created the landscape that we all see in our society today. I have never been disappointed at the day going by quickly just trying to manage or coach these sick folks. In recent years our rehab center took on the responsibility of merging the behavioral community that is saturated with Psychiatric issues and blending those patients with those primarily with addictive problems. To sort out and treat that combined population has been a tough job on every staff member. It would be easy to make a story of some kind out of almost every patient's life, but there would be for most of them not a happy ending. The staff members do see or get a visit on occasion from a former patient who has remained clean and is living a new life. That kind of feedback unfortunately is the exception rather than the rule.

For the first two years while I worked at the rehab I also stayed in the ICU. Going back and forth every other day between the two places made for an unusually busy time. It also gave me the opportunity to see things that others did not. One day I would take a dead overdose patient to the cooler at the morgue and the next day I would go to work at the rehab and listen to someone complain about the "green beans not being done enough in the cafeteria." I have wanted to grab some of them by the scruff of the neck and drag them over to the morgue and show them where they are headed. And I have also told them my experience about that quite often. The point that I always drive home the most is the fact that they have fooled themselves into thinking that there is some strange elusive reason why they keep using drugs and alcohol.

"There is none!" I bark all the time. "It is not an alcohol or a drug problem. It never was, is not, nor shall ever be a drug problem! It is a living problem! If you had learned how to live your life properly in the first place you wouldn't need something to medicate or anesthetize the pain or unsettledness in your life. Some of you have been beat, sodomized, talked down to, belittled, and only God knows what! The damage that other people have caused you in your life together with the trouble you have caused yourself as a result of it is what needs to be changed. Not some new way of trying to discover what the problem is. This is the problem!"

I always let them have it by the time I am done talking. Some are in tears and others are pondering what they just heard. Once in a while I tell them that, "If I was turned loose in the State Capitol I would really move the lawmakers to action. The general public and the State are over a barrel. We have been hoodwinked into thinking that there is some reason other than the deliberate choice to refuse the help that patients are offered. The same things are repeated over and over again and yet we finance a revolving door for too many who make a conscious decision not to apply themselves to get and stay clean and sober." Then I finish them off with this. "When you were on the streets you were a force to be reckoned with. There are people places and things out there that are ready willing, and able to assist you if you want to stay drunk or high for the rest of your life. You willingly and knowingly made decisions to use and apply those people and elements to further your own cause. You were willing to go to any length to get what you wanted. Now that you are on this side of the fence what are going to do? There are people, places, and things over here that are ready, willing, and able to help you stay clean and sober for the rest of your lives. Tell me, what is your cause now? I have just taken away every excuse that you can come up with as to why you can't stop. It's not because you can't it is because you won't. You can't stop just because you say you are going to. It takes hard work and applying yourself with the aid of other people. The simplest way to stay messed up is just refuse help as inconspicuously as possible. We are sneaky aren't we?" There has not been a time ever that people weren't shocked to hear things that had been going on in the mind for perhaps years. The battle would rage on.

I began to have trials of my own in the wonderful world of inventing. The beginning of that eight plus year stretch of grappling with people places and things to try and get Lifweb to market was easy. Always coming up with a new idea is the easiest thing to do. A nine or ten year old boy invented a biodegradable golf tee. Just stick it in the ground, hit the ball and leave the tee there. It breaks down and becomes part of the soil. The kid was a millionaire almost overnight, so it seemed. The biggest difficulty is getting attention from decision-makers in companies to see the value in an idea. I had been through the patent process before, but that does not guarantee a ticket into the marketplace. It can and does help, but ensures nothing by itself.

Filing a patent this time would require money that I did not have. I had born out a rule that if I couldn't pay the money up front...no go. I hated the payment thing to a lawyer a couple of years earlier and it pained me into making that decision. Of course, after all the designing and paperwork were done I hired a firm to file the patent. And, of course, it was rejected. This time I would fight. It turned out that the Patent Examiner in Washington did not fully understand the concept. I won in arbitration and got my first patent. I had sold all of my tools and used my savings, but at least did not owe a penny to anyone. The long process of trying to convince auto manufacturers to consider Lifweb going into their cars was futile to say the least. It took a long time before I would understand that adding anything on top of the cost of a car even if it would save a life would not happen the way I was doing it.. I had consulted with a lot of people to come to that dastardly conclusion. The "Big Three," Honda, Toyota, and Volvo all said no. I ended up hiring a marketing firm that contacted sixty-nine different companies that were supposed to be involved in that type of business. They all said no. Contacting another twenty-five companies myself brought the total to about one hundred different places that refused to seriously evaluate my concept. I did again what I do best. Set the idea down for a while. I needed a rest. The work and the money issue had brought me to the place where there needed to be a time of just living day to day without pressuring myself to hit the "big time." I hated the thought of doing what I was preaching against. Reaching out for all of the world and at any cost. The vision that I had for a future would come to pass. I wouldn't have to work myself into a heart attack or a stroke over it. I did have peace and I did not want to disturb that. Besides, there were things more important that I had to give attention to.

Ascent into Love

It would seem even before this point in my life, that my male intuition (if there is such a things for the guys), would have guided me into a safe and reliable relationship with a member of the opposite sex. Marriage is a decision that you can ask the whole world about, but it always comes back to you. No one else gets the blame or the credit.

I had written "The Beat Goes On" and lent a copy to a woman who was working at Park Ridge the same time as myself. I had seen her come and go in the ICU as a respiratory therapist as well as the other wings of the hospital.

We had a conversation about the life of a person in health care and I said, "I wrote a screenplay to a movie about a nurse who lost her husband and couldn't accept his death."

This had piqued her interest and I did not know at the time, but she had lost her husband in that very ICU at the same time I was working there and I didn't know it. She could have been visiting another patient for all I knew.

I brought a copy of the script to work and she took it home. Little did I know that this act would alter the rest of my life. She smiled and seemed to want to guard it closely. I was happy about that for I felt like my blood went into that piece of work.

After a week or so, she called me and said, "I read your screenplay and I loved it."

I smiled, of course, and responded. "Good, do you want me to come down and pick it up?"

She gave me the address. At that time I had no interest in Carol-Aynn, but I suppose I should wonder why I didn't promote the idea that she could have just brought it back to work in the first place.

Getting to the apartment complex wasn't a problem. I had heard of Spanish Gardens before. Having worked as a maintenance man at a nearby property kept me more than privy to the other businesses that competed against my former employer. I rang the doorbell and the sweet smiling therapist answered. I entered a beautifully decorated apartment that had nothing out of place.

"Like some tea?" she asked.

"No thanks," I said. "Water is fine. I don't drink tea."

We sat in the little dining area, which was actually part of the kitchen just a few feet from the front door. The screenplay lay on the table. I looked at it and then looked at Carol. She was now quite somber. Taking a sip of my water I knew I had to let her speak first. Something wasn't right.

Setting down her tea she looked away from me staring out the window. "I could relate to the movie," she said. "It had some things in there that happened to me."

In my mind's eye I quickly scanned my work and hoped that this sweet woman could not relate to the death of a husband. "I lost a husband," she continued. "He died a few years ago."

I froze and couldn't say a word. Then I fought to say, "I'm sorry, I didn't know."

Tears welled up in her eyes and looking at me and shaking her head. "No that's okay, its not your fault. I haven't had anyone here to talk about it in a long time. Excuse me," she said as she got up to get a kleenex.

Coming back into the room with a little more composure gave me a cue to ask, "How did it happen?"

Wiping her eyes she responded, "His heart, an infection in his heart from his tooth."

This man died in my unit and I hadn't heard of that kind of death before. Where was I? I needed her to connect the dots.

Taking a deep breath, Carol courageously continued on. "His name was Jeff. He had gotten an infection in his tooth. He wouldn't listen to me. He thought he would just gut it out. We didn't know that the tooth had gotten as bad as it did. The infection went to the valve in his heart and grew a lot of vegetation around it. He only lasted a few days."

"When did it happen?" I asked.

"September 17 back in1991,"she revealed.

Hmm, I thought. *This was the date of my anniversary of getting sober.* Looking at her with concern I slowly opened my mouth. "Are you okay?"

"Yea, I'm okay."

I must admit I was all thumbs because I didn't expect this, but I turned the screenplay around and then became at a loss for words. We talked for a little while longer and I shook her hand and left. My drive home had me thinking that I hope this hurting woman was comforted in some way. I saw too many people loose their loved ones on my new job to think that her loss was any easier.

The coming days at work were now different. We did not know it, but her revealing of this event in her life put both of us into a new light. It was therapeutic for her to tell it, but the fact that I knew the story so intimately drew Carol-Aynn Jones and me into a common relationship that was inescapable. I wrote it and she lived it. If it had been a disaster I would have given it a second thought about asking to see her again. The track record of two people meeting in a hurricane and trying to make something of it was not good.

Among the bells and whistles of our work environment we eventually saw each other again.

"Would you like to go for a walk sometime?" I asked.

It was a little nerve racking to mention it, but I thought, *What the hay?* She might say no, but what else is new. I never got the trophy for optimism anyway except when I played the ponies years earlier.

It was in room six of the Intensive Care Unit when she said yes to the walk.

We picked a day and I showed up right on time. A late spring day somewhere around the beginning of May saw our first planned encounter for a stroll in the evening. The weather was perfect. The area to walk in was perfect. There was much to talk about along the way. She was seven years older than myself, so I wanted to glean some good conversation about where she has been in her life. I, on the other hand, had become an expert in telling people about the experiences in my own. Getting a jump start many years earlier in the AA meetings presented me no problem in getting my life's story out in a conversation. Being holed up for over fourteen years as a single male, there was an accumulation of many more chapters of a life not told so maybe there was a subliminal desire to share those things with another person.

Our walks became a more frequent thing. I met her daughter Julie who was living with her at the time. She was a mature minded seventeen year-old girl who was attracted to men who were much older than herself. Her reason was simple. "Men my age are so immature," she would say. During one of my visits to Carol's it was discovered that Julie was going to be married to a man at least ten years older then herself. Carol seemed to endorse it, but though I didn't say it at the time I couldn't give approval to such a union.

A few strolls later I met some of Carol's family. Her sister Michelle had brought her kids over one evening. Two of the boys lived with Michelle and the two girls and another brother lived out of state in Ohio with their father. It was a little nerve racking at first because I was conditioned to playing basketball with only weekly acquaintances and now there was a little trepidation at the thought of any commitment toward a large family, which I only had heard of most of them up to that point.

The oldest son Brandon was a nine-year-old basketball player. Fortunately for all of them there was a court on the complex where Carol lived so we all went down to partake of our common factor. This seemed unimportant at the time because after all I thought I was just keeping the kid busy during one of the visits with his mother and Aunt.

A lesson yet to be learned was going to be a painful one. My relationship to other people was not to just consist of going home to myself just because the sun went down. I needed other people in my life and the exercise of bringing others into my "space" was irritating, inconvenient, and sometimes just a pure pain in the neck. But I knew I needed it. That realization and the will to fulfill it was greater than all of it. Inside I was ashamed of myself for having played it safe for so long. The reason I was in the safe zone for those many years was I had refused to grow and mature in several tracts of my life. It was convenient to do what I wanted, go where I wanted, when I wanted with no strings. But there is a price for everything. My choices were self fulfilling. Staying single and protected kept me that way. I couldn't expect to reap the benefits of family if I was going out the door forever.

You can't have it both ways, I thought. There was this pinnacle in my life, maybe a saturation point that told me enough is enough. I was not a fulfilled human being. That for which I was created did not exist in my life. It is fine for some to be single even for the rest of their lives, but to deny yourself the healthy relationships with other people results only in wrong identity. I watched some older people throughout my city get caught living in squalor. Only to find out that their decisions to avoid any relationships with any other people at all resulted in huge garbage piles in their homes, maybe keeping money out of the banks and letting their personal hygiene go by the wayside. Carol-Aynn was a wonderful example of all I had lacked. A very large family with many grandchildren, countless friends and a ready willingness to add more testified to her normal human basic commitment. The contrast between our lives was encouraging and the fears that I had at the time were somehow allayed by her natural gift of acceptance of other people. To put in bluntly, she lived it, I didn't.

Over the next month, Carol had made the decision to move. Her approach to me to help her in some way flattered me.

"Ron, I want to look for a house and will need someone to help, you know, look it over to make sure it doesn't have any real problems. Will you do it? I'm tired of living in an apartment.'

It didn't take long for my answer, which was yes. She knew that I had worked construction and remodeling for many years so I was able to look at things and give an honest opinion.

"No problem," I said.

The next couple of weeks saw us check out some houses in the neighborhood near the lake, which really wasn't far from Spanish Gardens. We ended up at 30 Petten Street, a small road that ran from Lake Avenue to the Genesee River. About a mile from the lake and a couple of stones throw from the river afforded anyone who wanted to live here a prime opportunity to walk in some of the best of environments. The proposed plans for the renovation of the waterfront didn't hurt any. The only problem at that time was that for many years there was only talk and no action. Well, she liked that house, and after my approval of the structure she bought it. An eighteen hundred square foot home including an apartment upstairs became the residence of Carol-Aynn Jones.

I can't quite remember at exactly what point she asked me to remodel the first floor in this home, but I do remember that it was before she moved in because the furniture was placed in the garage for that purpose. I said, "No I can't, I sold all my tools to finance a patent." Apparently not acknowledging my valid reason and some more prodding from her I said, "I'll tell you what, if you borrow the tools I will do the work." I really had two things in mind. One, I didn't think she could get the tools and if she did it would only take about six weeks to do what I felt she wanted.

Well, she got the tools from her brother John and that was the official start of a new life for yours truly. After the closing on the house and the furniture was delivered to the garage I began to remodel 30 Petten Street. Little did I know that Carol had perfected the art of changing her mind on things. Any job I had done before got the benefit of my talent for saving money as well as a unique creativity. This endeavor was no different and this was attractive to Carol. It wasn't so comfortable for me when the homeowner would not cooperate with some things that made common sense. The costs of some products varied from place to place as well as competition in the brands made for a good argument and Carol ended up listening to me…in the end.

A common problem with buying a home and leaving your former residence in that you never want to pay out to both places. Carol-Aynn needed to live in this house and rent out the upstairs at the same time. Could both happen? She did it. Renting out the apartment to a single mother who gave her nothing but grief while she herself slept on stacks of drywall for months proved she could do it.

"Are you sure you want to do this?" I exclaimed. There was evidence too often that there should be some other type of arrangement, but she always was willing to do what it took.

Over the next several weeks the entire first floor was a dust house. For a woman with asthma this was not good. Tearing out wall after wall consisting of that old lathe and plaster made for the worst type of dust. They used asbestos back then when plaster was made. Although the house was over one hundred years old we still found artifacts in some of the walls from the late 1800s. Newspapers from the 1930s insulated the wall separating the kitchen from the side porch. In all we had removed 7.4 tons of measured material from this house. Hardly the beginning of only a few weeks job. Every wall and ceiling in every room, the floor in the kitchen and bath were replaced. Carol started living on the drywall first in the master bedroom, then the living room. Her clothes hung on a makeshift line stretched across the bedroom. After about two months the line stretched so that the clothes started sagging toward the floor. The line was the white electrical Romex cable. This type of living was nothing short of "roughing it."

The work actually started in September 1998. In April of '99 the house was still in disarray. Added work took away any thoughts of a completion date. Tearing out a major support wall, enlarging the kitchen, adding a wood burning stove with a chimney and adding a sliding door were only some of the added projects to the overall scheme of things.

As the project advanced into the summer months, it became apparent that my time with Carol became more than the plutonic social relationship we had experienced. Having dinner from the grill in the back yard became a regular thing. We became fond of each other. Neither one of us believed in having sex before marriage so that wasn't something that factored into any decision about going further with any commitments. There came a day when I was sitting on the loveseat across from Carol-Aynn. We were talking about life in general. Then it became more specific. We talked about us. There comes a time in a man's life when there is that pinnacle about a subject and there is no more to be discussed. Action must take place or it is all just "putting it off." I gathered myself together and looked at her. I thought to myself, *How much longer am I going hold onto only thinking about it?* Now is the time or its no time. "Will you marry me?"

She looked at me with great intent and didn't move. For the first time in my life I wasn't afraid of the outcome, whatever it would be. She said, "Could you repeat that?"

I said, "Will you marry me?"

She got up from the sofa and we came together for a big hug. She was in tears. I was pleased with the outcome. We sat and planned the date. October 15 of 1999 was to be the big day. Back in Bradford during the fall of the year would be perfect.

There was a new mood around her house after the engagement. An electrician, Matt Trostle, was happy at the news. He came on occasion to wire the house to bring it up to code. I never did anything electrical, maybe replace a receptacle or two. Carol told her family and friends. Although there was skepticism and questions from some people close to her, Carol assured them that I was a keeper. There was a sense that their concern wasn't whether I was a keeper or not, but that since she had been married four times before they wanted to have some evidence that there was something drastically different this time. Something that would prove it would last. They would all have to wait, just like the rest of us. Time would tell.

Just a couple months earlier when the house was a mess I got a call from a local television station. The trade show where I had displayed my invention in had produced bit of publicity for Lifweb, the side impact collision concept that I had patented. Maureen Maguire asked me if she could come out to the house and do a story. I said sure.

Carol said, "What! The house is in shambles."

"Don't worry about it," I told her. "I'll just set up Lifweb on the sawhorses in the kitchen." That room had no drywall, no finished floor and the ceiling was open. My working model weighed one hundred fifty pounds and had to be set up on something that was fairly strong and a piece of plywood across the horses was perfect. After all that is where I had built part of it in the first place.

Maureen came out with her crew much to the chagrin of Carol. I did in some way agree with her that the house was a mess, after all, I made it. The major consolation for both of us was that the prospects for success in our new life together was being ratcheted up a notch. If this invention would take off it would be the cat's meow. I waited while the crew set up the camera and the lighting. They stayed for an hour and a half. That is a long time for any news channel to stay on the scene. I was nervous, but maintained my composure and demonstrated my invention under the lights from different angles. The news clip on television ran two minutes and twenty seconds for four days and nights. That was an exceptional amount of time for any local story.

It was interesting that I did not experience any of the questioning in my mind concerning the decision I had just made concerning Carol. Having been engaged twice in the last fourteen years should have made me a skeptic especially since those engagements ended at the last minutes before the wedding, and not by me. This time was different. I had not become a skeptic. My wife to be was a real treasure. I was moved by the contrast in her life from her previous commitments to marriage. She also had a reason to be skeptical of her own decision to marry me, but did so without reservation. The most outstanding quality that she had was that she was soft. Her gift in life is one of charity and I gravitated toward that. Maybe it was the mother image. I, on the other hand, was hard. Later on we both agreed that she was too soft and I was too hard. We hoped that there would be a working in our lives where that would balance out. Well it really doesn't work that way unless there is some give and take, as we have so humbly found out.

Carol endured much while the house was being done. She was a little trooper wearing her dust mask in the clouds of dusk sometimes so thick that you couldn't see across the room. With her asthma she still held up. She needed stitches once when she picked up a piece of sharp lathe and cut her leg. Also dealing with Crohn's disease kept her making trips to the bathroom upstairs because hers was all torn up. While the project continued and most of the major things got done there arose an unforeseen problem. Renting to other people has its moments and Carol Jones's initiation in landlordship was a difficult one. That single mother of three mentioned earlier had acted out the sweet innocent type just to get the apartment. She left out one minor detail. She was pregnant with a fourth child. To have all those kids in a two bedroom upper apartment was against the law. The crying, yelling screaming, and visits by her boyfriend for weeks at a time was a frustrating life for a woman who had just spent many weeks herself sleeping on a stack of drywall, all while working a full time job in a very busy hospital. Consulting the law and professionals was to no avail. This young mother had rights that made others' lives very uncomfortable. I had to hold my peace while a frustrating situation never got better until that golden day arrived many months later. Even while she was moving out, her boyfriend took every light bulb out of the apartment. In the beginning of all this I had acquired the position that I could do nothing because it was an agreement between Carol and this woman. The law was the law and I had to respect it.

It was a beautiful summer in 1999. The weather had cooperated very well and the descent into the fall announced the arrival of our wedding plans. Traveling to Bradford with Carol's side of the family was an interesting experience for me especially because I had never been treated so important that the bride to be in my life would consider such a thing. Her family was so big and mine so small that it was obvious that maybe the wedding should take place in Rochester. This was example of the working of me becoming soft. What was natural to her I had to work hard at, remember? She is soft, I am hard. I was becoming softer because of her humility. Love truly is such a beautiful thing.

We got to the motel and dropped off our things and got ready for the wedding. Pastor Palutro was to preside over the ceremony. The wise man of God now in his early fifties, Phil, as I sometimes called him, required that we come to Bradford for some sessions of marriage counseling before the wedding. A couple of trips down to B-town before we got married got us into a little better shape for the commitment. We anticipated hard questions and good counsel and we were not disappointed. The big day was here and the preparation at the church saw people start to wander in. We had only invited about forty people so it was going to be a little laid back. Carol's mother was one of the last ones to arrive. She embarrassingly had left her dress back in Rochester and had to buy a new one in Bradford. We didn't find that out until after the wedding. Her problem was compounded by having to find a store that had something she liked and fit, but the town of only twelve thousand people didn't have as much to offer as the stores back home. She got one at the wire and waltzed into the church just in time.

The ceremony went very well. We had given three yellow roses to Pastor Phil. He looked at them, held them up for all to see. The rose in the middle was higher than the other two. He gestured to the people in attendance that the rose in the middle that was higher was representative of the Lord ruling over this marriage of Carol and myself, the other two roses. We believed that neither by irony or coincidence, but by a divine appointment by God sealed this marriage and confirmed it by the message that was prepared for the service. The scripture in the Bible was read. Its reference was that "a three-fold cord in not easily broken." The translation that is widely accepted for that portion of scripture means that if the Lord is allowed to be the primary part of anything that it will not be disseminated while the Lord is sought. The Lord has been sought and the provisions of that message have been a sustaining force ever since.

We said our vows and the picture taking would commence. My friend Jon Moore had been doing the video thing for us and it turned out well. Back at the Holiday House motel, preparations were being made to get the buffet ready for the reception. This being the place for our first night made it very convenient. A toast, more pictures and good food gave what was already a good event a better touch.

Our first day saw another great bit of weather for traveling. Our honeymoon was to be in Provincetown, Massachusetts. Carol had purchased a timeshare near the ocean many years earlier and took her friends there for an occasional retreat. I had never been in the New England states before so this was a double treat. The Eastwood at Provincetown on Bradford Street became a very special place in my own heart. The whole area did. I must say that at the time of this writing I am enduring a pain with respect to our honeymoon. We have just received a letter from the administration at Eastwood that they were having financial difficulties and had to raise the maintenance fees again for the second times in two years. I called them yesterday to tell them that we wanted to sell our timeshare. I had to do this while I am sitting here writing about how this place meant so much to me. Literally, on the same day. It is painful. We have gone back there almost every year since. Maybe things will work out where we still can. But it will never be the same again. Well, its not over yet, but if and when it is, its okay. The reason for it all does not dwell in Provincetown, its here in this house in Rochester New York.

I was like a little kid on my first day in "P-Town." Since Carol knew her way around there so well it made it easier to see the best sights and eat at the best places. At the ripe old age of forty-six she led me by the hand through the streets lined with a myriad of art galleries and gift stores. The one thing that I was prepared for, at least in principle was the predominantly Gay life in that area. I wasn't used to seeing two guys walking down the street holding hands or two girls kissing on a main thoroughfare. That never deterred me from liking the place. In my mind they needed as much prayer as I did. Sometimes I know I needed more. Anyway, I had left most of my judgmental spirit in the past. At least I thought I did. I tell everyone that I am half Indian and half Jewish. The response usually is, "Gee that's an interesting combination."

"Yea," I say, "I don't know whether to keep everything or give it all away, you know. I'm still mad over that Manhattan deal, that one where the Indians sold it for twenty-four dollars worth of beads? Well, guess who is living in Manhattan now? My other half!" It usually gets a laugh or two and it always take the edge off of any conversation where I feel any discrimination is in the air. I have always thought that it is not so much that people disagree, but how they disagree. Don't be disagreeable in your disagreement.

As we went from store to store looking at some of the art I got the sense of some type of serenity there. What I discovered was that people were accepting each other like I had never seen before. It didn't make a difference how you lived your life or what you wore or how you did your hair, you became accepted. The quickest way to rock the boat in a community like that was how you displayed your disagreement about something. Nobody seemed to care enough to make someone else's business their own. I liked that. It was a principle that the rest of the world should take notice of.

The ocean was just about a hundred yards from all the shops. The next day or so depending on the weather would see us looking at the prospects for a whale watch. Halfway through October is not the best time. The sea gets choppy and it is too cold to try and "force fun on yourself."

The rest of the trip to Cape Cod was nothing less than what anyone could want in a honeymoon. It was a new birth. A pleasantly hopeful anticipation of the life had come with my newlywed. We returned home after that week, to start afresh, another aspect of our trek in fulfilling our vows in matrimony.

Carol and I had made an agreement about something that is not very common. Since my income was not such that I could support a family, there had to be a covering of my back while I invented and wrote. Her income was earmarked for most of the entire house with all of its needs. Working a couple of days a week at the drug and alcohol unit just wouldn't cut it with the expenses like house payments, insurance, taxes, etc. She had some help from renting the upstairs, but that had proved to be a decision that would haunt us for the remainder of the year. When that year was up, the plan was never to rent again. And that is the way that it went. My income paid for my own personal usage such as fuel in my truck, insurance, some food in the house on occasion, and, oh yes, did I mention that my wife and I have been going Dutch treat when we go out to eat. She pays for her own meals, I pay for mine. It has been like that since we got married seven years ago. This arrangement has been unique in many ways because on at least two occasions it has been hampered by decisions made concerning a decline in income. Making sure that the upstairs apartment became my office which removed five hundred a month, my job hours were cut back to eight hours a week from sixteen or twenty four. That extra burden Carol took on was gallant and to this day she runs the show in all this financial stress. Could I create more income the conventional way? Yes and no. Making money is the easiest thing for me to do, as far as getting a job or doing contract work. Carol would have none of it. My vision from a decade ago will come to pass. The woman who would marry me was going to have to at least bear the brunt of her own commitments. I would take care of mine. In any marriage, the talk of "mine and yours" should do nothing less that contribute toward contention, but in ours it doesn't. We pay our own way sometimes to the penny. I recently asked my wife if when I make a hit with a writing or invention, "Would you still like to go Dutch treat just for fun." The answer was an emphatic "No!" of course. In a scenario like that I would be generating income to pay for everything. And ultimately she would have the choice to work or retire. At this time I have three written screenplays, a patent expiring, and three patents pending, and of course the writing of this memoir.

Family issues arose almost immediately. One of Carol's daughters had begun to experience behavioral problems with her five-year-old son. My introduction to him consisted of watching him swear at his mother and run down the street saying he wanted to kill himself or his dad. His mother didn't marry and has relentlessly pursued building a family without a father figure in the house. Four times. The consequences of that decision is horrific. Talking of suicide or murder at any age is not right let alone a five year saying it. God help us. I could see that little Brandon had a rough road ahead of him. Maybe I did to.

After the boy got calmed down he became the sweetest youngster to be around. A bright creative young lad capable of anything he put his mind to should be an inspiration to others. It appears as though the opposite is true. A monster in the making. Many trips to emergency rooms, psych units, responses by the authorities to violent behavior by age ten doesn't make a stellar example for others to follow.

The rest of Carol's children had their own version of life to offer. Drugs, jail, prison for the boys, resentment, hatred and alienation for the girls. I had my work cut out for me. Being husband number five was brought up more than once. I didn't have a problem with that. After all, I could count too. And then there were the ex-husbands. After the initial entrance into this family the trials and testings would commence though I must admit that I remembered I had not entered this blindly. I was fully aware of what the status of each person was in this family and I would deal with each person, each incident, one at a time just like I have been trained to do. Working with drug addicts and alcoholics salted with various mental and emotional problems became part of the saving grace afforded this family. I saw it as Humpty Dumpty. However, it was possible to put the family back together I thought. It was going to take patience and hard work on everybody's part, but it was possible. Little did I know the extent of the stretching I would endure. Good thing I didn't. I would have quit.

Carol said to me one evening, "How are you dealing with all of this?"

It was right after there was a threat by one of the ex's. I gestured that all was well. My wife needed encouragement with the fact that none of this was her fault. She naturally took on a lot of guilt when anyone said anything negative about our relationship. Since all this fallout began before she had ever met me it was another burden that apparently belonged to her. I mentioned that "the past is the past, this is now." It's too bad that it takes much more than someone just saying it sometimes, but that is the way life is. The bumper sticker on some cars read. "Just Say No." The reference is to drugs. I tell my patients that "If life was as easy as reading a slogan to get clean then maybe the world would be different. The reality is that life is not like that. Oftentimes there are longterm affects of our decisions and whatever those affects are we must accept that as fact. The decision to change does not necessarily mean that the providential circumstances change."

I told my concerned wife that it will be okay. "To this day I have not regretted my decision to marry into this family. Hey, we all need worked on, including me. If that is truly realized, the perspective of other people changes. The judgmentalism or criticism of others may cease because of this revelation about myself. The thoughts are there, but they have to be stopped at the door. That is where the battle is. The mind, and for everybody.

It came to pass more than once when Carol needed reassured that I wasn't in a bad space. I was too at times, but the biggest problem I had to deal with was in the mirror not in the externals. Sometimes I have wanted to write a book entitled, "The Monster in the Mirror." Has a good ring to it.

The work on the house continued. One of Carol's trials was that she had always been a person who liked to entertain family and guests, especially during birthdays and holidays. The state that the house was is in, pretty much prevented that for quite a while.

This arrangement of me staying home, working on writing or researching inventions also saw the household chores gravitating in my direction. Doing laundry, all the cooking, running errands like banking, getting the groceries and doing some things for other family members became a normal part of my life, which continues to this day. The ongoing remodeling and working that I do on my projects, coupled with going to work a couple days a week makes for a busy life. It seems that the harder things got, the harder we have strived to make the system work. And change on the inside was most affected.

We have and are continuing to change, making what we describe as a wonderful marriage that just as I have recently told Pastor Phil that "It just keeps getting better and better." Oswald Chambers says in his devotional, My Utmost for his highest that "Prayer doesn't change things, prayer changes me and I change things." (See reference on page 513.) A point well taken and we couldn't survive on anything less. Our character is constantly scrutinized. The circumstances in our lives may be talked about and either envied or despised, but when it comes to the kind of person you are, that is what matters to everyone. I can be off center a bit in some circumstances, but if I am of a very undesirable spirit it doesn't matter about the other.

We needed a vacation. Before we got married we had made a trip to Carol's brother's house in Lake Havasu City. This resort town in western Arizona was quite a respite from an occasional harsh winter back in the east. My first trip there was very much liked. Steven Dunham had moved to accept a new position with an investment service as well as get as far away from the family trouble as possible. Meeting him for the first time in this new environment was very nice. He showed the absence of certain stresses so easily found in other family members. Being single for some time gave him some opportunities for moving on in life that he couldn't have otherwise. A beautiful home within clear view of the lake, especially in the evening made for a place of refuge from all the elements back home, not just the weather. To be so far away from your home gives you a new perspective on things. I guess that is what vacations were designed for in the first place.

Though it is easy to get into a lot of side stories, my wife and her affect on me is paramount. I believe that without her it would not have been possible to write and invent like I do. Before I met her I was paying someone else to do my typing for me. I vowed never to get near a computer. Shortly after that bold statement I had to learn a minimal bit of computer work at my job or what time I was putting in would cease. I avoided having a computer in my home once by buying that used word processor. After one or two attempts at working that thing it I made it history. Selling it out of frustration got a problem out of my life that I didn't want to deal with anyway. The prospect of continuing to pay for typing didn't seem so bad after all. It was a longer more expensive way, but that did not deter me. At the time there wasn't anyone in my life to contest that decision and all I felt I had to do was give the typist a copy of screenplay format to follow and that would be that.

About four years had passed and now I have someone in my life who may see things differently. I had been receiving subtle hints along the way that I should invest in a computer and with a wife in my life it was a day of reckoning. The mentor I had found to get me started in screenplay writing recommended that I get a computer and mentioned a specific program that was used for writing screenplays. If Carol had not been with me at that meeting I might still be without a computer. She listened intently to Nick after I had told her he knew his stuff. I had prepared my bed and now I was going to have to sleep in it. After the meeting I succumbed to letting Carol buy the whole shot. It was humbling to me. Her primary reason for wanting to buy it in the first place was that she said that she was thinking about getting one anyway and this was a good reason to make it happen. She wanted to do charts from work and maybe get into some craft projects. She hasn't gone near the computer during the several years it has been in the house. I even do all her E-mail retrievals.

The month of August of 2001 saw the entrance of computer technology enter 30 Petten street. I was intimidated to ever learn the use of one. The one at work was only for my e-mails and do a progress note which I have done only a few of those. To learn a special program on top on learning about running a computer was an insane idea. But, I did it. The Internet was another story. It is so big that nobody could ever see all there is. One time there was 4.6 million web sites for just one topic. However, what was impressive to me was only second nature to many others. I was just being groomed to catch up with most of the rest of the world.

Rewriting my first movie script and finishing several drafts to my second one was only the beginning. What had started out as a fear of change had ended up to be a revolution in my new household. I can never thank my wife enough for sticking to her guns about things she believed in. We make almost all of the decisions together. I once heard a man say, "If you love God you can do whatever you want." I had to think about that one for a while. It was explained to me that when you truly love someone you will not do anything that will hurt them. You essentially will do only things that will please them. On the surface, the cliché has a very negative ring to it. Anyone knows that loving a person doesn't give you a license to do whatever you want. I thought the lesson in that statement promoted the ideal for a desirable relationship and that is the potential I saw between Carol-Aynn and myself. For the last four years it has been very good as we have moved from one level to another in positive fashion.

It seemed to be sink or swim all the while cramming in the knowledge base for doing everything at once with writing. I guess it was just another lesson in a long list that I had to learn over the course of my life. I have been amazed at the size of the task and I wasn't falling apart. The prospect of failing really didn't dominate my mind. When people set me down and tell me the way something should be I most often listen.

Prior to the initiation into the world of computers I had fought the battle of self-sufficiency. The world is being inundated with this "You can do it" thinking. While the effort to promote this thought process has good some good intentions I was left in the quandary of observations that this is not entirely true. There are some of whom may have limitations. Ones that are put there by what I call divine design. Even then, many persons have overcome those barriers and accomplished great things. Stephen Hawking, the great physicist comes to mind. He has severe limitations in his entire muscular system and is wheelchair bound yet teaches physics to students and lives a life, which he makes the most of. However, there are things that are not meant to be or at least not to be right now. This is exampled by relationships, finances, promotion etc. just because you think it means it is going to happen. Countless people have the frustration of going nowhere in some endeavor and it shouldn't always be viewed as a failure on the part of the person.

The respect that I have had for the opinion of others has saved me a lot of trouble, but it is I who gets to choose which counsel I listen to. And my heart condition will be the biggest factor in that in that decision. What am I really after? I love to get off on a tangent about life once in a while. It is good for the soul to recount some of the lessons one has learned.

My allergies came back to visit me since I thought I left them with my childhood. Carol was home alone enough that she thought we should have a pet. Although I believed that cats may be a problem we could never know unless we tried. Felines in anyone's house were not really a test because most of went to hide when company came. I used to play basketball on Tuesday and Wednesday night. Working the evening shift at the rehab on Thursday evening made for a lonely stretch for Carol during the week. While she normally goes to bed earlier than me it still was a time to consider having a pet.

We started off with a dog. He was a cocker spaniel puppy. A fun dog who destroyed both of our respiratory tracts. He ended up with a close friend and is very happy there. The second attempt was a trip to the area's notable animal shelter, Lolly Pop farms. We went there in search of the perfect pet. We found them in two adorable little kittens. The thinking was that if we got them young that we could grow into them and the allergy problems we might have. Didn't work. Carol went to work and I had to take them back to the shelter. I was in tears. They huddled together in nervous anticipation of what was happening. It was very spooky that they knew what was happening.

By now we had gotten the computer and several people told us to look into pets with little or no shedding of hair. We searched online for such a pet and found a breeder of very shorthaired cats. Driving on a sunny winter's day about an hour away we met the woman with a Devon-Rex male cat named Elliot. The cat had a very tough time at the thought of leaving the one person he could trust. We could provide a home that every cat would envy, but this cat wouldn't know it if it bit him in the face and from that day on that is exactly how he acted, as if somebody bit him in the face. It was an agreed two-week trial time with this feline. No matter what we did he didn't like it. There was no attempt at any adjustment and it seemed as if I was just tolerating this whole thing just for the sake of running out the two weeks. We called the woman back and told the news. We needed to give him back. Trying to get Elliot into a cat carrier was the biggest trial of the whole relationship. I had to block off the bedroom so he couldn't run and hide. I made the mistake of using a big mirror. Elliot ran full speed into the mirror. Neither the mirror nor his head broke. Don't know how. After finally grabbing him with gloves on, he proved he was not cut out for this household. Now he was like trying to stuff a basketball into a medicine bottle. Spreading his legs out wide so he wouldn't fit, was complicated by his claws grabbing the edges. I guess that whole scene made it more difficult to accept that he had to go. There was relief that he had to go, but we still were affected emotionally that he was gone. We would try again.

Another trip to Lollipop Farms saw us looking for another dog. Carol saw a specimen that I thought was a poor excuse for a dog. He was a mangy Terrier type that had a diseased back. His demeanor was likable which attracted Carol. Daniel had been exposed to regimen of medicines, much more that we were told. We also were told that his prognosis for recovery from the disease was better than what was the truth. We had to take him back after learning that he was basically a dying dog. I sort of liked him and it was especially sad for Carol to have to give him up too. By this time we had wondered if we were really supposed to have a pet. We agreed to try one more time.

The Internet became a little touchy as a resource for finding a pet. There was something synthetic or unnatural about it. Like looking for a mate I viewed this method of research for anything other than an inanimate product such a used car was not meant to be. We ended up locating a breeder of Llasapoos through an acquaintance. These little dogs had a reputation for being almost hypoallergenic. Off to their home we went. Down the parkway about fifteen minutes we came upon the pet of our dreams. The story was that a litter of puppies to the parents was going to be the last. A group of four little Llasapoos were falling over each other when we got there. I don't think anyone would have passed up a chance at these dogs so we were glad to get there when we did. The parents of the puppies were very friendly and they all looked alike as was their colors…except for one. The puppy we chose stood out from the rest. We picked him up and did the trial thing again. I got the privilege of naming him Pippon. It doesn't really mean anything I just liked the way it sounded. After two dogs and three cats, our longing for a pet was fulfilled. Pippon worked out very well. Housebreaking and getting him to stop removing the tissue from the waste basket in the bathroom was the bulk of our work with him. Whenever we go on a vacation he gets to spend some time with his parents.

Not having a pet of my own in about two decades and never owning a computer saw me endure another pair of culture shocks.

Had I continued to play it safe all the time I would not have experienced either. Carol was profoundly good to me.

On the family front there continued much trouble. A suicide attempt, assaults, more jail time, threats of violence and murder, child abuse and trips to the psyche unit kept me on my toes as watched a host of family dynamics unfold week by week. Sometimes the thought of putting up with a mangy dog was looking pretty good. It wouldn't be fair to elaborate on the trials or errors of those in my newfound family. I have received much mercy in my own life so I shall just pass some of it on. Each situation was dealt with according to what kind of attention it needed. Some are resolved and others are in a holding pattern. Patience is a must in life and we always are in need of more.

After working for over thirty years in a hospital setting with emphasis on weekends and holidays Carol-Aynn had the opportunity to transfer in to a sleep disorder clinic. It was quite a decision to make. She was so attached to her co-workers in the Respiratory Department that the decision was difficult. The abuse that I saw her taking from her boss though prompted me to side with the move to another facility. She was well liked and her services would be missed. I could testify that Carol did everything that she was told and much more. Missing lunch and breaks was a common occurrence in the hospital setting. It still is. Carol's new job would be weekdays only and holidays off, a health care worker's dream.

We thought it was best that she moved to her new job and so she did. It was a great trial for the first few months. Getting used to a new crew and being plopped down into too many things that she knew nothing about rattled me also. There were too many times that she wanted to quit and I would just be there for her. She knew in her heart that throwing in the towel was not the right thing to do in this situation. I certainly would have endorsed such a move at the hospital. There is always a price to pay for progress and this was no exception. The silver lining to all this was growth. I discovered that I must be willing to pay that price and not just run all the time. So much of life is missed by taking what I thought was the easy way out. There was an element of tribulation going into this trial with Carol on her new job. She had a certain view about not having to do the weekend and holiday thing anymore and found out that all that glitters is not gold. She stuck it out and she was glad that she did. So was I. The last three years for the both of us with her at her job have been rewarding for us as individuals and as a married couple. Some of the things she was asked to go through made me think that I would have done the same thing in "hitting the road." But we thought, "We didn't get where we are by leaving all the time."

A mass exodus began a few months after she left the hospital. The other respiratory therapists who had worked closely with my wife for years had all of sudden wanted out and when they had discovered the schedule that Carol had it was in her direction that they looked. I definitely thought, "here we go." And go we did. The first of five therapists followed Carol out the door. I almost enjoyed it when it put the unreasonable boss on the spot. Four of those people came directly to the sleep disorder center to work with Carol. Before anybody could stop the bleeding, Carol not only started to get a handle on her job and got to enjoy bringing all her friends with her. Of course she did make sure that she really had nothing to do with it. They just acted like little kids. What little Carol got everybody else wanted. It took a while, but she got to enjoy something that is almost unheard of in any industry let alone health care. To this day I don't know why it happened, but it did and Jim the tyrant was in damage control at the hospital for a long time trying to keep the slots filled.

One of the fringe benefits I have enjoyed in this new arrangement is the Christmas holiday company party. A suit and tie affair, we meet every year in this old medical building that is a restored mansion. The food is catered, which I always like. (Remember that I was raised on the other side of the tracks, so this is my ongoing revenge on poverty.) A beautifully decorated dining room with an attractive loft accented the spacious walls of antique paneling and wallpaper. A secret door going into a wall on the way up the stairs boasts the grand entry into the loft.

What I was impressed with more than anything else was the people. Carol was given a very nice group of individuals to work with. All the doctors, secretaries and technicians that were already there were nothing less than a gift. Carol's initial problems when she arrived there consisted of the fact that more people believed in Carol's ability to perform work she had never done before. That gave her some encouragement to continue despite how hard it got. I recently heard that people almost always have a pretty good idea that they can handle the job before they get there. It's the people. "You don't hate the job, you have a problem with the people," a friend said. We just label the job that way because it may be an easy way to open the door to leave. Which brings to mind another saying. "Wherever you go, there you are." The problem again is usually "the monster in the mirror." That principle has come to my attention more than once, especially in my current line of work.

Carol's health has always been an issue. Crohn's disease has the characteristic that never lets you forget it. Unless there is a total divine healing of this digestive ailment, it never goes away. Flaring up whenever it wants, for life, it can get pretty rough. "Hopefully the worst episode is past us," has been my secret wish for her and for us. Many years ago the disease put in her in the hospital on life support. Even at about age twenty, when Carol was strongest, her life was almost taken. The fact that it happened in the first place keeps me in a place of wondering about this chronic problem. So far, in the first four years of marriage, there have been a few times when things have gotten a little trepidus. Right after landing in Las Vegas on one of our trips to Arizona an unusual and unrelated incident happened to her. She had acquired a small problem from the plane ride, according to the doctors. It didn't manifest until she got into bed for about an hour. We got to Lake Havasu City Arizona to see Steve her brother at six in the morning and went right to bed. It was about seven o'clock when my wife woke up with all the classic symptoms of a heart attack. Shortness of breath, cold sweats, nausea, and the pain in the chest. I called 911 and the paramedics gave her oxygen and nitro. They probably could have never guessed it was only vertigo, but that's is what the doctors said she had. Although there are incidents of this problem, it has showed up in an unlikely place and in an unlikely group of people. Movie stars and plan rides. Vertigo is somehow caused by altitude change or air pressure which affects the inner ear. Not many people get it, but there is an increasing incidence in famous people who travel. There are other groups of people who travel sometimes more often than movie stars, but no one could explain to us why this group was selected. Mimicking a heart attack is its earmark, but it still kept Carol in the hospital for a few hours.

There was a problem with dehydration on one occasion. Constant vomiting and not replacing the fluids in her body lead to a serious problem. Refusing to go to the hospital made matters worse. I did not know how bad until Carol collapsed in the bathroom. I rushed her to the emergency room and we discovered that she was probably minutes away from cardiac arrest. When the heart stops because of the lack of fluid in the body the death rate is almost one hundred percent. She got her fluids and a chastising from me when it was over. You know the drill. "I'll be okay." I said to something like "This isn't going to happen again on my watch." I still stay on her today about drinking plenty of water, especially when she is not feeling the greatest.

There is plenty to write home about when it comes to my own relationship with Carol-Aynn. I wish at times that the whole world had what we have in our lives together. The first installment for anything to be successful is a sincere desire. How bad do you want it? That is what I tell all my drug addicts and alcoholics. Human beings have the innate desire to succeed, but the price it may cost scare many off who have to pay that price. The lie that feeds itself is, "I can't." The truth is, "I won't," but too often is deceptively passed off as a weakness that needs rationalized and medicated. My marriage is no different. Humility, patience, love, and mercy all had better be a part of the equation or it is not going to work. And these qualities are not acquired easily. I want to dominate, win or be on top when the battle is over. It has been quite apparent that many people have a good quality or two in their lives. For some it seems to be a natural part of them. It is those characteristics that I have often envied. "Why can't I be like that," I have often wondered. Being single kept me at bay from learning some of the things that can only be learned in a marriage situation. I have also learned that it may also not be true. Both can be true at the same time. It would seem that it would be a contradiction. I can remember that certain lessons in life approached me when I was living alone. A story worth repeating comes to bear.

It happened that day when my job was taking care of the elderly in a nursing home. One of two nursing homes that I worked at through the years. Working on the sixth floor of St. Anne's nursing home for a few months saw me in a position to meet a whole new group of people, staff and residents alike. I was taking care of a ninety two year old man named Ed. Ed had one good eye and one good arm. I got old Ed cleaned up for the day. His wife was a ninety one year-old woman who lived in the "Heritage Home" located right next to St. Anne's. She was due to come and visit Ed that morning so I put an extra spit polish on her husband. I had noticed something special about these two people. They were going to celebrate seventy years of marriage in June of that year. I wanted to know how they lasted so long. I knew that they were from the "old school" and a lot of the morals and ethics were different back then, but they still had to do something right because like today, I also knew that every generation has its own set of problems and that these two were a dying breed. Nobody's marriage lasts that long anymore and I wanted a tip from the experts. "Mrs. Ed" walked in the room and I presented her to him. She liked the way he looked and gave him a smootch on the cheek. Before I left the room I had to ask. With his wife at the bottom of the bed I looked at Ed and asked, "You know, you two are going to be celebrating seventy years of marriage this coming June. What advice would you give a young buck like me if I were to ever get married? How did your marriage last so long?" Well, Ed looked at his wife and then at me with his one good eye and said, "keep your mouth shut." Those words still echo in my mind ten years later. The reason that they hit me so hard in the first place is that I cared enough to really hear what the answer was and not just in asking the question. That man continues to help me today by what he said. Could I have learned that lesson before I got married? Of course, but the depth may not be there because co-workers and friends cannot generally reach to the depths that a commitment to a wife can. I can however, get some of this growth in a sufficient degree and can continue to grow when I got married. Thank God that I got what I did get or it may have been curtains for Carol-Aynn and me. Between her mercy and me begging for it, we both have been brought to the place where there is a very working functioning life together.

What can I attribute any growth to? And have I arrived? The answer to the second question is a resounding no! What is responsible for me getting anything in this life? In this day and age it is very often an unapproachable subject to talk about God outside the cliches that we use in everyday conversation. I was once told that

"When your car breaks down you take it to the car repairman. When you break down you take yourself to the one who made you." Easier said than done for somebody who may squirm at the thought of God entering into any conversation in the first place. As mentioned earlier, there was a commitment in that direction and it continues to this day. People, places, and things are used to get messages to me if I would only watch and listen. Carol-Aynn is one of many tools used to forge character into this pathetic soul. I have needed simply to submit to the user of those tools. The people, places and things may irritate me, make me laugh or cry, bring me joy or sorrow, but it doesn't make any difference. What does matter is that I should have a trust in the user of those tools and not the tools themselves. People die or leave, money gets spent or stolen, anything of substance has the potential to fail, but God doesn't. When will we get that? Anyway, on with the story. My wife, who by the way has failed me on occasion, continues to seek the better things in life. Things that are not tangible. That is what makes for a mature person. I could be bribed with a favorite meal or a new car. But what is important is the heart from which it comes. Hot dogs, hamburgers, and corvettes may come and go, but the heart lives on. EVERY GIFT COMES FROM THE HEART. The real question is: what condition is the heart in? A Pause on September 17, 2003. I have never been too big on diaries, but an entry into this story comes in that form. Today is the anniversary of one of Carol's former husband's death. It is also my own 23rd anniversary of sobriety from alcohol. While these events may be worthy of note, we are awakened this morning by a phone call from a troubled sister in-law. Carol's younger sister Michelle is in one of her bad spaces. It is not unheard of in this family to get these calls at any hour of the day or night. Michelle is a mother of two boys whom she has interrupted their relationship by putting them into a very dangerous situation. They have been separated for a year with supervised visitations. The boys witnessed a violent act from their mother and have been in the care of a couple in which the wife works with Carol. This precarious position has brought much stress from two fronts. Being the aunt of the boys and being in the middle of continuing troubles from an uncooperative sister creates difficulties for myself also. About four months ago there was a court order handed down by a very good judge that Michelle was not to interfere with the welfare of her two children. They were placed in another home for a reason. This morning's phone call at six o'clock was non other then a communication to let us know that she was going to move to another part of town just around the corner from where the boys are staying. It is a time of staying cool for Carol while she tries to convince her sister that it would not be in the best interest of the boys, as well as herself, to move near them. At first it was apparently an innocent thing because although she has been seeing the boys on the supervised visits, she did not know where they actually lived. That was a wise move on the part of the appointed father figure in the house where the boys are. After it was discovered that Michelle picked the wrong place to move to, she was told about and appeared to respect the request not to move to that location. However, she changed her mind and has decided to do it anyway. Carol warned her not to, but Michelle's decision was supported by her counselor, at least that is what she has said. I listen in on the conversation for awhile and hung the phone up. Carol has been taking this issue hard. It makes her angry that her sister has this thinking that "It's all about Michelle." I have stepped in at this point and said that we have to let her do what she wants. It is the best thing to let her go all the way and put herself at risk by the law taking the rest of her parental rights away from her. The boys will be protected and they need a mother in their life that cares more about their welfare than what she wants for herself. That currently in not the case. After about an hour on the phone I asked Carol to get ready for work. I explained that it was important for her to be mindful of her reaction to this scenario. It was all right to accept that she was a part of it, but she had a choice of how she let it affect her. She went to take a shower, then it was my turn. The phone rang extra loud that day. My sister was cn the other end of the line. She wanted me to know that she can't take it any more. Back home in Pennsylvania, Mom continues to make for a great frustration in all of our lives. Mary had been a real problem to me the last time I was down there for a visit. Although Bradford is only a hundred and fifty miles away, I had made five trips down there to try and resolve these issues with our mother. The last one was bad. My relationship changed with my sister on that day and now she was acting as if nothing had ever happened. I held my peace and did not bring up the past, but I eventually will because I believe that I have to. With the

State making two trips into Mom's house and following up with Mary it still wasn't good enough. Somehow we have to get power of attorney she would say. Mom needs to get to a doctor. We had been over all that before and our options were nil at this point. My Mom was acting crazy, doing things that were not normal, but according to the State counselor, it was legal for Mom to be crazy. "There are a lot of crazy people out there," the counselor would tell me. A mental hygiene arrest was out of the question and our mother was hallucinating. As long as she was not a direct threat to herself or to others she was within the scope of the law. This frustration was bearing heavily on my sister and at this point she was reluctant to accept the facts even though they were presented to her by the state. At first I had told her what they had shared with me. That didn't work. I was fooled into thinking that if the counselor would have shared all this with Mary that it would be easier to accept. Nope. Didn't work. I told her the same things that I have said all along. Right now there is nothing less than a temporary patch to try and bring us to the place for an intervention. Not for my mother, but for my sister. I thought it was interesting that within two minutes of my conversation with Carol-Aynn, I was to be on the spot to practice what I preached. I am happy to report that my integrity seems to be intact. There was a time in my life when these types of conversations would not have gotten past first base. Stay tuned. Now, back to our originally scheduled program already in progress.

The advice that I had gotten from Ed at the nursing home had carried me into my marriage. It is the type of counsel and encouragement that I think everyone should have in their life. There seems to be a direct connection to what we want in life, and what is provided. It has been my hope that I would change and grow. The provisions for such an answer to this request are very compatible to the need. If I would only heed what is placed on my plate then I would be given more or given something different. This principle has showed up all the time. I know it works on the negative line as well. We see it run through the world of criminals. My continuing relationship with my wife affords enormous opportunities to be changed both from the outside and inside. It is apparent that these same opportunities are changed to meet the rising or falling of the inner man. If you don't grow you die.

All these family issues are compounded by Carol's mother being admitted to the hospital a couple of days ago. Dori Dunham had severe pains in her abdomen and was nauseous. Michelle called me while I was working on these memoirs. It seems hard to get to the former things when I have so much going on right in my face, but that's okay.

Carol spent all day yesterday at the hospital. Dori has had a lot of visitors. I saw her for about forty minutes. I make the visits, but it is easier for me because with the exception of my situation with my own family down in PA, everything else to me is non-intimate. I am touched by many people who have a lot to deal with in places that they are intimately involved. Big families and a lot of close friends are good to have in your life, but when there is a lot of dysfunction in those groups you must be prepared to take the bitter with the sweet. Have you ever noticed in the fall harvest season when the corn is ripe in the farm markets or grocery stores? Most food places do not remove the outside of the corn for you. They may have a sign up that says: Please do not remove the husk from the corn. Maybe you find a store that allows you to and they provide a bag or basket to take care of that, but most do not. The point is, that you are required by the store to take the bitter with the sweet. I have to take whatever card I draw in life and others may have a say in what cards are dealt. What do I do with that? It may be simple, but not easy. Unless I have had some things worked into my life, these family dynamics and other things like my own relationship with Carol will not be right.

I am affected by other people's responses to things in life also. It can and has been a reflection on me how those events happen.

"I am so angry," Carol told me when she heard from her sister. "I don't know if I can take it anymore," she retorted.

I listened intently and responded to help her. She was being taken to another level and I knew it. With all that was going on in her life I could see that she needed to hear the note of encouragement, that the truth that she has in her life, what it took, and was receiving that very moment the qualities necessary to be an overcomer concerning all these things. "Of course" I would say. It is a fact that you are intimately acquainted with the players and circumstances and you have not just a right to feel certain things, but it is a natural response. The choices one makes about exibiting that response is what is important. This thinking has come in handy right now as there are more opportunities to prove this point. Just three days ago I responded to a phone call from Michelle that she was concerned about Dori. Dori was having a problem with some kind of pain and I was called to take her to an appointment to have a scheduled test. Michelle had some appointments of her own and couldn't get her mother to hers. The call sounded a little frantic and I said, "Put Dori on the phone." She did not sound well so I went right over. When I got there my mother in-law was crumpled over with pain in her abdomen. I thought it was a little more serious than just taking her to a test so I call 911 and the paramedics came over in about ten minutes. They thought that Dori had a kidney stone and the pain that she had would certainly support that. I was not totally convinced, but they took her to the hospital to discover what the problem was. After a few hours in the emergency department the doctors decided to admit her. After a CAT scan her pains were attributed to a kidney stone, just like the medics had said. The stone was too large to pass so she was admitted for observation and to decide what course this problem was going to take. Dori went to a floor room for a day. Through more testing, the doctors became somewhat puzzled at the chemistry changing in her body. They ordered more tests, one of which could only be performed in another hospital on the other side of town. That machine also has temporarily broken down and the line for people needing it was becoming long. Dori would have to wait. During this time she would be transferred to another floor where the care would be more in line with her needs. I had visited her just minutes prior to her transfer and had come home. There was a message on our answering machine from Carol a few hours later. When I got home from my Inventors meeting the message from her said that Dori was moved to the intensive care unit. First I called my wife, who returned the call only to explain to me that Dori had a cardiac episode. I went right up and was told that I couldn't get in to see her. Carol wouldn't come out of the room away from her mother, so Michelle met me to explain why I couldn't see Mom. Dori was becoming septic and her state was worsening through the night. There were indications of more severe problems and doctors were still baffled. Many people had come to see her late at night and couldn't. When I got there, Carol's daughter Alicia and three of her kids were there. I had a problem with that and I went to the lobby back downstairs. Alicia still has not let her mother see the kids in the past sixteen months. I have been biting my tongue over that one all this time. The kids saw me and it was obvious that they were coached to ignore me. Michelle had said a lot of things to me that were not associated with Mom's condition, but we closed the discussion out on a good note and waited till morning so see any change in the situation.

The morning has come and Dori is stable enough to have a shunt put in. They do not have any choice because all others choices are limited by her condition and the case of the broken machine that would blast away a kidney stone.

My own mother continues to be seeing things that are not there, not cashing her checks and after talking with her former employer has accumulated at least ten months worth of pension checks and two payroll checks dating back three years. The social security checks were another thing. I needed Mom's social security number and that was the only way that I could find out how many checks from the Federal government were not cashed. They do not recognize power of attorney and they require a signed form from a doctor to transfer any mailing of funds to another account. Getting just the social security number was going to be a task. Mom wasn't willing to see a doctor and I was counseled by the state just the other day to try and trick Mom into it. Set up an appointment, go to Mom's unannounced and tell her "are you ready for your doctor appointment?" Even if she doesn't remember anything about a doctor visit I was supposed to act as if it really was true.

The woman said, "Hey, you have to do what it takes." I thought how I wished that also was true or I would have had Mom under a mental hygiene arrest before this. Getting trials thrown at you from both fronts has been interesting to say the least. This morning one of Carol's ex-husbands called to say his feeling toward Carol's mother and how he still doesn't like me. Oh well. You win some, lose some.

My continuous spot check of my relationship with my wife didn't really take any effort through all of this. The emotion running high and low, coupled with the gross dysfunction within this family, especially with all of them being drawn into one place at the same time is testing enough. It basically has been a distraction from other things. Disaster has truly brought enemies together, but not for anything else than a temporary forced tolerating and not real association or friendship. The study of relationships that came out of emotional responses to a trial have not had a good track record and that is surely evidenced by the September 11 event. We Americans will treat each other any way we want. But when someone else from the outside treats us the same way it drives us to stand together, side by side against the enemy. Emotions run high and low and a sense of real camaraderie, but as soon as the enemy is beaten away or the trial is lifted it is back to business as usual. It has been that way in this family before and it shall be that way again.

Carol has been very supportive in my troubles with my own family and, of course, I with hers. It is quite an interesting thing to see and experience all these events in both of our lives at the same time. A foundation has been built in our relationship that is fit for dealing with so many things at once. I love how the results of the work of a person on the inside prove whether it is real or not. However, it can be a painful road trip to get there and that may be something that is less then desirable. I currently have a Patented product that some people are interested in. There are three products that are patent pending and are being evaluated. One of my two screenplays is being marketed around the country, during all this other stuff going on. I mentioned it before, but it bears worth repeating because it is a new application. What people want most is not just something that is interesting, but something that is of real value. And most of the time we don't even know that, that is what we are looking for. It happens and we make the observation after the fact. Someone once said, "you are what you eat." That applies not just to food that goes through our mouth, but those things that contribute toward a good or bad life, depending on what it is we desire and take in through sight and sound. You become, what you take in. Carol and I have sought to take in some good things, both on an individual basis and together. Every morning since our marriage we have read a devotional together and sometimes a chapter from the Bible. When we are apart we have other readings or times of devotions. This has made for a marriage that continues to go in the right direction. In the process there is much testing to see if the work was real or what needs changed. The classic saying is "that trials reveal character." Trials don't change a person they reveal who we are. What we do in response to a trial is the process not the goal. The goal is to become a better person not in spite of, but because of, this opportunity to grow. A far cry from the resentments and confusion that abides within the human race. My own sins, if you will, are a stamped out copy of what every one else on the face of the earth has. Obviously in varying degrees of course, but you can look around and see that different people have different areas of their lives under control. I know that I have secretly envied a quality about someone else that should be a part of my own life and wasn't. That can smart and can do one of two things. It can cause me to be resentful at the thoughts of my lack or it may enhance my desire for change. No one is neutral in response to a pure quality. There is always a reaction. Grow or go.

I did again what I do best. Set the idea down for a while. I needed a rest. The work and the money issue had brought me to the place where there needed to be a time of just living day to day without pressuring myself to hit the "big time." I hated the thought of doing what I was preaching against. Reaching out for all of the world and at any cost. The vision that I had for a future would come to pass. I wouldn't have to work myself into a heart attack or a stroke over it. I did have peace and I did not want to disturb that. Besides, there were things more important that I had to give attention to.

Time to Care

My family life, which I did not have for a long time, was taking on a new shape. The part of my wedding vows that said, "For better or worse" now was about to be tested in new ways. Carol and I had obviously agreed that I was too hard and she was too soft. We would be good for each other. However, in order for that to happen it meant that there was going to be some bending and stretching. That hurts. My troubles with people for the fourteen years of singlehood consisted of being mostly at a distance. I couldn't escape this so easily now. Carol-Aynn and I got into our early arguments that ended up with yelling and leaving the house. Either her or myself would get away from the situation a couple of times and it seemed it was meant that we were to be apart for good. I was convinced that I had made a big mistake and was ready to call it quits. Fortunately the disagreements had nothing to do with money or unfaithfulness. Both being the ages that we were and having been living our own lives for a while there were some freedoms that weren't looking so bad to go back to. Who needed this anyway, right? One of the most prevailing factors that brought us back together was that each of knew that there certain things that God himself wanted to deal with in our lives. To walk away from the trouble this time was simply saying no to the growth that each one of us claimed that we wanted. It was hard to admit a wrong or to say, "I'm sorry." Pride and habits from the past prevent relinquishing of my right to myself to another. She had been the victim of many people who tried to get from her what they could and coldly walk away. I wanted to defend her against that, but at the same time had to deal with my own inadequacies. Trying to incorporate five children and several grandchildren into my life was a mistake. I wasn't supposed to be trying to "incorporate other people in to my life" in the first place. Their life was to be my life. My thinking was still selfish. For the first year of our marriage I kept contact with her family members to a minimum. I claimed that we needed to bolster our marriage with a little solitude in the early stages.

My introduction into the family presented its own troubles anyway. Carol-Aynn had been married four times before and the kids, as well as some of her friends, had their doubts about me. They really didn't know me personally, it was just that the track record that she had acquired concerning men did not welcome me with open arms. Minding my own business especially in these beginning months was crucial. My first assignment was to ignore her daughter Cherie following me around at a birthday party down by the lake with a video camera. She said that her father "wanted to know who I was."

"Help yourself," was the message that I had for her. "Could you pass the salt please?"

Having little babies in my life was a shock too, a far cry from all of my former life. Having never had any kids of my own, this change was welcomed most of the time. It was good to have them gone after a couple of hours of infant hoopla. I have always known that I wanted and needed change, but these ones could come in no other way than through actual events and people bringing the opportunities to my doorstep and laying them at my feet. Patience in greater degrees, kindness, meekness, being of few words had been in my life at various levels, but many things would be used to ratchet up those characteristics to heightened positions, that is, if I wanted to go along with the program. I have been shamed too often by the work that God was able to do in other people's lives while my reluctance to grow by playing it safe for so long was now coming home to roost. I would either get with that program or I would be gone. Carol-Aynn would be out of my life by now if I had chosen to avoid the pangs of growing into something better than I was. There was no excuse now. It is grow or go.

Working on the house presented its own challenges. Carol was used to having the best of everything that she bought. While I doing the work on the kitchen, she had purchased a door that was very expensive. I felt that a less expensive door would suffice. I took the twenty four hundred dollar one back and brought home a nine hundred dollar one. Having gone through that ordeal in Olean with the Housnecht family remodeling HoJo's gave me some experience in saving people money. For the most part, Carol-Aynn listened to lot of my suggestions for the house. The work got done right and she didn't have to pay through the nose for it. Of course now she didn't have to pay at all. She had married the guy who was doing the work!

One of the things that we liked to do when we could was travel. Since our honeymoon we take at least one trip in the late winter and if we can, one in the fall. Making that trip to Steve's when we can in Arizona is always a treat. Each vacation would have its own story to tell.

My old buddy Joe had been watching all of this go on. He was happy that I finally had found someone that I could spend my life with. After all I had gone through with him, I still had him in my life. He had shown a willingness to stay off the drugs for a while. I had him do some work with me on the house. It was interesting that when he fell off into the that scene again that he went out of his way to go to another neighborhood and steal things out of string of people's homes, including the electrician Matt who was doing our electrical work on the house. This time Joe would not be so lucky and just get a trip to a shock camp. He got seven straight years for his crime. I took Carol to see him once. He would be moved from place to place to keep him from becoming too involved with the personnel who worked the prison jobs. Joe had become a great manipulator and they were wise to it. It saddened me to lose a friend who once had been completely away from that stuff for some time. He is still in prison and may learn a lesson there.

The tandem of Carol-Aynn and Ron had to now deal with the world and with each other in ways never dreamed of.

I have been grateful at the health that I have had and my wife's willingness to cover me while I do my part in fulfilling the vision of long ago. My trip to the emergency room myself would have wiped me out if I had to pay for it. I had been hit in a basketball game across the wrist. I didn't begin to feel much pain until about a week later. After enduring the pain for another few days I finally decided to go and have it checked. X-rays showed it was broken and was beginning to heal wrong. I was told to consult with an orthopedic surgeon. A half-cast was put on my arm and I left with my appointment papers to meet the doctor. I had forgotten that I had a standard shift in my truck and when I got to the parking lot and got in to start it up. I looked at the shift and got a little frustrated. I ripped off the cast and did not keep any appointments to have surgery. Haven't had any problems since.

The decision to get a truck with the stick shift came because I got it for a song. I probably would have bought it without an engine, almost the deal that I got with the Grand Marquis. Even though it was only a two-seater, the box part of it became invaluable. Carrying the drywall and plywood for the house got sort of old hanging every other day out of the truck of the Chevy Caprice I had up until I got that Chevy S10. Even that old car that had served me well had a story to tell.

I had needed a truck and owning one many years ago left me with the knowledge of just how important one was. Right now was the time, but the blue Chevy had to go before I could get something else. After putting an ad in the paper I got me a couple of responses. After a few no's I answered the phone one day where this woman made the commitment without seeing it. I thought it was sort of strange that anyone could buy a car without seeing it and I wouldn't let her do it.

"I'll tell you what," I told her. "Just tell me where you live and I'll bring to you to look at it. The price will still be three hundred dollars. But I need you to see what you are buying. I don't want any problems afterward because you were disappointed. Do you understand?"

She agreed and I drove "old blue" to her address. It was in one of the roughest parts of the city. I crept up to her house and she came out to look at the car.

In tears she walked around the car. "Praise God! He has answered my prayers! I can't believe it! Thank you oh so very much!"

She obviously was content with what she saw. I let her get in and she felt right at home.

"How much?" she asked.

"Three hundred dollars" I answered.

"All I have is two hundred and ninety. Will you take that?"

My thoughts then were that she was a strange one. For ten dollars why would you want to come that far and then back down from three hundred? Didn't understand it.

"Okay," I said. "I'll take the two ninety."

Then her next pitch came. "Could you drive me to my father's garage? He works as a mechanic. He's going to give me the money."

By now I was beginning to think that I should have asked more, but I wanted to get rid of the car. I had told her about anything that was wrong with it. Nothing would deter her from owning this thing. And nothing would deter me now from selling it. We went to her Dad's garage, got the money and another license plate. I drove home and took my plate off. I put her plate on and she drove off into the sunset a happy customer. I never saw her again.

Six months had passed and I got an interesting piece of mail from the State. The letter said that I was to respond to an inquiry about why I had abandoned my car along the thruway a month earlier. The information on the car in question was certainly the Caprice that I had owned, but I now had to do a little investigating of my own. I ended up at the house of the woman who had bought the car. No one was around. In fact, the house was empty. I couldn't go inside, but the garbage cans outside were full of things that looked like someone did move out. I started to sift through the trash to discover maybe something about the woman that would help me answer the State. In the can were original copies of many unpaid telephone bills. The largest one was for over seventeen hundred dollars. There were other things that seemed to indicate that she was not the kind of person that she was portraying herself to be. I wrote a letter to the Government and explained that it appeared as though this woman did not register, inspect or do anything else to put it on the road. When it broke down, she just left it where it was and moved on with her life. The last record of ownership, of course, was me and that was the reason for the letter. Fortunately, I also could send them a copy of the receipt that I had sold the car. The State absolved me of any wrongdoing.

The leap from one car to another sometimes would leave me without a ride for a short time. Even selling one car to help finance another gave me no incentive to have something to drive all the time. It has been a habit of mine at times if it was necessary, to just borrow a car or have someone take me around to look at cars. I always took my time and was careful about what I bought. Scanning the newspaper for used trucks I came upon the 1997 Chevy S10 pickup. It was 1998 and the truck was less than a year old. I had saved enough money to buy something better than what I have had for a long time. I called the number and went to see the kid who was selling it. I didn't ask about the color, but when I got to his house I loved it. He was asking ten thousand dollars and I knew that it was worth every penny. With only 17,000 miles on it and a nice stereo to boot, this truck had to be mine. His story for selling it was that he had just had a new baby girl and the truck could not haul around the three of them. He hadn't been married a long time and wanted to start a family. After introducing me to his wife and baby I asked him the big and simple question.

"You know," I said, "when people sell a vehicle, they always have a rock bottom price in mind when they sell. What's yours?"

He knew immediately what his was. "Eighty-five hundred," he answered. Inside, my heart stopped. I couldn't believe what I was hearing. I knew that it was worth ten grand, but eighty-five hundred?

"Sold!" I said. I gave him some money to hold it and went to the bank and got the entire amount in cash. He was happy and I certainly was. We shook hands on the deal and I went to the Department of Motor Vehicles to do the paperwork. They wouldn't go for it. They refused to give me anything that said I now owned the car. When they looked into their books to check on the tax rate that they should charge me versus what I had actually paid for the truck, things in their mind just didn't add up.

The clerk said, "You actually paid Eighty-five hundred dollars for the truck? We need a signed written statement from the previous owner stating that is what you really paid. Just a receipt won't do it. Do you know what the truck is worth, sir?"

By then I was very confused and nervous. "Ahh, no, ma'am."

She enlightened me, but in an accusatory manner. Many people come to her desk and lie about what they paid for a vehicle only to try and get out of paying the accurate tax. "According to our books it is worth thirteen thousand four hundred dollars." She waited for my response.

"Well, I guess I got a good deal didn't I? I'll go and get a statement." My fear of believing that I had done something wrong and the jubilation inside about what I had really bought kept me in a trance. I had to go to this kid's workplace and get that written statement. That was embarrassing, but I didn't know why. He gave me what I wanted and it was hard asking for it because I had to reveal why. That bothered me.

A short time after I was driving my new truck there was nothing like a good old-fashioned accident to break it in. Driving on Ridge Road in Greece is like the traffic of a large funeral procession, very slow. Another accident had occurred up the road a ways and the cars had slowed from a tortoise's pace down to a snail's. As we were creeping along less than five miles an hour we stopped then started over and over again. I did not like to put that kind of wear on my clutch. During one of the stops during this crawl, the man behind me obviously wasn't watching and drove the front of his Chevy Cavalier into my bumper. I got out and looked. Even going less than five miles an hour the bumper was crushed in. I couldn't believe it. There was no damage to his car at all. The two guys got out and called the police. I have always hated to have accidents and have my insurance raised. After an officer questioned the men and then myself I had gotten the sense that somehow they tried to make it look like I was to accept part of the fault. It didn't turn out that way. They had tried to find a soft spot in me to work on and it would not work. The bumper was destroyed and they would pay.

My next job was to get estimates. I went to two repair shops, one of which was a well known Chevrolet dealership. Both of the men who gave me estimates said that they do a lot of work for the insurance company that the man had. They both also gave me an estimate of five hundred dollars. Within six dollars of each other and the fact that I would not tell either of them what the other was charging I thought I got an accurate one for the insurance company. I found it interesting that they would want to know how much other people's estimate were, but that is the day in which we live in I guess. I was content with my estimates and went to keep my appointment with the insurance company's adjuster. I drove into the bay of their garage and got a little lesson on fraud. The adjuster looked over the damage and both of my estimates.

"Please come over here," he said. "I want to show you something."

After sitting down next to him at his desk, he pointed to his computer. "Look at this chart for a minute. I want to make a call. Just listen." While he was on the phone waiting for an answer I saw numbers representing the prices on parts for my truck. His conversation with a man on the other end was at the dealership where I had gotten one of my estimates. What was happening was that the garage was charging the insurance company for one part at a time when they had had the whole bumper assembly in stock at their location and were lying about it. He caught them and would only pay two hundred fifty dollars for the entire assembly.

"Do you see what we mean about people messing us over? People think that the insurance company is doing the customer injustice with their rates. It just isn't the damage to the vehicle that we have to deal with, it's the fraud that these kinds of places hit us with."

I was astounded to actually see this going on live. I had heard the arguments, but never had witnessed it before. Every time I see documentary on 60 Minutes or 20/20 about fraud I think of that moment.

Family life was getting more interesting all of the time. With the number of people and all of their issues I was kept busy. Carol's mother was a very spry seventy-eight year-old woman when I met Carol-Aynn. She definitely was the matriarch of the family. Her social life would affect me greatly. I hadn't been around people for many years that I would respond to like she did to her family and friends. The last thing anyone could accuse Dori Dunham of was not "being with it." She is good in the thinking department and hardly ever misses a trick. Over the years and all of the things that she had to be concerned about I can understand many of the reasons why she feels the way she does about things. Doctors and medications are very often a sore spot with her and justifiably so. Carol's sister Linda is a deaf-mute. She had had a bout with a disease when she was a young child and with the ongoing seizure activity for the last fifty plus years no wonder her mother has to be on the lookout for wrong prescriptions. Maybe too much of one thing or not enough of another has kept Dori on her toes.

On one our trips to Arizona we had decided to ask Dori to come along. Of course she didn't want to be a burden to us, but we talked her into it. The long trips through the airports made it necessary to use a wheelchair. We would just pile the luggage in her lap and use her as a battering ram to gain control of the throngs of people that were in our way. Las Vegas airport seemed like quite a contrast between cultures as I would be pushing a devout elderly Mormon amongst the banks of slot machines. It was a particular joy to me for more than one reason. I loved the trip of course, but this woman who was my own mother in-law was on a long trip with me. In our society, mother in-laws have been stereotyped as somewhat as a disagreeable enemy of a son in-law who dare not cross the line anywhere her daughter. I refused to bow to that notion that this woman had to be a thorn in my side just because society wanted to dictate that.

We made it to Havasu City and stayed there for a few days. One of things that we all had to do was eat. Carol's other sister Michelle had been traveling across the country and met us there as well. I took all of the women to the grocery store to get some food for the week. Steve's wife Kay, Michelle, Carol-Aynn, and Dori now utilized me as their chauffeur. We got inside the store and I sort of went off by myself ahead of the girls. My favorite aisle in any grocery store, especially in other cities was the snack aisle. Potato chips and other "crunchies" made by unknown companies always tasted good. The same brands that I was used to were good, but I need to try other things.

As the women were slowly filling the cart they would stop and chat about "girl things." In this one particular aisle I happened to be walking along about thirty feet ahead of them with my hands locked behind my back. I had been pondering a minute about something on a shelf. I stopped and waited for the ladies to catch up. When they were taking "their good old time," I slowly turned around and said with a voice loud enough that they could hear me and said, "Come along!" I was trying to be funny and turned to walk away. While continuing down the next aisle, I did not notice that a man had been watching us.

He had gone up to the ladies and asked Dori, "Excuse me, are you Mormons? I noticed that man up there telling to you to come along and I was just thinking that he was the husband of you women." The women looked at each other in amazement while Dori stepped in.

"Why, yes. We are Mormons, but not the kind that you think that we are. Those are the Jack Mormons. We don't agree with that group. He is not our husband. He is my son in-law. This is his wife and sisters. Do you want to become a Mormon?"

The man was not interested in joining the Mormon church, he had just gotten an answer to his question and we got a little humor out of it.

We enjoyed the sun, played dominoes, and went to the Conference in the Mormon Church that happens every year about Valentine's Day. My attendance in the Mormon Church could easily bring ridicule from mainstream Christians. I could and may write a book about that some day. I had come to know a few of the folks in that church and especially the men. I was allowed to play basketball on their nice indoor court once or twice during the week. There was one common factor with all of the Mormons that I was meeting everywhere that I went. They were consistently delightful to be around. The discipline that exists in that group is impressive. The rules regarding participation in some of the influences of the world were left up to people's choices in most other churches. These folks kept themselves as a whole from a lot of troubles by turning suggestion into a mandate. If left unchecked, the consequences brought real disciplinary action. Accountability has made the purity aspect admirable.

We needed to take another trip from Havasu City in a rental car to Oceanside, California. This community outside San Diego was about eight hours away traveling across the hot desert. Carol's Aunt Norma who was Dori's sister in-law was a widow who needed a visit from a part of the family that certainly had a history together. Norm, as she was called had married Gordon Herrmann decades earlier. Though "Gordy" had been gone for quite a few years it obviously still made for a difficult life for Norm. Dori prepared us for the exhaustive conversations that she would be involving us in. We would not be disappointed. I felt bad for the lady. She kept herself well and still had other family near her. I guess it had been quite a traumatic event to loose her husband and she never really got over it, at least up to that point.

We arrived at 960 Vine Street in the middle of the afternoon. A nice hotel was right next to the townhouse complex where Aunt Norm was living. We could stay there for a couple of days. Dori could use a breather between trips anyway. She is still resilient to many things that other people would only buckle under to, but everyone still has their limits. We got to meet Norm (me for the first time) and it was good to see the welcoming and hugs between people who hadn't seen each other for a while. It was especially good for Dori. Since she was getting up years herself it might one of the last times that they would see each other.

Aunt Norma had a very nice place on the fourth floor. It was a good thing that they had elevators. Many of the people there were a little too old to use the stairs. We were greeted with a late lunch and good hospitality. After a short conversation to bring things up to date, out came the photo albums. It was the perfect excuse this time to talk about someone that I had only heard of. The pain of the loss of Gordy still echoed in this woman's heart. He was Dori's brother. She carried it well and I was more impressed about her dedication to another human being than the mourning period that maybe should have ended a long time ago. The apartment was beautifully decorated and the walls were filled with photographs of family, some of which I would soon meet.

After lunch and a couple of hours of conversation I decided to go for a walk and look around the area. Carol and Dori stayed back to talk about some of the things that only they could relate to within the family. I went straight to the administration office. I guess it was my intention all along. When we had first gotten there, this office had to be checked with in order to visit anyone who lived there. A couple on their late sixties ran the place and we had met them on our way in. When we had signed the visitors log I had noticed that the man was wearing a tee shirt with a unique logo on it. It had something to do with Area 51. I had had questions when I first saw it, but would wait for an opportunity to ask about it. This was it. I walked in the office and the man's wife directed me to another place on the grounds where her husband would be doing some work in the flowerbed. I found "Mike" and he was wearing a different shirt. I walked up to him slowly and made light conversation. Mike carried himself in a way that I would have never guessed that he would wear a shirt like that. Maybe someone a little younger or maybe someone who was a little fanatical about flying saucers and Government coverups.

"How ya doin," I would say, reaching out my hand to shake his.

He stopped shoveling and looked at me as if it put him on guard. "What can I do for you?" he answered.

"Well, I was wondering. When we signed in at the office I noticed that you had on a shirt that had to do with Area 51. Do you know anything about that place?"

That did it. He continued shoveling and responded abruptly, "Yea, I do. I used to work there, but I can't tell you anything about it." By now each shovel full of dirt was handled with authority. He was a little agitated. I quickly cut out.

"I hope you have a nice day," I quipped. As I turned to walk away he glanced at me with beady eyes that seemed to hold some secrets that were dying to come out.

"You too," he said.

I was intrigued by all of this stuff myself. But in spite of it all I would be confused as to why this man would draw attention to himself by wearing something like that in the first place. Maybe he had an emotional attachment to that place and thought it would safe to wear it thinking that others would only see it as just another logo. I would really never find out.

The next day Norma took us to a soup and salad place for dinner. It was a very nice place to eat, but I would have to tolerate not having the meat and potatoes that I was used to. It definitely cramped my style to eat like a rabbit. Smiling and trying to enjoy that world made me only get a little more cramped in my lower regions. My body was used to dealing with things that were tougher to digest than lentils and lettuce. Norm was happy to take us there and that seemed to really be the important thing to me. My consideration for others had been growing more over the years and the family that I had married into ensured that this principle would be exercised very often.

We said our goodbyes and headed back to Havasu City. Michelle hadn't been with us on that trip. She had stayed back to visit with Steve and Kay. Our drive back went well and the usual pitstops for bathrooms and gas took the edge off of any long straight stretches of highway. Of course, the highlight of the trip would be when I could stop and finally order a hot dog!

After our trip to Havasu City, our last leg of the journey would take us back to Vegas. We had flown into that city and rented a car to drive the few hours south to Havasu. Steve's friends Phil and Sue from church were pleasant people to be around. We had played dominoes with them, went to a church Valentines dinner and we would miss them. Our trip home was for me a hurtfully delightful one. I always miss people that I can't be around after meeting them for the first time. I have always hated leaving someone that had become part of my life and then must go. The rest of the trip went well.

Dori was going to turn eighty in 2001 and I hatched an idea to have a party for her. I talked it over with Carol and we rented a large pavilion at a nice park owned by the town of Greece. I thought that we had better take care of my mother in-law because "You never know how much longer she was going to be around." She has since enlightened me to the fact that that was what everybody was thinking when they threw a party for her when she turned seventy-five. I rented the place in the fall of the year for the following spring. Her birthday is May 14 and sometimes falls on Mother's day. I enjoyed doing it up big. My experience from the '70s had helped me plan the party and have a little fun. About eighty people would be invited from church, family and a few friends that had been by the wayside for a while.

The big day had come and it was miserable. Wet and rainy for most of the day wasn't a real deterrent for many of the people that were invited. However, some couldn't make it and frankly I couldn't blame them. At least we had a big indoor shelter and a large awning to cook the many hotdogs and hamburgers. There was more than enough to eat. We had decorated the hall with balloons and streamers which the bright colors helped a little in dealing with the gloominess of the weather outside. The gathering for Dori went pretty much the way I wanted it except for the rain. I felt like I was beginning to open up a little more and was willing to meet new people. There were plenty to meet in this family.

Like a flower to the rain I spread my wings,
Come water my soul I say.
I yearn for joy that eludes me, but however long it takes,
I shall wait for He who rejoices over me
And gives me life in the springs.

My own mother had started to become a little more forgetful. The attitude that she had at times made me think that that there was something working against her from the inside, but I couldn't put my finger on it. My phone conversations had to now be short. The accusations of me being down there in Bradford and stalking her when I was in Rochester the whole time had a bad ring to it. She would continue though, to refuse to see a doctor. Mary and Sam would become increasingly frustrated. Sam could handle it better. Mary has always been an emotional person and this would work on her feelings very much. She had worked in a nursing home and saw what it was like for old folks to endure the changes of losing their homes and possessions, while others were left out in the "halls of abandonment" by family members. I never understood why people lived like that. Having worked a couple of nursing homes myself I could not escape the reality of that plight. Traveling to Bradford would not be the same as I was used to over the years. Mom all of a sudden made it clear that I could never stay there again. There was never a reason given for the change. Sam would continue to call me less and less. It was though everybody was slowly dying.

After a couple years of the decline of my own mother, I needed another vacation. Carol and I decided to drive to Florida this time. It would be a little more expensive, but people by this time had cut down on the traveling by plane after the 9/11 attacks in New York. Our drive this time would take us to stay at a resort in the Orlando area. We would visit some friends for a couple of days over in the Ft. Myers area. One of the most interesting parts of this trip was the visit to Cape Kennedy. I had a longing all of my life to get there and it finally came. I remember when Dad had pointed up in the sky back in the early sixties when the Russians had put Sputnik into orbit. I acted like I saw it, but I really didn't. Now I could see all the rockets, the space shuttle and learn some things about the space program. We drove about an hour into the Cape. After we parked the car we approached the set of ticket booths. Walking over to enter the building there was a man with an Uzzi. The security around that place had been heightened, compliments of Osama bin Laden.

The weather was perfect as we entered the first area for exhibits. Walking around the grounds we could see the "Rocket Garden." Many of the rockets that had been used for space exploration and placement of satellites in orbit were planted like tall trees in an area that could be seen for miles. We sat in on a seminar and listened to a man speak about the cost of the space shuttle launches. He said it takes "four hundred million dollars to launch the shuttle every time. It takes three weeks for engineers to check out over two million circuits on the shuttle's control structure." I was like a little kid listening to all of the statistics. After lunch we went into a mock copy of the space shuttle and then boarded a bus that took us out closer to the launch site. We walked around the grounds and could see the next launch vehicle sitting on the pad about three miles away. Walking through a maze of tin roof buildings, the rocket motor displays gave you insight into just how complex these things really were. Then the highlight of the trip came for me. A special building had been built to house the Saturn V rocket. This behemoth of mechanical engineering had taken up so much space I wondered how they ever got the thing off of the ground. I had remembered that rocket from my youth and I did not even know that on that day I would see it. The huge assembly was in the original three sections. Each section would take up the space of many tractor trailers. The bottom where the engines were was the most interesting. There were five individual motors, shaped like cones. Each one was big enough to fit a large car in. I got to speak with an engineer that had worked on the original project. He had been retired and was volunteering his time to explain questions from visitors about that big rocket and the space program.

It came time for us to go. The whole day had been spent getting a crash course on some of my own curiosities about Cape Kennedy. Carol and I got into the car and drove into the sunset headed west back to Orlando. After we had gotten a few miles out and then it hit me like a ton of bricks. Depression. I never get depressed. But I was now. Everything had gone right that day and I still ended up in that place feeling like I had lost my best friend. I didn't have to look very far at all to know why.

I immediately looked over at Carol and said, "Honey, I'm depressed and I know why." Fighting back tears I continued. "You know that Saturn V rocket that we looked at?"

A concerned wife looked over at me. "Yea, what's the matter honey?" she said.

"Well, when I was a little boy and even all the way up into my teenage years I wanted to become a rocket scientist. I blew it and it didn't happen. I made a wreck of my life and I lost my chance to do it. That rocket should have been mine." I looked out the side window and was torn between embarrassment that an almost fifty year guy would be acting like this and at the same time acknowledging it as fact.

Carol went through her usual regimen of comforting me. "But look at where you are now. You changed your life around. You don't live like that anymore. You haven't for a long time. Honey, you have a lot to be thankful for."

A moment later the depression was lifted. What had become a very uncomfortable feeling of loss had turned into a very beautiful sweet sorrow that I had been part of something that I loved so dearly and now it was gone. I thought that this had been a message from Heaven to heal a broken wing. Now I can fly.

Sick Mothers and the Big Apple

The time had come, at least in my mind that everything was going to go wrong with both of our mother's. When there are hints of it you don't really believe though that it happening at the same time to two people who are close to you.

I have always wondered whether the things that others were finding important in this life were really what they were cracked up to be, our health and our wealth. Yours truly could be counted among them even while I believed the contrary. When times are tough with money issues or the threat of being sick or dead it just doesn't feel good. Carol and I would have to face this at the same time with Dori and Mom simultaneously.

It was September 2003 and I was already grappling with Mary about Mom. By then, our mother had been doing things that didn't do anything less than suggest Alzheimers. It had progressed to a greater stage by then and Mary in particular had become distraught about it. What had frustrated her the most was Mom's refusal to get medical attention while she was letting herself go to the skids. The trend of not cashing retirement checks had continued and the accumulation of unpaid payroll checks left us all in confusion. After consulting with a couple of lawyers we had come to the conclusion that nothing could be done to make our mother do anything against her will. She was still able to carry on a conversation and give anyone the confidence that she wasn't' in a place that could result in a Mental Hygiene arrest. She would go to the store with Sam or maybe take a ride in the country, maybe do the laundry and do a lot of the daily things that she always had. She plainly was doing enough to frustrate her family and the system. The new laws protected her from the imposition of other family when taking into account her current state of mind at the time. She was sick enough to be a pain in the neck, but not sick enough to be helped by force. Again, unless she was doing something to harm herself or others we couldn't touch her. Mary's frustration mounted. It was easier for me to bear it in some ways because I was not living there at the time. That fact was causing me more trouble than I knew.

Meanwhile, a couple years after Dori's birthday and a humbling trip to the hospital the decision was made to bring her home. Someone had to be there with her twenty-four seven for an undetermined amount of time. The kidney stones were still there and had to be dealt with. She was weak and could not do the same things for herself as before. The recovery that her body needed just from the time in the hospital was important.

During one of the family meetings we looked around the room for someone to volunteer to stay with Dori until things got to a better place. Carol and I looked at each other and took the job. And it was a job. The plan was that we all felt that about three weeks would be about right to help her get back on her feet. A doctor appointment or two and cooking a few meals would get this woman back to some normalcy. Whoopty-dee. I thought I learned not to plan out my life in every detail, but God had other plans for me too. For the next four months right down to the day we lived another life.

Carol and I packed up and moved into her mother's on October 1. We would be staying on the second floor in the room where she had grown up. She hadn't stayed in that room for decades and this would impact her in many ways. The only bathroom in the house was downstairs and that would be a problem for a wife who had to use it during the night and took measures faithfully not to do anything that would not wake her up any more than necessary. Lights glaring and going up and down the stairs certainly wasn't something that she wanted in her program.

Going into winter with the daylight hours getting shorter wasn't much of a help either. I had to make sure that Carol's car was cleaned off and running before she could drive to work. Fortunately I was only working one day a week by then so my time was a little more flexible.

Dori had to have her kidney stones "Blasted." Lithotrypsy was the medical term used to describe the procedure that would hopefully break up the stones and then she would pass them and we could all go home. Untold trips to the doctors for cardiac, kidney, and suspected neurological problems made the days go by quickly. Even though we never knew how long we would be there, it was a good thing that we didn't. Trips to the store for food and medications were aplenty as well. It was fortunate that those two items were in the same store and was right down the street. Other professionals came to help with some of the care that Dori needed. One of the biggest struggles for her was the threat of losing her independence. She submitted quite well in the beginning because she had no other choice at the time. But after some things started getting a little better the battle raged on. Some of my own freedoms had been compromised. Carol and I had watched television for a while in the evenings. There was no cable and the only TV at all was a little one with the rabbit ears. I was able to play my basketball on Tuesday nights, but even that got interfered with once through a power failure. Priorities were being scrutinized. Some things had to change or it would not work. We had to realize that we were there to take care of a sick mother and not just transfer our ways of doing things into another home. Whatever it required, we had to do what it took to get her well and back on her feet.

As I prepared meals I had to be aware of salt content and whatever we bought at the store had to be carefully examined. The first attempt at blasting the stones had not worked. We would have to plan some of the care all over again.

Dori's little dog "Makayla" quickly became my friend. Most people did not like her because she is a yippy white Maltese who always wanted her way. I guess it was the house that she grew up in.

One of my first days at the house I made a big mistake and almost cost Makayla her life. I was going up and down the stairs with some boxes of things and she would follow me around. I would always close the door after I passed through it. One of those trips when she was near me and my arms were full of things she got in my way at the top of the stairs. As I stood waiting for her to go down the stairs ahead of me she stalled and wouldn't move. With my right foot I tried to gently nudge her to move. My weight had shifted and the force of my foot became greater than I wanted it to. I shoved the little dog off of the landing and onto the stairs. She was running down the stairs on her front paws to keep from going head over heels. By the time she had gotten to the bottom she "Planed off," like a boat in the water. It was also that she got straightened before the bottom step because that closed door was coming up fast and her owner was sitting on the sofa a few feet away from it. If Makayla would have hit that door I couldn't have forgiven myself and I might have had some company.

My relationship with Dori began to change. We talked about things that we might never have if these things had not happened to her. The past, family experiences and my projects were just a few of things that we sat and discussed. She had been into the genealogy thing for a long time. It was encouraged in the Mormon Church and Dori certainly had a lot of family to try and keep track of. We would talk of the root of the Herrmann lineage which originated in Europe somewhere between Germany and Holland. Aunt Norm and Gordy had adopted a son from that area and he was living near Norm around San Diego. When we were out there visiting we had all gone out with his wife and kids for a nice dinner at an Olive Garden.

One part of our discussions still was to some degree difficult to talk about. I guess it depends on who is listening. Many times have I talked about the trials and woes in my life, but many of the people that heard me talk about those things had either been through it or could in some way sufficiently relate to it. That hardly ever produced any trepidation. This environment however became a little bit of a problem to discuss. Dori would talk about how some member of her family had learned to adjust to a new life in America or how someone was related to someone famous. When it came time for me to talk about my family, mentioning about how a drunken Dad used to sleep on a park bench in the public square just didn't cut it. The distinct contrast between family history discussion was hard. Dori would rescue me at times by asking me about my projects. I had plenty of good things to discuss, it was just that I didn't feel that I wanted to switch tracks just because I was uncomfortable about the topic that I thought we were on.

One important task that my mom in-law likes to do is take photographs. She does it so much that sometimes she is a pain in the neck. At the most strange times she wants the world to stop so she can "take a shot." I saw a picture of her husband lying on a lounge chair from a few years earlier. If he hadn't been dead I would never have questioned her commitment to get a photo of anything that moves. It doesn't have to be a party or celebration of any kind. It can be at the dinner table or coming in from the cold. "Don't move," she would say, as the shutter was ready to click. Her real desire is of course to capture a lasting memory for others, not just herself. While we were living with her we could not go through all of the collection of her snapshots from over the many years. The number of them was too great. Every one is marked with a date and a note about who or what it was. For a Christmas present one year the family put together a long film that took in the family history.

Carol and I eventually made it to the first of February and we moved back home. The last sixteen weeks had given Dori the jump start she needed. We made sure we followed up on help with the meds and food afterward. Our long awaited trip to see Steve in Arizona again had been earned, to say the least, this time.

I had hired a man to critique my second movie script a year or so earlier. He was living around Los Angeles and I would hope to see him personally on this trip. His job at the time was to write for one of the television series that I watched every Saturday night and I had been steered in his direction by another man that I eventually met at a seminar for screenplay writing.

Carol-Aynn and I got to Vegas and started our usual trek toward Havasu City. This whole trip would feel so much different than the other ones. After the pressures of the winter and living at Dori's and then be on a trip like this was nothing less then spectacular. The grass was greener and the sky bluer. Steve had sold his house and bought another one a few streets away. He still had a good view of the city that was built by Robert McCullough, the inventor and entrepreneur who also purchased the original London Bridge and brought it to America. It took literally my whole life to understand where that song, "London Bridge is Falling Down" came from. The first bridge had actually started sinking into the ground after many years at a rate that was calculated to be at a point where it would be useless to try and fix it. They had decided to remove it and build a new one. Mr. McCullough had the bridge dismantled and each marked piece was boated to the United States, thus giving rise to a town in the desert called Havasu City. It became the only bridge ever that was built on dry ground. They dug backwards under the bridge and the water from the manmade Lake Havasu went under it. It is a beautiful resort community.

During this trip we drove to LA and I was to finally meet Scott Little, the man that I had spent three hours with me on the phone after he took six hours to assess where I was with my skills in writing screenplays. The deal included all of that time in conversation and I was to tape the whole thing as he spoke about "East Wind Rain," my second screenplay.

We got to Los Angeles and it wasn't pretty. I had only seen and heard about the traffic problems in that area. My trip with the guys back in 1973 took us near that mess, but not in it. This time would be different. I tried to time it so that we wouldn't hit the rush hour traffic. It really didn't make any difference. We got held up enough where it got us anyway. Driving to Santa Monica gave us a little breather, but the Hotels there on the ocean were so expensive I just wouldn't do it. There were none of those cheaper motels around like Motel 8 near the highway. I called my friend and I told him to forget it. We were going back. We had gotten a call that Steve's newborn niece was at death's door so we headed back the same day. After driving fifty miles or so we came upon an affordable motel. I needed a rest just from the stress of the traffic. We eventually made it back in one piece and the baby was fine. Scott seemed to be disappointed, but I would wait for another time.

One of the days on this trip Steve would take us for a drive back to Vegas where his daughter was living. She was working as a waitress in a new restaurant named after one of one of Jimmy Buffett's songs. He owned a couple of the "Margaritaville's" and had sprung a good business at both locations. Our lunch there and then a visit to the large

Mormon church outside the city made for a full day. We had stopped at the Mormon book store and when we were leaving I ran into Tony Weeks, the man I recognized as a boxing referee on television. Carol got a picture of Tony and I together.

Whenever Carol and I would take a trip out west, one of my favorite things to do was drive at night. Out in the open desert in the wee hours of the morning was somehow mesmerizing. The big trucks with all of their lights and a hot dog with popcorn at a huge truckstop was fitting for me. Carol would sleep through much of that part of those trips, but it was always a part of my life. Running around in the night had never really left me. I was always wide awake. My wife on the other hand, having led a more sensible life than myself, needed her rest. This visit became only a memory in a very short time.

During my studies of screenplay writing I had gotten an advertisement about a seminar being held in New York City. David Freeman was hailed as one of the best teachers in the craft and I decided to go. He had been the man that referred me to Scott in LA for the critique of my work. What attracted me just about as much as going to the seminar was the fact that it was in the city that I had avoided all of my adult life. The closest that I have ever gotten was that Hotel in Jersey when I went to the top floor and drank myself into oblivion twenty-five years earlier staring at the "City that never sleeps." During that "decade of decadence" I had made that conscious decision to stay away from New York. It scared me. Many other major cities saw my face, but something was too wrong about this one. Never did put my finger on it.

My first legitimate train ride would be only the second time ever on one. The first trip obviously was the time Bob Cummins and I jumped the one on Main Street in Bradford in 1968. We rode it two miles and I had to jump off into a swamp at fifty-five mph. Bob landed in an abandoned railroad bed and still has cinders in his elbows to this day.

I booked my trip to NYC on Amtrak. The big day had come. I would be leaving the station at 5:55 am on a Thursday. It would take a full six hours to get to Penn Station in Manhattan. I was as excited as ever now to get there. Twenty years of television series, innumerable newscasts and certainly 9/11 all changed whatever fears that I had into an anticipation that was rivaled only by a ten year old kid

413

entering Disney World. A friend of mine had dropped me off at the station in Rochester. Carol needed her sleep for work and I didn't want her to miss it. I would be coming back on Monday. The Seminar went all day Saturday and Sunday so I took a day and a half to see what I could without any other commitments.

The ride down became nothing less than a joy. Reading a few pieces of literature that I had brought would easily keep me busy. And, of course, lunchtime on the train was a pleasant surprise. They sold National Hebrew hot dogs. I didn't remember the last time that I had one of those kind. They were more expensive and I didn't recognize the taste except from when I was a kid. Being a connoisseur of hot dogs I somehow had missed this brand for all of those years. Maybe it was because they are the most expensive ones on the market, I'm not really sure. The rest of the ride however went well as we traveled through the central and eastern part of the state. I was watching a map to where we were at all the time. The stops along the way in Utica, Albany, and a couple of other places kept me sure of when we would be getting closer to the big city. As we got about twenty-five miles or so away from New York I struggled to see the Skyline. The weather was perfect and my heart started to race. I had also printed out a map so that I could get to the Hotel easily just a few streets away from the train station. The thought of getting lost in New York City had made me take every precaution.

We pulled into Penn Station and I got off of the train. The people were everywhere. The first impression that I was getting was only a taste of what I would get when I went to the ground level outside during a nice day at lunch hour.

I emerged into the streets from the lower depths of "traindom" to see an awe-inspiring sight. What I had only seen on NYPD Blue and Law and Order was now the real thing. That trademark echo of sirens through the canyons of Manhattan greeted me as if to say, "Welcome, we've been waiting for you a long time." I didn't know I was standing outside Madison Square Garden until I turned around to try and get my bearings and saw the sign. My friend at work had told me one time that Penn station was under that building, but I had forgotten.

My new assignment was to get to the hotel. The Holiday Inn gave me clear directions and so it was a no-brainer to get to it. So with directions in hand and two suitcases, both of which fortunately had wheels, I got lost. I have to admit that my façade in the crowds of people at lunchtime in New York caught up with me immediately. When it was time to cross the street at an intersection I tried to act like I had been living there all of my life. You know when that little man on the pole lights up and tells you that it is okay to cross the street? Well, nobody told me to lead off with the other thousand people before he lights up. It was move with them "now" or look like an idiot. I chose the latter. I had gotten found out. They knew that I was not from there. There was something else more important than that though. They didn't care about it. I had never seen such a demonstration of individuality and at the same time a mysterious camaraderie among a group of people in my life. They moved as if they had all just broken out of the same meeting and were going to the same buffet lunch. After going in the wrong direction for a couple of streets I decided to ask one of those people that were moving less than one hundred miles per hour where my hotel was. They were all kind to me and I made it there safely. My shoulders were hurting though. Pulling the suitcases down the street was hard without having them veer off to the side and hit someone. I did that a couple of times, but made it alive to where I was going. The folks there are very forgiving, but they also meant business.

I got to the hotel and walked into the lobby to check in. The first words that I heard from one of the clerks was that the place was booked up and a man was a little agitated about it. Since I had made previous plans with them, my room would be a shoe-in. When it came my turn to sign in I was informed that I had no room. I just knew God wouldn't let this happen to me.

"I'm sorry Mr. Knott, but there are no empty rooms. We will have to work something out."

I had no intention of letting her know how I felt. My respect for this place had grown tenfold in less than an hour and she would get no beef from me about it. I just completely gave up my life and said to myself, "Whatever will be will be."

The lady said, "Wait here, I'll get the manager."

The manager came out and he went and got another person. After I was convinced that they knew who I was and where I had come from I believed that all would work out. The first clerk came back and issued me a penthouse reserved for the VIP's. I guess it would work out. My room was all I thought it would be, and more. Overlooking the streets from the fourteenth floor was very nice.

By now it was time for a late lunch. I had hoped to buy something from a street vendor just like the cops do it on "Law and Order," but I went to a cheap restaurant instead. It was a steakhouse that everybody went to. You got your food fast, but I was glad that I didn't have to eat fast. Since my classes wouldn't be starting until Saturday I had the rest of Thursday and all day Friday to see some things. Keeping a low profile for an hour or so I went for a walk down the street to Times Square. The New Year's Eve celebration and Macy's Parade on television over the years made sure that I would recognize this place when I saw it. I counted my steps on the sidewalk in front of Macy's. Three hundred of my paces measured the store's length at nine hundred feet, that is three football fields long! It was truly the longest storefront in the world.

The next day saw me buy a ticket to go up to the top of the Empire State Building. Just the process that it took to get up there was like someone going through the process of trying to get top secret security clearance for the Government. My group finally got off the elevator and we spread out to go our own ways. My view of the city from the eighty-fifth floor was more than I thought it would ever be. Central Park, the Statue of Liberty, the former sight of the World Trade Center, and the other buildings made for a breathtaking sight. I was not disappointed. I had also bought a ticket to a New York Knicks basketball game for that Friday night. It would be the capstone to the leisure part of the trip. I had gotten better at crossing the streets with my seven million new friends too. Without my suitcases I was able to blend in and feel accepted. Funny how I even cared about stuff like that at age fifty, but I did. Everything that I had planned out could be reached on foot. There would be no cabs for me. The stigma of watching my life savings go out the window by way of a meter run by a cabbie who could quickly sense that I was an easy out of towner kept me out of those yellow cars. At least that is what my perception was. The seminar was to be held at the Fashion Institute of Technology only a couple of streets down from the "Garden." Everything was easy to get to. My visits to a few of the shops run by foreigners was entertaining. All of the cop shows had characters that were informants who ran businesses so anything that I could somehow relate to, became fun.

My classes at F.I.T. were on one of those steep auditorium type inclines. I hadn't sat in one of those since high school, except for all of the movie theatres. The man who was teaching came with a battery of paperwork. We ran from early morning till late evening with a lunch break and two short breaks during the day. David Freeman made sure that he lived up to his reputation as one of the best. Plenty of video assistance, tons of paperwork and the skills to communicate verbally what he knew about the craft of screenplay writing drove the point home over the next two days. I had wondered how anyone could really learn anything about all of this in two days, but he had answered that question abundantly.

There were about one hundred twenty of us in the class and hardly 5% of the group had actually written a screenplay. I was so glad that I had studied this subject and subsequently wrote an entire script before I took that class. The sheer volume of information alone was overwhelming to me and had to be a trial for those that were just exploring the possibility of writing. He had warned the class about that before we started.

Mr. Freeman's video assistant was no ordinary one. Mark Say was also the man who took care of the works of many other clients such as the Rolling Stones. The Stones were on tour in Japan when we were there in New York. I had the chance to talk to Mark for a while after we had broke for lunch. During the verbal instruction Mark was responsible for changing the images on the screen for the class. A couple of times during the day if David would take a long time before he would need the image changed we would see Mark dosing off and it embarrassed David. He explained to the class that he had been up for the last seventy-two hours working on the "Stone's" tour material.

Even our lunch hours had a little drama. My first day during the time to eat it was rather fun to look for a place to eat. At least the weekend business crowd was a little less crowded. I picked a nice little place a couple of blocks down the street. Before I had come to New York, Carol made sure that I would be dressed appropriately. She helped me pick out clothes that would suit the affair. Today I was dressed in a casual sport jacket and solid black shirt. I carried my black briefcase of material wherever I would go. When I went in to the eatery for lunch I had felt like I looked like a terror suspect dressed the way that I was and carrying that briefcase. In my mind I could have gotten away with that in any other city, but not here. I felt that it would be some time before this abused populace would get over what had happened two short years earlier. The government's finger on the pulse of the terror community and letting the nation know what color the threat level was made sure all of us knew that those memories weren't going to just fade away. As I sat having lunch I could see a police car drive up in front of the building, then another, and another, and another. I got up out of my seat and walked over to the window to see what was going on. What attracted me to investigate was not only the cop cars, but how slow they actually pulled into their parking positions, all thirteen of them! I went back to my seat and became a little nervous that now I really had become a terror suspect. I slid my black briefcase out of the way so no one could see it and waited. Two officers walked in the front door. My heart is pounding heavily. They glanced in my direction for a moment and then ordered a bite. I knew they had to play it cool knowing they had me cornered. They left with their food and just sat in the patrol car waiting. After a few minutes they all left, down the street in single file. I had learned that they were just following a large crowd of about 100,000 people who were protesting the war in Iraq the next street over. My own imagination had to have a little overhaul.

After two days of intense study it was time for me to come home. My train again would bring me home in the early morning. I walked down the street to Penn Station at about 6:30 and I was again amazed at the sight of the people. The subway tunnels were emptying themselves of thousands of people into the streets. They were coming up out of the ground like giant ants in a horror movie. The street vendors were already set up for the lunch hour, whenever that was. There were already some customers having a hot dog or Teriyaki stick at that hour of the day. On my way to New York on the train I had noticed many small towns as far away from the city as a hundred miles that had a parking lot full of empty cars. The commuters had used the train and had to get up very early to get to work on time. The up side of that was that they wouldn't have to pay the cost of

Manhattan living. I got on the train and bid fond farewell to the "city that never sleeps." I found out that it is possible to have jet lag while on a train. The residual affect of having been in that place left me with a feeling that I had just been to a mythical metropolis. It was a good feeling and I felt that someday I would be back.

Although my vision for writing screenplays was definitely being fulfilled I needed to make more money than what I was making at the time. I wasn't dying of starvation, but Carol-Aynn had been covering my back and I wanted to deliver my end of the bargain much sooner than what seemed to be happening. A man that Carol had met through her job was introduced to me. He had gotten into a discussion with her about inventing and she had told him about me. I called him and had a meeting or two. He immediately wanted to go into business and create some entity to market our ideas. The experiences that I had had about that subject convinced Jim Trek that he had finally run into the person who could help make it all happen. I appreciated the offer, but refused. I had become one who wanted to be a solo if I was ever going to make any money inventing. I just plainly did not want to go into business with anyone else. Jim had introduced me to some of his friends who were starting a business and he wanted me on board to complement the group. I would be the finishing touch to a consortium that could catapult our ideas into the marketplace. I knew that it took more that just an idea, but I was still out of the corporate effort. I proved to myself anyway that I could accomplish something if I wanted to bad enough. There would be meetings in the Lennox Tech center, the building that we were holding our inventors meetings. Even two of the three men who wanted to be a part of Jim's efforts had their businesses at that address. I met all of the guys eventually and came on as sort of a consultant. After a couple of meetings or so, Jim convinced me to be a part of it all.

The first order of business was to address the invention that Jim had been working on for the last twenty years. A corporation was formed and we all were in the process of signing the final papers when I uncovered things that I did not agree with. The organization and the intent of one of the partners was not up to snuff. The last thing that I wanted to get into was babysitting other people that I had gone into business with. "Jim" I said. "I can't do this. One of the guys is talking like he is a millionaire and he has nothing. I don't want him around. That was an indication of bad things to come. If he hasn't taken care of that façade by now he might never and I don't want to try and find out when that is going to be." So, as the story goes I made sure that Jim and I were on the only ones that were going into business. It took some time and explanation, but it ended up being with what I really wanted anyway. The lesson in business that I had to learn was that limiting myself by not associating with others cost me too much already throughout life and I still had reservations about how far I would go with it. Discipline was a big factor.

Science Holdings Incorporated was born in May of 2004 and became the focus of our efforts. Much research, meeting new people in business, universities, and Government has become almost a weekly diet. Jim had been sort of a ship without sails for a long time. He had the ideas, but not the means to get them the attention they needed. Our joint efforts could now make that happen. There were some idiosyncrasies about Jim that irritated me. And if the truth were told, still do. Loudly slurping at a water fountain, emptying five packets of salt on a hamburger, rubbing his eyes constantly while I am talking to him are some of the irritants. I have yet to discover whether those are legitimate gripes or not. At this point I haven't said anything because my conscience tells me that I am making a big fuss over nothing. His character and integrity however are very good. That is what has always counted to me. I never seem to get the entire package, but at the same time I started to wonder what he got. Was he content? I think he is and the capability that he saw in me seemed to drown out any malfunction that he may see. I knew that I should view things the same way. Starting to watch "The Apprentice" on television about this time actually helped me make some adjustments in my assessments of other people, especially in business. The decisions that those folks had to make under the various imposed pressures was very interesting. The way they treated each other, the idiosyncrasies, faults, and the mounting stresses of having to win squeezed out a lot of who these people really were.

I secretly gave into my better judgment and did not bring anything up. I made a decision to weigh out what I should say if ever. Working on encryption for data security and a few other ideas had been moving to the forefront of our business. Attending seminars, filling out forms, maintaining two offices in our homes and keeping a rein on the tight finances was a constant chore. The plan was to use our creativity in every aspect of business to generate a legitimate reputation in the local community. We thought that "since necessity is the mother of invention," the lack of money forced us to be creative wherever we could. I was in some ways still intimidated by meeting all of the people in dark suits that had established businesses and were rubbing elbows with a lot of other people, including Government leaders and individuals in business who were influential. Shaking hands with those folks and acting like I was glad to meet them was a hard thing to do. One of the things that I would always look for was someone else that was going through the same feelings about things. By signing onto this world I was to again embark on a journey that reveal much about myself and would be given sufficient opportunity to make some adjustments.

Life wasn't all work after I helped start the business. Carol-Aynn had wanted to find something that she was interested in, in the form of a hobby. Something that would keep her busy that didn't include any distractions from family issues that kept pressing for attention. I had encouraged her to find anything that would be therapeutic. She chose "Beading." She had gotten interested in buying beads and all of the accessories for making jewelry. About a month or two after she made her first necklace and set of earrings she asked me if I would go to a beading class with her.

"You'll really enjoy it," she said.

Maybe in my mind I was only imagining that I was puckering at the thought of going to a beading class. The most important thing to her was that I was there and really, the most important thing to me was that she was happy. So, without further adieu she signed me up and I went. We got to the class and of course out of the thirteen people there I was the only male. Where had I seen that before? Unlike the screenplay writing seminar in New York City I had no preparation for this one. I didn't even know there was this other world out there called "beading." I sat down in a well-lit room. The instructor handed out some free beads and we were all going to make a DNA pattern. She was a kind lady about thirty-five who had been volunteering her time to promote the craft. I thought it was kind of her to do that, but did she have to pick something that looked like only a rocket scientist could make? I got my stuff and started to follow her directions. I also had a set of illustrated directions on paper in front of me. I just couldn't do it. The poor lady had to keep coming over and assisting me more than anyone else. I knew what my problem was right away. My apparent need to avoid directions over the decades was coming back to haunt me. The fact that I only knew how to spell bead was the closest I had ever gotten to the craft. *The Indian part of me had better kick in real fast*, I thought. *My marriage is riding on it.* I did not get it. There had been plenty of close attention paid to me by everyone in the room. Even keeping the teacher away from those people who needed help didn't work. I'm glad that no one got irritated with me. They could have easily, especially since I may have been invading female territory.

I became sincerely interested in the art of beading. The bright colors of my first class overwhelmed any doubt about that. I would not be discouraged by the events in that room and my ultimate failure at getting the "DNA pattern." Carol and I would now be able to go to the stores that carried beads and things as well as bead shows displaying other peoples work. We were due to go back to Provincetown that fall and we could check on available places before we even left. Our trip there would see me make my first necklace. I got into it so much quickly that I wanted to check out any and all of the stores that were in the area. I saw a good deal in one shop that was selling many of the necklaces that were already made up for a song. I bought thirty-four of them and brought them back home to sell over the holiday season. I found a vendor who was setting up his booth in one of the main runways of the Marketplace Mall. The necklaces were there throughout Thanksgiving and into the New Year. I sold not one and I tried to remind God that I was not in the shelving business anymore, but it didn't seem to make any difference. Carol and I would just continue to do this together whenever we could. I have been mostly teaching myself through the tips in beading magazines. It is fun and something that we both enjoy doing.

Nesting

Leisure time was becoming more and more an entity that you seemed to have to grab. I never wanted to live like that. I liked vacations, but those times should not be earmarked as the only time when you can say "Ahhh, I needed that rest." Carol had chosen a place to live that I was very happy to be in. The waterfront near the Petten Street area was to be worked on over the next five years. A private company that shared assets from Canada and the United States bought a forty two million dollar "Fast Ferry" to cart people back and forth between Toronto and Rochester. It was quite a build-up to the arrival of that boat which had traveled from Australia, up the East Coast and through the St. Lawrence Seaway. So much criticism came from people who wanted that money to go for things like school budgets at a time when school nursing programs were being eliminated, and whole schools were being shut down. The boat had hit a dock and was damaged around New York City somewhere. That only rattled those who didn't want it in the first place.

I was here at the dock in Rochester that cloudy day the boat arrived. I was really wondering how big this thing really was. On television, the images don't do it service as far as seeing real sizes of objects. TV station transmitters were lined up among about two thousand people. From a distance it was hard to tell anything about the boat until it got closer. As it approached the port, the thing seemed to get bigger and bigger. It was everything that they said it was and then some. The new dock that had been built over the last two years made for a good fit for "The Breeze" as it was called. A contest in the community netted what I felt was a silly name for something so majestic. Able to carry several hundred people and cars I hardly felt that a name like that was fitting. It became the brunt of cartoons and commentaries in the *Democrat* and *Chronicle*. Whatever the real story was about that new business, it was supposed to launch by a certain date and only ran for about three months. It did well it its short time of operation before the engines had trouble. The company went under and the city of Rochester ended up putting the boat up for bid at an auction before it would try to sail again. During that ninety day stint between the two cities it did well as far as getting people to ride it. The people had spoken regardless of the critics. That alone was an incentive for the city to look into the venture. Right after the city purchased the boat, it was discovered that the engines needed overhauled. The Germans who had built those motors have always had the reputation of superior engineering in all that they do. I still don't know what happened. Major engine work twice on a new car would not be tolerated by anybody. Maybe the fact that tax dollars were used for the project could explain the wide margin of tolerance.

The entire Port of Rochester was now being renovated. The Breeze had been used as a lever to upgrade that locale. No one could argue that the new appearance of that part of the city was looking nicer all the time. As the work continued it would inconvenience some people here and there, but it was nice to see the support of those who liked it. Boat or no boat the area was improving. We would be able to still go to the Wednesday night concerts in the summer time at the "Lake Ontario Beach Park." We are within walking distance to it all and certainly appreciate that fact when everyone else has to deal with the traffic problems. On concert night though we will drive and get there plenty early. Carol needs to have a rest after work and walking on that particular night with the chairs is just to much.

The music at the beach is of a different order every week. Barber shop, country, rock, and jazz are just some of the various venues. Wegman's grocery store chain has been sponsoring the event for quite a few years and it brings out at least several thousand folks for dance, food and conversation during the middle of the work week to take the edge off.

It hasn't been only Wednesday's that Carol and I would go to the lake. A good long walk through the back yards of homes along the lake has been a ritual. There is a paved path that was built for the public that travels between the back yard and the water. All of those who walk that path seem to pose no problem to the well-kept grounds of the affluent in that neighborhood. I haven't quite figured out yet why that arrangement is allowed. If I owned a million dollar home along the lake I don't think that I would want the general public walking through all of the time. I have to hand it to those who do. The flowers and lawns are immaculate and trying to fully enjoy them the homeowner always has traffic in the summer months.

My wife and I always take stock of were we are at in our relationship. When you see how others live and what they have to deal with in life it can provoke thought if you are one who really cares where you are traveling down this path called life. Anywhere, anytime, we will just reflect on where we have come from and how we are doing as individuals as well as us together. It makes for a great relationship. Something that it was supposed to be. Seeing people hold hands, especially the older ones, testifies that they have something that all people want. I wasn't able to feel comfortable walking down the street holding my wife's hand in the beginning. She was hurt and frustrated at that aspect in my life. She had a right to be. As time went on, I realized more and more that what I was embarrassed to do should be the norm. I knew that simply holding hands told your spouse something more than it was your responsibility. It creates a better bond. I had been holding onto the "touch thing," as it was related to other things. Starting over near the age of forty-seven I still had needed to grow up.

Festivals are one of our favorite things to do. All of them have arts and crafts, but there is a theme that is different for each one. Some of them are self-explanatory by their name alone. The "Hilton Apple Festival," the site of the world record that was set for the largest apple pie back in the early eighties had everything that you can make with apples. Pies, sauces, cakes, even apple sausages accompany the many concoctions made with apples. I won't go near those apple sausages.

Maybe some day, but for now I don't want to ruin my thoughts about what a sausage should really be. The "Naples Grape Festival," features some of the best recipes in pies, other desserts, and a wine tasting venue in one of the best wine regions in the world. There is the "Apple-Umpkin festival," the "Cornhill and Park Avenue Festivals," and dozens more around the region. And of course every large community had its own battery of ethnic festivals from around the world. My favorite one for the taste of food from the German Festival. All of the knockwurst, brockwurst, and all of the other wursts keep me coming back. Carol and I both enjoy the people in their native dress with the music and dancing. I am like my mother in that sense. She always likes to see people eat and have fun.

Although Carol-Aynn and I like to do the same things together, like attending festivals and going on walks, it was never meant to be looked at as the glue that keeps us knitted together. Our time apart from each other can be just as valuable as when we are hand in hand. Not as often of course, but time to meditate, pray in your heart, and take on the responsibility of the moment as God seems to deal to you is what really counts. I have discovered that you become like whomever you are spending your time with. That in itself says a lot. I recently had heard a preacher say, "Whatever you deem important in this life, you will find the time for." That became quite convicting to me.

What was important to me certainly got attention. I've had to be careful with my imagination. Being creative in many ways I can come to depend on my ability to create in my mind and leave the most important things out. If I were to use what my thoughts were as a measuring stick of success I am the greatest failure on earth. There was a rich man back in the early '90s. I read an article on him in the newspaper. The reason he was interviewed in the first place was because he was a billionaire and those people get all the attention that they want and some that they don't. His wife and he were going through an amicable divorce. She wasn't taking him to the cleaners and he wasn't trying to keep everything that he had. She was going to get twenty-six million dollars a month! Not a year, a month! I would have thought that to be a lot even per year. They weren't fighting over anything. The story went that when he was only a millionaire she got on his case about his potential. It seemed as though he was moping around the house as if he had come to the end of what he could do in life.

"Get out there and do it," she said. "You are capable of much more than what you have done."

The essence of the message that this woman was telling her husband was that you weren't supposed to ever think or live your life as if you had conquered all and now it was all over. Time to quit. She wouldn't allow him to continue on in that thinking. So, he went out and made billions. It is the principle that counts, not what or how much. The words by him that I will never forget is: "I never tell people what I am going to do, I change my mind so often that if they knew it they wouldn't want to do business with me." That was from about 1993. Making adjustments in my ways of thinking can be tempered by those who have been around or are more experienced than myself. He was eighty-four at the time and made a lasting impression on me.

During my times of leisure and moments of reflections, many issues would be vying for my time, some more than others. Mom had continued to get a little irritating on the phone, my alienation from Mary and the fading communication with Sam all had been crowned with a mutual concern for Mom's future. I have been taking care of her SSI monies and am waiting for a decision from the judge on whether I will be in charge of all of the affairs of a mother who seems to sit dead in the water awaiting her fate. She has been aware of some kind of trouble, but hasn't been able to put her finger on it. She has never asked one question as to where all of the bills in the mail or her social security checks went. I almost wished that she had. At least that would have given me some confidence in her cognition. It is difficult to say that you care and at the same time keep your distance from all of the negative aspects of this tangled relationship. If I would travel to visit Mom and Mary knew about it, she would be there to make sure that I wouldn't be a problem, at least in her mind. I could and did just show up when it was convenient for me. That kept things a little less stressful at times.

When a Mom gets sick, I have watched other families all too often go through their hurts and woes, going back in time to remember that person, the way they once were, family get togethers, good times and bad. Now it is my turn…again. I have found it difficult, but in a new way to have to deal with a mother that is slowly moving away from her ability to deal with life rationally. The fading memories, which both short and long term are affected. The hallucinations that keep me only a notch away from being her enemy one minute, and her dear son the next, all have me on my toes. I don't know who I am going to get when I talk to her on the phone or visit her face to face. The thing that still bothers me a lot is the prospect of her being in a nursing home. It is not the stigma of those facilities, but the fact that Mom started her life out in a children's home. I know from my conversations with her many years ago that she didn't like it and now to return to the type of place that she started her life in hurts me just to see it in my mind. I can see Mom hanging out the laundry to dry on the clothesline in the back yard. The smell of the fresh white sheets still goes through my nose on a cloudless sunny day. There was just enough breeze to let you know that everything was alive. She would wear her apron and make sure that we wouldn't travel too far just before lunch. Those kinds of days were on the weekends or during the years when she wasn't working her job at a factory. Peanut butter and jelly sandwiches, Oreo Cookies and milk made my day back then, but only if Mom made it. Anyone else, no matter how hard they tried couldn't match the mother's touch. Those memories are so strong that they seem more real than the current situation that we all face. I have to look back and see if Mom was happy. It is one of the most selfish thoughts that I have right now. I am really concerned about what I am feeling with respect to her history, not her sense of loss. I simply don't want to hurt. To think that she could have done better and couldn't kills me. She had so much restriction in her life that maybe I would have done better myself to acknowledge the value in some of that. But this is the way that I was conditioned to think. I continue to be amazed at the simple things in life that I avoided for so long, and now it is catching up with me. Again it is time for a change. Dori, on the other hand is holding her own. After a recent bout with some sickness and a few trips to the doctors she continues to battle back and do almost all of the things that she has always done. Still sharp as a tack, she shovels snow, does yard work, goes up and down the stairs, and makes meals, this woman will only give up when she has expired. She still is living proof that you should keep moving or you will freeze up. A woman comes to help her with some of the things a couple times a week. Dori had changed in the way that she cannot do everything herself. That can be an example for others especially me. There comes a time when you have to stop fighting the inevitable. There is that difference between common sense and a pride that will make you look like a stubborn mule. I still like to learn lessons from people who have been there rather than go through some hard things just because I wouldn't listen to good counsel. Some people just live their lives in such a way that you are feeling the guilt from the decisions that you make. Nobody has to say a word, you just know.

Carol is certainly not her mother's daughter. She has a sweet spirit that has produced that "lamb led to the slaughter" effect in her life. She also has been a trusting soul to a fault. In recent years however there has been a significant change where she can't be so easily fooled by many. This has been where hanging around me has come in handy. I have lived a life of suspicion. Making sure that unscrupulous individuals did not gain any footing in most creative ways had become the norm. The Joe thing with the football card and the tax refund episode ratcheted up my skills a notch or two. I have been teaching my wife to wait and think about the motives that are driving some people when they ask a question or want something. The track record with respect to "getting used" was too consistent. When I came on board it was going to stop. She is growing leaps and bounds.

Carol-Aynn likes plants. The yard around the back of the house has needed some attention in that area. Right after we had gotten married she was afflicted with a nasty bout with poison ivy. Digging around the small flowerbed and pulling up what looked like weeds got her to look like she had been burned. The itch and redness took a long time to go away. Her fair skin readily showed up any changes in color. Although there is still some limited space back there to grow things, it hasn't gotten the attention it needs. The front of the house however, has. Putting a short brick sidewalk leading to the house from the main walk added a touch that she has wanted. There has been enough room on the sides as well the front to put some plants. A very industrious neighbor makes sure that we have all the odd flowers that we want. Ray is a man who lives a couple doors down and owns a few rental properties. His access to free plants that the city discontinues keeps him and us in a constant supply of certain flowers and a shrub or two.

I have always wanted a white picket fence. I had been thinking about that dream when I was caught in my addiction. I thought that this life was something that would never be a part of mine. It was liberating to buy, paint, and especially install that white fence. I also made two decorative posts at the end of the sidewalk and capped them off with two gothic fixtures. Before I put in the fence, Carol had been for the last two years putting flowers in all of the yard except the back one. Her touch with those plants easily outshines anything I have ever done with things like that. A green thumb has not been on any of my lists to learn. I have always liked the big sunflowers. Carol had gotten a seed packet of those flowers from a gas station for a fillup. Who would have guessed that those flowers would have gotten over nine feet tall. I have examined many of that kind of flower and never had seen one that tall. There were several of them about that height. All of the other flowers that we planted, (most of them, she did) came up in full bloom. Her success with plants made the front of the house look spectacular. The white picket fence only added to the contrast of colors as some of the plants poked through the spaces near the long city sidewalk. There was one person though who thought that we overdid it. After two years of growing things and adding new flowers, our neighbor "Rosey" had walked past our house one too many times and had to let me know in private that it "was too much." I had done some work off and on over at her house. She had trusted me to take care of clogged gutters, repair her steps and remove some broken limbs after the wind and ice storm of 2003. I understood why she thought that we had too many flowers. It wasn't the volume of plants so much as the maintenance that was required to keep them. She had a very large yard and a few flowers. Those plants however did not need the attention that ours did. Most of hers were on many bushes anyway. At eighty-two years old, this little Italian woman mowed her lawn and did most everything else around her house. And her level of being "with it" was matched only my none other than my own mother in law. Neither of them did not miss a trick.

My favorite photo of my wife is when she is standing among the flowers in the front yard. The full height of those sunflowers made her look even shorter than the five foot height that she is. The contentment on her face cannot be totally captured by a camera when she is doing what she likes so much.

The days when Carol-Aynn can get into the flowerbed are contrasted by the job that she has. Being a respiratory therapist and working at the Rochester Sleep Disorder Center for the last five years has been tiring for her to say the least. It does not compare with the previous thirty-five years, however, when she had to run all over the hospital, answering calls to give breathing treatments or try to save a person's life. I didn't realize though just how much everything that happens to her affects me. The change from the hospital setting to where she now works was one of the best moves that she made in her life. Although she is busy, the required weekends and holidays are now nonexistent. Three and a half decades of that were enough.

I was very happy that she was happy. The new staff that my wife works around is stellar. The environment that houses the tight knit group keeps everybody in a space that encourages camaraderie. Dr. Israel leads the group and is quite a gentle jokester. A year or so after I met him we worked on a project together to try and develop a new mask for the patients to wear. It really did not accomplish what we wanted it to and the idea faded away. The other staff has been really supportive of Carol and many of them should be. After she had gotten this job, and four of the other therapists followed her from the hospital they had better be there to help. It had been a mass exodus from the clutches of Egypt. After everybody had heard of the conditions of the job they all wanted one. That had produced of course, a "stop hold" of anyone else leaving the hospital. I could tell why they all wanted it. When my wife came home from work at the hospital she needed to just lay down and rest. It was killing her. As previously mentioned, the boss on that job near the end had become somewhat undesirable at that point. Sometimes I wanted to go there and straighten him out. I had been made angry more than once at the stories I had heard about that man. Biting my tongue had become a ritual with me as I waited for the pains that Carol was going through to stop. God had been faithful again.

The affect that some of the trials in Carol's life had, has been dampened by the people that she has in her life. The support of others for her has been another good example for me as well. I have been in the people helping people business for years and these folks are the real deal. She can count on the help being there when the chips are down.

The support for me on my own job is similar in ways. The fact that I am there only one day a week now changed that a little. Some of the core group is still there with a few odd hires here and there, but I have seen some staff rally when there is a problem. The constant bickering still goes on there as well an anywhere else, but when I need something I can count on others, at least if it is some kind of problem where I am hurt personally. I haven't required that kind of attention yet. We have lost more than one staff member to the grave and too many patients who had captured our hearts. We help out where we can and that commitment gets exercised all too often. The more people that you are around the better the chances that you are going to hurt if you care. It is a principle that operates everywhere in humanity.

I have been frustrated though at the lack of continuity on the job. Dealing with so many patients with so many different problems can be trying, but when you have to cope with a staff that is nice as a people, but just don't get on the same page as a team it makes it harder for everyone. I had been asked to write a manual for the technicians. During the middle of the task I had to call Cheryl Martin and tell what I thought about quitting this piece of work.

"I am in a tough spot, Cheryl. I have gone around and personally handed out thirty-seven three-page informationals to staff. I requested some feedback and input in to the manual. The deadline was January 20, and now it is April 7. I've gotten responses from two people. My plan was to write the manual based on the input from the staff and I've got nothing from them. They were supposed to read the first draft and give me suggestions for honing it into a finished piece of work. Now, I want to write it once and force them to eat it. What do think? I have enough material that I have collected myself and I can finish it, but I don't want any of their ideas into it now."

My cool, calm, and collected boss heard me out and said, "We don't want to write anything negative, but write it and give it to me, Pat and Sheron. We will look it over and help you,.okay?"

I was a little tired now from expressing something that I had been carrying around for awhile. I couldn't go to the people that I was having a problem with. They haven't been listening for months. Everybody wants to do things their way and the unit did need a standard down on paper that would make people more accountable. I needed to finish the job that I had started regardless of what anyone else was doing or thinking. I have believed that I had experienced this before, but all of the other times I simply chose to make my own way, when it didn't require any feedback from others. This time was different. I needed the cooperation of others and I wasn't getting it. I was encouraged to finish it anyway. Now I had to go back and rewrite all of the first two pages that contained some hard line criticism of my co-workers.

Sometime within the last two months I felt something like the death of a job. I told Carol one evening that it felt like a ventilator had been pulled off of a patient who was dying. Sometimes it takes hours or even days for that person to expire. This job feels like the life support has been removed. It seems to be just a matter of time before I am gone. The business with Science Holdings, the inventing, the writing, all of the domestic issues in both families, and much more, are keeping me busy. I iron my own clothes, do all of the cooking, do the maintenance on the house, the laundry, run errands to the store, bank, gas station, hardware stores and some limited cleaning all vie for my time. It certainly is a much different life than when I was alone, but I am not overwhelmed by any of it. Not because I am strong, but because I am weak. It is of utmost importance to me to be right in all of my affairs. Home, family, work, and business are affected by what I have become. All of the players involved in my life will help me be what I am supposed to be, if only I can see that they too are Angels sent to do me nothing, but good.

Sweetie and Company

I came across a paper the other day. It was entitled: *Things on My Mind*. It had the date 6-29-00 on the top. The things that I was thinking about that day had compelled me to write them down. The sheer volume could overwhelm me if I had anything to do with letting them. Out of the thirty three items on that list from (now five years ago), only three were not about people. That was a definite improvement. I hadn't really thought about whether I had that many folks that I really cared about. Nineteen of those entries would not be there if I were not married to Carol. Her life of family and friends had a greater impact on me that I ever thought. A couple of lines stand out from the rest. My relationship to Carol's ex husbands, and a very nice man we met in Florida. Both had been a concern to me, though in different ways.

Even being abundantly clear that I was husband number five, I hadn't walked into my honey's life with eye's closed. One of her husbands had passed away. One may be dead, we aren't sure. The other two however, are very much alive and living around Rochester. I had been welcomed into the Dunham family by everyone. Carol's brother John had spoken some words of encouragement at our wedding reception in Bradford. Dori certainly had a wish come true after an embarrassing request that I should marry her daughter when we were at dinner for Aunt Raine's 80th birthday party. Steve became a staunch supporter of me after a trip to Arizona. The men that Carol had in her former lives, is another story. The beginning for me was rough, mainly on the inside. I have always liked peace, no trouble, just peace. At the same time, if was ever pushed far enough, the sky was the limit. And I did not want to find out how the sky was.

David was Carol's second husband and whom she was married to the longest. My introduction into the family caused a stir in him. I don't know what he felt for sure. His acceptance of me hasn't totally come around yet. Why should I care? They had four children together and all of them are still around Carol except for one of them who lives in Texas. He was adopted by David, and Sean was a son of Carol's first marriage. There has been a longstanding stigma between ex-husbands and the new ones. It is worse than the mother in-law rift. Maybe it is the male thing, I'm not sure. At any rate, there were legitimate ties in one way or another between Carol and Dave. One could not just forget that you spent time with the same children that you both reared. I had to respect that fact and it saved people a lot of trouble that I did. By that time the last child, being a girl had moved out of Carol's townhouse at Spanish Gardens at the time I started to see her mother. I never would be around David except for the occasional birthday party or when Carol and I would be here for the holidays. We try to switch off every other year. We go to Mom's in Pennsylvania in the odd years. There is always this space between David and I. We never talk about anything. We might shake a hand on the way in or out of a family gathering. It has been rather uncomfortable living this way.

The other husband, however, is much different. Dan married Carol-Aynn after her third husband died. He had been a good friend of Jeff Collins and seemed to catch the heart of a woman who was totally out of the hurt from it all. In the beginning it was as rough going for me, as my non-relationship was with David. There has even been times when all three of us have been at the same party. Maybe each one of should be given a trophy for some kind of tolerance.

The most interesting family gathering was the summer pool party and their daughter Cherie's. Dave, Dan and myself were all there in a game of volleyball. About a dozen or so of us were enjoying the hot day in the sun. Someone got us to stop for a moment and shot a picture. We all gathered into a position that made it look like an actual family picture at a reunion for the photo album. Carol and I have a copy of that and I treasure a lot. It still is amazing how everybody else accepts things the way that they are.

Dan had to return some things that belonged to Carol one day and he had dropped them off at the house when I was home alone. I hadn't had a good feeling about it, but I would accept him in his role too. He and Carol never had any kids, but he had certainly grown to like hers through a lot of trepidation. He got to be around them when they were younger and into their teen years. The pressures that he had dealing with them during that time were especially rough. Having no experience with having your own kids can make it unusually difficult picking up where somebody else left off. I met Dan and shook his hand when he came to the house. Carol had told me that his new wife was real nice. Much of this I just had to listen to. Things were moving so fast that I couldn't keep up with it. As time went on, I saw Dan more and more at the family functions. We eventually began to talk and relate to each other. He is an Indian and that fact had an influence on us. He would tell me about his rough riding days back in the '60s and '70s. I was an expert by then at telling my story. The Carol issue has never been a problem from that time on. Dan and I have gone on day trips together to other places. One time it was three hours away to pick up a special lamp at a store. Another time it was to buy some Indian patterned glasses at an outlet mall an hour and a half away. The four of us have been at each other's home for dinner as well as into the restaurants. We continue to be friends and that is the way I want to live. When I had taken some of the photos to Bradford to show my family, that one picture of the "three wise men" urks my sister. She can't understand how or even why ex-husbands can be around each other let alone be in the same picture. It is easy for me to understand why she feels that way. The stigma of ex's got her. Mom on the other hand just tries to stay out of those conversations. She has that much sense to her under the circumstances.

The children, on the other hand, continue to be in various places or stages in their acquisition of any trust with me. There isn't anything really that they can hang their hat on when it comes to acting or saying anything wrong. It has been a very slow process to gain any real note of confidence from any of them.

Probably the one son, Jeff, has made quite a turn around. He has had his problems with me entering his space. In that first year after Carol got married he had abandoned his mother. He thought that he was going to be in some kind of business with Carol. The house that she bought, he was going to be a part of that deal somehow. When things changed in her life he wouldn't talk to her a couple of years. During the first winter of our marriage a young Jeffrey came to our home in the middle of the night in a truck outfitted with a snowplow. It had been snowing hard for hours and his job was to take care of certain plow jobs for his employer. I heard a noise outside in the driveway. I got up to see what it was and I could easily see a pile of snow had been piled high into the back of Carol's car. In the distance about a half block away under the streetlight I could easily see a red pickup driving away. I got up, got dressed and tracked that truck in the snow. For five miles through the city at one o'clock in the morning I came upon that red Ford. He led me to his house on Aab Street. He was getting out of the truck as I jumped out of mine. I went over to tell him to stay away from the house. After putting his finger in my chest I pushed him as he was supposedly dialing the cops. He told me to leave his property and I did. I was very angry and he could have gotten hurt easily. We eventually became friends, but like all of the other kids, it takes time.

Jeff eventually went to work for his father, who was David. After a couple of years of that job, he got tired of it. He had started to get into a better place with Carol. They talked things out and I felt good that another one had "come around."

One of the more recent jobs, Jeff was sent on a temporary job in Florida. When he got there he fell in love with the place. I thought that it wasn't any big deal. Everybody in the entire northeast falls in love with Florida after the novelty of the holiday snow wears off in the middle of the winter. He called Carol.

"Mom, I'm not coming home. I'm staying here."

Carol tried to patronize her son thinking that he was just learning that a nice day away from the cold winter in Rochester is something that anyone would want, but he had responsibilities. He couldn't just stay in Florida because he had a job that was going to end soon. His wife Jane, three boys, and a fourth one who would visit on weekends needed a father around anyway.

"Yes, honey, I'm sure that you like it down there," she would say. He was smart enough to know that she thought he wasn't serious.

"No, really. I'm not coming home. I love this place. Jane and the kids are going to be moving down here."

Carol adjusts herself in her seat. "You're serious, aren't you? How are you going to move them down there if you aren't here?"

Jeff removed any doubt about what his potential was. "I'm going to have Jane get some help loading the truck and I will come home and get everyone. I got a good job offer with someone else. I can get a nice place to live."

As I was listening to all of this I was happy that he was making a change in his life. He needed it. He had gone through some kind of change while he was there and he was serious.

Carol was hurt a little, of course. She was going to lose the company of a son and his family. But it was also a sweet sorrow. He was starting over and the confidence that he was showing to do something he had never done before gave his mother some comfort. Only a Mom can experience that. Things went just as Jeff said they would. I volunteered to help load the truck. Carol and I spent the day with Jane and the boys. They had gotten rid of as many things as they could to lighten the load. We had plenty of help to load the truck and by 3:30 in the afternoon Jeff had come from Florida with two of his new friends. They had driven straight through without stopping. Hitting a snowstorm in Virginia slowed them up a bit, but they got to the Lilac City on time. I had never seen the process of deciding to move and then actually doing it so quickly. Jeff got to the house, we had it packed and off they went. Jane was hurting and nervous at the same time. She had all of her family near Rochester and this change caught her by surprise. I thought that it wasn't going to work out, but it did. We talked for a few minutes before Jeff came home. She had been smoking in the house and I had to ask her to take it outside. My heart starts to race with cigarette smoke in the air. As she went out on the landing I was able to have a word or two with her. I felt a loss because I hadn't really gotten to know them like a parent should and I had this urgency to make up for lost time.

"How are you feeling about all this?" I asked.

She was looking around at what she was going to miss. She had made it clear that she liked where she was at. They had only been living there about six months and Jane was becoming attached to the place. It was a cold out, but a bright sunny day.

Taking a puff, she looked at me with those sad eyes. "I'm all right. It is just going to take some time to adjust to a new place. Mom and Dad are doing okay with it. Mom, of course, doesn't want us to go."

I let her talk and felt a kinship develop that had not been with anyone else in the family. It is funny how things all of a sudden become important when they are not going to be around any more. I let Jane know that I wished her and the kids all of the best in their new life. After everyone packed the cars, we gave the normal hugs and bid the farewell. I hate those airport experiences! I saw Jane as she drove away, glancing over at the home that she was leaving behind. It killed me inside. I had done that many times in grand fashion. I knew what she was going through. It would all be worth it, but the feelings of loss are unavoidable if you have cared about those things. I walked to our car a sad man. My wife had feelings that I could never conjure up.

One of the consolations in all of this was that Carol-Aynn and I had planned a trip to Florida ourselves. It was to be right near this move of Jeff's. He wanted us to try and drive the one hundred miles north to see his new place. We were flying and we didn't know for sure if Carol's friend would want to do such a thing anyway.

We packed up and arrived on a flight to an airport near Naples, where we would be staying. Mary Ann Maggio had bought a condo on the west side of the state and would be picking us up at about 1:30 in the afternoon. My flight down was better than most. Over the last several years my tolerance of flying had improved. Things, of course, were going much better than my first Florida flight over the Bermuda Triangle thirty years ago. I was happy to be permitted to stay with a friend of Carol's who had nothing, but a high standard of living. She wasn't rich, she just had this thing about the having "the best." One thing that she did not have though was a complete knowledge of who I really was. I had visited her with Carol to her home in Rochester, but the two of them did the visiting thing while I would read or watch a sports program. The best thing for everyone who was watching Carol was that she was becoming happier than she has ever been in her life. That gave me a little clout when I was being assessed for my worthiness. The fact remained though that it had to ultimately be a one on one exposure for someone to get to know me, no matter what

Carol-Aynn was saying. This trip was going to be a test for Mary Ann. I didn't have a problem with her. I came for the trip away from the winter and she could get to know me the best that she could. I felt no pressure. Of course it was a nice sunny Florida day when we were picked up at the airport. I had to ride in the front of the new SUV. I still hadn't gotten over my problem with the sea sickness in the car. I have to be riding shotgun.

We got to the condo and sure enough it was the best. Another couple had planned to come and visit at the same time as us. It was a little trial for Mary Ann because some communications had gotten mixed up and five was too much, especially since there needed to be a settledness in her mind about me. She and Carol-Aynn had gone back a long ways and the bond was tight, she didn't want to see her hurt.

Carol and I unpacked into our room. As soon as she walked into the condo she said, "It's gorgeous."

I mouthed the same words in silence while Carol was speaking them because that is exactly what I have heard for the last fifty years. It's gorgeous! It's gorgeous! But what I really spoke was, "It's really nice. I like it. I'll take it." Mary Ann laughed.

We unpacked and got the royal tour around the property. We would be taken everywhere. The other couple who had arrived two days later would be going around the area by themselves except for a trip to dinner with us one time.

Mary Ann and I quickly hit it off. This wasn't just a stop by and chat for a minute deal. We were there to stay for a week and I made sure that I would be sociable. It was a new friend that I would acquire through that trip. We talked a lot and her trust about me grew. Going to the beach, arts festival, meals at home and in eateries, conversations along the way everywhere was a good thing for all of us. Mary Ann has the funny characteristic of laughing about whatever she is talking about even if what she is saying is not funny.

I like Geckos. To see the little lizard just sit there and stare at you and do nothing is humorous. Now they have one on the Geico Insurance commercials. Florida is full of these creatures. Everywhere that we went they seemed to follow me. Our trip through the Arts Festival got me thinking a lot about culture, what other people did for a living, and many other things that I don't give much thought to around Rochester. Geckos were used as images on many of the art exhibits.

Sunday morning we were taken to a buffet breakfast at the clubhouse where Mary Ann lives. The food there was phenomenal. The display, selections, and the amount, made a believer out of me that these people lived well.

One of our trips to the beach took us on a walk out on a pier. The pelicans were in the water waiting for the parts of fish that would drop off of the wharf. Men had been fishing and all of the catch were cleaned at several cleaning stations provided along the way. The blue waters of the Gulf of Mexico combined with the fine white sand ground into every fiber of my being that I was a blessed man to be here. I knew pretty much what was going on back north and you just know that there are many other people who would want to enjoy this kind of setting right now. I saw Mary Ann as an angel being used by God to give me some comfort along the way of this path in my life. It was very nice to be here.

Jeff, Jane and the kids were now down here. Maryann had considerately planned to take us the ninety-four miles to see them. We got in touch by phone and went up the Monday before we were to come back to New York. It was a good drive all the way. The hour and a half in this climate, riding shotgun was something I'm not used to anywhere. I do all the driving at home when Carol and I are riding around. Some of the drivers in the area where we were staying reminded me of the nuts that were on the road around Orlando the last time we were in the "Sunshine State." This time though, I had the luxury of being a passenger. My conversation with Maryann had mostly to do with the types of cars that she likes. Her favorite seems to be a misty blue Jaguar. We saw a man in one and she went ape. In her rearview mirror he came up and stayed directly behind us.

"Ohhh, look! There's a guy behind us in a Jag. I wonder if he's married. I can't tell if the passenger in a woman or not. I want a guy about fifty and loaded."

I looked over at her and smiled. She glanced back and said, "Really, the guy's got to have a lot." I couldn't say anything. I had heard it all before. The car passes us and there she was. The suspect passenger was a lady. Taking the wind out of Maryann's sails I felt sort of bad for her. I had asked her earlier about being married. "Been engaged a couple of times, but never got married," she said hesitantly. "I'm glad the one guy is not in my life, he turned out to be a kook anyway." My own life with Carol always gets some attention when I see what goes on in another relationship.

We got to Jeff's not knowing what we would see. They had moved into a neighborhood that seemed okay. There were only eight minutes from the waters of the gulf. The "Red Tide" was there at the time. It is a strange spore that kills fish and can make humans sick if you stand around the waters long enough.

The house was acceptable. It needed some work and was certainly getting it. Jeff is a go-getter and the move down there proved it. Leaving his father's business in the process was hard as well, but he did it. New carpet was being installed when we arrived. A large tin bin for storing the many boxes of packed items was outside on the driveway. The boys were glad to see us. It only took about ten minutes for me to end up pulling all three of them around in a wagon. Only two at a time, the third one would whine until he got a turn. Going around in circles about twenty times made me think of the times when my sister Mary and I were in that old buggy back in Bradford as youngsters.

"I want to ride next, Grandpa," the boys would say.

I still haven't gotten used to being called that title. At the same time I have seen too much of children getting abused or abandoned to let this opportunity slip by. It keeps me going to think just how much influence I am having on these little ones. I have still felt little traces of that old independence hanging around.

"You wait till it's your turn, let your brother have another ride and then you can go, okay?" I would say.

They have been mostly cooperative when I remind them of some structure. Little Joey is only two and, of course, already thinking like an adult. That hardly ever happened when I was a kid. Maybe it's something in the meat. Kids today know more than they ever did. At the same time it seems to be in the wrong areas.

The dogs were having their heyday. A front and a back yard provided a good place for them to romp and maybe leave a doggily deposit here and there. I hate that part of animals and had to watch were I stepped when I was pulling the boys around. "Purdy" is Jeff's

Dalmation who knows me too well. I had spoiled her back home by doing what all dogs love. I have won over many a mutt who had an attitude problem by a long scratching session. Dalmations have that reputation for an attitude. The other dog is a Shepherd mix with one blue eye. He also bows to a good scratching.

I personally wouldn't live where they had chosen to. But then, I wasn't in their shoes at the time either. When I had talked to Jane before they had come down there, I shared my experience about Lois before we had moved to Rochester.

"Not knowing what is going to happen when you make a drastic move can be a little scary," I said with a note of approval. "When the chips are down you have to do what you have to do," I continued. "I appreciate that you care enough to make the change when there is not a lot going on here. A lot of people can't or won't."

She seemed to be comforted a little, but at the same time looked like she was fighting back any thoughts of tears.

After the carpet was in we decided to go to the water and then go to dinner. The sand was coarse compared with the fine white beaches near Maryann's. The dead fish laying all up and down the strip was disconcerting, but we knew that would end soon. I got another taste of the large body of water that I have begun to get the "call of the sea," about. Even though the waters of the Gulf of Mexico are rather confined away from the main part of the Great Atlantic I still get that chill going up and down my spine when I see it.

The dinner was simple for me. Sometimes I will keep it light when there is a question of when who is going to pay for it. That can be taken two ways. I never know for sure which way I really mean it. And I know from watching people all of my life that I am in good company. I don't want to burden anyone by ordering something more expensive if someone else is going to pay. I'm sure I will like it when that doesn't matter anymore. And if I ever feel compelled to pick up the tab I want to make sure that I am doing the right thing. Jeff of course paid for us all. He likes to do that when he can.

We stayed with the family for another half-hour after dinner and had to head back to Maryann's. When we got back to the house the Siamese cat was still making her distinct whine that only those cats can. She was not used to the place yet and being in the carrier gave the animal some sense of protection. The trip down to Florida in the van included two adults, three kids, two large dogs, and a cat. When we had watched them pull out of Rochester it looked like Noah's ark.

Driving back to Naple's brought us a lot of delays. Road construction held us up almost two hours. Maryann had become irritated at the holdup, but was her usual laughing self. Even when the going was rough she still laughed when she spoke. "You know, this is crazy, ha-ha. Construction at this hour in the dark is ridiculous, Ha-ha. I hate it, Ha-ha." With my chin resting on my hand and looking out the side window at nothing, I just couldn't understand what I was hearing. She was really funny.

After one more day in the sun it was time to come back. Getting up at four in the morning would be Maryann's last act of martyrdom to make sure that our stay was a good one. She did not fail at any point. On the way to the airport she let me know what she thought.

"You know, Ron? I didn't really know what to think about you. Now I know. All the trouble that those guys brought into Carol's life made me wonder what the cat dragged home this time. You're okay. I'm happy for you and her. I have never seen her this happy before."

I tried to choke down the compliment, but had to add to it. "I understand how you all must have felt. I would have seen things the same way. I can say that you check out to. Carol is quite a treasure." I turned around to look at my wife who was sitting in the back seat fumbling around for something in her purse.

"What, honey?" she answered. The fact that she had not been listening made her look all the more innocent when she answered me.

"Nothing." I said. "We were just talking."

We flew home and had a two-hour layover in Newark, New Jersey. The sun was shining bright at ten in the morning when I looked out the large bay windows at the airport across the bay into Manhattan. I just couldn't get enough of a look at that place.

"Come here, hon, take a look at this. I want to bring you there and show you the sights," pointing to the spot where the World Trade Center had stood, I said, "It was right over there. The twin towers. I didn't get up close when I was there, but I could see the property from the top of the Empire State Building. We can go down there sometime."

Carol is always accommodating to me when I am excited about something. When we are on a trip like that she lets me know that she is interested, "but we are on a trip this very minute and to talk about another trip now, just doesn't fit in so well." She doesn't like to get ahead of herself too much. I just stared and finally realized that I can see a thing differently than her and there wasn't anything necessarily wrong with it. It is nice to have come to that place where we can disagree about something and it is all right. No one has to die over it.

We got home and had a few days to spare. Having planned out the vacation for Carol left days open on both ends. She never wants to get back on the Sunday before she has to go to work. It is too much to have to rush around and try and rest up from a trip while beating away patients who always need the attention that they can't get anywhere else. Pippon had stayed at Dori's house with her dog Makayla this time. They had a good time together. Our dog had certainly been in familiar territory since his four-month stay less than a year earlier. Dori was doing well. We thanked her and left.

After about two weeks I had to finally go down to the Port of Rochester to see a woman about a deal. Quite a few weeks earlier I had a conversation with the owner of a gift shop who was set up at the new Terminal for the Fast Ferry. When Carol and I were in the shop looking at the types of things that she had for sale I asked her if she would be willing to consider letting me put a screenplay in there for sale. Eileen was about to give birth and was going to take a month off after the child arrived. She agreed to take a look at the idea. I went home to get a copy of *East Wind Rain*, and brought it back to her.

"I'll take a look at it," thumbing through the pages. "Oh, you have the names of my husband and brother in here. I will read it and get back to you."

I waited at least two and a half months and stayed away from there. One of the trips to the terminal for something to eat gave me the idea to finally say something. We went into the shop and she was working. The baby was sleeping in the stroller behind the counter. We had a couple of the grandchildren with us at the time and I would wait to see if Eileen would recognize me. I hate to be pushy about anything even if I felt I had waited enough. I don't always know if my enough is enough. I'd rather test the waters if I can. Walking around the store for a few minutes watching the customers enjoy themselves, I walked to the counter and saw the baby.

"Look's like someone is tired" I said with a discerning eye.

Eileen looked down at her little girl and smiled. "Yea, she is a good sleeper. She doesn't give us much trouble at night either."

It was time to make my move by getting closer to home. "She's what, about three months now?" I asked.

She looked up at the ceiling and answered. "Two and a half, yea, she'll be three months. You keep good track."

I couldn't keep her in the dark any longer. "Do you remember me? I was the one who had given you a screenplay to read. Did you read it?"

The answer was too often a "no." People get excited about something at the moment and then it fizzles out. I don't hand out scripts like that anymore. The goal was to get my work into the store. She eventually read part of it and said no. The store moved.

Mom's Descent Into?

It is difficult dealing with the declining state of a loved one. For most of my life I had been only an observer of the afflictions of others in this area, but now it has come home to roost in my life. Being the firstborn has its responsibilities, some inherited and some dropped in my lap. Either way it has been fine with me as far as my role is concerned.

Mom's recovery from Dad's death has always been in question, at least in my mind. Sometimes we really don't know where a problem started we just have to fix the tire and not argue about how it got flat in the first place. About a year after he died Mom went out and got a driver's license for the first time. That was quite interesting as was the purchase of her first car which by the way was newer than any car we had ever owned. Even though this period of time in all of our lives was a new beginning, my life was manifesting a scenario that was all too familiar with Mom. I had started drinking. That may have been something comforting to a woman that endured the ravages of alcoholism through Dad. Sounds strange, but Mom never told me once in ten years of abusing alcohol ever to stop. The evidence was there that I should have never started in the first place and yet there was a nurturing woman ready to accept not an illness, but some type of profile to fill the gap of a lost husband and father. All the car wrecks, late nights, and spent money did not sway her one bit. There existed for Mom a bit of a perverted solace in my patterned dysfunctional presence. A mild reprieve was always in order when I did something Mom didn't like. It would be always obvious to everyone that my errors were not a matter that Mom just didn't like, no one would. "Could you turn it down," she would say, when I played Pink Floyd loudly back in the '70s. I would hardly ever answer, I would only turn it down or jump on the headphones. There was no evidence of any looming sickness of mind or body, she lived what appeared to be a new life and seemed to be content with many of the positive changes that would occur in a her husband-less world. Dad's presence did restrict her in many ways and now she was busting loose. She even went out with the gang of friends I had to the Holiday Inn and danced. So far from where we are now.

From 1971 to 1985 there was never a mention or a tear shed about the loss of Ronald W. Knott Sr., at least we never saw or heard any. I had assumed that Mom had a handle on things. Although she was very passive, maybe there has been a lot of internalizing going on and us kids never knew it. In many people it may come out in a temper flare or some form of lateral venting. In her it never did. But in 1985 something happened. When I came to visit she started to follow me around the house when I wanted to talk to my brother Sam. She always wanted to know what we were talking about. Of course I got ticked at times and just left, but it became the norm. I couldn't understand why she was doing that and never got a straight answer about it. To this day she has a desire to know what people are talking about. The only event that really seemed to coincide with this behavior is that I was abandoned by my wife. Mom did not like the fact that there was an influence in Lois's life that contributed to the feeling that there was an out no matter what. That psychiatrist had counseled Lois to commit adultery against me and Mom knew that.

He said, "It will help your marriage if you have a short affair with someone." What Mom really didn't like was the fact that Dr. Carter offered to be that person who would stand in for me for awhile. Of course my wife declined that kind of thinking...for a season. The pressure to be out of the marriage became too great and my wife ran off with another man. There were two things in my mother's entire life that I personally knew that she did not like because she said so. One, Dad's friends influencing him to drink ultimately causing his death. And two, the professional community's responsibility for breaking up my family.

Although it scared me, I decided to brush off Mom's ill gift of clairvoyance. I ended up coming home from Canada to a more determined mother. She would follow Sam and I up and down the stairs to hear what we were saying to each other. Fortunately I wasn't living there, just visiting. We avoided trying to talk in the house. I miss the older more sane Mom.

At the time of Mom's changes I was going through my own so maybe that was a distraction of some sort. Without really investigating this matter any further we wrote it off as being ultra-nosey, after all, the incident with knowing a person's mind was a one time deal. What became apparent though was a newfound ability to forget things, especially short term.

I moved away permanently and kept in touch by phone and for the first couple of years came home to visit on weekends. Being only one hundred fifty miles away afforded me the trips. Mom would call me off and on for a few years then it tapered off to none. For about a decade or so I had not gotten one phone call from her. Again, if anyone calls, it is me. I began to resent that a bit, but learned to accept it. Her reason for this is that, "I hate computers and answering machines." Her disdain for modern technology came when she saw a computer take the jobs of some of her friends at work while working at the Zippo lighter plant across the street. About five years before she retired the company brought in the techno-replacement. It irked her to no end to see an inanimate robotic machine bump people out of work, especially those she cared about. I have been suspicious that this event was the straw that broke the camel's back. Since her retirement she had let herself go. Her hygiene, the house, the bills, and many other things had fallen by the wayside.

Although the passiveness is tainted by words that I never thought I would use to describe my own mother I can still see that good sweet, passive woman through it all. We all as a family, have been approached with this problem and are currently trying to work it out, painfully so.

A frustrating footnote to all this is that Mom's responsibilities with the simple things in life have been shirked. She now is not cashing her retirement or her social security checks. I have sought the counsel of a lawyer and the State of Pennsylvania. At this point it has been discovered that Mom's problems do not manifest when being interviewed by a social worker. The state says that Mom may be a pain in the neck in enough ways that she falls into the category of innocence with respect to law.

Most recently the hallucinations have gotten worse and so is the memory lapse. I still have been accused of watching her from the aquarium in her living room and also from that neighbor's house, all while I am in another city. This problem is compounded, by asking the same questions over and over, within just a few minutes. We know it may be a symptom of the dreaded Alzheimers disease, which we cannot currently prove nor are we being given a chance. She is sick enough to play it out with a select few within the family, but doesn't manifest enough to require intervention through the law. The bills such as insurance, auto inspections, and utilities have to be paid with late charges, but only after she is assertively encouraged. To wrestle power of attorney from her would be "messy" according to the attorney. Obviously that would require a lot of money and that is where we get off. We believe Mom is carrying a lot of money in her two purses she hauls around wherever she goes, but we can't prove it yet, so we are stuck. We may be nearing a resolution to this problem, but it will require a strong gut to implement. Taping an episode and calling in a Mental Hygiene Arrest has been the choice of counsel thus far.

Things have moved so fast in my life that it would seem as though it doesn't have any affect on me. Sometimes it does, sometimes it doesn't. Being a counselor myself has helped me objectively explore options that we can work with for the betterment of Mom and the rest of the family.The most difficult aspect of all this worth repeating has been that Mom's history has been nothing short of much sadness. Starting her life out as a resident in a children's home on the east end of Bradford saw the first eighteen years of her life mostly as an orphan. Throughout those years she had run away to where Aunts Hilda and Julia lived their whole life here in the United States.. The last name being Bengson testified to the Swedish culture. They welcomed her all the time with open arms, but maybe their father "August" had something to do with Twila June Pilk (Pilk is Jewish) not staying there any length of time, I never found out. She always had to return to the "Home." Uncle August was the brother of Mom's father, a father who abandoned Mom at age three after her own mother died. At age eighteen, Mom was working in a little store across the street from the children's home. "Teaberry's," represented the modern style convenience store that is so prevalent across the country today. As the story was told when I was very young, Dad had come down from Canada looking for work. His sister Mary lived a couple of blocks from the store. She had married Allan Summers and they both worked at the world famous Case knife company conveniently located right next to their home.

Dad who was also eighteen, walked into the store and it was love at first sight. Mother said to me that Dad's jet black hair and dimples with his smile won her over immediately. Their birthdays are eight days apart in the month of July. Dad's is the 3rd and Mom's the 11th. They started dating and according to my calculations the summer of that year I was conceived. Later on I would regret being "made before marriage." However, that betrothal had a price…a big price. If there was thoughts of escape from living in a children's home by marrying an alcoholic Indian she was in for a rude awakening. Though there was some times of joy and fun, the next eighteen years of Twila Knott's life would become a shadow compared to the picnic at the Bradford Children's home.

My own memory has served me well, and the fact that Mom taught me to remember things by association, has preserved the specter of accuracy in almost all that I write. Later on I would discover that this method of recall has a downside. You also remember things that you don't want to. It is a part of her current existing torment.

After a time of courtship and then getting married, somehow Mom and Dad ended up at 414 Congress Street to live with the two sisters from Sweden. August had passed away and left the property to five children. The deed is still in his name to this day and we haven't discovered what the arrangement is yet, all we know is that no one has paid any attention to it for at least the last fifty or sixty years.

After my conception in May of 1952, I was born the following January. Mom had tender hands and a tender spirit. Those qualities only accentuated the abuse she would take from Dad for years to come. As a typical '50s mother, Mom wore a long dress even to do the laundry. Over the dress was an apron, one that was worn for baking also. I miss her fried cakes. Dad got his first job here working at Case in a department close to Aunt Mary. The paychecks were steady, but sometimes there was a layoff. My own sister Mary was born the year after me and she was a regular visitor to help pick up the Government surplus food.

It became apparent that Mom was quite industrious. The laundry, cooking, and cleaning occupied most of her day. I can still seeing her wiping the wet hair from her forehead with her wrist. Wearing rubber gloves to handle hand scrubbing the floor did not afford to clear the sweat with her hands. "Please go in the other room," she would say. "The floor is still wet." After us kids graduated from the "Jolly Jumper" and could walk, we could accommodate her.

Discipline was a page right out of Mom's playbook. It did not seem out of order to have been spanked with an open hand by a woman who always had a quiet and orderly disposition. I knew that I was wrong all the more when Mom did it because of the contrast in her life. She never swatted us on the behind with a mean spirit. That only made us understand all the more that she was right and we were wrong. But of course there were times that the second wave of personal contact would be made after the feared words, "Wait till your Dad gets home," were spoken. The most memorable spanking from Mom was when she got a phone call that me and my old pal Kirk had been seen throwing clay at a neighbor's house. I was laying in the field of tall grass next to our property when Mom came to the edge of the yard looking for me. I knew that she knew I was there, but I would not answer her call. She walked back to the house and then it dawned on me that she was just waiting me out. I had to go home sometime, but I didn't realize that when I was hiding. The fear of getting caught and punished blinded me to that fact. We stood up. I watched in envy as Kirk walked away scott free and I had to face my tormenter. As soon as I walked onto the back porch, Mom came to the door and grabbed me by the wrist to spin me around. Of course I resisted, but she was too strong and she spanked me till I wailed.

"Don't you ever throw clay at the neighbor's house again, do you hear me?"

With a wrinkled face I responded, "Yes."

Mom never had to address our errors a second time in conversations like that unless we were naïve enough to repeat the crime, which was rare. The fact that she had the ace in the hole with Dad arriving a little later didn't hurt, at least her.

I have often wondered, what ever happened to that type of discipline? There is too much of wrong, mean spirited correction in homes today. That is one of the many obvious reasons that some kids turn out the way they do. As mentioned, I got a taste of both worlds in my own house. Dad hardly ever used his hand on a pair of jeans. It was the belt on a bare behind. Mom never objected to that. That type of punishment from Dad never really did any mental or emotional harm to me. It was other things that did. I knew even with Dad that I was wrong, at least in principle. It was also these very things that would be I believed, divinely used to shape and mold me on the inside. What I do know of this disease brings a strange type of grief in us kids. We are all in a better space now, but *we all want Mom back the way she was*. It is not the same. Maybe all of this might be a factor in what would happen to me next.

Seeing Double Again

And what good story would be complete without me suffering a stroke. That "Black Friday," all hell broke loose...and then so did Heaven. It began on Thursday with the usual hard workload working with a very dysfunctional group of patients at the rehab. I had just turned in the Technician's Manual that I was working on for the last few months just two days earlier after a tech meeting. I had been frustrated for five months because almost all of my co-workers did not turn in any requested feedback for this new piece of work. I needed some cooperation and wasn't getting it. What made it especially difficult was that I let everyone know from the beginning that after the first draft I would be passing out a copy for all to see and give me further input so I could complete the project. After that earlier conversation with Cheryl, I did do the first draft and was certainly happy about that.

Working until 10:30 the night before a trip to Bradford had been done before, but not under these circumstances, ever. We were all scheduled to be in court at 10:30 that Friday morning. The anticipation of it was quite tough. I never would tell anyone that I hated court for any reason. This time it had to do with Mom. After I got home on Thursday I did my usual routine of winding down from the night of "caring for my fellow man." After getting to bed at 1:15 and getting up at six for two and a half-hour trip to Bradford I had no problem staying awake. Carol was, of course, concerned about my schedule.

"Honey, are you alright? I'll be praying for you. Pace yourself," she said, with her hands on my shoulder.

That is what I always tell her. I was upstairs cramming like a kid before a test. Gathering all the paperwork for court at the last minute wasn't my norm. I had planned to do it at the last minute to become more intimate with the trouble that was coming. In my mind there was going to be a fight and I am good at getting ready for one.

I gave my wife a hug and a smooch and off I went into a world I hated, one of useless conflict. All of these problems could have easily been avoided, but I was ready to engage my enemy…who turned out to be me. I had nothing on my mind other than to let the whole world know what really was going on in my family situation.

After about an hour into the trip I had to stop at a Mickey D's to grab a "Sausage McMuffin." Keeping in a good mood meant keeping food in my belly. At least there would be less chance of any bad attitude when I wasn't hungry, especially under the pressure of being in court. Having another hour and a half to drive gave me time for much thought. The scenery traveling across New York State in the southern tier was always beautiful. This morning however somehow dimmed the bright sunny day that one should be having. The pressure was great and the rolling hills, winding highway complimented by the solitude of traveling alone still didn't cut it. I just wanted this trip to be over.

I pulled into "Top's" supermarket in Bradford at about 9:15 that Friday morning. Not a lot of people were shopping at that hour, but I had to use the restroom. Even though Mom and Mary lived less than five minutes away they were the last people that I would be asking for anything on that stressful morn. I went in the store and walked by an elderly man eating a muffin at the café.

"Good morning," he said with a smile.

I smiled back, though I was not as sincere as I should have been and responded in kind. "Morning," was all I could get out as I bobbed my head in friendly gesture. His approach to me was reminiscent of small town America. It also made my problems stand out a little more. I used the little boy's room and went back to the truck.

As I pulled my keys out of my pocket and went to put them in the ignition, it hit me. Everything that I was now looking at was double...vertically. I closed my eyes and slowly opened them thinking that it was only my imagination. It wasn't. I went outside the truck and stood to look around at the hills and other buildings. I was seeing two of everything, one on top of the other. What I wanted to do was get to the courthouse, which was another twenty minutes away. Whatever was going on wasn't going to stop me from this important appointment. I started the truck and tried to drive around the parking lot. I went about five feet and had to stop. I now became afraid.

It must be related to the stress of it all, I thought. *Am I having a stroke or what?* Having finally relinquished the thought of making it to court I started to really get concerned.

Carol had given me the cell phone for just such emergencies and this was quickly developing into one. Sitting down for a moment, I remembered my lawyer's phone number. The only problem was that as I started to dial numbers, the people on the other end had never heard of me. Seeing two phones had caused me to punch in all the wrong digits. After a couple of quick apologies I discovered that if I closed one eye I could see straight. I called the secretary and told her what was happening.

She said, "You had better call 911, I'll call Steve at the courthouse and tell him that you're having this problem."

"Thank you, Barb," I answered. I got off the phone and had to call Carol at work. I got through to her answering machine. By now the thought of my situation getting worse had taken over. Working in the medical field for the last fifteen years made me wonder if I had an aneurysm that was going to blow all the way. Bleep, bleep, bleep, on the phone to my wife I went. Even though her voice was on a mechanical device I felt some kind of comfort.

"Hello, this is Carol-Aynn Knott at the Sleep Disorder center of Rochester. Please leave your name, number, and a brief message at the sound of the tone and I will get back to you as soon as I can."

I couldn't wait until my turn came to talk. By then I thought I was going to pass out. My message to my dear wife was short, vague and justifiably frightening. "Honey, it's me. I'm in Bradford. Something is happening to me. I have to dial 911." Click! I then called 911.

The ambulance came in about five minutes and the two young men were good at their job. I had to close my eyes while they got me on the gurney. The double vision had made me more dizzy and uncertain about what would happen next. It was a short trip to the hospital. This was the last place that I wanted something like this to happen. The Bradford Hospital had been the source of resentment ever since Dad had died. I knew that I took care of that problem in my own mind, but now I guess it was time to back it up with a little action.

Coming into the emergency room created a little stir. Although throughout the years smalltime Bradford had its share of accident victims and other patients, my case on a slow Friday afforded me some extra attention. Nurse Mary from Hinsdale, New York gave me good care. She was good. The first time that she left me alone for a few minutes I could hear a conversation from across the room between a doctor and another patient. The doctor was chiding him for his bad habit. "I'm telling you that if you continue to smoke you will die!"

The man responded, "I am not giving up. I can't. It is something that I have been doing for most of my life."

The doctor interrupted with a raised voice louder than the first time. "What is the matter with you? Don't you want to live? You must give up smoking those things. You and I both know that they will kill you, especially in this condition. Stop it!"

There was silence. Then I heard footsteps coming in my direction. In my mind I thought, "Oh no, this is not going to be my doctor!" The curtain was hastily thrown back out of the way. There stood the man who knew that I had heard every word from across the way.

His Russian accent was distinct as he said, "Hello, my name is Dr. Shupac. Don't pay any attention to that conversation. I know him and he is acting stupid. How are you doing?"

Seeing two of him made it hard to look directly at which one was actually talking to me. I quickly closed one eye and answered. "I feel alright. It is just that I don't know what is going on. I'm seeing double."

Dr. Shupac got a piece of gauze bandage and covered one eye so that I could see one of everything that I was looking at for the time being. He was polite and kind to me from the get go.

"We are going to get a Cat Scan of your head, Mr. Knott. We want to see what is going on there. Your blood pressure is up a bit. We will run a Nitro drip after the patch is taken off." He stood there and smiled as if he had known me for a long time. "You are a nice person and we will take care of you," he said.

I couldn't help but wonder why he did say that. I had never met the man in my life. Anyway, I will take it. Right now I can use all the attention I can get. My "return" maybe from giving other people their due attention should have been much less...at least in my mind.

My care continued well as the nurse faithfully watched my blood pressure stabilize. A trip to the Cat-Scan and a MRI did not find the site of the stroke. My vision began to return to normal, although there was apparently still the drooping of my face. Nurse Mary had informed me that Carol-Aynn was on her way and would be here at about 4:30. Carol had called Pastor Phil from the old church that I had attended in Bradford. We had kept in touch and when we would travel to visit Mom and Mary we still go to that church on Sunday mornings. Phil faithfully came and sat with me a while. After I had explained to him what had happened I had to tell him something else that was on my mind.

"You know, I have been getting some attention from the Lord about Him as Creator. He created us and the revelation about Him having made me, even surpassed the principle of Lord and Master. To understand that we are made, all that I could have a concern about seems to be unimportant."

As usual, the pastor contemplated. "Hmm, Job had to learn that lesson. God did not reveal himself to Job in that capacity. He had to remind Job that he had created all things and the awesomeness of that revelation made Job more humble than he was."

I agreed that Job knew in his mind that God had created all things as many people believe, but there is evidence that it is not fully birthed among mankind today or ever.

Shortly after a quick conversation with Pastor Phil and a few visits from the nurse, in walks my sweetie. Carol gave me a big hug with that worried wife look on her face.

"Are you all right, honey? I missed you." She had brought a visitor, her ex-husband Dan. It is a good thing that I see some things different in this life than many folks. My relationship with an ex-spouse of my own wife is what everyone should have. I had refused again to bow to the pressures of a society that says I should be at odds over an ex. It has paid off over and over again not only for us, but for many others as well. Dan had driven Carol all the way to Bradford. For a woman who doesn't really like to drive in the first place and to have to drive two and a half-hours on top of it made Dan look almost look like a saint. He has been obviously as opened-minded as myself and certainly unbeknownst to him, listening to God about some things. We shook hands as he stood there with concern for me. I had introduced him to Pastor Phil as Dan the friend rather than an ex-spouse of Carol. I had been placed in that awkward position before and this experience has paid off as well.

After all day in Bradford, the doctor came and said, "Mr. Knott, we do not have a neurologist on board right now. Do you want to go back to Rochester? You can take a helicopter or an ambulance. I can call and talk to them as soon as you say." It didn't take me long to decide where I wanted to be in the first place. My spirit revived knowing that I had that choice.

"Yes, I want to go back home doctor." I thought for a moment about my options of getting there. The way my day was going I had better stay on the ground. "I'll take an ambulance please. Thank you." I sent Carol and Dan on ahead and waited for my ride. Dr. Shupac became unusually attached to me as a patient. I don't know what kind of other patients he was seeing day to day, but maybe he needed more cooperative ones in his life. The way he was acting, he needed that.

The ambulance came and the two paramedics were both good at what they did. One of them had heard of me back in high school. Before we left the hospital another order came down to have a second Cat-Scan. After the scan we waited in the lobby near the entrance of the Emergency Department. Waiting for the paperwork, I got sick. The Nitro-drip and whatever else I was taking made the room spin around. That was the first time that I had done that since nineteen years earlier back in Olean when I ate that whole chicken at four in the morning. One of the medics gave me a pan to vomit in. I was momentarily embarrassed. My own experience in health care helped me in this situation. With a lot of people nearby I knew that they were not paying a lot of attention to me, and my belching. After I felt a little better I asked the other medic what his name was. One of the interesting things about being away from my hometown was that I could be in the presence of someone that was only a baby of a few years old when I left. Many kids back in the mid-eighties weren't even born yet.

"Jim," the guy said.

"What's your last name," I asked.

"Valentine," was the answer.

"Are you a Bradfordian," I continued.

"From day one," Jim responded, now looking at an obese man coming into the ER with an apparent heart attack. "I suppose that he would be mine if I wasn't going to Rochester."

"What year did you graduate?" I prodded further.

"1972," came the answer. "I remember you from high school. You were fast."

I leaned back and pondered my Dad's death. He had died in this hospital across the street from the high school we were talking about. I did not want to die here. "I think my name is still on the board over at the track isn't it?" I asked.

"Yea, it's still there," Jim answered.

It was now time so saddle up and head out. The final strapping of myself into the gurney was complete and out into the cold rainy evening I went. It was pouring and I felt glad that I chose an ambulance. What I was most happy about though was the fact that I was going back to Rochester. My two and a half-hour journey though, would not be a snap.

Getting secured onto the floor of an ambulance and just the gurney itself is quite a feat for the medic. Click, strap, snap goes the nylon and metal as I wait for "Jason" the second paramedic who would making the trip with us to buckle me in.

"How are you doing?" he asked as the final click is heard.

"I'm doing alright," I answered as I looked around at the equipment.

Jim jumped in the driver's seat and we were off. Jason sat down on a bench next to me. Glancing at the bottle of nitroglycerin swinging back and forth on the IV pole I wasted no time in getting to know my second caretaker.

"And how are you doing? How long have you been doing this?" I asked.

Adjusting his clipboard and then grabbing a bar on the seat he gave me his answer. "Been around this for twenty years."

I thought he didn't look any older than thirty, but then he went into the story of how it all got started.

"I'm from outside Pittsburgh. Came here, went back and here I am back again. My Dad had been a paramedic as I used to ride the ambulance with him when I was young. I've actually been doing this myself for fifteen years." That explained his age of thirty-four

One of things that I really didn't pay much attention to when I had been loaded into the vehicle was the cool temperature. It had been raining heavy for quite a while and those April showers brought more than May flowers that day. It had cooled the inside of that ambulance and "cold and immobility" are the combination that I hate, for one reason. Cramps. Ever since I was a child I could always count on something cramping up if I am unable to move around and the temperature was too low. It took about an hour for it to happen, but it did, royally. After much conversation about my experiences in health care and what I am doing now, both legs cramped at the same time. They were locked solid as I grimaced in pain. Jason did not really know just how much pain I was in as I reached down and unlocked the first belt around my waist.

"Cramps!" I said, grinding my teeth and trying to stand up. He unlocked the second strap around my legs and I climbed off of the gurney to try and stand up. I grabbed another railing attached to the ceiling and tried to rub my legs with the other hand. The ambulance was rocking as we would pass car after car along Route 17. The IV line had to take second place until the pain started to subside. I remembered that the only other time in my life that both legs went down like was after that workout in track season back in high school. That put me in a snowbank as I buckled under the pain.

The cramps were gone, but the residual pain, which lingers for days, remained. Jason strapped me back in and we were back in business. Another hour and a half to go as I flexed my legs all the rest of the way. I couldn't rest or it would happen again.

"Do you want some heat?" he asked.

Of course my first thought was, *No, why would I want that?* But I wasn't in the cynical mood. Here was a good kid who was comfortable with the temperature himself so I could see that he might not be so sensitive to how this was really affecting me.

"Ah, yes. I'd like some heat, thank you," was my answer. Jason turned on a blower that immediately filled the vehicle with a warm air. That was a good thing, but it also was too late. My legs had cooled too much and my right one started to cramp again. I reached down to rub it. Jason was watching my struggle.

"Do you want me to rub it?" he asked, staring at my grimacing face.

I thought for only a split second. "No, that's okay, I got it." I said. In my mind I would rather suffer a bit than try and guess where he was really coming from. I managed to grind it out until we got to Rochester.

We pulled into Park Ridge Emergency and it was the most comfortable feeling that I had in years. I felt so at home. A nurse that I knew met us at the door and welcomed me into trauma room number one. I knew that room all too well. I had done CPR on that thirty-eight year-old twelve years earlier and lost him with his wife holding his hand. But there was something else about this department that touched me. This was the first time that I realized just how much trouble Lois was in twenty-two years ago when we almost lost her. I had always known what the facts were, but to actually be on this side of things hit me differently. It was now very interesting to see where I was at, compared to the kicking and screaming I had done to refuse to even come to Rochester, let alone end up working at the place that now would taking care of me. My, how times have changed.

The nurse, Cindy quickly recognized me. "Well, what brings you here? I never thought you would have a problem like this."

As she and the others gave the heave ho to get me into the bed, I grunted. "You just never know what can happen, do ya?" I answered. I thanked the guys for the "wonderful" trip and they headed back to B-town. The first comment that Cindy made had to do with replacing "THEIR nitro patch with one of OURS." Having that patch and the drip at the same time became a bone of contention with others later on.

While I lay there and waited for all of the "domestic hookups" I watched many other folk come into the unit. It was Friday night and I was feeling all right. To be on my back at prime time in a hospital should have made me depressed or angry, but it didn't. I was so happy to be there and I knew that whatever happened was okay with me. The other patients coming in at that six o'clock hour I knew was only the start of the usual beginning of the weekend swamping of the emergency department. All the hospitals, especially with the weather the way it was could count on some good business.

Carol came in with her daughter Cherie. Dan had gone to his home only minutes away. I was so grateful to have all these people in my life. Cherie was demonstrating again that she would show up for support at any time. Her schedule was full enough, but to come there and see me was nothing less than admirable.

The goal now was to get a room upstairs for me. I didn't know if I would have to wait for one in the hall on a gurney for six or eight hours like some people did. I didn't. They sped me through the system and I went to 2405, the telemetry floor. This wing was right next to the Intensive Care unit that I had put a few years in. My own room for the next four days was very nice. The only inconvenience was that during any hour of the night I would be awakened to the sound of a nurse or a tech coming into the room to take my vital signs. Due to the nature of my problem I had to have my blood pressure taken very often.

The staff on the 2400 floor were all stellar. I would now have to go through many more tests to try and determine just what happened and where. The care I received from each person on each shift for the entire stay was reflective of the kind of care that I wanted for everyone that I cared for in that hospital. Maybe I was getting what I gave out. I had worked on that floor too.

Dr. Jaeger was filling in for my personal doc who was out of town. He came to see me the next day. With his accent from who knows where he kindly laid out what they wanted to accomplish. "We will be sending for another Cat-Scan and an MRA. We need to find out where the problem is. It is likely that after looking at your chart from Pennsylvania that you had a small stroke. We haven't looked at the disc that they sent us yet of your tests down there. I will be on duty for another day until Dr. Christidis comes home. If you have any questions you can let me know."

Carol listened to the man and was pleased to meet him. He was clear and concise about what they wanted to do.

I finally got to eat hospital food. My entire life had been inundated with this stigma that the eats that get while you're sick was the pits. It was not bad at all. I ate almost everything that I was given every day. It was, of course, the low-sodium diet so the only additives that I got on my trays were a packet of "Mrs. Dash" spice and some pepper. I did not miss anything that I was eating before this all happened. It had been said throughout my life that God does not give you more than you can handle. It is quite clear that in order for that to be true you had better be closely knit to Him. That is the secret. I wouldn't have imagined being stopped in a moment's notice from all of my everyday habits and routines and excepting the entire change gracefully. I was happy as a lark to be where I was. My experience with patients throughout that hospital was that "most of the people had been traumatized merely by the fact of inconvenience of being sick and not just the sickness itself." With some exceptions of course it definitely was the norm.

I had been in the habit of keeping track of things in my life and all of the people, places, and things during my "downtime" were no exceptions. Two Cat-scans, two MRA's, an MRI, a Doplar study of my carotid arteries, and a study of my heart down through my throat made sure at least what condition my body was in. We never found the sight of the stroke, but found an old stroke site. I never knew that I had it. I could only guess when it might have happened. Either the time that I had gotten knocked out in that boxing ring in Smethport twenty-three years ago or the strange dizziness that I had a few months ago playing basketball, I'll never know. They also found a small hole in my heart that was closing up.

Working in a hospital and being a patient there has its perks. I saved myself a lot of trouble on a couple of occasions just because I had been in the industry. One of the male nurses came in my room about eight in the morning.

"You are going now to get the MRA test," he said.

I was wearing a halter monitor at the time under my gown and he unhooked me from it. That monitor sent signals about my heart to a station down the hall and they could watch and record all the information that was sent. The problem was that he left the patches on. In the center of those patches was a metal bead that held the leads in place. He had left them there and that was a big no-no. A transport came to take me to my test and I got to the room away from the main part of the hospital containing the MRA machine. I knew that those leads were not supposed to on me when I went into that tunnel.

I handed the technician the chart and she asked me, "Do you have anything in your pockets?"

"No," I said. I would wait until the last second to let her check everywhere for any metal. She did not, and now sitting on the table ready to lay down I said, "but I do have this," lifting up the gown off of my chest revealing eight metal leads.

She gave me a look like "someone had better catch this the next time before something happens." I knew what a machine like that can do. In another hospital outside the state a young boy was killed when an oxygen tank was pulled from across the room and crushed his head. I know enough to make sure that any metal that can be affected by that million-dollar baby had better be gone.

It came time for me to get my first MRA. As I slid closer to the unit, which had not even been turned on yet, I felt a pull on one of my front teeth. The post was metal that held the tooth to my jaw.

"I have metal in this tooth," pointing to it with my mouth open.

The tech said, "It will be okay, we have people come through here all the time with that and it was alright."

I thought for a second and believed her, but just in case she was wrong I would close my mouth tightly and then slowly open it to see if the powerful electromagnetic force would pull it and down through the back of my neck. If it did, I would have a contingency plan to kick and scream as loud as I could. There was an intercom inside the unit so she could talk to me. As I went into the tunnel it was tight. I could see why people had a fit being in those close quarters. I just closed my eyes and listened to all of the clicks and other sounds that occur in those things. Backing off from a closed mouth I have to admit that I was concerned as I could feel the continuing pull on the tooth. *Could she be wrong?* I was thinking. I was able to open my mouth and enjoy the prospect of making it through the procedure.

All was well as the transport took me back to my room. I would not write that off to incompetence on anyone's part because knowing what I know about health care, things do happen and it was just fortunate that I knew what I knew. Carol wasn't particularly happy to hear that news, but she also knows what can happen in this field, she had been working here longer than myself. It seems to be different when it is your loved one that endures the mistakes of others.

The second mistake that happened was the fact that not all of the required tests were done during that first MRA. They were supposed to inject dye into my veins and do a special study of the arteries in my head. Back to the machine I went again. The next day came and this time would be a little scarier than the first. I was asked to lay down as they ran a line into the vein on my left arm. The tooth was being pulled again as I was moved back into that tunnel. The noises started and I believed that this would a snap. I closed my eyes so that I wouldn't feel the closeness of that roof over my face. This test would last longer than the previous one. The technician spoke to me over the intercom and told me that the last phase was to last only twenty two seconds. At least that is what I thought that she said. It seemed like hours as I "wasn't supposed to move my face at all." No deep breaths, no yawning, and especially no clearing my throat. It was murder not to do any of those things. But what happened next made it all the more complicated. With my arms at my side I couldn't get to see whether the fluid that was running down my arm and my back soaking the sheet was blood or the IV contrast that was being injected. The line had come apart and the technician had turned off the intercom. I didn't know it.

"Hello, I said. No answer came. "HELLO!" Silence. I prepared to die by bleeding out. I had a peace about it. Closing my eyes, I had accepted to depart from this earth. Then the call came. "Mr. Knott, you are done."

They had turned on the intercom, came over to find the line detached and said, "We got the pictures despite the leak of the contrast. Are you okay?"

Looking down at my wet arm, I answered calmly. "I'm fine. I didn't know what that was."

Spending four days in the hospital gave me a unique type of rest even with the sporadic wakeups for vital signs throughout the nights. My discharge back into the world had created a deeper contrast between being sick in the hospital and being out prancing around a healthy individual. I now know what it is like to be helpless and under someone else's care. For the next few weeks I would walk to the store and get adjusted to some small doses of medications. The summer was coming and Dr. Christidis made it clear that I not overdo anything, especially in the heat.

The newly discovered hole in my heart may have been the culprit for throwing a clot into my system and causing my stroke. While that was not necessarily a good thing, the doc said the hole was closing up. I was glad that the prospect of other reasons for my condition had been reduced. Tissue stress, an embolism, or especially an aneurysm, were ruled out. I followed the doctor's orders to a tee that summer until the call came to help someone else.

Biloxi

In the late summer of 2005 the hot days had been accented by a record string of hurricanes particularly in the southern part of the United States. Those of us in the north had experienced off and on some of the residual effects from rains and wind that occasionally would be gentle reminders of what could have been, but was not. News travels fast these days and that made us "Yankees" appreciate not living near the Gulf coast. The images on the television screens almost twenty four hours a day throughout the entire summer allowed us to hope and pray for those who became victims of some damage and loss of loved ones. Those aspects of the hurricane season are well known. Simply put, the folks living around the coastal areas and the Gulf of Mexico had the highest risk of losing something or someone due to a hurricane.

There was one hurricane that had gotten a lot of attention early on. Her name was Katrina. No doubt a lot has been and will continue to be written and told about her. She had gathered strength in the Atlantic and took a unique path into the gulf across the southernmost end of it and hooked back up toward the gulf coast states. As she slowly moved across the water at about eight to ten miles per hour she had wind speeds exceeding at times one hundred fifty miles per hour. Hurricane after hurricane had been around that area all year long, but this one was about to pack a punch no one really expected.

The usual coverage on TV by all of the stormtrackers made it interesting this time. Many of the storms that year had either veered off away from people and property or just fizzled down to an obnoxious inconvenience that kept people indoors. Katrina showed no signs of fizzling out though and concern grew as she targeted land with the deadly threat tandem of wind and water. I wondered what would happen as the satellite images showed us the large white swirling cloud that I must admit looked deceptively harmless. Maybe it was because I was sitting safely fifteen hundred miles away eating popcorn and no other hurricane earlier that year did anything worth being concerned about.

The nation watched as Hurricane Katrina slammed into southern Mississippi and Louisiana. The two states seemed to slowly disappear off of the screen as this big white cloud engulfed their borders. Reporters did their usual thing with almost sacrificing themselves to their gods of wind just to get us the story. We knew that Katrina hit with full force, but the jury was still out as to what problems she would actually cause that area. Then the reports started coming in as the large spiral cotton moved out of the south and started to dissipate over the land north of the immediate coast. Hour by hour the assessment grew worse. Small towns had been completely destroyed, many people killed or missing. New Orleans was a city entirely flooded. Floating casinos were picked up and moved inland by a water surge that was at least thirty feet high. Reports of homes being wiped off of their foundations, trees uprooted and many people being swept back out to sea when the waters receded were becoming the norm. No one expected it would come to this, but it did. Throughout the many decades those storms seemed to cry wolf, but never made good on a threat as a people had decided to "ride out" another one. It was a mistake. Maybe the Sunami that had killed thousands in another part of the world had something to do with it I don't know. Events like that have a way of making us believe that our own situation is not going to be that bad. In either case it didn't matter now. It was that bad and now it was damage control.

There was obvious contention arising between the survivors and the response from the Federal Government. F.E.M.A. was to be responsible for helping our own in their time of need and were unpredictably slow in getting food, water, and shelter to that area. That debate will continue for some time to come on how to make that organization better.

The churches across the country reacted swiftly. The Mormons sent in their first fleet at least 128 tractor trailer loads of supplies to those people. Although there would be some red tape to slow them up they still got through much faster than a government agency that found itself wrapped in a mesh of politics and mismanagement. Full gospel, evangelical, Catholic churches and many other groups of faith crossed the lines of separation to help their fellow man in time of need. It was heartwarming to see that effort also covered by the media.

After a short time had passed the call came for our pastor to step up to that plate. Pastor "Pat" Medieros had proved himself to be a true lover of God and a lover of people. This is the banner he has flown since he had become senior Pastor a decade ago.

"We are going to put together a team of about a dozen or so to go to Biloxi, Mississippi," he said. "We need volunteers." By that time Biloxi had been labeled clearly as the hardest hit town out of all the entire affected area. All we knew at that time was that the small town took a direct hit by that powerful wall of water. The real extent of the damage was only communicated by word of mouth. All communication was out and even the mainstream media couldn't cover the entire losses suffered.

As my dear wife and I sat in church that one Sunday we looked at each other after Pastor Pat had announced the need for men to go to Biloxi. We both knew that I should take the call. It was interesting because normally we wouldn't want to be separated for a week, even for something like that. We had set a little extra money aside for charitable cause and it all came together. Many of our expenses were to be covered by the church, but there would still be some need for personal funds. I signed up and got the list of items to get for the trip. The last time I saw a list like that was during the summers in my early childhood when we had the scavenger hunts back in Second Ward Park. This list though was one in which I would find everything. A sleeping bag, bottled water, energy bars, cans of nuts, clothing, a chain saw, first aid items, were some of the things necessary for this trip.

I was excited to say the least. We never knew what to expect. We knew that we were supposed to meet another group there, but some of this required faith when people were starting to talk about the deadly "black mold," bodies of people still in buildings, and many other scenarios that certainly demanded trusting that "all would be well with my soul."

Including Pastor Pat, there would be a total of thirteen men going. The date was set and we would all meet at the church on Sunday September 18, 2005. It was a beautiful day with hardly a cloud in the sky. Quite the contrast in my mind with what I expected to see in about twenty-four hours or so. Three vehicles would make the trip. A white van carrying Pat and several others. Then our crew of three in a brand new Ford heavy-duty pickup with that "Triton ten cylinder" engine. We would be needing all of that extra power. A new buddy Steve would be driving out of Rochester for an indefinite period of time. Doctor "Waseem Gazoly" would making the trip and was riding shotgun. He was a general practitioner at Park Ridge Hospital and had just made a commitment to the Lord a couple of years earlier.

I had the entire rear seat to myself. Only one problem though. I get carsick if I'm not driving or at least up front. I dealt with it and did not tell a soul. It was time for me to start changing some things and the opportunity was at my doorstep. Some of my quirks and idiosyncrasies were about to be washed away in a flood of humble submission. I must confess that most of my life has been racked with pure stubborness when it came time to change my safe little comfort zones. This event gave me beauty for ashes.

Our vehicle would be towing the trailer that housed most of the supplies. Generators, gasoline, and most of the personal items would be in tow. That truck drove so well that it seemed as thought there was nothing behind us. Between the power of that engine and handling through the suspension it would be a breeze to drive. The third vehicle was a small camper that carried the remainder of the crew. Of course they had the luxury items such as place to sleep and a bathroom. We would all be connected by walkie talkies. The Nextel phones with their now infamous "bleeps" would keep us in constant contact with each other, sometimes too much.

We were scheduled to leave about five p.m. and we weren't far off of that. Three of the grandchildren came to see us off. Pictures were taken, hugs and kisses and a final prayer for our protection and example punctuated all of the anticipation. Off we went, down to Interstate 90 towards Ohio.

The trip down was pretty interesting. Although there was a little scenery I hadn't seen before (couldn't see much at night anyway) which gave our journey a little pizzazz was that we all were around people we really didn't know well at all. Some had associated with others, but no one knew me. That made for much conversation.

"What do you do Ron?" asked Dr. Gazoly.

I know that whenever I am asked that question there cannot be a short answer. "Oh, I work at Park Ridge too, up on the hill with the drug addicts and alcoholics. I'm down to one day a week. I am primarily a writer and an inventor."

Then we get into what I have invented and some of things that I had written. People's usual response is that "You lead an interesting life." Some say, "I wish I would have done that."

"Waseem," as he wanted to be called is one of the most friendly people I have met. His nickname given to him by Steve is "Holy Gazoly." They have dinner every Friday night at each other's home. Since I was the stranger in their midst it is fair to say that my questions were fewer than theirs.

We made our way through the Buckeye State down into Kentucky. Bathroom and meal stops were kept to a minimum. We wanted to get there as soon as we could and set up camp. Switching drivers was never a problem especially since I liked to drive. The trip had a little essence of the journey that us boys took back in 1973 across the country in that new Chevy pickup. On into Nashville and further south we went. Some singing, praying and some joking over the Nextel phones sometimes crowded out what we were there for in the first place...communicating directions. More than once there arose a little contention about that. Fortunately, I never was involved in that. We were all tested, many times in the same things. Being hungry, tired and any untried pet peeves that we possessed which had escaped the throngs of conviction now all came out. I was glad to keep my mouth shut. I was a little surprised at an occasional attitude that came forth, but those things always got ironed out. Once I stepped in and made it clear that communication was very important. They were basically a great bunch of guys and I was happy to be with them.

About halfway down I discovered something. One of the constant things that I have told people for years is the fact that when I had decided to step off of the alcohol freight train bound to Hell, everybody stopped talking or hanging around me. Even though I had been clean and sober for a quarter of a century I haven't spent any real time with any of the guys that I had run with back in the '70s. I was experiencing some abandonment, loneliness, and frustration at not having any friends close by for all of those years. Most of that time I discovered that it was my own fault. I could have sought new ones, but it just didn't happen. Most of my acquaintances were convenient. Basketball, a smiling handshake in church, and mostly women at work made for quite a small crowd in my life. That is why I'm glad I married Carol. Many people came out of nowhere and now I don't have to work that much at all in the way of looking for people to associate with. I suppose that will get better with time as well. The men that I found myself with on the trip to the south became important in many ways. I looked at them as a long awaited replacement on my 25th anniversary of abstaining from that old life. Being twelve in number made me feel like I was symbolically the "Thirteenth Apostle." A high and low position at the same time. Whatever the case, I made sure that I listened and participated in almost every conversation. Sounds immature especially for a fifty-three- year-old, but being teachable and correctable is of value in this world no matter what age you are. At least that is what I tell others.

We arrived in southern Mississippi a little over twenty hours after we left home. The light rains started as we traveled along the gulf toward Biloxi. Getting held up once for two hours because of an accident and congested traffic made the final leg of the trip very slow. People were dying on the highways trying to get out of that area while relief efforts were clogging the inbound traffic. Sometimes entire roads were destroyed so that four lanes sometimes were rigged to accommodate only two. That crunch going both ways made life even more difficult for those leaving behind death and destruction. Local reports kept us all updated on that front.

The closer we got, the apparent damage to property became obvious and ever increasing with each mile that we logged, particularly the last fifty miles or so. The evening had come, the clouds were lifting and the sun was setting. The big beautiful bright orange ball in the west was right in front of us as we made our last leg of the journey. I always love sunsets, especially up on Race Point near Provincetown, Massachusetts when Carol and I go there for vacation. This sunset was nice, but because of all that had happened in recent days and weeks, I wasn't to be fooled by its beauty this time. Something about it kept my awe in check.

The damage done to homes, business, and highways seemed to increase with each passing mile. Signs reading "Biloxi" still stood among the paper and plastic decorated trees. Power was still out in most of the areas. We pulled into the area where we were to be stationed. Cars were stacked on top of each other, a few buildings with all of their windows out, roofs caved in and displaced waterlines showed up everywhere. I couldn't believe that the highway we were sitting on showed the depth of the water to be several feet above the roof of the car, above the roof of the camper for that matter. I gazed around the landscape with Steve while Waseem was to be found pointing his camera, taking picture after picture.

"Look at this," he would say.

Glancing right, left, right, left, out the windshield and back again gave me a sore neck. I was impressed and once I got over the novel aspect of it I began to be grateful for my own life. A voice now came over the walkie-talkie.

"You guys see this? This is nothing." It was Pastor Pat. He had been given a description of the real damage that we hadn't seen yet.

Our caravan pulled into our destination twenty-six hours after departing from Rochester. Our handle on the squawk box had been "Corn Dog," something that I suggested and had taken it from calling "Pippon" our dog that name once in a while. I had also teased Waseem about us traveling in a camel train because he was originally from Egypt. The small town we came to a rest at was named D'Iberville, only a couple of miles from Biloxi.

The night was setting in while we made our way to the place in the huge parking lot of this big warehouse. Two huge tents were set up side by side. There were a few other large campers parked along the outside of the property up against the curbs. Several people were walking around carrying a few items. We all got out of our vehicles and stretched our tired bodies.

"Praise God, we made it," Steve said.

"Amen to that, brother," was pastor's response.

We had circled our wagons in one corner of the lot and now it was time to set up camp. I had no idea where I was going to sleep. The camper was looking like the premium place to be, but I was sure that it was accounted for. Will, our nurse practitioner who would be assisting Waseem with the medical mission set up his little tent on the surface of the parking lot. It was hot there and I made an early decision not to try and bed for the night anywhere near that hot black pavement. I have always known that the day's heat is held in that material into the wee hours of the morning and "moi" doesn't get along with high temps while trying to count sheep.

John, a new convert from just a couple of months ago was probably the most vibrant of the bunch. He had seen the error of his way through an evangelist who had come to tell his story of waywardness. Kirk Cameron had made quite an impression on John as he had come full circle from the life of drugs and all the trimmings.

What was interesting to me was that each person had certain talents that would come into play as to where they could be assigned. That would not be discovered until the next day.

After being introduced to the director "Tom," we had a little time to explore the grounds. Inside one of those big tents were enough facilities to cook hot meals for over three thousand people per day. In one corner of that tent was the medical area. Waseem and Will would man that place the next morning bright and early. The second tent would be the place for orientations and was also used as the distribution area for four thousand cold meals per day. Paper bags filled with enough for food for one family for a day was the current plan. Folks in need would have to come there every day to get what they needed.

By the time came to lie down for some sleep I had scouted every place that I thought was possible to get the job done. By that time two more pup tents had been set up next to Will's between our truck and the camper. The air conditioner for the "premium estate on wheels" was the only sound after dark other than the generator working into the night. Everyone had staked their claim as to where they would be for the night. That is everyone except me. What appeared to be a mistaken case of musical chairs was really an opportunity to get the best seat in the house. After being warned about sleeping in the grass because of the cottonmouth rattlesnakes, that is where I would sleep anyway. On the other side of the tent away from my party I spread a blanket on the grass and then opened my sleeping bag and laid it on top. I knew the grass would keep me cool and the noise from the generator and AC unit would not be a nuisance. I had heard about this man who was found sleeping under a boat and turned his life around from a life of alcohol and he would be sleeping it a little tent near where I had chosen to bed for the night. Maybe I would meet him.

The next morning had come and everyone got to compare notes as to how their night went. I had the best one, hands down. The men in the camper couldn't sleep because of the noise and the air conditioner wasn't what it was cracked up to be. A couple of guys slept in the truck and were too hot, had to get up turn the truck and its AC on, then turn it off and do it all over again…all night! The few men who tried to sleep in their tents were admittedly too hot being so close to that hot pavement. They didn't sleep much at all. Then there was me. I got to sleep about eleven thirty (my usual time) and slept like a baby until I had to get up and use the bathroom. Sometimes I would end up taking a flashlight and walk through the tents to make sure that everything was intact. The grass did keep me cool and no snakes came around. I remember seeing documentaries where campers in the western states would wake up the morning with a rattlesnake in their sleeping bag. What a thing to open your eyes too!

That first morning was a bit strange. I did not know what to expect. We were given all of our meals free of charge. I thought I was going to have to do those nuts, energy bars and Slim Jims for a week. All of the workers from some other churches came into the tent for breakfast. My wakeup call came in the form of two workers firing up a new Honda generator about eight feet from the bottom of my sleeping bag. They didn't care about it at all. What was funny was that they apparently were quiet until they got the engine running. No talking, and walking lightly, then "ROAR!" the sound of the motor running at high speed. Don't want to wake the baby up. That scenario went on all week long. The rest of the time though, I was ready for them. Being a light sleeper, I grew to expect them promptly at 6:30 every morning.

After our first meal came orientation and our assignments. We were issued official nametags and given instructions as to what to expect. Some of the men including pastor were going to be going to people's homes and delivering bags of food to those who couldn't make it in for themselves. They would have stories to tell. Another crew went to cut up trees in people's yard's that blocked the progress of other efforts. I originally went with a crew of three others right into East Biloxi to a distribution center set up in a "Save a Lot" grocery store parking lot. The store's owner had been gracious enough to let the large rescue effort literally occupy about ninety percent of the property. I arrived with Peter, Dominic, and Herb. It was going to be a very hot day, one that would break records for that area.

Our workday began with a word of prayer and then each one of us would listen to our final marching orders. About a dozen other people from churches around the country would be working with us to dispense food, water, ice and non-perishables to victims coming to get what they could. Cars, wheelchairs, walkers, bicycles, and some on foot came for items just to stay alive. I had been warned about the Vietnamese people living in that community, that they would try and steal if they could. They tried and I stopped them. They knew that if they did not listen to me that the heavily armed National Guard just a few feet away would give them their final warning. One lady went as far as to change her appearance to come back and get another load of supplies. Having done that myself back in my hey days I can easily spot what someone wears looks different and changes their clothes to throw me off. She went to great lengths to alter herself, but it didn't work. I sent her away empty handed. She did not resist.

My day mainly would consist of handing out bags of ice, bottled water, and some food items. People who drove had to park their cars and come into our stockade to "shop" for what they needed. We averaged two hundred fifty cars a day. I didn't know where they were getting their gas.

We were about three miles from where we had camped the night before. The damage to East Biloxi was quite severe compared to the area near our campsite. Although some houses were still standing, the curbs along the streets were piled high with water damaged possessions such as home furnishings and building materials that had removed from the affects of the flooding.

My duties also would include restocking the items that ran low. Tractor trailers were unloaded with forklifts and many man-hours of labor were required to put each item in its final place. Canned food, paper products, and clothing were found in abundance. We hardly ever ran out of anything. I worked hard on that site from about 7:45 a.m. until five p.m. It was the hardest job physically that I have ever worked. Harder than any construction job during the ten years in the '70s or any other role I had. My doctor would have had a cow if he knew that I was working like that. One of the last things that he had told me after my stroke was "You don't play basketball in the hot sun for an hour and a half. You don't have anything to prove." Well as this story goes, every day was at least ninety-five degrees and I drank more fluids than at any other time in my life. I felt no problems related to my stroke that had occurred only five months earlier and it was good being around this environment because it was teaching me much about life.

Probably the most interesting aspect of this trip was the people who had suffered loss. This is why I was there. Still not seeing this principle in its entirety gave me a lot of room for the expansion of my own horizon. When you get into a situation like that there is a tendency to be in the "giving only" mode. You just don't expect "to get." It is not something that is on your mind until it hits you in the face. For instance, one lady drove up in her car and asks for some ice and water to be put in the rear of her car. She requests for an item that I have to shag. She pulled up out of the way and I retrieved what she wanted.

As I loaded it into her vehicle, I asked the same question that I asked everyone. "How are you holding up?"

Her response came in the form of a question. "Where are you from?" she asked.

"New York," I answered. "Rochester, New York."

With her hands still firmly on the steering wheel she lowered one of them to shut off the engine, looking at me the whole time. "I hate New York!" she retorted. "My son lives in New York City and I have hated New York ever since September 11. I have had a bad relationship with him because he won't move away from there." She looked straight ahead and stopped talking.

Of course I do not know what to say. I knew that she needed to say what she did, but I couldn't put my finger on the real problem.

She looked back at me in tears. "You people are angels. I could never do what you are doing. Thank you, oh so very much for coming all the way down here and helping us. I'm going home and try to call by son and apologize to him."

Inside, my mouth dropped. I thought by the way that she was talking just a minute ago that a gun barrel was going to be sticking out the window and then this. "Well, I hope everything works out for you and the family, God bless and have a good day," was my answer.

The lady started the car up, put it in drive and reached out a hand. I squeezed it and said not a word. She then drove off and left me with a gold mine. Here was a woman who had been humbled by the kind acts of others. I thought how I had hoped that I would never miss that opportunity when it came my way.

Many stories came from each of us workers as hundreds of people came from everywhere just to get something to survive on. One man lost his entire family while another had one of those floating casinos land on top of his house, completely flattening it. Death and destruction was the common message from anyone who came through our gates. But there was one person who stood out from the crowd. A man in his early sixties drove up and parked his pickup across the street. Sometimes that meant that they were going to steal something while others just didn't want to tie up the line so they could take their time shopping. I always kept my eye on them because this street was on the back side of our supplies and we were vulnerable. This stately looking man came over to our displays and I approached him.

"Can I help you, bud?" I asked.

He adjusted his cowboy hat and said, "Yeah, I could use some water and ice."

"No problem, I'll help you," I said, shaking his hand. "Step right over there."

We both went and got what he wanted and walked back to his truck. As I threw the last bag of ice into the bed of the truck, I had to ask that question.

"How ya holding up." I adjusted my language to the cowboy hat.

The man looked me in the eye and said, "Angry, very angry. I am angry with people, the government." The man looked up into the sky and said, "especially him."

I saw again that most of the time you really don't know what is going on in the hearts of others. I must confess that at the moment I saw what I thought was an opportunity to tell him a lot of things about the character and nature of God. But instead I delicately spoke. "You know, I had a lawyer come to me one day. He was an acquaintance and lived in the same apartment complex as myself. We were walking to a park to watch fireworks on the Fourth of July back in 1988 with his wife and a little girl. 'Ron,' he asked. 'What does it mean to be born again? What does it mean to be saved?' Now, I knew at the time that his wife had been going to the same church that I was and I also knew that they would argue over her commitment to the faith. He hated her going to Bible studies and I was being put on the spot. 'Well, Steve. You are a lawyer. You committed yourself, your money and a lot of hard work to know the laws of the land. There are things that I cannot ask you because I have not committed hard work, time, and money to that effort. I would need to do that in order to comprehend many of the answers to my questions. 'I understand,' the man said, putting his head down. 'I need to get back to God.' Now in tears he firmly shook my hand and looked intently into my eyes. 'I will be praying for you,' I said." We parted ways and I went back to work. I was a little taken back at how easily I could have said other things that may have caused him to pull back rather than acknowledge the story the way that he did. I was very happy for him.

Each day ended with all of us meeting back at the "Big Top," as I liked to call it. Actually each of the two tents could house a small circus. Our crew would come back at different times from different places to compare notes about our experiences of the day. Even the crews working in the tents had their share of stories to tell. Waseem and Will took care of many people during the days that we were there. Waseem's usual number of patients back at Park Ridge averaged about 120 patients a week. Here in the tent near Biloxi he averaged between one hundred eighty and two hundred twenty per day! The physical consequences of a catastrophe seem to equally be matched by the mental and emotional trauma a person suffers.

Waseem said that he never had gotten so many hugs from a hurting people in all of his life. Over in the other side of that tent where he was working, people with million dollar homes stood in line every day for food. The stories of the "black mold," loved ones still missing, homes gone and the death of spouse or children filled the air every day.

After a hard day of sweating and working there is nothing like getting those two complete showers out of every twenty ounce bottle of water. And that included brushing the teeth. One day while on the job I made the mistake of washing my face with gasoline. Fortunately none really got in my eyes. I didn't realize it till I got back to the campsite. I thought someone had a leaky gas tank on their vehicle. By the time I was brought back to be around all the other guys my face and scalp had started to sting. Every scrape and scratch on my head now was inflamed with unleaded. My washcloth that I had stashed back at work was accidentally stored near a leaky supply barrel of gasoline. I came back the next day and used it like all of the other days. Wrong move. You would have thought that I would know right away what had happened. I just looked around for someone that had that leaky tank after smelling all of the explosive fuel. It was good that not a soul smoked on those grounds.

It was usually in the evening when I would call Carol-Aynn. She was such a trouper in letting me come down here with her being alone with Pippon. The cell phone towers had been down just before we had gotten to Biloxi, but were back up in time for some of us to call our families.

Nighttime was special to me. Looking up at the stars and wondering what it was like for the all of these people down here made me hurt a little. A calm still fright resonated in my soul. I could feel the violence from not so long ago lingering in the air. It happened to me at that airplane wreck in 1968 and now it was back. You weren't there when it actually happened, but your spirit feels the event as though it was continuing, but you just can't see it. It does have some elements of fear with it.

I befriended that man they called Dennis. He was in that little tent about twenty-five feet away from where I lay every night. I introduced myself and thought he may need a little help with some things considering that he was a new Christian. We would set up till about the midnight hour talking about what had happened there and each one of our own stories as well. It was true that he had slept under a boat after the hurricane hit. He had survived by being on top of a building.

"The water came in and went up about eight feet or higher in some places" he said, pointing to a group of buildings across the street.

Those people didn't have flood insurance and they started breaking out their own windows to get money from the insurance companies. Some clause in some other kind of insurance paid for them. In my own mind I had made a mental note when I had heard that the waves had come thirty feet and as I looked at the place where Dennis was pointing I agreed with his assessment of eight feet or so. I would find out later this week why someone had said thirty feet.

My new friend was I think, about fifty years old. He told me and I forgot. He admitted that he had been an active alcoholic for many years. Being much of a loner and frequenting the bars kept him broke and in the street for much of the time. Rejected for being a bum by his own family and just living off of society all came to a halt only a couple of weeks or so earlier. After the waters had receded he said that he laid under the bow of a boat that had gotten washed inland.

When he woke up he said, "I thought I had died and went to Heaven. Spread all over the landscape were cans and bottles of beer."

The waves had pilfered many of the bars and washed the beer out through the doors and windows. It was a real beer garden. Dennis got up and started drinking the warm beer all day. After he gotten drunk he became sick. He staggered down the street to the place where the church had set up the tents. He wanted some kind of medical attention for his very aching stomach. The folks who were there obviously before us brought him to the medical tent and prayed over him.

He said "The power of God must have come over me because all of my pain went away. They prayed with me that I would accept the Lord into my life, and I did. Haven't been the same since. Don't want any alcohol in my life and don't swear hardly at all anymore. Got to get rid of these things," he said, flicking a cigarette butt into a hole in the ground.

"Hmm," I snorted, listening intently. "Do you have time for a story?" I asked.

"Yeah, I guess so," he said.

Of course I let him have it with both barrels. I didn't take very long, but he was glad that we had met up. That first night I helped him with a couple of scriptures and then called it quits. We talked each night until it was time for me to go.

If I were hard pressed for the most profound experience that I had that really lasted it would be the strongest sense of freedom that one gets from doing something like this. I wasn't being paid a nickel. I wasn't thinking about any of my own responsibilities. In my mind I was set free of all connections to this world. I owed no one and no one owed me. The minor inconveniences of bathing and bathroom privileges being mostly absent, the sleeping arrangements and anything else that was off center in my life did not matter in the least. I saw and felt that principle mostly at night when everyone else was asleep. The only thing that I can use for an illustration is when an astronaut is outside of his spaceship and his line gets cut. He drifts endlessly into a space that demands nothing more than just his presence.

It was near the time to go and we had just one more night left. During that day before quitting time Pastor Pat had come over to our site and told us that he wanted to take us and show us something. We quit about 4:30 and took a ride just three minutes from where our campsite was. I sat in the front of the white van as Pastor drove. I couldn't believe my eyes. We had been right in the area hardest hit and I had thought that I had seen it all. It had crossed my mind that there were worse areas than what I had already seen because of the stories the locals who had suffered loss were telling us, but I had no idea. The thirty-foot waves now came into play. We were taken right to the neighborhoods and business districts along the coast. Homes were flattened or completely gone. Some only had a concrete slab. I could see the water line in some of the trees that were still standing. Cars and trucks were driven into the ground. Plastic bags, insulation and splintered lumber were stuck on branches. I could readily see that anyone occupying any of these homes when that wave hit wouldn't have a chance. When anyone would tell me that bodies were floating as far as ninety miles out into the Gulf of Mexico I could see how they would have gotten there. It was frightening to look at. We were taken to the areas where the big shrimp boats and large buildings had been. I also saw that casino that rested on top of that man's house. He had told me at the work site, but I wouldn't have dreamed that I would have actually seen it. That building was built on pontoons and had been floating out in the Gulf because the laws in Mississippi said that no casinos were to be on land. I was told that "they are rethinking that now." This casino had been lifted up over top of telephone poles and the roadway and then dropped into that neighborhood. If that man would have been home at the time he would have just been another casualty. The water came in, did its thing and receded in a short time. How it was explained to me was that the waves had started way out in the gulf and by the time it had hit land they were too big and too fast to get out of the way from. It was almost as if they were something alive.

After our short tour of the most afflicted areas it was time to go back to camp and prepare to spend our last night there. A feeling of loss had started to set in with me. There were new people coming and going from everywhere. Churches from North Carolina, California, Indiana, Florida and many other places sent crews to help out. It seemed hard for everyone to leave when their time came. There was nothing more we could do for these people physically. Our prayers and hope for some more relief would continue, but somehow being there and then going away actually hurt. We packed up what we could and stayed the night. We planned on working all the next day and heading back north that evening. Something we had not really planned on began to happen though. Another uninvited guest named Rita had formed out in the Atlantic and was headed our way. Everyone around the globe was watching of course and she made no bones about where she wanted to go.

It was about ten o'clock in the morning on the job site. I knew along with several others from other areas that we were going to part ways. We had started to say our goodbyes early. The skies began to darken with that ashen gray look. It happens only before some event like a hurricane or tornado. By one in the afternoon those dark clouds began to swirl like whipped cream in a mixer. Pastor Pat showed up much earlier than before.

"We got to get out of here guys," he said. "I don't have a good feeling about all of this. I know we planned on leaving later, but I think that would be a mistake."

The winds started to pick and the entire crew decided to call it quits. We covered everything up with tarps and plastic in record time. We gave our final hugs and got in the vehicles. The light rains started as we headed back to get the rest of the crew. Looking around as we headed out I had a fear for that area again. After what the last hurricane had done, the memory of it had not time to fade.

Everyone was back in their vehicles and we headed north. The plan was to get to a place about a hundred miles away and book a hotel. Pastor made that announcement well after we had gotten under way and it was the best news that we had heard all week. Someone had sprung for a donation for our hotel rooms and after a job like this the hot running shower would seem like Heaven. We stayed in contact with Tom the director who stayed near that area. He had been hailed as a top-notch, relief effort man after having spent nine months at ground zero after September eleventh. The word that we got on our way north was that two tornadoes were spawned off of Rita and one of them killed someone just one street over from where we had been working. Pastor Pat had made a good decision and maybe saved some of our lives in the process. Our hotel was five star, complete with all of the amenities. The weather was nice. This trip had made an impact on all of us and I could see it in the rest of the guys. You just are never the same again. The contrast between what we had just experienced and now I found myself standing in a warm shower staring at the ceiling and weeping like a baby. This was real life. I appreciated what I have a lot more and realized that it all can be gone in an instant. Those people, including the churches and Tom had not wanted us to go. That was a little heartening, but I had gained some valuable experience to help someone else.

We arrived back home with all of our loved ones waiting in the parking lot. Sorting out our belongings was a little difficult after hurriedly stuffing them into the trailer. John, the young new convert just gave away a lot of the things that he didn't need. I ended up with some food and other things I could use over time. It was nice to be back home and be with Carol. She had been very faithful to support me in any way that she could.

Many lessons would continue to come out of this experience. Not the loss or loss of material things so much, but the real substance of life's lessons that are meant for everyone. Love, forgiveness, compassion, self-control. I had been stretched to many different shapes just with my own little habits. I always eat lunch at home about 10:30 in the morning. I get the paper from the little store up the street and enjoy a good meal at a special time every day during the week. Being home alone while Carol was at work gave me free reign to do this. In Biloxi though, that never happened. I knew what I was going to experience when I got there and immediately I went with the flow. I ate meals delivered at all times. I wish I could say I change that easy with all things. But some lessons come a little harder. I would dare to say that what matters most, is that one really cares enough to change...however that may happen. A caring heart comes emanates from many people, sometimes unexpectedly. Only a few days after I had finished this story I got the following note from the folks back in that crushed little town.

February 28, 2006

Dear Volunteer:

The stars shine brightest against the blackest sky. As the winds of Hurricane Katrina moved away from our little town of D'Iberville, Mississippi, it was soon apparent that they left behind the dark clouds of destruction, desolation and despair. Then the stars came out—volunteers like you.

There is no way to adequately express our gratitude for all you have done. Your physical presence put a "body" to the face of compassion; your expressions of love and caring renewed our spirits. You have lifted us from the debris physically, mentally, emotionally, and spiritually.

From the depths of our hearts, we thank you.
D'Iberville Volunteers Foundation
And the citizens of D'Iberville

For the Love of Pippon

This is a story that is hardest to write purely because it is so fresh. It bears resemblance to the throng of so many other people that I had quietly criticized for acting like their world was ending because of the death of their pet. In my mind I would say; "You are just a whimp, suck it up, it's only a dog for cryin' out loud." Now it was my turn again to force feed myself a large slice of that humble pie.

We had picked up Pippon our dog about four years ago. He was different from his brothers and sisters. His colors, the way he acted, even then made him standout from the rest of the crowd. In the beginning after Carol and I had heard of the litter being born we still approached with caution. So, after those five attempts with three cats and two dogs we would not be sure whether this cute puppy would not make our allergies or Carol's asthma kick up. We drove down the parkway to the owner's home and were quickly invited in. The parents of these darling Llasapoos were about as friendly as you could get. Both were solid white and jumped around like show dogs. Mom had a little off color in her coat. These dogs were actually a mix of the Llasa Apso and a Poodle. Their reputation for being "hypoallergenic," still made us wonder. Of course, after the episode with "Elliot the cat," nothing was a shoe-in.

When we arrived, the puppies were all in a makeshift corral in the kitchen. There was supposed to be five puppies, but one had been missing. The teenage daughter in the house had been hiding the one we would actually pick. It was her favorite. Though we hinted at relenting on our choice for her sake, her parents had made it clear that they all had to go. We took Pippon, a little fluffball of a dog, who had the cutest face of all of them. Everyone knew right away what the young girl saw in him. I felt for the girl, but now entirely for all of the right reasons. Having never understood myself how anyone could become so attached to an animal, it was not hard to discount any compassion for her.

We brought Pippon home and welcomed him into our two-person family. Carol really needed a pet. I was going to basketball on Tuesday evenings and she would be home alone. Between that and the fact that it had been a long time since she had had a pet, this would be the perfect opportunity for her to have a little company. Initially, of course I had rejected another attempt to have one. I felt I would be "stuck" at home during the day cleaning up after him, a now embarrassing fact that I hate to mention. The owners of the whole litter had done a remarkable job potty training Pippon. My responsibilities with that area of his life were kept to a minimum as a result.

I grew quickly to take on my new role as father of the house. Never having children of my own it was apparent that taking care of a dog was my limit anyway. Pippon became quite a thinker. He would sit and stare at you without moving as if waiting for some marching orders or maybe studying your body language to see what you were going to do next. His first experience with snow was probably as humorous as any dogs. His short legs kept his body well below the top of the drifts as he would disappear into the yard burrowing his head as if looking for a rabbit. Then halfway across our fenced in property a head would pop up and check to see where we were. I would have to start making a path through the snow for him. He needed a place to go to the bathroom and doing it in his own path wouldn't cut it.

Carol's side of the family loved Pippon. Although to me he was obnoxiously loud when he heard the doorbell, he would ultimately settle down and be playful with anyone who came by, children and adult alike. A tug of war with a piece of "rope toy" was something that he would grip on and tug at with anyone who was game for it.

Pippon and I grew to be fond of each other. I began to take him on my runs to the store, post office or a short visit to the mall. Our walks around the neighborhood were especially good for him. After I had my stroke those times of strutting down the neighborhood sidewalks became a staple for me anyway. Pippon had one thing in his little mind that was peculiar. He would not step on a manhole cover or a metal utility plate that happened to be a part of the sidewalk.

He was a particularly cautious dog. Though he trusted all who entered our home there would be some that you could see where he had some doubts about. We knew he was right about them. Some things you just cannot explain to an animal. You don't have to.

When Carol's mother became sick, Pippon had quickly taken his role as watchdog at her side. She had explained that her own dog Makayla as well as Pippon would switch their positions as sentries for the ill matriarch of the family. One dog lay at the bedside and then would leave while the other one took over the duty. We called Makayla, Pippon's cousin. They were good friends all of the time. Makayla being a spoiled little Maltese who looked like she should have been eating out of a goblet quickly realized that she was going not to be in total control of the whole house when Pippon came to town. She would nip at the side of his face to try and steer him in the direction that she wanted, but our dog never succumbed to it. Those four months that we had lived with Dori gave us all including our pet some valuable experience about living in tight quarters with others.

When I need to take one of those trips to the store Pippon did what so many dogs do. "Do you wanna go for a ride?" I would say. His ears would perk up and very often he would wait to get excited to run a check to see if he heard right. If I stared at him for a moment he would start jumping up in the air. Or, if I repeated myself he would do the same. Early on in our travels I think he was getting carsick so I would have him sit on my lap while I drove. That gave him a good view of what we traveled by and in the summertime that also made the air blow in his face, something that I have never seen a dog not like. Unless we were traveling down the Parkway for a few miles I tried to keep his body in the passenger seat as much as I could. I was afraid that if we were in an accident I could never forgive myself if the airbag went off while he was still sitting on my lap.

My office is upstairs in our house. With all of the typing that I do it was good to have him nearby. My day job only being one evening a week afforded me being around Pippon every day. When Carol and I would go on a trip for a week or so, he went to cousin Makayla's house or in the case of the first couple of times, he went back to his parents and the teenage girl got to keep him with her.

His trips to the groomers he always looked forward to. Every six weeks or so he and sometimes Makayla would both go to "Happy Tails," a local group of folks who did good work with grooming dogs in particular. Our dogs always came back with little bandanas around their necks. If it happened to be near a holiday the colors would reflect the season.

A trip down to Pennsylvania was certainly in order for Pippon once in a while. Being about a two and a half-hour trip, he just slept in the back seat and we would take him out once for a stretch and his "duty." Mary and s/o Fritz both loved him. Mom liked him, but it brought some memories back about "Pepper and Pretzel," that at times were uncomfortable. She had those dogs from their youth and now they had been gone for a long time, never to be forgotten. They never were replaced for many years.

I even on two occasions took Pippon into work on an off day. The patients loved him. I am trying to get a little more animal therapy into that environment. The nursing homes have their dogs and it works quite well. The down side is that any dog that gets that job gets too heavy quickly. The food mysteriously makes it way from the resident to the animal.

At home it took a couple of years, but Pippon ended up coming to bed with us. I never thought that I would allow something like that, but he was one creature that was capturing my heart and I didn't know it. He had been expanding his own horizon by being the dog that he was. Although he wasn't really a spoiled pet he got a lot of attention from me. More than I would have imagined. There was a special sound he would make when he wanted to come up to sleep with us. Politely waiting near the door and waiting for our response, the unique growl reminding us of a low hum of a man with a base voice while his mouth was closed. Either Carol or I would say "come" or maybe I would snap my finger once and Pippon would be in the air on the way to our covers. He had attuned himself to act on cue immediately.

Stories about an animal could be a dime a dozen. I would dare to say that I have heard and seen many of them, some of which really moved me, mostly as a child. But in real life I have never paid a lot of attention to other people's woes at their loss of a pet. Many of us grew up on the movies like *Bambi*, *The Incredible Journey*, and *Old Yeller*. Now it's the likes of *The Lion King*, *Iron Will*, and *Finding Nemo*. We all root for the character in trouble. I remember hating it when Bambi's mother died at the hands of a hunter. As a kid who also suffered greatly when Dad killed all of my puppies, reality and fiction didn't seem far apart. Buried hurts and resentments did not change me as one who felt affected by the afflictions in an animal's life. It took another forty years to really find that out.

Pippon started to act a little strange toward the middle of February 2006. We were all still coming off of the holiday season. A trip to Mary and Fritz's for Christmas had been a necessary capstone to seal the beginning of a new relationship between us all. Pippon, of course, traveled with us and would steal the show. He would always run up the stairs at Mom's too, knowing that she would try and break the rule of "no people food."

Our dog seemed to start moving slower than usual. Finally we saw him getting sick and wrote it off as "maybe he just got into something bad out in the yard" or is just a sick dog and will get over it with a little TLC. He worsened and we called the veterinarian. By that time I saw Pippon had stopped eating and drinking and would pick him up and use a baby bottle to try to get him to drink. I wasn't very successful. Food was out of the picture. Although I was concerned I wasn't concerned about whether he would recover or not. If it would get worse, the vet would just take care of it. That was my attitude. Well, it did get worse and he was weakened to the point that we had to help him up onto the bed. He would shake and quiver as if he was freezing. Trying to keep him warm didn't work. He wasn't cold. Becoming more and more agitated by whatever was bothering him he started to whine and yelp unceasingly. At night I moved him to the bathroom on the other end of the house. We could hear him yelp too loud for us to sleep. Then I moved him to the upstairs bathroom still on the other end of the building. That did not do it either. He was in pain and started to look like he was drunk. I took him to the vet and they checked him out and found nothing. Blood, urine, and stool samples gave us nil. He had a little temperature and the doc gave us an antibiotic as a precaution. We brought him home and he got worse still. The next trip would require him to be admitted to the hospital. Fluids under the skin and intravenously as well were going to be his norm until we found out what was going on. I did not know that a dog could go as long as a month without food. That to me would buy us the time to correct whatever was wrong. There seemed to be good news in the fact that he was responding to the fluids, which indicated that his kidneys were functioning. The liver enzymes were good also. All the tests were revealing nothing worthy of pointing us in the direction of a particular treatment. X-rays and a subsequent trip to another animal hospital in the next town for an ultrasound did nothing. Over a week in the hospital, and still no answers. Dr.Hughes had the best nature than a vet could have. He spent a lot of time making sure that Pippon had the best treatment. But he was baffled and frustrated. By this time Carol and I had to discuss putting Pippon to sleep. I did not want to think about it. I would never bring it up as an option to the doctor.

We had made a couple of trips to see our dog during his stay at Northgate Animal Hospital. Pippon could only lay on his side and look as if he was just going along with everything. Our last trip was met with a feeling of deep darkness. Pippon in the beginning of his stay there had been slowly following Dr. Hughes around and he had captured the hearts of the staff. His worsening condition had affected them all. Our dog lay on the steel tray looking the most ragged that he ever had. On that day before I got there I had determined that if Pippon would ever have to be put down that I would be far away. Sometimes things in life just didn't go the way that I planned. As Carol was holding him Dr. Hughes came in and looked at us with a sense of a loss for words as to what else could be done for him.

"I don't think there is anything more we can," he said. I knew at that moment that the statement was the cue to end it.

Carol-Aynn picked up on it immediately and looked at me. "Ok doctor," she said.

I turned my palms up in submission and the doctor left the room. I did not expect him to return so quickly and with a syringe filled with a red colored fluid.

As he reached down to find a vein in our dog's leg he said to me, "This acts very quickly."

I had gone against all that I planned on. I was going to be there went my Pippy-pops died. Dr. Hughes injected the red fluid and I watched the breathing stop within fifteen seconds.

Cooly I said, "That does act fast." Then it hit me. He is really gone. I let go of my dog and walked away to the other side of the small room, breaking down. Dr. Hughes had an assistant with him who had become accustomed to Pippon. She asked if we wanted a couple of chairs to be with him. My back was to them and I couldn't answer. This event hurt me more than my own father dying, my wife leaving me, or the other ten deaths that had occurred over that span of those four years back in the '70s. In a strange way, even more than being deceived about becoming a preacher, or my puppies being murdered. It would seem as though almost none of these things could be related, but they all had one common factor. I remembered them all. Now nothing else mattered. I couldn't even respond to say no about the chair. With my back to everyone I just shook my head no. A seemingly insignificant story about a dog all of sudden meant something. It was me this time. Over the period of a little more than four years I was the one who had slowly come to learn what it was to be loved and as two friends put it "unconditionally loved." No ifs, ands, or buts. I was loved by an animal without reservation or conditions attached.

The recovery from all of the attention to Pippon's sickness and subsequent death will continue in ways that I have never known. Now I am not so quick to say how things are going to be. As the days go on I am more amazed at the true lessons of love that are coming at the hands of a dog. My wife and who she really is, is now coming more out of the mist. I thought I knew her. Her love toward me is easier to acknowledge.

For the third time in my life I have felt like I was being carried by someone else. Being totally helpless with not a care about anything is again absolute freedom. When I was on my back in the hospital and on my back looking at the stars at night down in Biloxi I got the beautiful sense of release from this life that only God can give. In my mind, the pain of it all only arrested me and made me a captive to Him who is really in control of all. Why can't I live like that all of the time? Why does the path that takes me through the city of suffering seem to be the only boulevard to true life? Maybe when I wake up and learn some things when I am supposed to, some of it will come by another means, I don't know for sure. Either way I want to finally love and be loved.

I am now open to compassion, caring, and kindheartedness in ways never known to me before. Having been away from the direct affects of alcohol for over twenty-five and a half years one could easily think that I knew more than what I really did on the subject of love. Sorry, I didn't. And I'm not sorry that I'm leaning it now. Many other people can now benefit from the experiences that I go through and learn from.

Pippon left this earth on February 20, 2006 at 3:15 in the afternoon. I had planned a trip to Los Angeles a few weeks earlier. My flight was to leave Rochester at six in the morning that following Thursday. I questioned for a moment whether I should even go. Getting blasted unexpectedly by the events surrounding Pippon made me think that what I had to do in Beverly Hills could never be done under this pressure. Remembering that I had used the trials of others for inspiration I decided to go anyway. My job out there in Tinseltown was to sit before at least eight executives and pitch my new screenplay "Shadow." I had finished it just before Pippon got sick. Fortunately I had been through this daunting pressure only two years earlier, so I knew much of what to expect. I kissed Carol-Aynn goodbye at four in the morning that Thursday and hopped the plane to LA.

The flight to Chicago went quite well. I had found my seat beside a woman who told me she was from downstate New York.

"I'm going to Nebraska," she said. "My mother is dying and I have to go there to help my sister."

I looked out the window and then tried to comfort her. "Sorry to hear that. I hope all goes well with that. Are you and your mother very close?"

"No," she answered. "We haven't been close for a long time, but I'm still feeling something about it."

She didn't really show any signs of stress from the fact that she was going to lose her mom, but wasn't void of having some deep thought along the way. I try not to get into a lot about what I do for a living, but a note about helping drug addicts and being a writer usually suffices in situations like this. During my four-day trip I never said a word about my experience with my dog. I was so inundated with other people's stories that it was easy to be grateful that I was going through only my ordeal. It could have been much worse, that I already knew.

When I got to the windy city I had to wait a bit for my final leg to California. Killing time in situations like that is always easy for me. I'm a natural at thinking just about anything to keep my mind occupied. Liking some layover time in the first place doesn't let me be concerned about missing my flight. I don't particularly care to remove my shoes at the x-ray machine, but like many others I write it off to "protecting ourselves."

When I'm in airports I don't usually strike up conversations especially with women. I'll engage when I'm spoken to, but sitting beside anyone on a plane sort of puts us in the position to talk no matter who it is. Having been infatuated with the 747 jumbo jets I always get a good look at them in Chicago and LA. I have never been on one and want to. There are many places that I want to go that require that size of plane to get there. Hong Kong for one, New Guinea for another. I'll have to wait. I remember that statement a man said during the second season of the "Apprentice." He said, "If you haven't made it by the time that you're fifty, you won't make it." I knew that his brother had had a problem with alcohol and I have often wondered if that relationship factored in that line of thinking. Whatever the case was I set out to prove him wrong. Not a one-man show, just an opportunity to tell him after I do make it that even a late bloomer like me can't be counted out. Maybe I could try to help his brother in the process sometime, you never know. I had those thoughts come to me time and again including on the plane to LA. After the first trip out there, I also knew that many stories of the people started a long time ago in other parts of the country. Doubters were in abundance then and they still are.

I arrived at LAX at my scheduled time. The famous airport again lived up to its reputation. Thousands of people coming and going looked like as I had described New York City to one man "What happens after you kick an anthill." Having gone through all of this before I knew that I really wouldn't rest until I opened my door to my hotel room. But as I found out soon after, the welcoming committee to one of the largest cities in America wasn't all smiles.

I got my baggage and went to the front of the airport to look for some kind of a ride to the Sheraton Universal, the hotel at Universal Studios , my home for the next four days. Shuttle service came back to mind as I knew a taxi would be very expensive. Going to the outside curb near a sign that indicated a shuttle, I waited. A dispatcher walked that area getting addresses from other people leaving from the airport. I did not know at the time that he was doing that.

Another man approached me from behind and said, "You looking for a shuttle?" He wore headphones and a jacket with the company logo of a competitor of the other shuttle service. And carrying a clipboard with names and addresses on it made him look official. And he was.

"Yes," I said, "I'm going to the Sheraton Universal."

Pressing the walkie talkie on his shoulder he phoned ahead looking for a loose shuttle coming to his spot on the curb where we now stood. After about ten minutes, one came and I was off. There was only one other person in the shuttle as a passenger and that made it a little tedious as we circled the airport at least three times before we actually left. Picking no one else up was probably a little discouraging to the driver who obviously made more money from tips if we could have filled the vehicle with other paying customers.

Traveling down the highway on a beautiful sunny day on the West Coast after leaving a state in the cold northeast was nice. Looking around at the sights that would take me through parts of LA that I hadn't seen before, I spotted something homegrown. Big steel horses pumping oil. Couldn't believe it. For a couple of minutes these small rolling hills were dotted with many of these mechanical monster looking pumps that I never dreamed I would see out here.

"Those things pumping oil?" I asked the driver. "I am from Pennsylvania and I never knew that you had oil out here."

The polite well-groomed Hispanic young man piloting the shuttle answered. "Yeah, there's a lot of here. Just in this area, though. It is owned by all the people who are rich. We've had it for a long time. I'm surprised that you didn't know."

One other thing that I did not know. By asking that question I was grooming myself for a little fraud. As we drove on farther and farther I became concerned about the price for the fare. Scanning the inside of the shuttle I found a list of sample fares posted above the door. None of the destinations listed showed the area where I was going. The prices that I did see went from twenty to sixty dollars one way. I wanted to ask what my own fare was, but felt I shouldn't. I ended up asking and shouldn't have.

"What is my fare?" I asked.

The young man did not answer. I waited another minute and then repeated my question thinking that he hadn't heard the question.

He finally responded. "Didn't the guy at the curb tell you?"

Leaning forward in my seat to hear him I made things clear to him. My simple answer of 'no' obviously gave him a license to be quiet for another minute.

"What is my fare?" asking a little louder.

"Thirty six," he answered.

We had to take a detour around some construction traffic and I didn't mind that. I planned on giving the young man a four dollar tip bringing the total to forty dollars even. I also felt that he was earning his money driving for as long as we did.

We arrived at the hotel and I paid the driver. "You coming back?" he asked.

"Yes, on Sunday night," I answered, reaching into my wallet. "If you call the shuttle, ask for me. Here is my van number," he requested.

I shook his hand and told him, "You earned your money on this trip, good job!" I said.

He took the money and left. It gave me a little comfort to know that I didn't have to fidget around looking for another shuttle when it came time for me to leave. And a smiling polite person did it all for me. He had doubled my fare and I did not know it. The only thing that I can think of was that song from back in the late '60s. "Smiling faces, they don't tell the truth." As I was unpacking my things in my room, I began to wonder why this kid would be so excited over a four-dollar tip that took him a long time to get. In my mind I replayed every conversation that we had on the way to the hotel. Then I called the shuttle service and asked what the fare from the hotel back to LAX was. Twenty-one dollars was the answer. The fare was the same going as it was coming. On the phone I snaked my way through management and was instructed at one point to do as the driver requested and when we would get to the airport to just "Get out of the van and run."

"It happens all of the time," the dispatcher said.

After two days of talking to people off and on including some newfound friends who lived in the area, I decided to take another shuttle service and file an official complaint when I got back home. I did and the money is supposed to be on its way. The event taught me a lesson. Even though I had assumed that there was a standard fee for everywhere that you could go, (and it was true) I opened myself up by asking what it was and creating an opportunity to not just get taken once, but twice. You know the old saying? "Lie to me once, shame on you. Lie to me twice, shame on me." He was setting me up to do it again. I don't believe for a second that he thought he would get caught. And with my complaint there is no guarantee that he was punished even if I get my money back. Time to drop it. On to why I came there in the first place.

The hotel was all I had expected and more. Pictures on the web and the downloaded literature described quite accurately what I was now partaking of. Built on the steep hill above the tall Universal office that was sitting in the valley, this luxurious place held a place of its own. Just watching the valet parking service operate, the concierge and the bell-hops doing their duties accented the grandeur of the building and well kept grounds. My room was on the 14th floor, the same floor as my trip to the Holiday Inn back in Manhattan. The view down the valley was nice. I could see the well protected pool area and some of the shops down on the floor of the valley.

I called Carol every night and sometimes more when I could. Having to play the three hour difference in the time zones sort of kept my eye on the clock to make sure that I didn't make a mistake and call her after midnight, particularly on a work night. One little story that

I told her was typical of the way I sometimes discover things. Although there was a small balcony outside of my room, the full-length sliding glass window would slide open only five inches. A sign on the lower section said it was "For my protection." At night I could see the well-lit streets and many shops that were open for business. They would be easier to spot at night and I needed to know where they were. My budget did not accommodate four and a half-dollar bagels down in the dining room. There was a limited view to the right of the building down on the streets. I had to find a gas station. None were within my view. That first night, for a few minutes I searched, nothing. I couldn't go out on the balcony and look in the direction that I wanted. I then pulled the mirror out of my suitcase that had a handle on it. Opening the sliding door to the max I put my arm fully extended with the mirror in my hand out through the space and bingo! There it was, just as I thought. Where there are people there must be gasoline. Glowing brightly in my mirror was a gas station. I could rest tonight knowing that some of my food would be here without having to take out a loan to get it. I told Carol and she laughed.

Getting here on Thursday night afforded me to spend my planned Friday as expected. The seminars were scheduled for all day Saturday, and Sunday was surely accounted for with the actual Pitch going on. Getting up Friday morning had me looking forward to discovering what was going on out there. I started the day by going to the exercise room and riding the stationary bike. Going for a walk down the hill in the sunshine then got me on my way to find a place to eat. There was a whole string of places that I could afford. Chain restaurants that I knew kept me from going broke. And any extra staples such as crunchies would come, compliments of that gas station. The common folk frequented this area and I had to relent from again stereotyping people from Hollywood. Every town has its diversity and even though my last trip out here let me know that, this area being new to me made somehow think it would be different. A couple of people carrying baggage collected from the curbs came around the hamburger joints. That was all below the grounds of Universal studios down in the valley only a half mile away.

The property above the hotel was different though. I had no idea what I had signed on to. I was told that shuttles came and went every fifteen minutes all day out in front of the hotel until 9:30 at night. They went up to the studios. What were the studios? I had to find out. My first trip up the steep hill had me in awe as we climbed the winding road taking us through the adjoining property of the Hilton Hotel, a place we would stop to pick up other tourists. The shuttle was not loaded too heavily and we stopped in front of this entrance into what was called the City Walk at Universal Studios Hollywood. I got off and had no idea where I was. Inside the grounds was a world that reminded me of the City Walk in Orlando a few years earlier. I had forgotten. Eateries, shops with the latest fashions, theaters, and plenty of entertainment made this the place to be. There weren't really many people there on Friday afternoon, but I discovered two things interesting. My favorite foods have been hot dogs and popcorn my whole life. Walking along the strip in this place I came upon a café named "The Sausage Kingdom." Guess where I had dinner? I sat down to eat my meal and straight across the walkway in front of me was a store called "Popcornopolis." I ended up getting a large white popcorn with real butter. I had hit the jackpot. And the price didn't break me. Sitting and watching the people, while seeing the sights and sounds of this place, was really fun for this fifty-three-year-old man. I believed that I needed anything that could help me enjoy my stay here. It was obvious that I didn't have to look very far.

My biggest problem up to this point wasn't having to deal with the fraudulent shuttle driver or the cost of food, but my actual pitch to these executives that I was going to see face to face on Sunday. Saturday would afford me some time to listen to top notch producers and panel discussions with Hollywood's best agencies, but I was still concerned about my own presentation. I had a full page down on paper, but there was still something wrong. It was too much and I did not know it. Help was on the way. During the day of meetings I met a woman who appeared to be a very busy minded individual. Marie was into marketing and backed it up with a superior knowledge of the trade.

"How's your pitch going," she would say.

"Oh, I think it might be a little too long, but I've got it down to the size of an index card," I answered.

"Let me hear it" she quipped.

Being in her business and me being who I was, I knew at the moment that God had sent her to push me up to the next level. I was reserved, she wasn't, by any means.

I got one sentence out and she said, "Stop! that's it. That's all you have to say. Make them ask questions. You know, just enough out to make them wonder for more."

I felt liberated. The day before I had been stuck on all the things that I felt they should know and now I by George I think I've got it.

Sunday came and my eight pitches went well every time. I generated some interest this time. We'll see how it all turns out with those who said they would make official requests for my material.

That day came and went. The usual cramming in line for the extra impromptu sessions gave me a little more exposure, but I was ready to come home. I had met some great people who are helping me continue with my work.

My shuttle had come and several out of the one hundred seventy-five people who had been there were on their way to LAX. I had been told that there was a man all the way from Australia. Having not met him during the weekend, it was pleasant to have him on the same shuttle as myself. He said he lived in one of Russell Crowe's apartments down around Sydney. He was dropped off at one terminal, I another. We met up in a McDonalds for a hamburger unexpectedly and found that our flights were leaving from gates next to each other an hour apart. Working for United Airlines as a maintenance mechanic he got all of his flights free. Only one catch though. He could only be on flights that had not filled up.

"How do you know ahead of time whether or not you have a seat?" I asked. "Don't you have to wait up until the last minute to see if someone cancels?"

Looking around at the long lines that were checking in to get on the big 747 he answered, "Yeah, you gotta gamble on it all of the time. The next flight for Sydney leaves tomorrow at 8:30 at night."

I looked at my watch and easily calculated that would be a twenty-two hour wait.

"You watch my bag," he said as he gave me the big "hold your breath and dive" look, and went to the ticket counter to see what his fate was.

I sat watching the crowd. Leo came back with a downcast face. "Didn't make it," he said.

I was a little taken back and felt for him. "Can't somebody still cancel," I asked.

"They got ten minutes to do it," he said.

I reached down in my briefcase and came out with an apple. Looking at it, I offered it to him and he swept it out of my hand. The "thanks," came from a disheartened young man who wanted to go home as he devoured the forbidden fruit. In my heart I started to pray for this man with a situation that I would not want to be in. I petitioned the Lord to open the door.

"What is your last name?" I quipped.

"Osborne," came his answer, taking the last bite.

"If you get a seat how will you know?"

"They will call out my name," he said looking around nervously. "I guess I will have to get a hotel and just ride it out."

Then the call came. "Leo Osborne to the ticket counter Gate 79," twice echoed over the intercom.

I was excited for him. He jumped up and went to the counter and came back to show me his stamped ticket. Someone had canceled at the eleventh hour. I stood up and shook his hand. I watched as he went through the gate to the Jumbo Jet. I felt a little heartsick and happy at the same time. I still do not like meeting people and have them go out of my life, perhaps forever. I walked over to the window and looked at the nose of that big jet. I knew where this one was going. *Someday I can be on one of these*, I thought.

I waited for my own flight that was due in another hour and headed home. One of the things that I try to do is schedule my return flight on the redeye shift. It is a little cheaper and I don't really care about sleep when I am typing in my request on the Internet, but now it was time to pay the piper. Leaving Los Angeles at eleven at night and getting to Washington capital at 6:30 in the morning was going to make for a long night. And it always comes on the end of the day at work, not the beginning. I just can't sleep on a plane. Choosing an aisle seat this time I thought would give me some leg room being six feet tall. I tripped the stewardess twice trying to doze off. She had actually kicked my foot both times as if she was trained to clear the aisles that way. She never missed a step either time and didn't look at me or try to catch herself. Whatever state I had gotten to in my quest to slumber was quickly shattered by her low hard strut shaking me completely awake. The young man with his two year old daughter who had to get out of his seat a couple of times didn't help any. They were very quiet in their seats, but this was life on a plane.

I got to Washington and waited for my United Airlines Express Jet to pick up the new load of passengers. It was very cold as I was shuttled to the area away from the main terminal built exclusively for shorter, smaller flights. My plane arrived and I was getting tired. I also started thinking about what I was coming home to, a life without Pippon. After so many hours without sleep one can feel things with a little more sensitivity. The AA'rs had told me many years ago to "beware of H.A.L.T. Don't get hungry, angry, lonely, or tired. It will drag you down."

I got on the tight seated jet and sat next to a woman in her mid forties. We went through the "Where ya coming from, where ya headed," routine as our discussion gravitated into a deeper dialogue. She was coming from Nashville where her father was in St. Mary's hospital suffering from many ailments. The prognosis was not great for the long term as her mother was a victim of Alzheimers disease and couldn't care for her husband even under the best of circumstances. There was pain all over the face of my seatmate on this plane. It spoke volumes to me as she looked out the window thinking about her life's circumstances, something that I seemed to grow accustomed to lately. It was in a strange way comforting to be in the presence of someone else who was enduring some of the trials of life. I felt compassion for her as I thought about my own life, especially at the moment. I still would not say a word about Pippon. I guess it would have been pale in nature by comparison to what this lady was going through anyway.

"What is your Dad's name?" I asked.

"Paul," she answered.

I said, "I'll be praying for him, your mom and you."

"Thank you," was her response, as she didn't seem to care about much else at the moment. She could have been believing in just about anything at that moment, but I knew that she was open to the suggestion of intercession through God.

Her name was Tara and was a nurse living in Syracuse who took care of children with disabilities. She was meeting her daughter in Rochester at the airport. They were going to investigate the possibility of attending Nazareth College. After a few more minutes of conversation, the short hop home from Washington came to an end. We parted ways and I went to a very cold truck. This was my usual circumstance when I came home from a long trip, unless I went to Provincetown in the summer.

I drove right to Carol's office and gave her the big hug. My eyes would be a dead giveaway, that sleep had eluded me for a grand total of thirty straight hours that trip. She made it clear that I needed to "hit the hay" as soon as I got home.

Walking in the door of my now very quiet home was a hurtful time. I really hadn't been thinking about that at all until I walked in the door. No barking, no jumping up to meet me...nothing. When I got all of my luggage inside the door and looked around, the silence overwhelmed me. Weeping, I couldn't even look up at the framed picture of Pippon when he was a puppy. Always concerned that I would have another stroke, I didn't care this time. The pressure and intensity of this pain did not subside for a few minutes. I had ignored to some degree the reality of all of this to accomplish my mission in California. I dried my eyes and had to take a quick shower and call it a day. A couple of hours of sleep on a cold sunny day would do the trick.

I started to discover that a couple of things had started to surface while I was away. I knew about one of them, but the story about a teenager had made quite a stir during a basketball game. They called him J-Mac, short for his real name. That first night home I noticed a rerun on the eleven o'clock news of some kid making basket after basket and the crowd during that high school game would erupt into a frenzy after each shot. I had the sound off as usual so I didn't know what the story was really about. A kid making shots like that wasn't uncommon until I made a mental note that it seemed that both sides of the basketball court were going crazy. Writing it off as some kid maybe breaking a record I went to bed.

Going through the usual routine of putting my things away and reflecting on the trip I bought the paper and had lunch. The main story on the front page and another one in the sports section highlighted what I had discounted as just another "good game" that someone had. J-Mac was a kid with Autism. As a senior in high school he had been the manager of Greece Athena's varsity basketball team. In Greece, New York all of the high schools are named using Greek names. Apollo, Odessey, Olympia, Arcadia, and Athena are about as Greek as you can get. J'mac's school Athena is right next door to the Greece Assembly of God church that I attend. (Lois's daughter Kim had attended there for a short while before we had moved back to Bradford).

The newspaper gave an account of what had really happened on that night of the basketball game against Spencerport, the team from about twenty five miles from Greece. The game was in Spencerport and it was "senior night." As the story goes, Coach Johnson had promised to consider letting J-Mac suit up for the game and play a short while. He had tried out for the team for the second straight year and didn't make the cut, so he was offered the manager's duty again. He humbly took it and again became the servant of the job he knew best. Handing out towels and drinks, he would shout, "Stay focused!" to a team that seemed to listen to him. This night would be different, however. Coach Johnson had made the decision to let J-Mac suit up and give him a few minutes to play. It was the decision of a lifetime. This teenager with Autism lit up the court with twenty points in three minutes and eleven seconds. That is unheard of even in college and the pro's. As I read the story, it became apparent the story was gaining momentum. I came home on Monday morning and by Thursday it had been splattered all over not just the United States, but the world!

On that Thursday, Carol had to get to her six-month visit to the dentist. In this metropolis of over a million strong who would have thought that J-Mac's mother would have been my wife's dental hygienist! Carol came home and told me that movie producers from everywhere had contacted the family. I was encouraged that they were really looking for stories. Sometimes you just don't know what the truth is until something happens to draw it out. Even though I had poured out my heart to try and sell my idea to executives in Hollywood I came home to someone that would unexpectedly be an inspiration to me. There is apparently more coming from the story in the future, especially if they make the movie.

The other events that were unfolding was the nomination of Philip Seymour Hoffman for an Academy award. He also was a local hero. He had just won a Golden Globe Award for his main character role in "Capote," the life and trials of Truman Capote. His memoirs have been sitting on my desk and I haven't read them yet. I never really knew much about him over the years, but when I was into mimicking famous people he was one that I would imitate. His strange high-pitched voice was something to behold when I saw an interview with him on television about thirty years ago. All I knew was that he was a writer and that is what made me buy the book at a local garage sale only two years ago. Now I have a little incentive to pick the thing up.

Sunday night came and the Academy Awards were going to be on the TV in our house. Hoffman was in a serious running and that is what I was hoping for. His mother is a family court judge and presides currently over a case involving my family. I seem to invite tire-kickers, but no one seems to want to go the whole way and sign. Hollywood producers, directors, Hoffman, J-Mac all around me, but nobody invites me to the party. That is the other side of inspiration. Around it, but not in it. Can this refugee from Pennsylvania make it? I'm doing my part for sure. But in the meantime, character, and integrity must abound. I am finding out more and more that a good name is better that all the riches in the world. To get that type of reputation you have to go about your business just like an animal. Care about nothing, but do what you are supposed to.

I rooted for Hoffman and he won. He was sitting alone, but I knew his mom was there. It was said that she had raised four kids alone and had plenty of experience for the bench. She would not disappoint. She had raised a kid that had more than dabbled in drugs and alcohol, but straightened out to become the proud owner of an Oscar. It is interesting to see where life takes other people. Philip Seymour Hoffman couldn't give enough credit to the one who had raised him from his youth. Moms seem to get leaned on when there is emotional drama in her child's life, whether it is good or bad. I'm sure that watching her son receive an Academy Award is a lot different than answering one of those phone calls at three in the morning from a jail or hospital. But he was another inspiration to me, especially being a local.

Carol-Aynn has been going through trials of her own and what affects her affects me. The continual presence of health issues and family concerns keeps us both on our toes. Four years ago while I still playing basketball, she needed some company and of course, as I mentioned, that company came in the form of Pippon. He would become part of the family and while I was shooting hoops he could help with the companionship role. Being down to one night a week playing with the guys, I agreed to get our dog. For the next four years Pippon would be the third member of our little entourage, wherever we would go. Now he was gone and it didn't take long for that to be a problem for my wife. I hadn't played b-ball since my stroke last April, but there still was a void in Carol's life. If the truth was told, Pippon's absence created many holes in my life too. While I type this sentence he is not near me now, watching and listening to the click's of the keyboard.

"Honey," my wife says. "Can we get another dog?"

I started to cringe inside. I did not like the thought of getting another dog, especially so soon. "I'm sorry dear, I can't bear something like that right now. You know when I'm committed to something I really am committed and I must let go of one thing before I latch onto another. You know when Lois left, it took fourteen years to find someone like you. Just let me deal with this a bit, okay?"

I could tell that even though she could see my point I needed to see hers again. She was starting to go through the process of loneliness again without a pet. I understood that when I was away, especially after this recent trip to LA that she was going to need some help through my understanding her a little better.

After a week or two had gone by she brought it up again. "Honey, Carol Gilson has this friend who has a litter of puppies. They are half Shitzu and half Maltese. Do you think we could take a look at them?"

I looked at my wife and realized that my grief, no matter at what stage it was at, it had to be dealt with. Would the presence of another dog so soon in the house affect me? I didn't really care after that question.

"We can," I said.

My wife's eye's lit up like a flashbulb. "Oh, thank you, honey!" she said. "I'll call Carol right now. Everyone wants those dogs. Here is a picture of them."

I looked at the photo from the e-mail and the little pups were certainly cute, but that couldn't all of a sudden make me feel better. I had talked to a couple of people before I had gone to California and they said that getting another dog soon was the way to go. In my mind I was not like everybody else and I had to wait until I was ready. Wrong! I have known too long that people, places, and things are all instruments in the master's hands, to get me to move beyond what my definition of "far enough" is. Being stretched to the limit is only a perspective of the person being stretched. I have watched little children my whole life act like they are losing their life only when they have a candy bar taken away from them. This new step of getting a dog before "I'm supposed to" is good for me. I would pay a little price for doing the right thing, but so what.

Carol-Aynn went to arrange a meeting with Carol Gilson's friend to let us see the puppies. All of the dogs were taken and the one left had been sold more than once and even with a waiting list we were moved up on that list after hearing of our situation they would have compassion on us.

We drove up to Larry and Barb Cardone's on a Friday evening. I was a little nervous giving in to this, but I knew that it didn't matter. I drank castor oil more than once as a kid. Larry answered the door and politely invited us in. After the introductions we went to see the proposed "Object of our affection." They still had all four of the puppies. The parents of the dogs were both still there and had greeted us at the door like old friends. I had fought back the tears the whole time. Carol sat on the kitchen floor and held a couple of the little dogs. I did not know which one was to be ours. Then they pointed him out. He was the only male and a dominant one. They called him the alpha male. He showed us all why. Always on top of the wrestling matches with his siblings even at six weeks you could see he was the boss. Being the same colors as Pippon made me aware that I was having another blessing plopped in my lap and all of the players handled this with cotton gloves. I felt as if I was being carried by someone else again. Barb handed me our dog.

"This one is yours," she said.

I held him as if he was a newborn baby. I really felt strange. My actual healing hadn't been complete before I walked in the door, but there was something going on inside that told me, "All is well…just do it."

We spent the next couple of hours at that house. The history of the dogs, where we worked, many things about all of us came out as Larry and Barb sought to make sure that the home that this dog was going to was more than fit. Once a month they have twenty-four people come over to play "Texas Hold'em," that game that is taking the nation by storm. People started arriving and we had to go. Larry took me into the basement to show me the three tables set up to accommodate the players. As I looked at the intricate setup I knew they were serious players. Green felt covered tables and overhead hanging lights made that all clear.

Carol and I left after thanking them for letting us have the last dog. At the advice of the vet, we would have to wait another week before we could pick up our puppy. He needed to spend a little more time with his parents and that would make things easier raising him ourselves.

There was evidence somewhere that I hadn't let go completely of Pippon.

"Honey, did you think of any names yet?" Carol would ask.

I did not want to answer that question simply because I didn't want to name him. "No, I haven't," I answered. "I don't want to name him. If you think of a name, that will be fine," I would say. After a week went by it was time to pick up the dog. On our way home we would stop at a pet store and pick up some things to complete our list. I carried the puppy in my arms like a little baby. Weighing less than two pounds and very cute, I still would not let him in all of the way. Even though I had participated in preparing our home like the arrival of a new baby he would not get too close.

The baby came home and cleaning up mess after mess became the norm. One of the things that did not change was that I would be home every day and have to take care of him. The food had to specially prepared, how he played and with what, his sleeping habits and training him to go to the potty on those new training pads all required much attention. Those pads are expensive, but they work well. It took a couple of days, but Carol called home from work to hit me with that question again.

"They thought of a name here at work. What do you think about Sami? It's short for Samwise, a character from a movie." She waited a moment for my answer.

"That's good, that name had crossed my mind anyway," I finally said.

So, Sami it was. We agreed on the first selection. The only thing left to do was get rid of my apprehension. I knew that I needed to move on, but some of me would not budge. This cuts across the grain of modern psychology, but there comes a time when one knows what is best for them. That shoe might not fit someone else, but if it fits me, I had better slip it on...sooner or later. It can be a painful thing to cross over from selfishness to being sensible. I haven't yet.

I care for Sami, in every way that one should, but when Paul the barber asked me, "Has he won your heart yet?" My answer was a resounding "no." So we play, eat, drink, exercise, and write together. Even took him on a trip to Pennsylvania to see my side of the family. They loved him. Mom wants a dog now, Fritz wants a dog, they all want a dog. Sami is making quite a hit wherever he goes. His cousin Makayla over at Dori's hasn't accepted him yet. She tries to ignore him. (I suppose Ron and Makayla will come around soon.)

During that first week that Sami came to be with us, President Bush came to Rochester and met with J-Mac and his Mom. It was heartwarming to see the President of the United States say, "I heard of your story and it moved me to tears." This was another thrust of inspiration for me. He had been inspired himself, by a person that he did not know. Glancing from the television, I looked at the corner where Pippon had slept, then at the puppy in my arms, I remembered that I can't help, but to be faint sometimes with the cards that I have been dealt in this life. Sometimes it feels as though I am being kept alive only to be killed right out of my socks. One thing is for sure though. I need others to help me through it all. So, for all of you people out there, some I have met, some I haven't...thank you!

Epilogue

Many years ago a senator from Texas was speaking to a large group of people, maybe at a college baccalaureate. When asked why he wasn't using notes like the other politicians his answer was, "The truth is the easiest thing to remember." That sort of stuck in my craw. In my quest to undertake this writing with only my two pointing fingers I kept in mind the need for accuracy. Though there may be some dialogue that could never be recalled with every dot dash and tittle, the work as a whole is put forth with truth as its earmark. There was and apparently is no need in my life to "pump up a story," for affect. What happened, happened. Some I caused some I didn't. It has been painful, healing, a joy and sometimes a sorrow to think and write about things past. Whatever the case it has been worth it.

As I looked at the world around me it became quite obvious that I became a little different. Shaped by circumstances, heredity, culture, or pure choice I may never know. But one thing is for sure. God has made it abundantly clear. Love Him and others as myself and all will be well with my soul. The peace that surpasses understanding rules the heart. What else could one ask for? I continue to tell my patients that we are made to love and be loved. From that baby on my mother's wet sink to my current age of fifty-three, it has been a remarkable ride. Maybe I will live long enough to have my diapers changed again I don't know. Whatever happens, I hope that I am treated as I have treated others. Can everyone say that?

My skin is clear now what can I say?
No yellow toxic wasteland,
where my eyes beheld dismay.
As I moved through this myriad called life,
committing adultery with one called death,
Who would have thought I would turn about to face the other way?
I cried I begged, I saw that which I could not grasp,
that life that others had so far out of reach.
A voice then said "give up that you may win" then I began to preach.
"Look what I found" I said, but deaf ears to prevail.
"We are happy for you, but don't tell us about the nail."
I live to die and die to live, my rest has finally come.
The trip has been worth the wait and pang,
Now Heaven has made my home.

QUOTE REFERENCE

Quote on page 373: Taken from *My Utmost for His Highest* by Oswald Chambers, edited by James Reimann, © 1992 by Oswald Chambers Publications Assn., Ltd., and used by permission of Discovery House Publishers, Grand Rapids MI 49501. All rights reserved.

Printed in the United States
73480LV00003B/27